15th European Workshop on Natural Language Generation (ENLG 2015)

Brighton, United Kingdom
10 – 11 September 2015

ISBN: 978-1-5108-1401-1

Printed from e-media with permission by:

Curran Associates, Inc.
57 Morehouse Lane
Red Hook, NY 12571

Some format issues inherent in the e-media version may also appear in this print version.

Printed by Curran Associates, Inc. (2015)

Association for Computational Linguistics
209 N. Eighth Street
Stroudsburg, Pennsylvania 18360

Phone: 1-570-476-8006
Fax: 1-570-476-0860

acl@aclweb.org

Additional copies of this publication are available from:

Curran Associates, Inc.
57 Morehouse Lane
Red Hook, NY 12571 USA
Phone: 845-758-0400
Fax: 845-758-2634
Email: curran@proceedings.com
Web: www.proceedings.com

ENLG 2015

Proceedings of the 15th European Workshop on Natural Language Generation

10-11 September 2015
University of Brighton
Brighton, UK

Co-organised by:

COST Action IC1307, The European Network on Vision and Language (iV&L Net)

Endorsed by:

SIGGEN, the ACL Special Interest Group in Natural Language Generation

This page intentionally left blank.

Introduction

We are pleased to present the papers accepted for presentation at the 15th European Workshop on Natural Language Generation (ENLG 2015), to be held on 10th and 11th September in Brighton, UK.

ENLG is a biennial series, which started with a workshop in Royaumont, France in 1987 and was most recently held in Sofia, Bulgaria in 2013. Together with the International Conference on Natural Language Generation (INLG), held in alternate years, ENLG is the main forum for research on all aspects of the generation of natural language.

This year, ENLG has a special theme on Image and Video Description. Vision and Language more generally has, over the past five years, become a research field in its own right, a development reflected for example in the recently introduced Vision and Language areas at ACL and EMNLP. Image and video description is the obvious vision and language application for NLG and with this special theme we are aiming both to provide a forum for existing work and to stimulate new research. We are delighted to have two invited speakers addressing the special theme in different ways. Mirella Lapata reports her work investigating how best to interpret and verbalise visual information, while Pinar Duygulu-Sahin provides a broader overview of image and video description work with a focus on weakly labelled images.

We received a total of 41 submissions for the workshop, from all over the world — not only Europe, but North and South America, Asia and Australasia — and accepted 11 as long papers for oral presentation, 13 as short papers for poster presentation, and 3 as demos. This volume contains all the accepted papers, as well as the abstracts by the two invited speakers.

We would like to thank all the authors who submitted papers, and the members of our program committee, for helping to ensure the high standard and continuing health of ENLG 2015 and of NLG research in general.

Anja Belz, Albert Gatt, François Portet and Matthew Purver

Organising Committee

Organisers:

Anya Belz (University of Brighton, UK)
Albert Gatt (University of Malta, Malta)
François Portet (Univ. Grenoble Alpes, France)
Matthew Purver (Queen Mary University of London, UK)

Program Committee:

Anya Belz (University of Brighton, UK)
Bernd Bohnet (Google, Germany)
Aoife Cahill (Educational Testing Service, USA)
Pinar Duygulu-Sahin (Hacettepe University, Turkey)
Marc Dymetman (Xerox Research Centre Europe, France)
Desmond Elliott (Centrum Wiskunde & Informatica, Netherlands)
Claire Gardent (CNRS/LORIA Nancy, France)
Albert Gatt (University of Malta, Malta)
Pablo Gervás (Universidad Complutense de Madrid, Spain)
Dimitra Gkatzia (Heriot-Watt University, UK)
Jordi Gonzalez (Computer Vision Center, Spain)
Markus Guhe (University of Edinburgh, UK)
Helen Hastie (Heriot-Watt University, UK)
Raquel Hervás (Universidad Complutense de Madrid, Spain)
Julia Hockenmaier (University of Illinois, USA)
Julian Hough (Bielefeld University, Germany)
Marina Ivasic-Kos (University of Rijeka, Croatia)
John Kelleher (Dublin Institute of Technology, Ireland)
Alexander Koller (University of Potsdam, Germany)
Guy Lapalme (RALI-DIRO, Université de Montral, Canada)
Kathleen Mccoy (University of Delaware, USA)
Margaret Mitchell (Johns Hopkins University, USA)
Neil O'Hare (Yahoo! Research, Spain)
Patrizia Paggio (University of Malta and University of Copenhagen)
Francois Portet (Univ. Grenoble Alpes, France)
Matthew Purver (Queen Mary University of London, UK)
Ehud Reiter (University of Aberdeen, UK)
Horacio Saggion (Universitat Pompeu Fabra, Spain)
Advaith Siddharthan (University of Aberdeen, UK)
Mariet Theune (University of Twente, Netherlands)
Juan-Manuel Torres-Moreno (Laboratoire Informatique d'Avignon / UAPV, France)
Kees Van Deemter (University of Aberdeen, UK)
Leo Wanner (ICREA and University Pompeu Fabra, Spain)
Michael White (The Ohio State University, USA)

Invited Speakers

Pinar Duygulu-Sahin (Hacettepe University, Turkey):

Words and Pictures: Mining Weakly Labeled Web Images and Videos for Automatic Concept Learning

The increasing number of images and videos resulted in new challenges for computer vision community. The requirement for manual labeling continues to be one of the most important limitations in large scale recognition. Alternatively, massive amount of images and videos with annotated metadata or descriptions are available on the Web. Although incomplete and errorful,availability of these annotations recently attracted many researchers to build (semi-)automatic methods to learn from weakly labeled data. However, images on the web are "in the wild" resulting in challenges that makes the data collections gathered from web different from the hand crafted datasets.

In this talk, first I will discuss the challenges in learning from weakly labeled images, Then, I will describe our recent efforts on recognition of visual attributes, as well as objects, scenes and faces on the large scale using weakly labeled images. Going beyond images, finally I will briefly discuss the issues in videos.

Mirella Lapata (University of Edinburgh, UK):

Learning to Interpret and Describe Abstract Scenes

Given a (static) scene, a human can effortlessly describe what is going on (who is doing what to whom, how, and why). The process requires knowledge about the world, how it is perceived, and described. In this talk I will focus on the problem of interpreting and verbalizing visual information using abstract scenes created from collections of clip art images. I will introduce a model inspired by machine translation (where the task is to transform a source sentence into its target translation) and argue that generating descriptions for scenes is quite similar, but with a twist: the translation process is very loose and selective; there will always be objects in a scene not worth mentioning, and words in a description that will have no visual counterpart.

Our key insight is to represent scenes via visual dependency relations corresponding to sentential descriptions. This allows us to create a large parallel corpus for training a statistical machine translation system, which we interface with a content selection component guiding the translation toward interesting or important scene content. Advantageously, our model can be used in the reverse direction, i.e., to generate scenes, without additional engineering effort. Our approach outperforms a number of competitive alternatives, when evaluated both automatically and by humans.

Joint work with Luis Gilberto Mateos Ortiz, Carina Silberer, and Clemens Wolff.

Table of Contents

This page intentionally left blank.

Conference Programme

Day 1: Thursday, 10th September 2015

8:00–9:15	Registration
9:15–9:30	Introduction
	Session 1: Surface Realisation *(Chair: Michael White)*
9:30–10:00	*A Simple Surface Realization Engine for Telugu* Sasi Raja Sekhar Dokkara, Suresh Verma Penumathsa and Somayajulu Gowri Sripada
10:00–10:30	*Input Seed Features for Guiding the Generation Process: A Statistical Approach for Spanish* Cristina Barros and Elena Lloret
10:30–11:00	*Coffee*
	Session 2: Sentence Planning and Evaluation *(Chair: Ehud Reiter)*
11:00–11:30	*A Domain Agnostic Approach to Verbalizing n-ary Events without Parallel Corpora* Bikash Gyawali, Claire Gardent and Christophe Cerisara
11:30–12:00	*Inducing Clause-Combining Rules: A Case Study with the SPaRKy Restaurant Corpus* Michael White and David M. Howcroft
12:00–12:30	*Reading Times Predict the Quality of Generated Text Above and Beyond Human Ratings* Sina Zarrieß, Sebastian Loth and David Schlangen
12:30–1:30	*Lunch*
1:30–2:30	**Invited Talk: Mirella Lapata** *(Chair: Matthew Purver)* *Learning to Interpret and Describe Abstract Scenes*
2:30–5:00	**Poster and Demo Session** *(with coffee 3:00-3:30)*

Posters

Moving Targets: Human References to Unstable Landmarks
Adriana Baltaretu, Emiel Krahmer and Alfons Maes

A Framework for the Generation of Computer System Diagnostics in Natural Language using Finite State Methods
Rachel Farrell, Gordon Pace and M Rosner

A Snapshot of NLG Evaluation Practices 2005 - 2014
Dimitra Gkatzia and Saad Mahamood

Japanese Word Reordering Executed Concurrently with Dependency Parsing and Its Evaluation
Tomohiro Ohno, Kazushi Yoshida, Yoshihide Kato and Shigeki Matsubara

Sentence Ordering in Electronic Navigational Chart Companion Text Generation
Julie Sauvage-Vincent, Yannis Haralambous and John Puentes

Natural Language Generation from Pictographs
Leen Sevens, Vincent Vandeghinste, Ineke Schuurman and Frank Van Eynde

Translating Italian to LIS in the Rail Stations
Alessandro Mazzei

Response Generation in Dialogue Using a Tailored PCFG Parser
Caixia Yuan, Xiaojie Wang and Qianhui He

Generating Récit from Sensor Data: Evaluation of a Task Model for Story Planning and Preliminary Experiments with GPS Data
Belén A. Baez Miranda, Sybille Caffiau, Catherine Garbay and François Portet

Generating and Evaluating Landmark-Based Navigation Instructions in Virtual Environments
Amanda Cercas Curry, Dimitra Gkatzia and Verena Rieser

Summarising Unreliable Data
Stephanie Inglis

Generating Descriptions of Spatial Relations between Objects in Images
Adrian Muscat and Anja Belz

Towards Flexible, Small-Domain Surface Generation: Combining Data-Driven and Grammatical Approaches
Andrea Fischer, Vera Demberg and Dietrich Klakow

Demos

JSrealB: A Bilingual Text Realizer for Web Programming
Paul Molins and Guy Lapalme

A Game-Based Setup for Data Collection and Task-Based Evaluation of Uncertain Information Presentation
Dimitra Gkatzia, Amanda Cercas Curry, Verena Rieser and Oliver Lemon

Generating Referential Descriptions Involving Relations by a Best-First Searching Procedure – A System Demo
Florin Haque and Helmut Horacek

5:00 *End of Day 1*

Day 2: Friday, 11th September 2015

9:00–10:00 **Invited Talk: Pinar Duygulu-Sahin**
Words and Pictures: Mining Weakly Labeled Web Images and Videos for Automatic Concept Learning

Session 3: Generation from Visual and Geographic Input *(Chair: Amy Isard)*

10:00–10:30 *Generating Image Descriptions with Gold Standard Visual Inputs: Motivation, Evaluation and Baselines*
Josiah Wang and Robert Gaizauskas

10:30–11:00 *Designing an Algorithm for Generating Named Spatial References*
Rodrigo de Oliveira, Yaji Sripada and Ehud Reiter

11:00–11:30 *Coffee*

Session 4: Narrative and Discourse *(Chair: François Portet)*

11:30–12:00 *Narrative Generation from Extracted Associations*
Pierre-Luc Vaudry and Guy Lapalme

12:00–12:30 *Topic Transition Strategies for an Information-Giving Agent*
Nadine Glas and Catherine Pelachaud

12:30–1:30 *Lunch*

Session 5: Data to Text *(Chair: Claire Gardent)*

1:30–2:00 *Creating Textual Driver Feedback from Telemetric Data*
Daniel Braun, Ehud Reiter and Advaith Siddharthan

2:00–2:30 *A Personal Storytelling about Your Favorite Data*
Cyril Labbé, Claudia Roncancio and Damien Bras

2:30–3:00 **Closing Session**

3:00-3:30 *Coffee*

3:30-4:30 **Discussion Session on Generation Challenges Initiative**
(Chairs: Anya Belz, Albert Gatt)

4:30 *End of ENLG 2015*

A Simple Surface Realization Engine for Telugu

Sasi Raja Sekhar Dokkara, Suresh Verma Penumathsa
Dept. of Computer Science
Adikavi Nannayya University, India
dsairajasekhar@gmail.com,vermaps@yahoo.com

Somayajulu G. Sripada
Dept. of Computing Science
University of Aberdeen, UK
yaji.sripada@abdn.ac.uk

Abstract

Telugu is a Dravidian language with nearly 85 million first language speakers. In this paper we report a realization engine for Telugu that automates the task of building grammatically well-formed Telugu sentences from an input specification consisting of lexicalized grammatical constituents and associated features. Our realization engine adapts the design approach of SimpleNLG family of surface realizers.

1 Introduction

Telugu is a Dravidian language with nearly 85 million first language speakers. It is a morphologically rich language (MRL) with a simple syntax where the sentence constituents can be ordered freely without impacting the primary meaning of the sentence. In this paper we describe a surface realization engine for Telugu. Surface realization is the final subtask of an NLG pipeline (Reiter and Dale, 2000) that is responsible for mechanically applying all the linguistic choices made by upstream subtasks (such as microplanning) to generate a grammatically valid surface form. Our Telugu realization engine is designed following the SimpleNLG (Gatt and Reiter, 2009) approach which recently has been used to build surface realizers for German (Bollmann, 2011), Filipino (Ethel Ong et al., 2011), French (Vaudry and Lapalme, 2013) and Brazilian Portuguese (de Oliveira and Sripada, 2014). Figure 1 shows an example input specification in XML corresponding to the Telugu sentence (1).

`vAlYlYu aMxamEna wotalo neVmmaxigA naduswunnAru.`
`(They are walking slowly in a beautiful garden.)` (1)

```
<?xml version="1.0"encoding="UTF-8"standalone="no">
<document>
<sentence type=" " predicate-type="verbal" respect="no">
<nounphrase role="subject">
<head pos="pronoun" gender="human" number="plural" person="third" case-marker=" " stem="basic">
vAdu</head>
</nounphrase>
<nounphrase role="complement">
<modifier pos="adjective" type="descriptive" suffix="aEna">
aMxamu</modifier>
<head pos="noun" gen-der="nonmasculine" number="singular" person="third" casemarker="lo" stem="basic">
wota</head>
</nounphrase>
<verbphrase type=" ">
<modifier pos="adverb" suffix="gA">
neVmmaxi</modifier>
<head pos="verb" tense-mode="presentparticiple">
naducu</head>
</verbphrase>
</sentence>
</document>
```

Figure 1. XML Input Specification

2 Related Work

Several realizers are available for English and other European languages (Gatt and Reiter, 2009; Vaudry and Lapalme, 2013; Bollmann, 2011; Elhadad and Robin, 1996). Some general purpose realizers (as opposed to realizers built as part of an MT system) have started appearing for Indian languages as well. Smriti Singh et al. (2007) report a Hindi realizer that includes functionality for choosing post-position markers based on semantic information in the input. This is in contrast to the realization engine reported in the current paper which assumes that choices of constit-

Proceedings of the 15th European Workshop on Natural Language Generation (ENLG), pages 1–8,
Brighton, September 2015.

uents, root words and grammatical features are all preselected before realization engine is called. There are no realization engines for Telugu to the best of our knowledge. However, a rich body of work exists for Telugu language processing in the context of machine translation (MT). In this context, earlier work reported Telugu morphological processors that perform both analysis and generation (Badri et al., 2009; Rao and Mala, 2011; Ganapathiraju and Levin, 2006).

2.1 The SimpleNLG Framework

A realization engine is an automaton that generates well-formed sentences according to a grammar. Therefore, while building a realizer the grammatical knowledge (syntactic and morphological) of the target language is an important resource. Realizers are classified based on the source of grammatical knowledge. There are realizers such as FUF/SURGE that employ grammatical knowledge grounded in a linguistic theory (Elhadad and Robin, 1996). There have also been realizers that use statistical language models such as Nitrogen (Knight and Hatzivassiloglou, 1995) and Oxygen (Habash, 2000). While linguistic theory based grammars are attractive, authoring these grammars can be a significant endeavor (Mann and Matthiessen, 1985). Besides, non-linguists (most application developers) may find working with such theory heavy realizers difficult because of the initial steep learning curve. Similarly building wide coverage statistical models of language too is labor intensive requiring collection and analysis of large quantities of corpora. It is this initial cost of building grammatical resources (formal or statistical) that becomes a significant barrier in building realization engines for new languages. Therefore, it is necessary to adopt grammar engineering strategies that have low initial costs. The surface realizers belonging to the SimpleNLG family incorporate grammatical knowledge corresponding to only the most frequently used phrases and clauses and therefore involve low cost grammar engineering. The main features of a realization engine following the SimpleNLG framework are:

1. A wide coverage morphology module independent of the syntax module
2. A light syntax module that offers functionality to build frequently used phrases and clauses without any commitment to a linguistic theory. The large uptake of the SimpleNLG realizer both in the academia and in the industry shows that the light weight approach to syntax is not a limitation.
3. Using 'canned' text elements to be directly dropped into the generation process achieving wider syntax coverage without actually extending the syntactic knowledge in the realizer.
4. A rich set of lexical and grammatical features that guide the morphological and syntactic operations locally in the morphology and syntax modules respectively. In addition, features enforce agreement amongst sentence constituents more globally at the sentence level.

3 Telugu Realization Engine

The current work follows the SimpleNLG framework. However, because of the known differences between Telugu and English SimpleNLG codebase could not be reused for building Telugu realizer. Instead our Telugu realizer was built from scratch adapting several features of the SimpleNLG framework for the context of Telugu.

There are significant variations in spoken and written usage of Telugu. There are also significant dialectical variations, most prominent ones correspond to the four regions of the state of Andhra Pradesh, India – Northern, Southern, Eastern and Central (Brown, 1991). In addition, Telugu absorbed vocabulary (Telugised) from other Indian languages such as Urdu and Hindi. As a result, a design choice for Telugu realization engine is to decide the specific variety of Telugu whose grammar and vocabulary needs to be represented in the system. In our work, we use the grammar of modern Telugu developed by (Krishnamurti and Gwynn, 1985). We have decided to include only a small lexicon in our realization engine. Currently, it contains the words required for the evaluation described in section 4. This is because host NLG systems that use our engine could use their own application specific lexicons. More over modern Telugu has been absorbing large amounts of English vocabulary particularly in the fields of science and technology whose morphology is unknown. Thus specialized lexicons could be required to model the morphological behavior of such vocabulary. In the rest of this section we present the design of our Telugu realizer.

As stated in section 2.1, a critical step in building a realization engine for a new language is to review its grammatical knowledge to understand the linguistic means offered by the language to express meaning. We reviewed Telugu grammar as presented in our chosen grammar reference by Krishnamurti and Gwynn (1985). From a realizer design perspective the following observations proved useful:

1. Primary meaning in Telugu sentences is mainly expressed using inflected forms of content words and case markers or postpositions than by position of words/phrases in the sentence. This means morpho-phonology plays bigger role in sentence creation than syntax.

2. Because sentence constituents in Telugu can be ordered freely without impacting the primary meaning of a sentence, sophisticated grammar knowledge is not required to order sentence level constituents. It is possible, for instance, to order constituents of a declarative sentence using a standard predefined sequence (e.g. Subject + Object + Verb).

3. Telugu, like many other Indian languages, is not governed by a phrase structure grammar, instead fits better into a Paninian Grammar Formalism (Bharati et al., 1995) which uses dependency grammar. This means, dependency trees represent the structure of phrases and sentences. At the sentence level verb phrase is the head and all the other constituents have a dependency link to the head. At the phrase level too, head-modifier dependency structures are a better fit.

4. Agreement amongst sentence constituents can get quite complicated in Telugu. Several grammatical and semantic features are used to define agreement rules. Well-formed Telugu sentences are the result of applying agreement rules at the sentence level on sentence constituents constructed at the lower level processes.

Based on the above observations we found that the SimpleNLG framework with its features listed in section 2.1 is a good fit for guiding the design of our Telugu realization engine. Thus our realization engine is designed with a wide coverage morphology module and a light-weight syntax module where features play a major role in performing sentence construction operations.

Having decided the SimpleNLG framework for representing and operationalizing the grammatical knowledge, the following design decisions were made while building our Telugu realizer (we believe that these decisions might drive design of realizers for any other Indian Language as well):

1. Use wx-notation for representing Indian language orthography (see section 3.1 for more details)
2. Define the tag names and the feature names used in the input XML file (example shown in Figure 1) adapted from SimpleNLG and (Krishnamurti and Gwynn, 1985) for specifying input to the realization engine. It is hoped that using English terminology for specifying input to our Telugu realizer simplifies creating input by application developers who usually know English well and possess at least a basic knowledge of English grammar. (see section 3.2 for more details)
3. In order to offer flexibility to application developers our realization engine orders sentence level constituents (except verb which is always placed at the end) using the same order in which they are specified in the input XML file. This allows application developers to control ordering based on discourse level requirements such as focus.
4. The grammar terminology used in our engine does not directly correspond to the Karaka relations (Bharati et al., 1995) from the Paninian framework because we use the grammar terminology specified by Krishnamurti and Gwynn (1985) which is lot closer to the terminology used in SimpleNLG. We are currently investigating opportunities to align our design lot closer to the Paninian framework. We expect such approach to help us while extending our framework to generate other Indian languages as well.

3.1 WX-Notation

WX notation (See appendix B in Bharati et al, 1995) is a very popular transliteration scheme for representing Indian languages in the ASCII character set. This scheme is widely used in Natural Language Processing in India. In WX notation the small case letters are used for un-aspirated consonants and short vowels while the capital case letters are used for aspirated consonants and long vowels. The retroflexed voiced and voiceless consonants are mapped to 't, T, d and D'. The dentals are mapped to 'w, W, x and X'. Hence the name of the scheme "WX", referring to the idiosyncratic mapping.

3.2 The Input Specification Scheme

The input to the current work is a tree structure specified in XML, an example is shown in Figure 1. The root node is the sentence and the nodes at the next level are the constituent phrases that have a role feature representing the grammatical functions such as subject, verb and complement performed by the phrase. Each of the lower level nodes could in turn have their own head and modifier children. Each node also can take attributes which represent grammatical or lexical features such as number and tense. For example the subject node in Figure 1 can be understood as follows:

```
<nounphrase role="subject">
<head
pos="pronoun"gender="human"number="p
lural"person="third"casemarker="    "
stem="basic">
vAdu</head>
</nounphrase>
```

This node represents the noun phrase that plays the role of subject in the sentence. There is only one feature, the head to the subject node whose type is nominative. The lexical features of the head "vAdu" are part-of-speech (*pos*) which is pronoun, person which is third person, number which is plural, gender which is human, and case marker which is null.

3.3 System Architecture

The sentence construction for Telugu involves the following three steps:

1. Construct word forms by applying morpho-phonological rules selected based on features associated with a word (word level morphology)

2. Combine word forms to construct phrases using 'sandhi' (a morpho-phonological fusion operation) if required (phrase building)

3. Apply sentence level agreement by applying agreement rules selected based on relevant features. Order sentence constituents following a standard predefined sequence. (sentence building)

Our system architecture is shown in Figure 2 which involves morphology engine, phrase builder and sentence builder corresponding to these three steps. The rest of the section presents how the example sentence (1) is generated from the input specification in Figure 1.

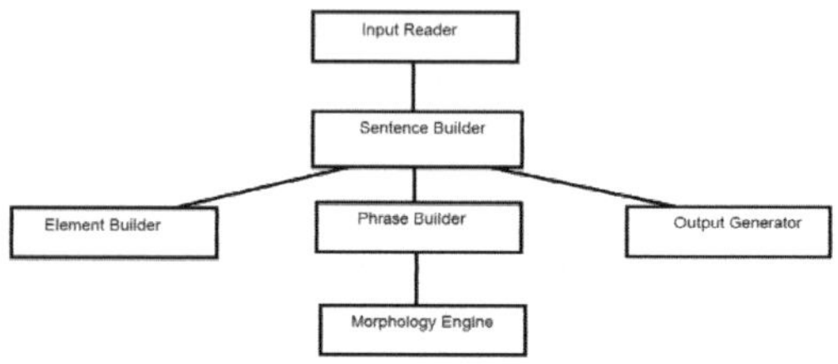

Figure 2. System Architecture

3.4 Input Reader

The Input Reader is the module which acts as an interface between the sentence builder and the input. Currently the input reader accepts only our XML input specification but in the future we would like to extend it to accept other input specifications such as SSF (Bharati et al., 2007). This module ensures that the rest of the engine receives input in the required form.

3.5 Sentence Builder

The Sentence Builder is the main module of the current system which has a centralized control over all the other modules. It performs four subtasks:

1. Sentence Builder first checks for predefined grammatical functions such as subject, object, complement, and verb which are defined as features of the respective phrases in the input. It then calls the appropriate element builder for each of these to create element objects which store all the information extracted from the XML node.

2. These element objects are then passed to appropriate phrase builder to receive back a string which is the phrase that is being constructed according to the requirements of the input.

3. After receiving all the phrases from the appropriate phrase builders the Sentence Builder applies the agreement rules. Since Telugu is nominative-accusative language the verb agrees with the argument in the nominative case. Therefore the predicate inflects based on the gender, person and number of the noun in the nominative case. There are three features at the sentence level namely *type*, *predicate-type*, and *respect*. The feature *type* refers to the type of the sentence. The current work handles only simple sentences therefore

it is not set to any value. The feature *predicate-type* can have any one of the three values namely *verbal*, *nominative*, and *abstract*. The feature *respect* can have values *yes* or *no*. The agreement also depends on the features *predicate-type*, and *respect*.

4. Finally, the sentence builder orders the phrases in the same order they are specified in the input.

In the case of the example in Figure 1 the sentence builder finds three grammatical functions - one finite verb, one locative complement, and one nominative subject. In the example input (1) the values for the feature *predicate-type* is "*verbal*" and for *respect* is "*no*". The Sentence Builder retrieves appropriate rule from an externally stored agreement rule base. In the example input (1) where *predicate-type* is set to *verbal*, the *number* of the subject is *plural* and the *gender* is *human* the Sentence Builder retrieves the appropriate suffix "nnAru". This suffix is then agglutinated to the verb "naduswu" which is returned by the morphology engine to generate the final verb form, "naduswunnAru" with the required agreement with subject.

"naduswu"+ "nnAru"----→ "naduswunnAru"

After the construction of the sentence the Sentence Builder passes it to the Output Generator which prints the output.

3.6 Element Builder

The element builder of each grammatical function checks for lower level functions like head and modifier and calls the appropriate element builder for the head and modifier which converts the lexicalized input into element objects with the grammatical constituents as their instance variables and returns the element objects back to the Sentence Builder. Our realizer creates four types of element objects namely SOCElement, VAElement, AdjectiveElement, and AdverbElement. The SOCElement represents the grammatical functions subject, object and complement. The subject in the example of (1) is "`vAdu`" for which a SOCElement is created with the specified features. Similarly a SOCElement is created for the complement "`wota`" and its modifier "`aMxamu`" which is an AdjectiveElement. Finally a VAElement is created for the verb "`naducu`" and the modifier "`neVmmaxi`" which is an AdverbElement.

3.7 Phrase Builder

Telugu sentences express most of the primary meaning in terms of morphologically well-formed phrases or word groups. In Telugu the main and auxiliary verbs occur together as a single word. Therefore their generation is done by the morphology engine. Telugu sentences are mainly made up of four types of phrases - Noun Phrase, Verb Phrase, Adjective Phrase, and Adverb Phrase. Noun phrases and verb phrases are the main constituents in a sentence while the Adjective Phrase and the Adverb Phrase only play the role of a modifier in a noun or verb phrase. There is one feature at the Noun Phrase level "role" which specifies the role of the Noun Phrase in the sentence. The phrase builder passes the elements constructed by the element builder to the morphology engine and gets back the respective phrases with appropriately inflected words. In the example input in (1), there are three constituent phrases, viz, two noun phrases for subject and complement and a verb phrase. One of the noun phrases also contains an adjective phrase which is an optional modifying element of noun heads in head-modifier noun phrases. The adjective phrase may be a single element or sometimes composed of more than one element. The verb phrase also contains an adverb phrase which is generally considered as a modifier of the verb. The phrase builder passes five objects i.e., two SOCElement objects, one AdjectiveElement object, one VAElement object, and one AdverbElement object to the morphology engine and gets back five inflected words which finally become three phrases, viz, two noun phrases "`vAlYlYu`", "`aMxamEna wotalo`", and one verb phrase "`neVmmaxigA naduswu`".

3.8 Morphology Engine

The morphology engine is the most important module in the Telugu realization engine. It is responsible for the inflection and agglutination of the words and phrases. The morphology engine behaves differently for different words based on their part of speech (*pos*). The morphology engine takes the element object as the input, and returns to the phrase builder the inflected or agglutinated word forms based on the rules of the language. In the current work morphology engine is a rule based engine with the lexicon to account for exceptions to the rules. The rules used by the morphology engine are stored in external files to allow changes to be made externally.

3.8.1 Noun

Noun is the head of the noun phrase. Telugu nouns are divided into three classes namely (i) proper nouns and common nouns, (ii) pronouns, and (iii) special types of nouns (e.g. numerals) (Krishnamurti and Gwynn, 1985). All nouns except few special type nouns have *gender*, *number*, and *person*. Noun morphology involves mainly plural formation and case inflection. All the plural formation rules from sections 6.11 to 6.13 of our grammar reference have been implemented in our engine.

The head of the complement in the example (1) has one noun "`wotalo`". The word "`wota`" along with its feature values can be written as follows:

"`wota`", `noun, nonmasculine, singular, third, basic,` "`lo`"`---wotalo`

The formation of this word is very simple because the word "`wota`" in its singular form and the case marker "`lo`" get agglutinated through a sandhi (a morpho-phonological fusion operation) formation as follows:

`'wota'+lo----- wotalo`

3.8.2 Pronoun

Pronouns vary according to *gender*, *number*, and *person*. There are three persons in Telugu namely *first*, *second*, and *third*. The *gender* of the nouns and pronouns in Telugu depend on the *number*. The relation between the *number* and *gender* is shown in table 1.

Number	Gender
singular	masculine, nonmasculine
plural	human, nonhuman

Table1: Relationship between number and gender

Plural formation of pronouns is not rule based. Therefore they are stored externally in the lexicon. The first person pronoun "nenu" has two plural forms "memu" which is the exclusive plural form and "manamu" which is the inclusive plural form. In the generation of the plural of the first person a feature called "exclusive" has to be specified with the value "yes", or "no". Along with *gender*, *number*, and *person* there is one more feature which is *stem*. The stem can be either *basic* or *oblique*. The formation of the pronoun "vAlYlYu" in the example of (1) which is the head of the subject along with its feature values can be written as follows:

"`vAdu`", `pronoun, human, plural, third, basic,`""`-vAlYlYu`

In this case the stem is *basic*. The *gender* of the pronoun is *human* because the *number* is *plural* as mentioned in table 1. The word "vAlYlYu" is retrieved from the lexicon as the plural for the word "vAdu" and the feature values.

3.8.3 Adjective

Adjectives occur most often immediately before the noun they qualify. The basic adjectives or the adjectival roots which occur only as adjectives are indeclinable (e.g. oka (one), ara (half)). Adjectives can also be derived from other parts of speech like verbs, adverbs, or nouns. The adjective "aMxamEna" in the example of (1) is a derived adjective formed by adding the adjectival suffix "aEna" to the noun "aMxamu". The formation of the word "`aMxamEna`" in the example (1) along with its feature values can be written as follows:

"`aMxamu`", `adjective, descriptive,`"`aEna`"`--aMxamEna`

The current work does not take into consideration the type of an adjective and will be included in a future version. The formation of this word is again through a sandhi formation as follows:

`aMxamu+aEna-------- aMxamEna`

Here the sandhi formation eliminates the "`u`" in the first word; "`a`" in the second word and the word "`aMxamEna`" is formed.

3.8.4 Verb

Telugu verbs inflect to encode gender, number and person suffixes of the subject along with tense mode suffixes. As already mentioned gender, number and person agreement is applied at the sentence level. At the word level, verb is the most difficult word to handle in Telugu because of phonetic alterations applied to it before being agglutinated with the tense-aspect-mode suffix (TAM). Telugu verbs are classified into six classes (Krishnamurti, 1961). Our engine implements all these classes and the phonetic alternations applicable to each of these classes are stored externally in a file.

The verb in the example of Figure 1 has one verb "naducu" along with its feature values. The formation of the verb "naduswu" can be written as follows:

"naducu",verb, present participle------naduswu

The word "naducu" belongs to class IIa, for which the phonetic alteration is to substitute "cu" with "s", and therefore the word gets inflected as follows:

naducu----------------nadus

The tense mode suffix for present participle is "wu", and the word becomes "naduswu". The gender and number of the subject also play a role in the formation of the verb which is discussed in section 3.5.

3.8.5 Adverb

All adverbs fall into three semantic domains, those denoting time, place and manner (Krishnamurti and Gwynn 1985). The adverb "neVmmaxigA" in the example (1) is a manner adverb as it tells about the way they are walking "neVmmaxigA naduswunnaru (walking slowly)". In Telugu manner adverbs are generally formed by adding "gA" to adjectives and nouns. The formation of the adverb "neVmmaxigA" in the example (1) along with its feature values can be written as follows:

"neVmmaxi", adverb,"gA"--------------neVmmaxigA

The formation of this word is a simple sandhi formation.

3.9 Output Generator

Output Generator is the module which actually generates text in Telugu font. The Output generator receives the constructed sentence in WX-notation and gives as output a sentence in Telugu based on the Unicode Characters for Telugu.

4 Evaluation

The current work addresses the problem of generating syntactically and morphologically well-formed sentences in Telugu from an input specification consisting of lexicalized grammatical constituents and associated features. In order to test the robustness of the realization engine as the input to the realizer changes we initially ran the engine in a batch mode to generate all possible sentence variations given an input similar to the one shown in Figure 1. In the batch mode the engine uses the same input root words in a single run of the engine, but uses different combinations of values for the grammatical features such as tense, aspect, mode, number and gender in each new run. Although the batch run was originally intended for software quality testing before conducting evaluation studies, these tests showed that certain grammatical feature combinations might make the realization engine produce unacceptable output. This is an expected outcome because our engine in the current state performs very limited consistency checks on the input.

The purpose of our evaluation is to measure our realizer's coverage of the Telugu language. One objective measure could be to measure the proportion of sentences from a specific text source (such as a Telugu newspaper) that our realizer could generate. As a first step towards such an objective evaluation, we first evaluate our realizer using example sentences from our grammar reference. Although not ideal this evaluation helps us to measure our progress and prepares us for the objective evaluation. The individual chapters and sections in the book by Krishnamurti and Gwynn (1985) follow a standard structure where every new concept of grammar is introduced with the help of a list of example sentences that illustrate the usage of that particular concept. We used these sentences for our evaluation. Please note that we collect sentences from all chapters. This means our realizer is required to generate for example verb forms used in example sentences from other chapters in addition to those from the chapter on verbs. A total of 738 sentences were collected from chapter 6 to chapter 26, the main chapters which cover Telugu grammar. Because the coverage of the current system is limited, we don't expect the system to generate all these 738 sentences. Among these, 419/738 (57%) sentences were found to be within the scope of our current realizer. Many of these sentences are simple and short. For each of the 419 selected sentences our realizer was run to generate the 419 output sentences. The output sentences matched the original sentences from the book completely. This means at this stage we can quantify the coverage of our realizer as 57%

(419/738) against our own grammar source. A more objective measure of coverage will be estimated in the future.

Having built the functionality for the main sentence construction tasks, we are now in a good position to widen the coverage. Majority of the remaining 319 sentences (=738-419) involve verb forms such as participles and compound verbs and medium to complex sentence types. As stated above, we intend to use this evaluation to drive our development. This means every time we extend the coverage of the realizer we will rerun the evaluation to quantify the extended coverage of our realizer. The idea is not to achieve 100% coverage. Our strategy has always been to select each new sentence or phrase type to be included in the realizer based on its utility to express meanings in some of the popular NLG application domains such as medicine, weather, sports and finance.

5 Conclusion

In this paper, we described a surface realizer for Telugu which was designed by adapting the SimpleNLG framework for free word order languages. We intend to extend the current work further as stated below:

1. Extend the coverage of our realizer and perform another evaluation to characterize the coverage of the realizer more objectively.
2. Create a generalized framework for free word order language generation (specifically for Indian languages). The existing framework could be used to generate simple sentences from other Indian languages by plugging in the required morphology engine for the new language.

Reference

Albert Gatt and Ehud Reiter "*SimpleNLG: A realization engine for practical applications*", Proceedings of ENLG 2009, pages 90-93, 2009.

AksharaBharati, Vineet Chaitanya, Rajeev Sangal "*Natural Language Processing A Paninian Perspective*" Prentice-Hall of India, New Delhi, 1995.

Akshara Bharati, Rajeev Sangal, Dipti M Sharma "*SSF: Shakti Standard Format Guide*" LTRC, IIIT, Hyderabad, Report No: TR-LTRC-33, 2007.

Benoit Lavoie and Owen Rambow "*A Fast and Portable Realizer for Text Generation Systems*" Proceedings of the Fifth Conference on Applied Natural Language Processing (ANLP97), Washington, 1997.

BH. Krishnamurti and J P L Gwynn, "*A Grammar of Modern Telugu*" Oxford University Press, 1985.

BH. Krishnamurti "*Telugu Verbal Bases a comparative and Descriptive Study*" University of California Press Berkley & Los Angeles, 1961.

Brown, C.P., "*The Grammar of the Telugu Language*". New Delhi: Laurier Books Ltd, 1991.

Elhadad M. & Robin J. (1996). "*A reusable comprehensive syntactic realization component"*. Paper presented at Demonstrations and Posters of the 1996 International Workshop on Natural Language Generation (INLG '96), Herstmonceux, England.

Ethel Ong, Stephanie Abella, Lawrence Santos, and Dennis Tiu "*A Simple Surface Realizer for Filipino* " 25th Pacific Asia Conference on Language, Information and Computation, pages 51–59, 2011.

HabashN. (2000). *OxyGen: "A Language Independent Linearization"*Engine. Paper presented at AMTA. London: Ablex. Available as USC/ISI Research Report RR-83-105.

Knight K. and V. Hatzivassiloglou. NITROGEN: "*Two-Level, Many-Paths Generation*". Proceedings of the ACL-95 conference. Cambridge, MA 1995.

MadhaviGanapathiraju and Lori Levin "*TelMore: Morphological Generator for Telugu Nouns and Verbs*", 2006.

Mann, W.C. and C.M.I.M. Matthiessen. Nigel: "*A Systemic Grammar for Text Generation*". In R. Benson and J. Greaves (eds), Systemic perspectives on Discourse: Proceedings of 9th International Systemics workshop 1985.

Marcel Bollmann, "*Adapting SimpleNLG to German*" Proceedings of the 13th European Workshop on Natural Language Generation (ENLG), pages 133–138, Nancy, France, September 2011.

Pierre-Luc Vaudry and Guy Lapalme "*Adapting SimpleNLG for bilingual English-French realisation*" Proceedings of the 14th European Workshop on Natural Language Generation, pages 183–187, Sofia, Bulgaria, August 8-9 2013.

Rodrigo de Oliveira, Somayajulu Sripada "*Adapting SimpleNLG for Brazilian Portuguese realisation*", 2014.

Smriti Singh, MrugankDalal, Vishal Vachhani, Pushpak Bhattacharyya, Om P. Damani "*Hindi Generation from Interlingua (UNL)*" in Proceedings of MT summit, 2007.

Sri BadriNarayanan.R, Saravanan.S, Soman K.P "*Data Driven Suffix List and Concatenation Algorithm for Telugu Morphological Generator*" International Journal of Engineering Science and Technology (IJEST), 2009.

Uma MaheshwarRao, G. and Christopher Mala "*TELUGU WORD SYNTHESIZER*" International Telugu Internet Conference Proceedings, Milpitas, California, USA 28th -30th September, 2011.

Input Seed Features for Guiding the Generation Process: A Statistical Approach for Spanish

Cristina Barros
Department of Software
and Computing Systems
University of Alicante
Apdo. de Correos 99
E-03080, Alicante, Spain
cbarros@dlsi.ua.es

Elena Lloret
Department of Software
and Computing Systems
University of Alicante
Apdo. de Correos 99
E-03080, Alicante, Spain
elloret@dlsi.ua.es

Abstract

In this paper we analyse a statistical approach for generating Spanish sentences focused on the surface realisation stage guided by an input seed feature. This seed feature can be anything such as a word, a phoneme, a sentiment, etc. Our approach attempts to maximise the appearance of words with that seed feature along the sentence. It follows three steps: first we train a language model over a corpus; then we obtain a bag of words having that concrete seed feature; and finally a sentence is generated based on both, the language model and the bag of words. Depending on the selected seed feature, this kind of sentences can be useful for a wide range of applications. In particular, we have focused our experiments on generating sentences in order to reinforce the phoneme pronunciation for dyslalia disorder. Automatic generated sentences have been evaluated manually obtaining good results in newly generated meaningful sentences.

1 Introduction

The task of Natural Language Generation (NLG) comprises a wide range of subtasks which extend from an action planning until its execution (Bateman and Zoch, 2003). This subtasks are commonly viewed as a pipeline of three stages: document planning, microplanning and surface realisation (Reiter and Dale, 2000).

The NLG can be applied to several fields, not only to the task of reporting, such as text simplification (Reiter et al., 2009), recommendation generation (Lim-Cheng et al., 2014), text summarisation (Portet et al., 2007) or text that attempts to help people having any kind of disorders in therapies (Black et al., 2012).

Despite the applicability of NLG, this is not a trivial task. There is still a lot of room for improvement, and small steps in this task would be useful for being integrated or applied in larger NLG or NLP systems.

Therefore, the main goal of this paper is to present and evaluate a statistical NLG approach for Spanish based on N-grams language models. Our approach is focused on the surface realisation stage, and it is initially designed and tested for Spanish, but it can be extrapolated to other languages as it is statistical-based. The novelty of this approach lies in its input data, which can be a concrete seed feature or aspect (communicative goal) that we will be used to guide the generation of the new sentence (i.e., for guiding the generation process). This seed feature could be a word, a phoneme, a sentiment, etc.

This type of generated sentences can be useful in many different ways such as helping in therapies as has been outlined above. Specifically, we have chosen stories generation as our experimental scenario, so that a person with dyslalia, a speech disorder that implies the inability of pronounce certain phonemes, can reinforce the pronunciation of several problematic phonemes through reading and repeating words. So the aim of these sentences for dyslalia would be to contain a huge number of words with a concrete phoneme.

At this stage we are not exhaustively evaluating how syntactically and semantically correct a sentence is, but just whether to what extent a sentence fulfilling a communicative goal can be generated from a functional point of view. We consider that the communicative goal of our experimental scenario is to teach how a phoneme should be pronounced, so, by repeating the desired phoneme along a sentence this goal can be reached. Therefore, we will evaluate and analyse the output from our approach based on the seed feature appearance along the sentence and the sentence correctness.

Proceedings of the 15th European Workshop on Natural Language Generation (ENLG), pages 9–17,
Brighton, September 2015.

The remainder of this paper is as follows. Section 2 discusses some related work concerned with surface realisation statistical systems. Section 3 presents our statistical approach for NLG based on seed features. Section 4 shows the experimentation carried out over the approach. In Section 5 the evaluation and the results obtained is discussed. Section 6 presents the potentials and limitations of our approach. Finally, section 7 draws some conclusions and outlines ideas for future work.

2 Related Work

The use of statistical techniques in NLG have been widely spread since Langkilde and Knight (1998) used them for the first time, where they used language models (LM) to choose words transformations after applying generation rules. Most of these techniques use language models, such as n-grams, or stochastic grammars. An example of these statistical techniques are given in (Kondadadi et al., 2013) that presents a statistical NLG system which consolidates macro and micro planning, as well as surface realisation stages into one statistical learning process. Moreover, many other statistical examples can be found in (Lemon, 2008), where a new model for adaptive NLG in dialog, showing how NLG problems can be approached as statistical planning problems using reinforcement learning, is presented. In the BAGEL system (Mairesse et al., 2010), a statistical language generator which uses dynamic Bayesian networks to learn from semantically-aligned data is integrated.

These statistical LM have been employed with several languages including Chinese, English, German and Spanish (Bohnet et al., 2010), where they take advantage of multilevel annotated corpora and propose a multilingual deep stochastic sentence realiser.

On the other hand, regarding to the application of NLG in order to help people having any type of problem or disorder there are several systems. For instance, STOP (Reiter et al., 2003) that generates letters to dissuade users from smoking, or systems to reduce anxiety of patients with cancer by providing them with information (Cawsey et al., 2000). These two systems employ templates that are filled with information from a data base or a knowledge base selected from user profiles.

There are approaches, such as the one in (Fernández et al., 2008) that generates sentences in Spanish containing words related to a specific restricted scenario, but, to the best of our knowledge, there is not a research in NLG focused on generating sentences in Spanish with the restriction of containing words with a specific seed feature. Moreover, since we use probabilistic techniques, these are language independent allowing its application to others languages adapting the necessary resources (e.g., semantic features) for the language-specific part.

3 Our Seed Feature Guided Language Generation Process

We propose a statistical approach using n-gram LM guided by an input seed feature. This approach is focused on generating a sentence with the highest number of words containing a certain seed feature. This seed feature, used to guide all the generation process, can be anything, such as letters, phonemes, POS tag, sentiments, etc.

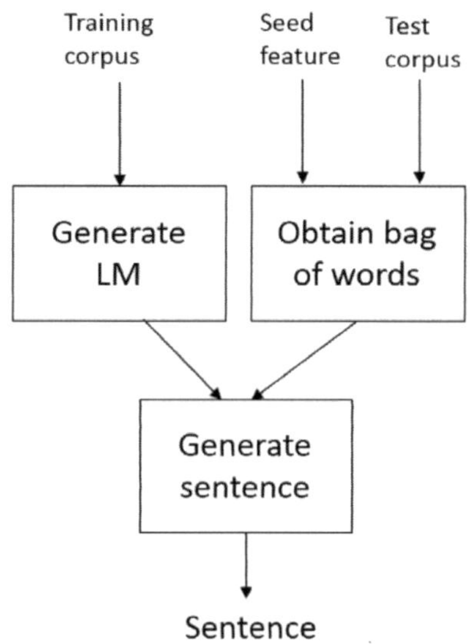

Figure 1: Our approach diagram

The input of this approach are: i) a training corpus, ii) a test corpus and iii) the seed feature. In Figure 1 a diagram of the process flow can be seen.

In the following paragraphs it is explained how the approach works.

1. **Generate the language model**: Before starting with the process, we train the LM over a training corpus in the desired language.

2. **Obtain the bag of words**: We obtain from the test corpus a bag of words having the seed

feature which is going to be used for the generation. This bag of words includes the word itself and its frequency of occurrence in the test corpus.

3. **Generate the sentence**:

   This step of the process can be executed with two different configurations. The default configuration only generates one sentence based on the seed feature; and, with the overgeneration configuration, the system generates several sentences based on the seed feature. Next, we will explain the overall functioning of the process.
   The approach is an iterative process in which this stage is repeated until either the desired length, or the special token end of sentence (</s>) are reached.
   Assuming that there is a word that has been obtained from the previous iteration, we first search in the bag of words if there is a word in it that follows the word from the previous iteration. If so, we check which one has the highest probability based on the LM depending on that word, and in case of a draw between two or more words, then the word chosen is the one with a higher frequency in the test corpus.
   Otherwise, we look for the word which has the highest probability of appearance with the word selected from the previous iteration in our LM, and if there are more than one word in our LM with the same probability, we check if any of them contains the seed feature. In that case, we pick the word with the seed feature; in another case, we choose the first appearance of the word with highest probability. As we said before, the process runs, prioritising the selection of words containing the seed feature, until the desired length or the token (</s>) are reached.
   We took several issues into consideration during the implementation of our approach. For the first iteration, we initially set the special token start of the sentence (<s>) as our starting word. Moreover, when we choose the words it is taken into account that, if the chosen word is a stopword, then the process returns the stopword accompanied with the most probable next word. Another issue taken into account is that a stopword is not selected as the next word on the last iteration, to prevent sentences ending inappropriately. Finally, a word cannot be chosen if it has been chosen before. This is to avoid words or word's sequences repetitions along the sentence.
   The main difference between our two configurations lies on the first iteration of the generation process. With the default configuration, we only choose one initial word, so a single sentence is generated. With the overgeneration configuration, for an input seed feature, a list of words is chosen. This list contains the words that i) have the same probability as the one with the highest probability of appearance with the token (<s>), and ii) are within a range of less than a 0.5% of probability with respect to the words with the highest probability of appearance with the token (<s>) (this was empirically determined). In the remainder iterations, for each word contained in the list, the process runs likewise the default configuration.

4 Experimental setup

In this section we are going to discuss both the scenario, resources and tests performed to the approach.

4.1 Scenario

We place our research in the context of generating text to help people with a any kind of disorder. In particular, generating stories in order to help children with dyslalia could be one of the applications encapsulated within this application area (Barros and LLoret, 2015). Dyslalia is a disorder in phoneme articulation which implies the inability to correctly pronounce certain phonemes or groups of phonemes (in Spanish some of this phonemes are: /ch/, /ll/, /rr/ or in English are: /zh/, /ng/, /j/). This disorder is estimated to have a 5-10% incidence among the child population (Conde-Guzón et al., 2014).

Consequently, and based on the dyslalia disorder, the seed feature selected in order to generate the sentences is a problematic phoneme. Therefore, our main objective is to generate Spanish sentences containing a large number of words with a concrete phoneme, so that a child with dyslalia can reinforce the phoneme's pronunciation through reading and repeating words. In Figure 2 an illustrative example in Spanish for the phoneme

/a/ obtained from a real story[1], being part of an educational project of the Spanish Government, can be seen. This type of sentences can be useful for dyslalia disorder because they reinforce the phoneme pronunciation of the child by constantly repeating that concrete phoneme.

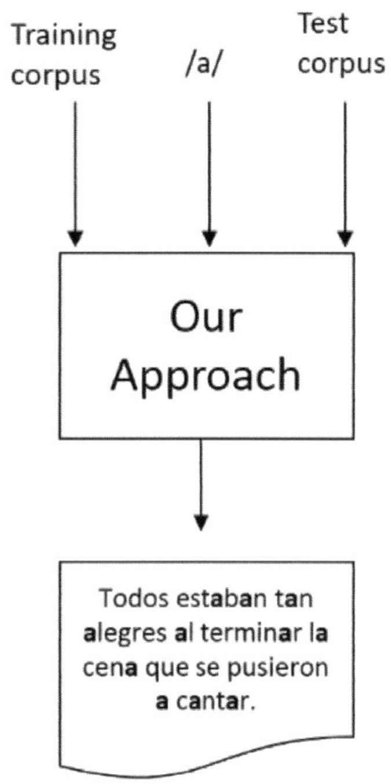

Figure 2: Illustrative example sentence. (*Translation: Everyone was so happy after dinner that began to sing.*)

4.2 Corpus and Resources

Since, as seen in the previous section, the scenario proposed is focused on generating stories which would improve the pronunciation of phonemes in children with dyslalia, the chosen corpus selected to perform the test is a collection of Hans Christian Andersen[2] stories in Spanish.

This collection consists of 158 children's stories (containing 21,085 sentences in total) of which 25% has been used as the test corpus from where the bag of words is obtained. For training the LM we have used the 75% of the corpus, in our case, we have trained a bigram LM and a trigram LM, being these models the most commonly used in n-gram language model (Rosenfeld, 2000). If we had chosen any higher n, we will have to confront with data sparseness problems, where most possible grammatical n-grams would never appear even in huge training corpora.

These LMs have been trained using the SRILM (Stolcke, 2002) software that is a toolkit for building and applying statistical language models. We have chosen this software for its usability and because factored languages models (Bilmes and Kirchhoff, 2003) are implemented in it, and, in the future, we want to introduce them to the approach.

Obtaining words containing a concrete phoneme was performed according to the correspondence between phonemes and letters, employing some of the phonetic restrictions exposed in Morales (1992).

Furthermore, the stopword's file used in the experimentation has been obtained from the NLTK software data[3].

4.3 Experiments

We have performed several experiments dividing them in two groups that will be explained in more detail in the following paragraphs:

- Preliminary experiments
- Overgeneration experiments

To determine the length of the sentences to be generated, the average sentence length of the corpus was computed (16 words), using also this value for our experiments.

4.3.1 Preliminary experiments.

This type of experiments were conducted in order to check if it was worthy to carry on with this statistical-based approach, employing bigrams and trigrams LM, and to what extent the approach's behavior could be affected by the inclusion (or not) of stopwords. In addition, these experiments were carried out with the default configuration of the approach and testing all the Spanish phonemes. In this sense, we performed three types of experiments:

- First experiment: we removed the stopwords from the generation approach but we did not remove them from the training corpus.

[1] http://redined.mecd.gob.es/xmlui/bitstream/handle/11162/30643/00920082002857.pdf?sequence=1

[2] http://www.ciudadseva.com/textos/cuentos/euro/andersen/hca.htm

[3] http://www.nltk.org/nltk_data/

[4] English translation is shown in brackets.

Phoneme:ñ **Letters**: ñ

1st experiment.
Bigram: <s> añadió niño pequeño ruiseñor </s> (*said little boy nightingale*)
Trigram: <s> añadió aguja niños pequeño ruiseñor siguió cantando acompañado soñar mañana sueños </s>
(*said needle kids little nightingale continued singing accompanied morning dreaming dreams*)

2nd experiment.
Bigram: <s> mañana pequeña </s> (*little morning*)
Trigram: <s> *mañana siguiente niño pequeño ruiseñor siguió cantando acompañado novia domesticada* </s>
(*next morning little boy nightingale sung accompanied domesticated girlfriend*)

3rd experiment.
Bigram: <s> añadió niño pequeño ruiseñor </s> (*said little boy nightingale*)
Trigram: <s> *añadió la aguja* </s> (*said the needle*)

Figure 3: Preliminary experiments output[4]

- Second experiment: we trained both LMs without stopwords, and consequently the generation was made without stopwords.
- Third experiment: we trained both LMs with stopwords and we also removed the words repetitions on the final sentence. Furthermore, the stopwords were included in the final sentence.

4.3.2 Overgeneration experiments.

This experiment was performed after checking the results from the preliminary experiments. The main objective of this experiment was to test the overgeneration configuration of the approach with all the Spanish phonemes, and, check if it generates some meaningful sentences, as well as the most common types of errors.

5 Evaluation and Discussion

In this section we report the results from our two types of experiments: preliminary and overgeneration experiments. Furthermore, for the resulting generated sentences we made a manual analysis and evaluation. With this evaluation we needed to check if there was any meaningful sentence, ensuring that the sentence contained at least one word with the concrete phoneme.

5.1 Preliminary experiments evaluation.

As previously explained in section 4.3.1, within these preliminary experiments we performed three types of tests regarding the approach behavior and the utilisation or not of stopwords. Some sentences obtained from this test can be seen in the Figure 3.

Concerning our first experiment, in many cases the approach did not find the next word and the generation ended before reaching the limit length of the sentence using both LMs, bigram and trigram. This was due to the fact that there are verbs or words that only appears next to stopwords. We also tested in this experiment that, when a stopword was found, the next function word returned the stopword accompanied with its next word, but the stopword was not included in the final sentence and it was only used for the next word prediction. Yet still, most generated sentence were meaningless and presented quite a lot repetition.

As a result of our second experiment, the generated sentences tend to be a sequence of nouns, verbs and adjectives without any relation between them.

Finally, in our third experiment we observed that the generated sentences with trigrams ended with the special token end of sentence (</s>), containing at least one word with the phoneme, and some of them where meaningful sentences. Regarding the bigrams generated ones, most of them contained a huge number of words with the phoneme but the words itself did not have any connection with each other.

Thanks to these results we found that our approach worked well in some cases and because of that we decided to try the overgeneration configuration of the approach.

Sentences	**Local percentage (based on 95 sent.)**	**Global percentage (based on 208 sent.)**
Generated sent. from bigram LM with (</s>)	46.32%	21.15%
Generated sent. from trigram LM with (</s>)	78.95%	36.06%
Newly generated not included in the corpus	73.68%	33.65%
Meaningful total sentences	56.84%	25.96%
Meaningful sentences included in the corpus	25.26%	11.54%
Newly meaningful generated sent. not included in the corpus	31.58%	14.42%
Newly meaningful generated sent. from bigram LM	9.47%	4.33%
Newly meaningful generated sent. from trigram LM	22.11%	10.10%

Table 2: Statistics of the generated sentences ended with (</s>)

5.2 Overgeneration experiments evaluation.

Based on the results of the preliminary experiments, we further test the overgeneration configuration (section 4.3.2).

In this case, the approach generated 208 sentences, which 119 of them contains the special token end of sentence (</s>). All these sentences were generated from the bigram and trigram LMs, so it can occur that the same sentence could be generated by both LMs. These sentences ended with the token (</s>) are important because they can be comparable to a complete sentence. Of the 119 sentences generated containing the token (</s>), 95 of them are different. This can be seen on Table 1.

Sentences	**Number of generated sentences**	**Percentage**
Total	208	100%
Not ended with (</s>)	89	42.79%
Ended with (</s>)	119	57.21%
Ended with (</s>) without repetition	95	45.67%

Table 1: Statistics of the generated sentences from the overgeneration configuration

We then focused the evaluation and analysis of our results on the sentences ending with the token (</s>). This is because we consider these sentences as complete sentences being this token comparable to a full stop. The statistics of Table 2 were calculated according to the total number of different generated sentences ended with the token (</s>), 95 sentences. In this Table we also include the comparative percentage regarding the total number of generated sentences, that is 208 sentences. As we can see in this Table, the statistics of meaningful sentences are really encouraging.

These meaningful sentences do not include punctuation marks so, although some sentences at first glance do not seem coherent, with the inclusion of some punctuation marks they become meaningful.

<s> allí se quedó con la doncella había llegado el invierno </s>
(P: /a/ L: a T:*stayed there with the maid had come winter*)
<s> añadió el niño pequeño ruiseñor </s>
(P: /ñ/ L: ñ T: *said the little boy nightingale*)
<s> dónde está el cielo </s>
(P: /n/ L: n T: *where is the sky*)
<s> finalmente llegaron a la superficie del agua </s>
(P: /f/ L: f T: *finally they reached the surface of the water*)
<s> nadie conoce la princesa </s>
(P: /n/ L: n T: *nobody knows the princess*)
<s> pues bien hecho está </s>
(P: /e/ L: e T: *well done*)
<s> quién pudiera verlo </s>
(P: /u/ L: u T: *who could see*)
<s> verdad que es la vida </s>
(P: /b/ L: b,v,w T: *really that is the life*)
<s> verdad vieja bruja perversa </s>
(P: /b/ L: b,v,w T: *really wicked old witch*)

Figure 4: Newly meaningful generated sentences. P: phoneme, L: letters and T: translation in brackets

Meaningful sentences cover almost the half of the different sentences ended with the token (</s>), and those newly sentences that not explicitly exist on the training corpus are about 30% of

Error types		Number of sentences	Local percentage (95 sent.)
Grammatical concordance	Nominal	2	4.88%
	Verbal	7	17.07%
Non words semantic relations		36	87.80%
Missing main verb		7	17.07%
Incorrect syntactic order		38	92.68%

Table 3: Common types of generated sentences errors

the 95 different sentences with the token. These result are quite positive considering that we are only focusing on the appearance of words with the phoneme within the sentence. Moreover, trigram LM is more suitable than bigram LM since it generates a higher number of newly meaningful sentences. Some of these newly generated sentences, that have been created employing different phonemes, can be seen in the Figure 4.

5.2.1 Error Types and Analysis

After analysing the generated sentences ending with the special token end of sentence (</s>), they may have some common errors along the meaningless sentences. These errors affects the coherence and cohesion of the sentence leading to make the sentence meaningless.

We manually analysed all the generated sentences and classified these errors attending to frequent grammatical errors[5] and frequent drafting errors[6]. In this classification we do not take into account punctuation marks errors because, when we train the language models we remove the punctuation marks from the corpus and, consequently, when we generate the sentences we do not introduce them.

We have found morphosyntactic errors of concordance. We subdivided concordance into two levels: nominal and verbal. Errors in nominal concordance refers to errors regarding with gender and number of the words, and, on the other hand, errors in verbal concordance refers to discordance between verb and subject in number. We also found errors regarding semantics relation between words, that is, the meaning of the words are unrelated to each other. Furthermore, we also found sentences not having a main verb conjugated. The most common error was found in the order of the words, having an incorrect order leading to nonsense sequences of words.

Because not all the sentences presents only one type of errors, in Table 3 we have counted each type of error independently, for the meaningless sentences ended with (</s>) that have that error. As it can be seen in the table, and it was already noted, the most common errors among the sentences are syntactic errors and non semantic relation between words. We will see some examples below with its translation in brackets. For example, a sentence with a missing main verb conjugated is:

<s>ahora **hacer** </s>*(now do)*

An example sentence having only nominal concordance error is:

<s>aquell**o** era demasiad**o** fina (</s>) *(this was too thin)*

Where *aquello* and *demasiado* are masculine and *fina* is feminine. And finally, an example sentence with ordering errors, non semantic words relations and verb concordance error:

<s>allí orgullo y aquella belleza brillan en aquellos pajarillos de ello </s>*(there pride and beauty that shine in those birds of it)*

These errors can be corrected employing grammars for generating a sentences with a correct syntactic order or using some kind of semantic information in order to select words related semantically to one another.

6 Potentials and Limitations of the approach

Considering this approach as our research starting point we have to take into account some key as-

[5] https://ciervalengua.files.wordpress.com/2011/11/errores-gramaticales-frecuentes.pdf

[6] http://blog.pucp.edu.pe/blog/blogderedaccion/2013/04/18/errores-m-s-comunes-en-la-redacci-n/

pects from where we can improve the approach until we can achieve a fully correct generation of correct syntactic and semantically generated sentences based on a seed feature.

This approach has a great potential since it is a statistical approach, that means that these type of techniques are language independent, so we only need to adapt the language-specific approach's input, resulting this adaptation cost not really high. Moreover, an advantage of our approach is that we can make a more flexible generation adapted to different scenarios and applications guided for the input seed feature, being our surface realisation approach flexible and adaptive.

There is much information to consider in order to form a correct sentence. On the one hand we need syntactic information in order to get a correct syntactic structure of the sentence. This syntactic structure information can be achieved via grammars or trees. We will check existing Spanish resources in order to decide if we use one of them or develop our own. For the other hand, we need semantic information to make the generated sentences coherent. There are several linguistic theories that refers to discourse coherence such as the rhetorical structure theory (Mann and Thompson, 1988) or the systemic functional linguistic (Matthiessen and Halliday, 1997), that could be further exploited and integrated in the approach.

7 Conclusions and Future Work

We have presented a statistical NLG approach for Spanish guided by a seed feature. This approach allow us to create sentences containing a large number of words with a concrete seed feature. We also outlined a possible NLG scenario where these sentences can be helpful in speech therapies. For example, if the selected seed feature is a phoneme, this kind of sentences can be used in order to improve phoneme pronunciation.

Furthermore, we have shown that the approach obtains good results generating meaningful sentences not contained in the training corpus, taking into account that we are only focusing on the appearance of words with the concrete seed feature. Although the results obtained are promising, we must improve them because we do not generate meaningful sentences in all cases.

In the future, the approach will be modified to include both semantic and syntactic information to ensure that the generated sentences will be syntactic and semantically correct. We also want to test and subsequently include to the approach factored language models. In this model enunciated by Bilmes and Kirchhoff (2003) a word is viewed as a vector of factors that can be anything, including morphological classes, stems, roots, semantic information, etc. The main goal of this model is to produce a language model taking into account these factors. So, this type of model can serve us as a way of combine different information at a word level with our seed feature-based approach. In addition, once we have consolidated this model with our approach, we will test it with an English corpus in order to compare its results with the ones obtained from employing a Spanish corpus.

Finally, we need to investigate diverse ways of evaluating the generated sentences instead of manually evaluate this sentences. This will allow us in the future to have an homogeneous way of evaluating the generated sentences from an objective point of view.

Acknowledgments

This research work has been partially funded by the University of Alicante, Generalitat Valenciana, Spanish Government and the European Commission through the projects, "Explotación y tratamiento de la información disponible en Internet para la anotación y generación de textos adaptados al usuario" (GRE13-15), DIIM2.0 (PROMETEOII/2014/001), ATTOS (TIN2012-38536-C03-03), "LEGOLANG-UAGE (Técnicas de Deconstrucción en la Tecnologías del Lenguaje Humano)" (TIN2012-31224), and SAM (FP7-611312), respectively.

References

Cristina Barros and Elena LLoret. 2015. Proposal of a data-to-text natural language generation approach to create stories for dyslalic children. In *1st International Workshop on Data-to-text Generation*, Edinburgh.

John Bateman and Michael Zoch. 2003. *Natural Language Generation*. Oxford University Press.

Jeff A. Bilmes and Katrin Kirchhoff. 2003. Factored language models and generalized parallel backoff. In *Proceedings of the 2003 Conference of the North American Chapter of the Association for Computational Linguistics on Human Language Technology*, pages 4–6. Association for Computational Linguistics.

Rolf Black, Annalu Waller, Ross Turner, and Ehud Reiter. 2012. Supporting personal narrative for children with complex communication needs. *ACM Trans. Comput.-Hum. Interact.*, 19(2):15:1–15:35.

Bernd Bohnet, Leo Wanner, Simon Mille, and Alicia Burga. 2010. Broad coverage multilingual deep sentence generation with a stochastic multi-level realizer. In *Proceedings of the 23rd International Conference on Computational Linguistics*, pages 98–106. Association for Computational Linguistics.

Alison J. Cawsey, Ray B. Jones, and Janne Pearson. 2000. The evaluation of a personalised health information system for patients with cancer. *User Modeling and User-Adapted Interaction*, 10(1):47–72.

Pablo Conde-Guzón, Pilar Quirós-Expósito, María Jesús Conde-Guzón, and María Teresa Bartolomé-Albistegui. 2014. Perfil neuropsicológico de niños con dislalias: alteraciones mnésicas y atencionales. *Anales de Psicología*, 30:1105 – 1114.

Carles Fernández, Xavier Roca, and Jordi Gonzàlez. 2008. Providing automatic multilingual text generation to artificial cognitive systems. *Vigo International Journal of Applied Linguistics*, 5:37–62.

Ravi Kondadadi, Blake Howald, and Frank Schilder. 2013. A statistical nlg framework for aggregated planning and realization. pages 1406–1415. The Association for Computer Linguistics.

Irene Langkilde and Kevin Knight. 1998. Generation that exploits corpus-based statistical knowledge. In *Proceedings of the 36th Annual Meeting of the Association for Computational Linguistics and 17th International Conference on Computational Linguistics-Volume 1*, pages 704–710. Association for Computational Linguistics.

Oliver Lemon. 2008. Adaptive natural language generation in dialogue using reinforcement learning. *Proc. SEM-dial*, pages 141–148.

Natalie R. Lim-Cheng, Gabriel Isidro G. Fabia, Marco Emil G. Quebral, and Miguelito T. Yu. 2014. Shed: An online diet counselling system. In *DLSU Research Congress 2014*.

François Mairesse, Milica Gašić, Filip Jurčíček, Simon Keizer, Blaise Thomson, Kai Yu, and Steve Young. 2010. Phrase-based statistical language generation using graphical models and active learning. In *Proceedings of the 48th Annual Meeting of the Association for Computational Linguistics*, pages 1552–1561. Association for Computational Linguistics.

William C. Mann and Sandra A. Thompson. 1988. Rhetorical structure theory: Toward a functional theory of text organization. *Text - Interdisciplinary Journal for the Study of Discourse*, 8(3):243–281.

C.M.I.M. Matthiessen and M.A.K. Halliday. 1997. *Systemic Functional Grammar: A First Step Into the Theory*.

Juan Luis Onieva Morales. 1992. *Nuevo método de ortografía*. Colección Cervantes. Verbum.

François Portet, Ehud Reiter, Jim Hunter, and Somayajulu Sripada. 2007. Automatic generation of textual summaries from neonatal intensive care data. In *Artificial Intelligence in Medicine*, pages 227–236. Springer.

Ehud Reiter and Robert Dale. 2000. *Building Natural Language Generation Systems*. Cambridge University Press.

Ehud Reiter, Roma Robertson, and Liesl M Osman. 2003. Lessons from a failure: Generating tailored smoking cessation letters. *Artificial Intelligence*, 144(1):41–58.

Ehud Reiter, Ross Turner, Norman Alm, Rolf Black, Martin Dempster, and Annalu Waller. 2009. Using NLG to help language-impaired users tell stories and participate in social dialogues. In *Proceedings of the 12th European Workshop on Natural Language Generation*, pages 1–8. Association for Computational Linguistics.

Ronald Rosenfeld. 2000. Two decades of statistical language modeling: Where do we go from here? In *Proceedings of the IEEE*, pages 1270–1278.

Andreas Stolcke. 2002. Srilm - an extensible language modeling toolkit. In *Proceedings International Conference on Spoken Language Processing, vol 2.*, pages 901–904.

A Domain Agnostic Approach to Verbalizing n-ary Events without Parallel Corpora

Bikash Gyawali
Université de Lorraine/LORIA
Nancy, France
bikash.gyawali
@loria.fr

Claire Gardent
CNRS/LORIA
Nancy, France
claire.gardent
@loria.fr

Christophe Cerisara
CNRS/LORIA
Nancy, France
christophe.cerisara
@loria.fr

Abstract

We present a method for automatically generating descriptions of biological events encoded in the KB Bio 101 Knowledge base. We evaluate our approach on a corpus of 336 event descriptions, provide a qualitative and quantitative analysis of the results obtained and discuss possible directions for further work.

1 Introduction

While earlier work on data-to-text generation heavily relied on handcrafted linguistic resources, more recent data-driven approaches have focused on learning a generation system from parallel corpora of data and text. Thus, (Angeli et al., 2010; Chen and Mooney, 2008; Wong and Mooney, 2007; Konstas and Lapata, 2012b; Konstas and Lapata, 2012a) trained and developed data-to-text generators on datasets from various domains including the air travel domain (Dahl et al., 1994), weather forecasts (Liang et al., 2009; Belz, 2008) and sportscasting (Chen and Mooney, 2008). In both cases, considerable time and expertise must be spent on developing the required linguistic resources. In the handcrafted, symbolic approach, appropriate grammars and lexicons must be specified while in the parallel corpus based learning approach, an aligned data-text corpus must be built for each new domain. Here, we explore an alternative approach using non-parallel corpora for surface realisation from knowledge bases that can be used for any knowledge base for which there exists large textual corpora.

A more specific, linguistic issue which has received relatively little attention is the unsupervised verbalisation of n-ary relations and the task of appropriately mapping KB roles to syntactic functions. In recent work on verbalising RDF triples, relations are restricted to binary relations (called "property" in the RDF language) and the issue is therefore intrinsically simpler. In symbolic approaches dealing with n-ary relations, the mapping between syntactic and semantic arguments is determined by the lexicon and must be manually specified. In data-driven approaches, the mapping is learned from the alignment between text and data and is restricted by cases seen in the training data. Instead, we learn a probabilistic model designed to select the most probable mapping. In this way, we provide a domain independent, fully automatic, means of verbalising n-ary relations.

The paper is structured as follows. In Section 2, we discuss related work. In Section 3, we present the method used to verbalise KB events and their participants. In Section 4, we evaluate our approach on a corpus of 336 test cases, provide a qualitative and quantitative analysis of the results obtained and discuss possible directions for further work. Section 5 concludes.

2 Related Work

There has been much research in recent years on developing natural language generation systems which support verbalisation from knowledge and data bases.

Many of the existing KB Verbalising tools rely on generating so-called Controlled Natural Languages (CNL) i.e., a language engineered to be read and written almost like a natural language but whose syntax and lexicon is restricted to prevent ambiguity. For instance, the OWL verbaliser integrated in the Protégé tool is a CNL based generation tool, (Kaljurand and Fuchs, 2007) which provides a verbalisation of every axiom present in the ontology under consideration. Similarly, (Wilcock, 2003) describes an ontology verbaliser using XML-based generation. Finally, recent work by the SWAT project[1] has focused on pro-

[1]http://crc.open.ac.uk/Projects/SWAT

Proceedings of the 15th European Workshop on Natural Language Generation (ENLG), pages 18–27,
Brighton, September 2015. ©2015 Association for Computational Linguistics

ducing descriptions of ontologies that are both coherent and efficient (Williams and Power, 2010). In these approaches, the mapping between relations and verbs is determined either manually or through string matching and KB relations are assumed to map to binary verbs.

More complex NLG systems have also been developed to generate text (rather than simple sentences) from knowledge bases. Thus, the MIAKT project (Bontcheva and Wilks., 2004) and the ONTOGENERATION project (Aguado et al., 1998) use symbolic NLG techniques to produce textual descriptions from some semantic information contained in a knowledge base. Both systems require some manual input (lexicons and domain schemas). More sophisticated NLG systems such as TAILOR (Paris, 1988), MIGRAINE (Mittal et al., 1994), and STOP (Reiter et al., 2003) offer tailored output based on user/patient models. While offering more flexibility and expressiveness, these systems are difficult to adapt by non-NLG experts because they require the user to understand the architecture of the NLG systems (Bontcheva and Wilks., 2004). Similarly, the NaturalOWL system (Galanis et al., 2009) has been proposed to generate fluent descriptions of museum exhibits from an OWL ontology. These approaches however rely on extensive manual annotation of the input data.

Related to the work discussed in this paper is the task of learning subcategorization information from textual corpora. Automatic methods for subcategorization frame acquisition have been proposed from general text corpora, e.g., (Briscoe and Carroll, 1997), (Korhonen, 2002), (Sarkar and Zeman, 2000) and specific biomedical domain corpora as well (Rimell et al., 2013). Such works are limited to the extraction of syntactic frames representing subcategorization information. Instead, we focus on relating the syntactic and semantic frame and, in particular, on the linking between syntactic and semantic arguments.

Another trend of work relevant to this paper is generation from databases using parallel corpora of data and text. (Angeli et al., 2010) train a sequence of discriminative models to predict data selection, ordering and realisation. (Wong and Mooney, 2007) uses techniques from statistical machine translation to model the generation task and (Konstas and Lapata, 2012b; Konstas and Lapata, 2012a) learns a probabilistic Context-Free Grammar modelling the structure of the database and of the associated text. Various systems from the KBGEN shared task (Banik et al., 2013) – (Butler et al., 2013), (Gyawali and Gardent, 2013) and (Zarrieβ and Richardson, 2013) perform generation from the same input data source as ours' and use parallel text for supervision. Our approach differs from all these approaches in that it does not require parallel text/data corpora. Also in contrast to the template extraction approaches described in (Kondadadi et al., 2013), (Ell and Harth, 2014) and (Duma and Klein, 2013), we do not succeed in directly matching the input data to surface text in the sentences obtained from non-parallel biomedical texts. Instead, we must extract the subcategorization frame and learn the linking between semantic and syntactic arguments.

3 Methodology

Our goal is to automatically generate natural language verbalisations of the biological event descriptions encoded in KB BIO 101 (Chaudhri et al., 2013) whereby an *event description* is assumed to consist of an event, its arguments and the roles relating each argument to the event. In the KB BIO 101 knowledge base, events are concepts of type EVENT (e.g., RELEASE), arguments are concepts of type ENTITY (e.g., GATED-CHANNEL, VASCULAR-TISSUE, IRON) and roles are relations between events and entities (e.g., AGENT, PATIENT, PATH, INSTRUMENT).

We propose a probabilistic method which extracts possible verbalisation frames from large biology specific domain corpora and uses probabilities both to select an appropriate frame given an event description and to determine the mapping between syntactic and semantic arguments. That is, probabilities are used to determine which event argument fills which syntactic function (e.g., subject, object) in the produced verbalisation.

We start by giving a brief overview of the content and the structure of KB BIO 101(Section 3.1). We then describe the steps involved in building our generation system.

3.1 KB Bio 101

The foundational component of the KB is the Component Library (CLIB), an upper ontology which is linguistically motivated and designed to support the representation of knowledge for automated reasoning (Gunning et al., 2010). CLIB adopts four simple top level distinctions: (1) enti-

```
SubClassOf(:Hydrophobic-Compound :Entity)
SubClassOf(:Plasma-Membrane :Entity)
SubClassOf(:Block
  ObjectIntersectionOf(:Event
    ObjectSomeValuesFrom(:instrument :Plasma-Membrane)
    ObjectSomeValuesFrom(:object :Hydrophobic-Compound)))
```

Figure 1: Example Event Representation in KB Bio 101

ties (things that are); (2) events (things that happen); (3) relations (associations between things); and (4) roles (ways in which entities participate in events).

Figure 1 shows an example representation for a blocking event between a plasma membrane and hydrophobic compounds which could be verbalised as *The plasma membrane blocks hydrophobic compounds*. In this representation, *Block* is a subclass of the event class. *Plasma-Menbrane* and *Hydrophobic-Compound* are subclasses of the entity class. The *Plasma-Menbrane* and the *Hydrophobic-Compound* concepts stand respectively in an *instrument* and in an *object* role relation with the *Block* event.

KB Bio 101 is organized into a set of concept maps, where each concept map corresponds to a biological entity or process. It was encoded by biology teachers and contains around 5,000 concept maps. KB Bio 101 is available for download for academic purposes in various formats including OWL[2] .

To test and evaluate our approach, we focus on the subpart of KB Bio 101 isolated for the KBGen surface realisation shared task by (Banik et al., 2013). In this dataset, content units were semi-automatically selected from KB Bio 101 in such a way that (i) the set of relations in each content unit forms a connected graph; (ii) each content unit can be verbalised by a single, possibly complex sentence which is grammatical and meaningful and (iii) the set of content units contain as many different relations and concepts of different semantic types (events, entities, properties, etc) as possible.

That is, the KB content extracted for KBGen isolate event descriptions which can be verbalised by a single, coherent sentence. To evaluate the ability of our generator to generate event descriptions, we further process this dataset to produce all KB fragments which represent a single event with roles to entities only. The statistics for the resulting dataset (dubbed KBGen+) are shown in Table 1.

[2] http://www.ai.sri.com/halo/halobook2010/exported-kb/biokb.html

Items	Count
Total nb of Event Descriptions	336
Avg (min/max) nb of roles in an Event Description	2.93/1.8
Total nb of events	126 (336)
Total nb of entities	271 (929)
Total nb of roles	14 (929)

Table 1: Test Set. The numbers in brackets indicate the number of tokens in KBGen$^+$

3.2 Corpus Collection

We begin by gathering sentences from several of the publicly available biomedical domain corpora.[3] This includes the BioCause (Mihil et al., 2013), BioDef[4], BioInfer (Pyysalo et al., 2007), Grec (Thompson et al., 2009), Genia (Kim et al., 2003) and PubMedCentral (PMC)[5] corpus. We also include the sentences available in annotations of named concepts in the KB Bio 101 ontology. This custom collection of sentences will be the corpus upon which our learning approach will build on. Table 2 lists the count of sentences available in each corpus and in total.

	#Sentences
BioCause	3,187
BioDef	8,426
BioInfer	1,100
Genia	37,092,000
Grec	2,035
PMC	7,018,743
KBBio101	3,393
Total	44,128,884

Table 2: Corpus Size

3.3 Lexicon Creation

To identify corpus sentences which might contain verbalisations of KBGen$^+$ events and entities, we build a lexicon mapping events and entities contained in KBGen$^+$ to natural language words or phrases using existing resources. First, we take the lexicon provided by the KBGen

[3] Ideally, since KB Bio 101 was developed based on a textbook, we would use this textbook as a corpus. Unfortunately, the textbook, previously licensed from Pearson, is no longer available.

[4] Obtained by parsing the ⟨Supplement⟩ section of html pages crawled from http://www.biology-online.org/dictionary/

[5] ftp://ftp.ncbi.nlm.nih.gov/pub/pmc

challenge. The KBGEN lexicon is composed of entries that provide inflected forms and nominalizations for the event variables and singular and plural noun forms for the entity variables, such as :

Block, blocks, block, blocked, blocking
Earthworm, earthworm, earthworms

To this, we add the synset entries of Mesh[6] and the BioDef[7] vocabularies containing the KBGEN$^+$ events and entities . Some example synsets obtained from Mesh and BioDef are shown below:

Block, prevent, stop
Neoplasm,Tumors,Neoplasia,Cancer

Finally, for generalisation purposes, we automatically extract the direct parent and siblings of the KBGEN$^+$ events and entities in the KB BIO 101 ontology and add them as a lexical entries for the corresponding KBGEN$^+$ event/entity. For example, for the KBGEN$^+$ event **"Block"**, the direct parent and siblings extracted from the KB BIO 101 are, respectively:

make inaccessible
conceal, deactivate, obstruct

Our lexicon is then a merge of all entries extracted from either a lexicon or the ontology for the KBGEN$^+$ events and entities. In Table 3, we present the size of lexicon available from each source (Total Entries) and the count of KBGEN$^+$ event and entity types (Intersecting Entries) for which one or more entry was found in that source. Table 4 shows the proportion of KBGEN$^+$ event and entity types for which a lexical entry was found as well as the maximum, minimum and average number of lexical items associated with event and entities in the merged lexicon.

3.4 Frame Extraction

Events in KBGEN$^+$ take an arbitrary number of participants ranging from 1 to 8. Knowing the lexicalisation of an event name is therefore not sufficient. For each event lexicalisation, information about syntactic subcategorisation and syntactic/semantic linking is also required. Consider for instance, the following event representation:

```
SubClassOf(:PC/EBP beta :Entity)
SubClassOf(:TNF-activation :Entity)
SubClassOf(:Myeloid-Cells :Entity)
SubClassOf(:Block
 ObjectIntersectionOf(:Event
  ObjectSomeValuesFrom(:instrument :C/EBP beta)
  ObjectSomeValuesFrom(:object :TNF-activation)))
  ObjectSomeValuesFrom(:base :Myeloid-Cells)))
```

Knowing that a possible lexicalisation of a *Block* event is the finite verb form *blocked* is not sufficient to produce an appropriate verbalisation of the KB event e.g.,

(1) *C/EBP beta blocked TNF activation in myeloid cells.*

In addition, one must know that this verb (i) takes a subject, an object and an optional prepositional argument introduced by a locative preposition (subcategorisation information) and (ii) that the INSTRUMENT role is realised by the subject slot, the OBJECT role by the DOBJ slot and the BASE role by the PREP-LOC slot (syntax/semantics linking information). That is, we need to know, for each KB event e and its associated roles (i.e., event-to-entity relations), first, what are the syntactic arguments of each possible lexicalisations of e and second, for each possible lexicalisation, which role maps to which syntactic function.

To address this issue, we extract syntactic frames from our constructed corpus and use the collected data to learn the mapping between KB and syntactic arguments.

Frame extraction proceeds as follows. For each event name in the KBGEN$^+$event set, we look for sentences in the corpus that mention this event name or one of its several verbalisations available in the merged lexicon (ALL in Table 4).

We then parse these sentences using the Stanford dependency parser[8] for collapsed dependency structures and extract frames from the resulting

	Total Entries	Intersecting Entries
KBGen	469	397
Mesh	26795	65
BioDef	14934	99
KBBio101	6972	397

Table 3: Lexical Entries and Number of KBGEN$^+$ event and entities for which one or more entry was found (Intersecting Entries)

[6]http://www.nlm.nih.gov/mesh/filelist.html

[7]Obtained by parsing the entries in ⟨Synonyms⟩ section of html pages crawled from http://www.biology-online.org/dictionary/

[8]http://nlp.stanford.edu/software/lex-parser.shtml

	KBGen	Mesh	BioDef	KBBio101	ALL	Min/MAx/Avg
Event	100%	10.31%	25.39%	100%	100%	5/97/22
Entity	100%	19.18%	24.72%	100%	100%	3/91/16.18
All	100%	16.37%	24.93%	100%	100%	3/97/18.03

Table 4: Proportion of Event and Entity Names for which a Lexical Entry was found. Min, max and average number of lexical items associated with event and entities

parse trees. A frame is a sequence of dependency relations labelling the local subtree originating at a node labelled with an event name (or one of its variants). For instance, given the sentence and the dependency tree shown in Figure 2, the extracted frame for the event *Block* will be :

nsubj,VB,dobj

indicating that the verb form *block* requires a subject and an object.

That is, a syntactic frame describes the arguments required by the lexicalisations of an event and the syntactic function they realise.

When extracting the frames, we only consider a subset of the dependency relations produced by the Stanford parser to avoid including in the frame adjuncts such as temporal or spatial phrases which are optional rather than required arguments. Specifically, the dependency relations considered for frame construction are:

agent, amod, dobj, nsubj, nsubjpass, prep_across, prep_along, prep_at, prep_away_from, prep_down, prep_for, prep_from, prep_in, prep_inside, prep_into, prep_of, prep_out_of, prep_through, prep_to, prep_toward, prep_towards, prep_via, prep_with, vmod_creating, vmod_forming, vmod_producing, vmod_resulting, vmod_using, xcomp_using, auxpass.[9]

A total of 718 distinct event frames were observed whereby 97.63% of the KBGEN$^+$events were assigned at least one frame and each event was assigned an average of 82.01 distinct frames. Each event can be lexicalised by several natural language words or phrases and each natural language expressions may occur in several syntactic environments.

[9] *vmod_creating, vmod_forming, vmod_producing, vmod_resulting, vmod_using, xcomp_using* are not directly given by the Stanford parser but reconstructed from a *vmod* or an *xcomp* dependency "collapsed" with the lemmas *producing* or *using* much in the same way as the *prep_P* collapsed dependency relation provided by the Stanford Parser. These added dependencies are often used in biomedical text to express e.g., RESULT or RAW-MATERIAL role relations.

3.5 Probabilistic Models

Given F a set of syntactic frames, E a set of KB event names, D a set of syntactic dependency names and R, a set of KB roles, we next describe three probabilistic models that will be used to generate natural language sentences.

- The model $P(f|e)$ with $f \in F$ and $e \in E$, which encodes the probability of a frame given an event.
- The model $P(f|r)$ with $f \in F$ and $r \in R$, which encodes the probability of a frame given a role.
- The model $P(d|r)$ with $d \in D$ and $r \in R$, which encodes the probability of a syntactic dependency given a role.

We have chosen generative models for frames and dependencies given events and roles, and not the other way around, because such models intuitively match the generation process at test time. Each of the three models $P(f|e)$, $P(f|r)$ and $P(d|r)$ is assumed multinomial with maximum likelihood estimates determined by the labelled data built as described in Algorithm 1. Intuitively, C_e is the corpus consisting of all frames found in the corpus to be associated with a lexicalisation of e. Similarly, C_r nd C_d gathers all pairs of (frame,role) and (dependency relation, role) that could be identified given the KBGEN$^+$ KB, the corpus described in Section 3.2 and the lexicon described in Section 3.3. A Symmetric Dirichlet prior with hyperparameter $\alpha = 0.1$ is further used in order to favor sparse distributions. Training thus gives:

$$P(f|e) = \frac{counts\left((f,e) \in \mathcal{C}_e\right) + 0.1}{\sum_{f'} \left(counts\left((f',e) \in \mathcal{C}_e\right) + 0.1\right)}$$

This first model allows to choose a syntactic frame that will be used to verbalize a given event.

For the second distribution:

$$P(f|r) = \frac{counts\left((f,r) \in \mathcal{C}_r\right) + 0.1}{\sum_{f'} \left(counts\left((f',r) \in \mathcal{C}_r\right) + 0.1\right)}$$

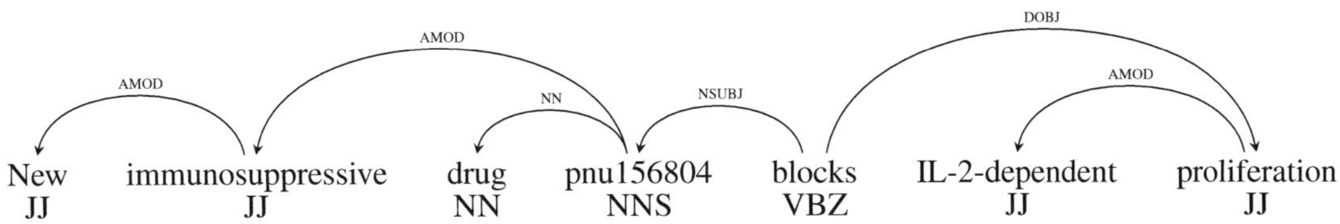

Figure 2: Example Dependency Parse Tree

This second model also ranks the frames, but this time based on the given set of roles.

The third model is trained in a similar way:

$$P(d|r) = \frac{counts\,((d,r) \in \mathcal{C}_d) + 0.1}{\sum_{d'} (counts\,((d',r) \in \mathcal{C}_d) + 0.1)}$$

It is used to choose which dependency in f shall represent the role r.

3.6 Surface Realisation

In our approach, surface realisation takes as input an even description. To verbalize an input event description containing an event e and n roles $r_1 \ldots\ldots r_n$, we first identify the event and the roles present in the input. The arity of the event is then defined as the count of distinct role types present in the input (to favor aggregation, in case of repeating roles)[10]. Among all the frames seen for this event during training, we select only those that have the same arity (same number of syntactic dependents) as the input event. All such frames are candidate frames for generation.

We consider two alternative scoring functions for choosing the n-best frames[11]. In the first case, we select the frame which maximises the score (M1):

$$P(f|e) \times \prod_{i=1}^{n} P(f|r_i) \qquad \text{(M1)}$$

To determine the mapping between roles and syntactic dependencies, we then look for the best permutation of the roles for every winning frame $f = (d_1, \cdots, d_n)$:

$$(\hat{r}_1^f, \ldots, \hat{r}_n^f) = \operatorname*{arg\,max}_{(r_1,\ldots,r_n) \in \mathcal{P}(\{r_1,\ldots,r_n\})} \prod_{i=1}^{n} P(d_i|r_i)$$

where $\mathcal{P}(\{r_1, \ldots, r_n\})$ is the set of all permutations of the roles[12].

In the second model (M2), we first compute the optimal mapping $(\hat{r}_1^f, \ldots, \hat{r}_n^f)$ for every possible frame and then use this information to select the n-best frames for generation:

$$P(f|e) \times \prod_{i=1}^{n} P(f|r_i) \times \prod_{i=1}^{n} P(d_i|\hat{r}_i^f) \qquad \text{(M2)}$$

Note that (M1) (and (M2)) can be viewed as a *product of experts*, but with independently trained experts and without any normalization factor. It is thus not a probability, but this is fine because the normalization term does not impact the choice of the winning frame.

Both (M1) and (M2) alternatives output a winning $\hat{f}$, i.e., a sequence of dependencies that shall be used to generate the sentence, as well as their mapping with roles $(\hat{r}_1^{\hat{f}}, \ldots, \hat{r}_n^{\hat{f}})$. Thus, generation boils down to filling every dependency slot in sequence with its optional preposition (e.g., for d_i = prep_to or d_i = prep_at) and the lexical entry of the entity bound to the corresponding role. For repeating roles of the input, we aggregate their bound entities via the conjunction "and" and fill the corresponding dependency slot.

The results obtained by verbalising the n-best frames given by models (M1 & M2) are separately stored and we present their analysis in Section 4.

4 Results and Discussion

We evaluate our approach on the 336 event representations included in the KBGEN$^+$ dataset. For each event representation, we generate the 5 best natural language verbalisations using the method described in the preceding section. We then evaluate the results both qualitatively and quantitatively.

[10]Thus if the input event description contains e.g., 2 object roles and an instrument role, its arity will be 2 rather than 3. This accounts for the fact that the two object roles will be verbalised as a coordinated NP filling in a single dependency function rather than two distinct syntactic arguments.

[11]n=5 in our experiments

[12]Here, we assume the order of dependencies in f is fixed, and we permute the roles; this is of course equivalent to permuting the dependencies with fixed roles sequences.

Input KBGEN$^+$
Lexicons $\mathcal{L}_e$ for events and $\mathcal{L}_t$ for entities as described in Section 3.3
Raw text corpus $\mathcal{T}$ with dependency trees as described in Section 3.4
Output Corpus (multiset) $\mathcal{C}_e$ for model $P(f|e)$
Corpus (multiset) $\mathcal{C}_r$ for model $P(f|r)$
Corpus (multiset) $\mathcal{C}_d$ for model $P(d|r)$

1. For every event e $\in$KBGEN$^+$, let $lex(e)$ be all possible lexicalisations of e taken from $\mathcal{L}_e$:
2. For every lexicalisation $l \in lex(e)$:
3. For every occurrence $e_t \in \mathcal{T}$ of l:
   (a) Extract the frame f governed by e_t
   (b) Add the observation f with label e in the frame-event corpus:
   $$\mathcal{C}_e \leftarrow \mathcal{C}_e \uplus \{\{(f, e)\}\}$$
   (c) For every entity $w_t \in \mathcal{L}_t$ that is a dependent of e_t with syntactic relation d, add every role r associated with this entity in KBGEN$^+$ to both role corpora:
   $$\mathcal{C}_r \leftarrow \mathcal{C}_r \uplus \{\{(f, r)\}\}$$
   $$\mathcal{C}_d \leftarrow \mathcal{C}_d \uplus \{\{(d, r)\}\}$$

Algorithm 1: Preparation of the corpora used to train our probabilistic models

4.1 Coverage

We first consider coverage i.e., the proportion of input in the test set for which a verbalisation is produced. In total, we generate output for 321 (95.53%) of the test data.

For 3 input cases involving two distinct event names (PHOTORESPIRATION, UNEQUAL-SHARING), there was no associated frame because none of the lexicalisations of the event name could be found in the corpus. Covering such cases would involve a more sophisticated lexicalisation strategy for instance, the strategy used in (Trevisan, 2010), where names are tokenized and pos-tagged before being mapped using hand-written rules to a lexicalisation.

For the other 12 input cases, generation fails because no frame of matching arity could be found. As discussed in Section 4.3 below, this is often due to cases where a KB role (mostly the BASE role) is verbalised as a modifier of an argument rather than a verb argument. Other cases are cases where the event is nominalised and there is no matching frame for that nominalisation.

4.2 Accuracy

Because the generated verbalisations are not learned from a parallel corpora, the generated sentences are often very different from the reference sentence. For instance, the generated sentence may contain a verb while in the reference sentence, the event is nominalised. Or the event might be verbalised by a transitive verb in the generated sentence but by a verb taking a prepositional object in the reference sentence (Eg: *A double bond holds together an oxygen and a carbon* vs. *Carbon and oxygen are held together by double bond*). To automatically assess the quality of the generated sentences, we therefore do not use BLEU. Instead we measure the accuracy of role mapping and we complement this automatic metric with the human evaluation described in the next section.

Role mapping is assessed as follows. For each input in the test data, we record the mapping beween the KB role of an argument in the event description and the syntactic dependency of the corresponding natural language argument in the gold sentence. For instance, given the event description shown in Section 3.4 for Sentence 1 (repeated below for convinience as Example 1), we record the syntax/semantics mapping: INSTRUMENT:NSUBJ, OBJECT:DOBJ, BASE:PREP-IN.

Example 1

```
SubClassOf(:PC/EBP beta :Entity)
SubClassOf(:TNF-activation :Entity)
SubClassOf(:Myeloid-Cells :Entity)
SubClassOf(:Block
 ObjectIntersectionOf(:Event
  ObjectSomeValuesFrom(:instrument :C/EBP beta)
  ObjectSomeValuesFrom(:object :TNF-activation)))
  ObjectSomeValuesFrom(:base :Myeloid-Cells)))
```

C/EBP beta blocked TNF activation in myeloid cells.

Accuracy is then the proportion of generated role:dependency mappings which are correct i.e., which match the reference. Although this does not address the fact that the generated and the reference sentence may be very different, it provides some indication of whether the generated mappings are plausible. We thus report this accuracy for the 1-best and 5-best solutions provided by our model, to partly account for the variability in possible correct answers. We compare our results to two baselines. The first baseline (BL-LING) is obtained using a default role/dependency assignment which is manually defined using linguistic introspection. The second (BL-GOLD) is a strong, informed baseline which has access to the frequency of the role/dependency mapping in the gold corpus. That is, this second baseline assigns to each role in the input event description, the syntactic dependency most frequently assigned to this role in the gold corpus. The default mapping used for BL-GOLD is as follows: *toward/prep_towards, site/prep_in, result/dobj, recipient/prep_to, raw_material/dobj, path/prep_through, origin/prep_from, object/dobj, instrument/nsubj, donor/prep_from, destination/prep_into, base/prep_in, away-from/prep_away_from, agent/nsubj*. The manually defined mapping used for BL-LING differs on three mappings namely *raw_material/prep-from, instrument-with,destination-to*.

On the 336 event descriptions (929 roles occurrences) contained in the test set, we obtain the following results:

Scoring	5-best acc	1-best acc
BL-Ling		42%
BL-GOLD		49%
M1	48%	30%
M2	49%	31%
M2-BL-LING	57%	43%

As expected, the difference between BL-LING and BL-GOLD shows that using information from the GOLD strongly improves accuracy.

While M1 and M2 do not improve on the baseline, an important drawback of these baselines is that they may map two or more roles in an event description to the same dependency (e.g., RAW-MATERIAL and RESULT to *dobj*). Worse, they may map a role to a dependency which is absent from the selected frame (if the dependency mapped onto by a role in the input does not exist in that frame). In contrast, the probabilistic approach is linguistically more promising as it guarantees that each role is mapped to a distinct dependency relation. We therefore take advantage of both the linguistically inspired baseline (BL-LING) and the probabilistic approach by combining both into a model (M2-BL-LING) which simply replaces the mapping proposed by the M2 model by that proposed by the BL-LING baseline whenever the probability of the M2 model is below a given threshold[13]. Because it predicts role/dependency mappings that are consistent with the selected frames, this new model is linguistically sound. And because it makes use of the strong prior information contained in the BL-LING baseline, it has a good accuracy.

4.3 Human Evaluation

Taking a sample of 264 inputs from the KBGEN$^+$ dataset, we evaluate the mappings of roles to syntax in the output. The sample contains inputs with 1 to 2 roles (40%), 3 roles (30%) and more than 3 roles (30%). For each sampled input, we consider the 5 best outputs and manually grade the output as follows:

1. Correct: both the syntax/semantic linking of the arguments and the lexicalisation of the event and of its arguments is correct.

2. Almost Corrrect: the lexicalisation of the event and of its arguments is correct and the linking of core semantic arguments is correct. The core arguments are the most frequent ones in the test data namely AGENT, BASE, OBJECT.

3. Incorrect: all other cases.

Three judges independently graded 264 inputs using the above criteria. The inter-annotator agreement, as measured with the Fleiss Kappa in a preliminary experiment in these conditions, was $\kappa = 0.76$ which is considered as "good agreement" in the literature. 29% of the ouput were found to be correct, 20% to be almost correct and 51% to be incorrect.

One main factor negatively affecting results is the number of roles contained in an event description. Unsurprisingly, the greater the number of roles the lower the accuracy. That is, for event descriptions with 3 or less roles, the scores are higher (40%, 23%, 37% respectively for correct, almost correct and incorrect) as there are less possibilities to be considered. Another, related issue, is data sparsity. Unsurprisingly, roles that are less frequent often score lower (i.e., are more often incorrectly mapped to syntax) than roles which occur more frequently. Thus, the three most frequent roles (AGENT,OBJECT, BASE) have a 5-best role mapping accuracy that ranges from 43% to 77%, while most other roles have much lower accuracy. These

[13]We have empirically chosen a threshold that retains 40% of our model's outputs; this is the only threshold value that we have tried, and we have not tuned this threshold at all

two issues suggest that results could be improved by using either more data or a more sophisticated smoothing or learning strategy. However linguistic factors are also at play here.

First, some semantic roles are often verbalised as verbs rather than thematic roles. For instance, in Sentence (2), the event (INTRACELLULAR-DIGESTION) is verbalised as a nominalisation and the OBJECT role as a verb (*produces*). More generally, a role in the KB is not necessarily realised by a thematic role.

(2) Intracellular digestion of polymers and solid substances in the lysosome produces monomers.

Second, in some cases, entities which are arguments of the event in the input are verbalised as prepositional modifiers of an argument of the verb verbalising the event rather than as an argument of the verb itself. This is frequently the case for the BASE relation. For instance, Example (3) shows the gold sentence for an input containing EUKARYOTIC-CELL as a BASE argument. As can be seen, in this case, the EUKARYOTIC-CELL entity is verbalised by a prepositional phrase modifying an NP rather than by an argument of the verb.

(3) Lysosomal enzymes digest nucleic acids and proteins in the lysosome of eukaryotic cells.

5 Conclusion

We have presented an approach for verbalising biological event representations which differs from previous work in that (i) it uses a non-parallel corpora and (ii) it focuses on n-ary relations and on the issue of how to automatically map natural language and KB arguments. A first evaluation gives encouraging results and identifies three main open questions for further research. How best to deal with data sparsity to account for event descriptions involving a high number of roles or roles that are infrequent? How to handle semantic roles that are verbalised as modifiers rather than as syntactic arguments? How to account for cases where KB roles are verbalised by verbs rather than by syntactic dependencies?

References

G. Aguado, A. Bañón, J. Bateman, S. Bernardos, M. Fernández, A. Gómez-Pérez, E. Nieto, A. Olalla, R. Plaza, and A. Sánchez. 1998. Ontogeneration: Reusing domain and linguistic ontologies for spanish text generation. In *Workshop on Applications of Ontologies and Problem Solving Methods, ECAI*, volume 98.

Gabor Angeli, Percy Liang, and Dan Klein. 2010. A simple domain-independent probabilistic approach to generation. In *Proceedings of the 2010 Conference on Empirical Methods in Natural Language Processing*, pages 502–512. Association for Computational Linguistics.

Eva Banik, Claire Gardent, and Eric Kow. 2013. The kbgen challenge. In *the 14th European Workshop on Natural Language Generation (ENLG)*, pages 94–97.

Anja Belz. 2008. Automatic generation of weather forecast texts using comprehensive probabilistic generation-space models. *Natural Language Engineering*, 14(4):431–455.

K. Bontcheva and Y. Wilks. 2004. Automatic report generation from ontologies: the miakt approach. In *Ninth International Conference on Applications of Natural Language to Information Systems (NLDB'2004)*. Lecture Notes in Computer Science 3136, Springer, Manchester, UK.

Ted Briscoe and John Carroll. 1997. Automatic extraction of subcategorization from corpora. In *Proceedings of the fifth conference on Applied natural language processing*, pages 356–363. Association for Computational Linguistics.

Keith Butler, Priscilla Moraes, Ian Tabolt, and Kathy McCoy. 2013. Team udel kbgen 2013 challenge. In *Proceedings of the 14th European Workshop on Natural Language Generation*, pages 206–207, Sofia, Bulgaria, August. Association for Computational Linguistics.

Vinay K Chaudhri, Michael A Wessel, and Stijn Heymans. 2013. Kb_bio_101: A challenge for owl reasoners. In *ORE*, pages 114–120. Citeseer.

David L Chen and Raymond J Mooney. 2008. Learning to sportscast: a test of grounded language acquisition. In *Proceedings of the 25th international conference on Machine learning*, pages 128–135. ACM.

Deborah A Dahl, Madeleine Bates, Michael Brown, William Fisher, Kate Hunicke-Smith, David Pallett, Christine Pao, Alexander Rudnicky, and Elizabeth Shriberg. 1994. Expanding the scope of the atis task: The atis-3 corpus. In *Proceedings of the workshop on Human Language Technology*, pages 43–48. Association for Computational Linguistics.

Daniel Duma and Ewan Klein, 2013. *Generating Natural Language from Linked Data: Unsupervised Template Extraction*, pages 83–94. ASSOC COMPUTATIONAL LINGUISTICS-ACL.

Basil Ell and Andreas Harth. 2014. A language-independent method for the extraction of rdf verbalization templates. *INLG 2014*, page 26.

D. Galanis, G. Karakatsiotis, G. Lampouras, and I. Androutsopoulos. 2009. An open-source natural language generator for owl ontologies and its use in protégé and second life. In *Proceedings of the 12th Conference of the European Chapter of the Association for Computational Linguistics: Demonstrations Session*, pages 17–20. Association for Computational Linguistics.

David Gunning, Vinay K Chaudhri, Peter E Clark, Ken Barker, Shaw-Yi Chaw, Mark Greaves, Benjamin Grosof, Alice Leung, David D McDonald, Sunil Mishra, et al. 2010. Project halo updateprogress toward digital aristotle. *AI Magazine*, 31(3):33–58.

Bikash Gyawali and Claire Gardent. 2013. Lor-kbgen, a hybrid approach to generating from the kbgen knowledge-base. In *Proceedings of the 14th European Workshop on Natural Language Generation*, pages 204–205, Sofia, Bulgaria, August. Association for Computational Linguistics.

K. Kaljurand and N.E. Fuchs. 2007. Verbalizing owl in attempto controlled english. *Proceedings of OWLED07*.

J.-D. Kim, T. Ohta, Y. Tateisi, and J. Tsujii. 2003. Genia corpusa semantically annotated corpus for biotextmining. *Bioinformatics*, 19(suppl 1):i180–i182.

Ravi Kondadadi, Blake Howald, and Frank Schilder. 2013. A statistical nlg framework for aggregated planning and realization.

Ioannis Konstas and Mirella Lapata. 2012a. Concept-to-text generation via discriminative reranking. In *Proceedings of the 50th Annual Meeting of the Association for Computational Linguistics: Long Papers-Volume 1*, pages 369–378. Association for Computational Linguistics.

Ioannis Konstas and Mirella Lapata. 2012b. Unsupervised concept-to-text generation with hypergraphs. In *Proceedings of the 2012 Conference of the North American Chapter of the Association for Computational Linguistics: Human Language Technologies*, pages 752–761. Association for Computational Linguistics.

Anna Korhonen. 2002. Semantically motivated subcategorization acquisition. In *Proceedings of the ACL-02 Workshop on Unsupervised Lexical Acquisition - Volume 9*, ULA '02, pages 51–58, Stroudsburg, PA, USA. Association for Computational Linguistics.

Percy Liang, Michael I Jordan, and Dan Klein. 2009. Learning semantic correspondences with less supervision. In *Proceedings of the Joint Conference of the 47th Annual Meeting of the ACL and the 4th International Joint Conference on Natural Language Processing of the AFNLP: Volume 1-Volume 1*, pages 91–99. Association for Computational Linguistics.

C. Mihil, T. Ohta, S. Pyysalo, and S. Ananiadou. 2013. Biocause: Annotating and analysing causality in the biomedical domain. *BMC BioInformatics*.

VO Mittal, G. Carenini, and JD Moore. 1994. Generating patient specific explanations in migraine. In *Proceedings of the eighteenth annual symposium on computer applications in medical care. McGraw-Hill Inc.*

C.L. Paris. 1988. Tailoring object descriptions to a user's level of expertise. *Computational Linguistics*, 14(3):64–78.

Sampo Pyysalo, Filip Ginter, Juho Heimonen, Jari Bjrne, Jorma Boberg, Jouni Jrvinen, and Tapio Salakoski. 2007. Bioinfer: A corpus for information extraction in the biomedical domain. *BMC Bioinformatics*.

E. Reiter, R. Robertson, and L.M. Osman. 2003. Lessons from a failure: Generating tailored smoking cessation letters. *Artificial Intelligence*, 144(1):41–58.

Laura Rimell, Thomas Lippincott, Karin Verspoor, Helen L Johnson, and Anna Korhonen. 2013. Acquisition and evaluation of verb subcategorization resources for biomedicine. *Journal of biomedical informatics*, 46(2):228–237.

Anoop Sarkar and Daniel Zeman. 2000. Automatic extraction of subcategorization frames for czech. In *Proceedings of the 18th conference on Computational linguistics-Volume 2*, pages 691–697. Association for Computational Linguistics.

P. Thompson, S. A. Iqbal, J. McNaught, and S. Ananiadou. 2009. Construction of an annotated corpus to support biomedical information extraction. *BMC Bioinformatics*.

Marco Trevisan. 2010. A portable menuguided natural language interface to knowledge bases for querytool. Master's thesis, Free University of Bozen-Bolzano (Italy) and University of Groningen (Netherlands).

G. Wilcock. 2003. Talking owls: Towards an ontology verbalizer. *Human Language Technology for the Semantic Web and Web Services, ISWC*, 3:109–112.

Sandra Williams and Richard Power. 2010. Grouping axioms for more coherent ontology descriptions. In *Proceedings of the 6th International Natural Language Generation Conference (INLG 2010)*, pages 197–202, Dublin.

Yuk Wah Wong and Raymond J Mooney. 2007. Generation by inverting a semantic parser that uses statistical machine translation. In *HLT-NAACL*, pages 172–179.

Sina Zarrieß and Kyle Richardson. 2013. An automatic method for building a data-to-text generator. In *Proceedings of the 14th European Workshop on Natural Language Generation*, Sofia, Bulgaria, August.

Inducing Clause-Combining Rules: A Case Study with the SPaRKy Restaurant Corpus

Michael White
Department of Linguistics
The Ohio State University
Columbus, Ohio 43210, USA
mwhite@ling.ohio-state.edu

David M. Howcroft
Computational Linguistics and Phonetics
Saarland University
66123 Saarbrücken, Germany
howcroft@coli.uni-saarland.de

Abstract

We describe an algorithm for inducing clause-combining rules for use in a traditional natural language generation architecture. An experiment pairing lexicalized text plans from the SPaRKy Restaurant Corpus with logical forms obtained by parsing the corresponding sentences demonstrates that the approach is able to learn clause-combining operations which have essentially the same coverage as those used in the SPaRKy Restaurant Corpus. This paper fills a gap in the literature, showing that it is possible to learn microplanning rules for both aggregation and discourse connective insertion, an important step towards ameliorating the knowledge acquisition bottleneck for NLG systems that produce texts with rich discourse structures using traditional architectures.

1 Introduction

In a traditional natural language generation (NLG) system (Reiter and Dale, 2000), a pipeline of hand-crafted components is used to generate high quality text, albeit at considerable knowledge-engineering expense. While there has been progress on using machine learning to ameliorate this issue in content planning (Duboue and McKeown, 2001; Barzilay and Lapata, 2005) and broad coverage surface realization (Reiter, 2010; Rajkumar and White, 2014), the central stage of sentence planning (or microplanning) has proved more difficult to automate. More recently, Angeli et al. (2010) and Konstas and Lapata (2013), inter alia, have developed end-to-end learning methods for NLG systems; however, as discussed further in the next section, these systems assume quite limited discourse structures in comparison to those with more traditional architectures.

In this paper, we describe a method of inducing clause-combining rules of the kind used in traditional sentence planners. In particular, we base our approach on the architecture used in the SPaRKy restaurant recommendation system (Walker et al., 2007), where a sentence plan generator is used to map a text plan to a range of possible sentence plans, from which one is selected for output by a sentence plan ranker.[1] To demonstrate the viability of our method, we present an experiment demonstrating that rules corresponding to all of the hand-crafted operators for aggregation and discourse connective insertion used in the SPaRKy Restaurant Corpus can be effectively learned from examples of their use. To our knowledge, these induced rules for the first time incorporate the constraints necessary to be functionally equivalent to the hand-crafted clause-combining operators; in particular, our method goes beyond the one Stent and Molina (2009) develop for learning clause-combining rules, which focuses on learning domain-independent rules for discourse connective insertion, ignoring aggregation rules and any potentially domain-dependent aspects of the rules. As such, our approach promises to be of immediate benefit to NLG system developers, while also taking an important step towards reducing the knowledge acquisition bottleneck for developing NLG systems requiring rich discourse structures in their outputs.

2 Related Work

Angeli et al. (2010) present an end-to-end trainable NLG system that generates by selecting a

[1]The sentence plan ranker uses machine learning to rank sentence plans based on features derived from the sentence plan and its realization, together with accompanying human ratings for the realizations in the training data. As such, the SPaRKy architecture differs from traditional ones in using machine learning to rank potential outputs, but it follows the traditional architecture in making use of lexicalization, aggregation and referring expression rules in a distinct sentence planning stage.

Proceedings of the 15th European Workshop on Natural Language Generation (ENLG), pages 28–37,
Brighton, September 2015.

sequence of database records to describe, a sequence of fields on those records to mention, and finally a sequence of words for expressing the values of those fields. Though Konstas and Lapata (2013) generalize Angeli et al.'s approach, they acknowledge that handling discourse-level document structure remains for future work. Given this limitation, under their approach there is no need to explicitly perform aggregation: instead, it suffices to "pre-aggregate" propositions about the same entity onto the same record. However, in the general case aggregation should be subject to discourse structure; for example, when contrasting the positive and negative attributes of an entity according to a given user model, it makes sense to aggregate the positive and negative attributes separately, rather than lumping them together (White et al., 2010). Consequently, we aim to learn aggregation rules that are sensitive to discourse structure, as with the SPaRKy architecture.

Other notable recent approaches (Lu et al., 2009; Dethlefs et al., 2013; Mairesse and Young, 2014) are similar in that they learn to map semantic representations to texts using conditional random fields or factored language models with no explicit model of syntactic structure, but the content to be expressed is assumed to be pre-aggregated in the input. Kondadadi et al. (2013) develop a rather different approach where large-scale templates are learned that can encapsulate typical aggregation patterns, but the templates cannot be dynamically combined in a way that is sensitive to discourse structure

Previous work on aggregation in NLG, e.g. with SPaRKy itself or earlier work by Pan and Shaw (2004), focuses on learning when to apply aggregation rules, which are themselves hand-crafted rather than learned. The clause-combining rules our system learns—based on lexico-semantic dependency edits—are closely related to the lexico-syntactic rewrite rules learned by Angrosh and Siddharthan's (2014) system for text simplification. However, our learned rules go beyond theirs in imposing (non-)equivalence constraints crucial for accurate aggregation. Finally, work on text compression (Woodsend and Lapata, 2011; Cohn and Lapata, 2013) is also related, but focuses on simple constituent deletion, and to our knowledge does not implement aggregation constraints such as those here.

3 SPaRKy Restaurant Corpus

Walker et al. (2007) developed SPaRKy (a Sentence Planner with Rhetorical Knowledge) to extend the MATCH system (Walker et al., 2004) for restaurant recommendations. In the course of their study they produced the SPaRKy Restaurant Corpus (SRC), a collection of content plans, text plans and the surface realizations of those plans evaluated by users.[2]

While the restaurant recommendation domain is fairly narrow in terms of the kinds of propositions represented, it requires careful application of aggregation operations to make concise, natural realizations. This is evident both in the care taken in incorporating clause-combining rules into SPaRKy and in subsequent work on the expression of contrast which used this domain to motivate extensions of CCG to the discourse level (Nakatsu and White, 2010; Howcroft et al., 2013). Five kinds of clause-combining operations are included in SPaRKy, most of which involve lexically specific constraints. These are illustrated in Table 2, using propositions corresponding to sentences (1)–(4) from Table 1 as input (combined with either a CONTRAST or INFER relation). MERGE combines two clauses if they have the same verb with the same arguments and adjuncts except for one. WITH-REDUCTION replaces an instance of *have* plus an object X with the phrase *with* X. REL-CLAUSE subordinates one clause to another when they have a common subject. CUE-WORD-CONJUNCTION combines clauses using the conjunctions *and*, *but*, and *while*, while CUE-WORD-INSERTION combines clauses by inserting *however* or *on the other hand* into the second clause. Table 2 also shows two operations, VP-COORDINATION and NP-APPOSITION, which go beyond those in SPaRKy; these are discussed further in Section 5.5. Finally, it's also possible to leave sentences as they are, simply juxtaposing them in sequence.

For the experiments reported in this paper, we have reimplemented SPaRKy to work with OpenCCG's broad coverage English grammar for parsing and realization (Espinosa et al., 2008; White and Rajkumar, 2009; White and Rajkumar,

[2]Available from `http://users.soe.ucsc.edu/~maw/downloads.html` under *the textplans/utterances*. To our knowledge, the SRC remains the only publicly available corpus of input–output pairs for an NLG system using discourse structures with rhetorical relations.

Operator	Sents	Result
MERGE	1, 2	Sonia Rose has good decor and good service.
WITH-REDUCTION	1, 2	Sonia Rose has good decor, with good service.
REL-CLAUSE	1, 2	Sonia Rose, which has good service, has good decor.
CUE-WORD-CONJUNCTION	1, 3	Sonia Rose has good service, but Bienvenue has very good service.
CUE-WORD-INSERTION	1, 3	Sonia Rose has good service. However, Bienvenue has very good service.
VP-COORDINATION	3, 4	Bienvenue is a French restaurant and has very good service.
NP-APPOSITION	3, 4	Bienvenue, a French restaurant, has very good service.

Table 2: SRC clause-combining operations plus two additional operations we examined.

(1) Sonia Rose has good decor.
(2) Sonia Rose has good service.
(3) Bienvenue has very good service.
(4) Bienvenue is a French restaurant.

Table 1: Example sentences from the SRC domain.

2012).[3] As in the original SPaRKy, the sentence planner takes as input a text plan, which encodes the propositions to be expressed at the leaves of a tree whose internal nodes are marked with rhetorical relations. The sentence planner then rewrites the text-plan tree using a sequence of lexicalization, clause-combining and referring expression rules. The obligatory lexicalization rules straightforwardly rewrite the domain-specific propositions into a domain-general OpenCCG lexicosemantic dependency graph, or logical form (referred to as a TPLF in Section 5.1). After lexicalization, the clause-combining and referring expression rules optionally apply to rewrite the logical form into a set of alternative logical forms, among which is ideally one or more options that will express the content concisely and fluently after each sentence is realized; if none of the clause-combining and referring expression rules apply, the text will be realized as a sequence of very simple one-clause sentences, with proper names used for all restaurant references.

As noted earlier, the task of choosing a particular logical form alternative belongs to the sentence plan ranker; since its task is largely independent of the task of generating alternative logical forms, we do not address it in this paper. Indeed, to the extent that our sentence planner produces logical forms that are functionally equivalent to the alternative sentence plans in the SRC, we can expect the output quality of the reimplemented system with a suitably trained sentence plan ranker to be essentially unchanged, and thus an evaluation of this kind would be uninformative.

An example aggregation rule for the OpenCCG-based system (going beyond the options in the SRC) appears in Figure 1, and an example input–output pair for this rule appears in Figure 2. As the latter figure shows, a dependency graph consists of a set of nodes and relations between them, where sibling nodes are taken to be unordered. Nodes themselves comprise an identifier, a predicate label and an unordered list of attribute-value pairs. The graphs have a primary tree structure; the graphs in Figure 2 are in fact trees, but in the general case, node references can be used to represent nodes with multiple parents or even cycles (in the case of relative clauses). The alignments between nodes in the input and output graphs are shown in the figure by using the same identifier for corresponding nodes.

Clause-combining rules such as the one in Figure 1 are applied by unifying the left hand side of the rule against an input dependency graph, returning the graph specified by the right hand side of the rule if unification succeeds and any further specified constraints are satisfied. The rules are implemented in Prolog using an enhanced unification routine that allows sibling nodes to be treated as unordered, and which allows list variables (shown between dots in the figure) to unify with the tail (i.e., remainder) of a list of child nodes or a list of attributes. In the example at hand, the variables `G`, `C`, `E` and `I` are unified with node identifiers `n(1)`, `n(2)`, `n(7)` and `n(8)`, respectively. The list variables `...D...` and `...F...` unify with the empty list since the nodes for *Bienvenue* have no child nodes, while `...L...` unifies with a list consisting of the relation `Arg1` together with the subgraph headed by `n(3)`, and `...K...` unifies with a list consisting of the relations `Det` and `Mod` together with their respective subgraphs headed by `n(9)` and `n(10)`. The list variables over attributes unify trivially. Finally, after checking the

[3] The lexicon is extended by the addition of the restaurant names as proper nouns to avoid spurious bad parses resulting from unknown words.

```
rule:
_ infer-rel [ .._.. ]
  Arg1
    G have [ ..H.. ]
      Arg0
        C A [ ..B.. ]
          ...D...
      ...L...
  Arg2
    _ be [ .._.. ]
      Arg0
        E A [ ..B.. ]
          ...F...
      Arg1
        I restaurant [ ..J.. ]
          ...K...

s.t. [equiv(node(C,A,B,D),node(E,A,B,F))]

==>

G have [ ..H.. ]
  Arg0
    C A [ ..B.. ]
      ApposRel
        I restaurant [ ..J.. ]
          ...K...
      ...D...
  ...L...
```

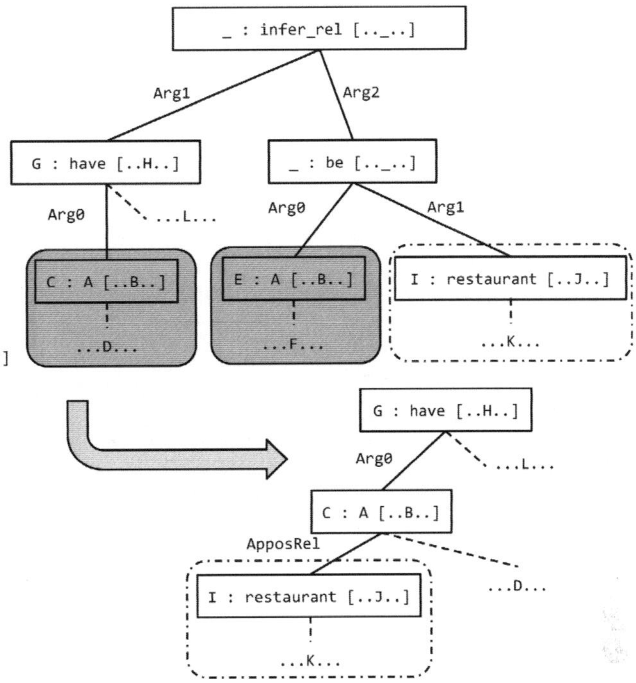

Figure 1: On the left is a textual representation of an NP-APPOSITION operation inferred from combining sentences 3 and 4 as shown in Table 2; on the right is a graphical representation. Capital letters represent variables, and underscores represent anonymous variables; variables over lists of attributes or dependencies are shown between dots. The solid rounded boxes highlight content that must be equivalent for the rule to apply, while the dotted rounded box shows the content preserved by the rule.

nodes headed by `n(2)` and `n(7)` for equivalence (i.e, isomorphism), the right hand side of the rule is returned, where the root `infer-rel`, `be` and second `Bienvenue` nodes have been left out, and the `restaurant` node `n(8)` has been retained under `n(2)` via an `ApposRel`.

In comparison to Angrosh and Siddharthan's (2014) lexical rewrite rules—which consist simply of a list of edit operations—we find the clause-combining rules induced by our approach to be quite readable, thus in principle facilitating their manual inspection by NLG developers.

4 Rule Induction Algorithm

In this section, we present the rule induction algorithm at an overview level; for complete details, see the rule induction code to be released on the OpenCCG website.[4]

[4] `http://openccg.sf.net`

4.1 Input–Output Pre-Processing

The induction method takes as input pairs of text plans (taken to be ordered) and sentences realizing the text plans, and returns as output induced rules, such as the one just seen in Figure 1. To begin, the text plans are lexicalized using simple hand-crafted lexicalization rules, as noted above, yielding initial OpenCCG logical forms (LFs). Meanwhile, the sentences are parsed to LFs serving as the target output of the rule, after any anaphoric expressions have been resolved (in an ad hoc way) with respect to the source LF; in particular, the LF nodes for the expressions *it*, *its* and *this CUISINE restaurant* are replaced with versions using the proper name of the restaurant, e.g. LF nodes for *Bienvenue*, *Bienvenue's* and *Bienvenue, which is a French restaurant*.[5]

[5] The restaurant name is located by searching for the first predicate under an `Arg0` relation, unless there is a `GenOwn` (possessor) relation under it, in which the predicate under `GenOwn` is returned. This method is generally reliable, though errors are sometimes introduced when multiple restaurants are mentioned in alternation. A more accurate method would take alignments into account.

Input dependency graph for *Bienvenue has very good service. Bienvenue is a French restaurant.*

```
n(0) infer-rel
  Arg1
    n(1) have [ mood=dcl tense=pres ]
      Arg0
        n(2) Bienvenue [ num=sg ]
      Arg1
        n(3) service [ det=nil num=sg ]
          Mod
            n(4) good
              Mod
                n(5) very
  Arg2
    n(6) be [ mood=dcl tense=pres ]
      Arg0
        n(7) Bienvenue [ num=sg ]
      Arg1
        n(8) restaurant [ num=sg ]
          Det
            n(9) a
          Mod
            n(10) French [ num=sg ]
```

Output dependency graph for *Bienvenue, a French restaurant, has very good service.*

```
n(1) have [ mood=dcl tense=pres ]
  Arg0
    n(2) Bienvenue [ num=sg ]
      ApposRel
        n(8) restaurant [ num=sg ]
          Det
            n(9) a
          Mod
            n(10) French [ num=sg ]
  Arg1
    n(3) service [ det=nil num=sg ]
      Mod
        n(4) good
          Mod
            n(5) very
```

Figure 2: Example input–ouput dependency graphs for NP-APPOSITION clause-combining rule

Input dependency graph for *Mangia has very good food quality. Mangia has decent decor.*

```
n(0) infer-rel
  Arg1
    n(1) have [ mood=dcl tense=pres ]
      Arg0
        n(2) Mangia [ num=sg ]
      Arg1
        n(3) quality [ det=nil num=sg ]
          Mod
            n(4) food [ num=sg ]
          Mod
            n(5) good
              Mod
                n(6) very
  Arg2
    n(7) have [ mood=dcl tense=pres ]
      Arg0
        n(8) Mangia [ num=sg ]
      Arg1
        n(9) decor [ det=nil num=sg ]
          Mod
            n(10) decent
```

Output dependency graph for *Mangia has very good food quality, with decent decor.*

```
n(1) have [ mood=dcl tense=pres ]
  Arg0
    n(2) Mangia [ num=sg ]
  Arg1
    n(3) quality [ det=nil num=sg ]
      Mod
        n(4) food [ num=sg ]
      Mod
        n(5) good
          Mod
            n(6) very
  Mod
    n(11) with [ emph-final=+ ]
      Arg1
        n(9) decor [ det=nil num=sg ]
          Mod
            n(10) decent
```

Figure 3: Example input–ouput dependency graphs for WITH-REDUCTION clause-combining rule

The next step is to align the nodes of the input and output LFs. We have found that a simple greedy alignment routine works reliably with the SRC, where nodes with unique lexical matches are aligned first, and then the remaining nodes are greedily aligned according to the number of parent and child nodes already aligned. After alignment, the parts of the output LF corresponding to each sentence are rebracketed to better match the grouping in the input LF (revising an initial right-branching structure). To rebracket the sentence-level LFs, the adjacent pair of LFs whose aligned nodes in the source LF have the minimum path distance is iteratively grouped together under an INFER relation until the structure has a single root.

4.2 Edit Analysis and Rule Construction

Following alignment and sentence-level rebracketing, the difference between the input and output dependency graphs is calculated, in terms of inserted/deleted nodes, relations and attributes. Next, these edits are analyzed to determine whether any equivalent nodes have been **factored out**—that is, whether a node that is isomorphic to another one in the input has been removed. For example, in Figure 1, nodes C and E are derived from the isomorphic nodes for the restaurant name NPs, with node E left out of the output.

Based on the edit analysis, one of four general kinds of clause-combining rules may be inferred: two kinds of aggregation rules, one involving a shared argument and one a shared predication, as well as two kinds of rules for adding discourse connectives based on discourse relations, one where clausal LFs are combined, and another where a connective is inserted into the second LF. The kinds of rules for discourse connectives correspond directly to those in SPaRKy; for aggregation, shared predication rules correspond to oper-

```
rule:
_ one_of(_,[infer-rel,justify-rel]) [ .._.. ]
  Arg1
    G H [ ..I.. ]
      Arg0
        C A [ ..B.. ]
          ...D...
      ...N...
  Arg2
    _ have [ .._.. ]
      Arg0
        E A [ ..B.. ]
          ...F...
      Arg1
        J K [ ..L.. ]
          ...M...

s.t. [equiv(node(C,A,B,D),node(E,A,B,F))]

==>

G H [ ..I.. ]
  Arg0
    C A [ ..B.. ]
      ...D...
  Mod
    _ with [ emph-final=+ ]
      Arg1
        J K [ ..L.. ]
          ...M...
  ...N...
```

Figure 4: Inferred WITH-REDUCTION clause-combining rule with generalized lexical constraints

ations of the MERGE kind, with shared argument rules accounting for the rest.

To keep the rule induction straightforward, exactly one node is required to have been factored out with the aggregation rules, while with the discourse connective rules, the edits must be localized to the level directly below the triggering discourse relation. When these conditions are satisfied, an induced rule is constructed based on the edits and any applicable constraints. First, the left hand side of the rule is constructed so that it matches any deleted nodes, attributes and relations, as well as the path to both the factored out node (if any), the one it is equivalent to, and the parents of any inserted nodes. Along the way, lexical predicates are included as requirements for the rule to match, except in the case of factored out nodes, where it is assumed that the lexical predicate does not matter. Next, the right hand side of the rule is constructed, leaving out any matched nodes, attributes or relations to be deleted, while adding any nodes, attributes or relations to be inserted. Finally, any applicable constraints are added to the rule. (Though both kinds of aggregation rules are triggered off of factored out nodes, shared predication rules actually involve a stronger constraint, namely that all but one argument of a predicate be equivalent.)

4.3 Constraints and Generalization

The constraints included in the aggregation rules are essential for their accurate application, as noted earlier. For example, in the absence of the shared argument constraint for an inferred RELATIVE-CLAUSE rule, adjacent clauses for *Sonia Rose has good service* and *Bienvenue has very good service* could be mistakenly combined into *Sonia Rose, which has very good service, has good service*, as nothing would check whether *Sonia Rose* and *Bienvenue* were equivalent. The lexical predicate constraints are also essential, for example to ensure that only *have*-predications are reduced to *with*-phrases, and that only *be*-predications are eligible to become NP-appositives.

After a first pass of rule induction, the rules are generalized by combining rules that differ only in a lexical predicate, and if a sufficient number of lexical items has been observed (three in our experiments here), the lexical constraint is removed, much as in Angrosh and Siddharthan's (2014) approach. For example, the rule in Figure 4—induced from the input–output pair in Figure 3 and others like it—has been generalized to work with either the `infer-rel` or `contrast-rel` relations, and the predication for the first argument of the relation (`H`) has been generalized to apply to any predicate.

4.4 Rule Interaction During Learning

Since evidence for a rule may not always be directly available in an input–output pair that illustrates the effect of that rule alone, rule induction is also attempted from all subgraphs of the input and output that are in an appropriate configuration—namely, where either the roots of the source and target subgraphs are aligned, or where at least one child node of the root of the source subgraph is aligned with the root of the target subgraph or one of its children.

Inducing rules from subgraphs in this way is a noisy process that can yield bad rules, that is, ones that mistakenly delete or insert nodes for words: nodes can be mistakenly deleted when the target subgraph is missing nodes supplying propositional content in the source, while nodes can be mistakenly inserted if they supply extra propositional content not present in the source rather than discourse connectives or function words, as intended. An example bad deletion rule appears in

```
rule:
_ quality [ .._.. ]
  Det
    E A [ ..B.. ]
      ...F...
  Mod
    G among [ ..H.. ]
      Arg1
        I restaurant [ ..J.. ]
          Det
            C A [ ..B.. ]
              ...D...
          ...K...
      ...L...
  Mod
    _ best [ .._.. ]
  Mod
    _ overall [ .._.. ]

s.t. [equiv(node(C,A,B,D),node(E,A,B,F))]

==>

G among [ ..H.. ]
  Arg1
    I restaurant [ ..J.. ]
      Det
        C A [ ..B.. ]
          ...D...
      ...K...
  ...L...
```

Figure 5: An undesirable rule that mistakenly reduces *the best overall quality among the selected restaurants* to *among the selected restaurants*, induced from LF subgraphs for these phrases

Figure 5. Another common cause of bad rules is errors in parsing the target sentences, especially longer ones. To lessen the prevalence of bad induced rules, we take inspiration from work on learning semantic parsers (Kwiatkowksi et al., 2010; Artzi and Zettlemoyer, 2013) and embed the process of inducing clause-combining rules within a process of learning a model of preferred derivations that use the induced rules. The model is learned using the structured averaged perceptron algorithm (Collins, 2002), with indicator features for each rule used in deriving an output LF from and input LF. With each input–output pair, the current model is used to generate the highest-scoring output LF using a bottom-up beam search. If the highest-scoring output LF is not equal to the target LF, then the search is run again to find the highest-scoring derivation of the target LF, using the distance to the target to help guide the search. When the target LF can be successfully derived, a perceptron update is performed, adjusting the weights of the current model by adding the features from the target LF derivation and subtracting the ones from the highest-scoring non-target LF. At the end of all training epochs, the parameters from the final model and all the intermediate models are averaged, which approximates the margin-

For input–output pairs satisfying increasing size limits:

1. **Direct Epoch** Starting with an empty model, clause-combining rules are induced directly from input–output pairs.
2. **Generalization** The current set of rules is generalized and the training examples are revisited to update the weights for the newly added rules. Subsumed rules are removed, and the initial weight of the generalized rule is set to the maximum weight of the subsumed rules.
3. **Subgraphs Epoch** Rules are induced from all applicable subgraphs of the input–output pairs.
4. **Generalization** As above.
5. **Partial Epoch** For any examples where the target LF cannot be generated with the current ruleset, rules are induced from an n-best list of partially completed outputs paired with the target LF.
6. **Generalization** As above.
7. **Pruning** After switching to the final averaged model, any rules not used in the highest-scoring derivation of an example are pruned.

Figure 6: Algorithm Summary

maximizing voted perceptron algorithm.

It is often the case that desired rules cannot be induced either directly from an input–output pair or from their subgraphs: instead, other learned rules need to be applied to the input before the example illustrates the desired step.[6] Accordingly, for input–output pairs that cannot be derived with the current set of rules, we generate an n-best list of outputs and then attempt to induce a rule by pairing each partially complete output with the target LF as an input–output pair.

[6]Consider a text realizing the same content as (1) and (2) in addition to the content in *Sonia Rose is an Italian restaurant.* A single sentence realization of this content is *Sonia Rose, an Italian restaurant, has good decor and good service.* In order to learn NP-APPOSITION from this input–output pair, the system must first have learned and applied a MERGE rule to (1) and (2) so that the structures are sufficiently parallel for inference to proceed.

4.5 Staged Learning

A summary of the rule induction algorithm appears in Figure 6. In the outermost loop, the algorithm is run over input–output pairs that meet a given size limit on the output LF, with this limit increasing with each iteration. Since during development we found that rules induced (i) directly, (ii) from subgraphs and (iii) from partially completed inputs were of decreasing reliability, such rules are induced in separate training epochs in that order. A final pruning step removes any rules not used in the highest-scoring derivation of an input–output pair, using the averaged model. The pruning step is expected to remove most of the bad rules involving undesirable node insertions or deletions, as they are typically downweighted by the perceptron updates.

5 Evaluation

5.1 Data preparation

We convert the text plans used in Walker et al. (2007) to a more concise logical representation as described in Section 3.

Using OpenCCG's broad-coverage grammar, we then parse the SRC realizations corresponding to these text plans, resulting in one LF for each sentence in the SRC. Since nearly all realizations in the SRC include multiple sentences, this results in multiple LFs for each. In order to combine these sentence-level LFs into a single sentence plan LF (SENTLF), we impose an initial binary right-branching structure over the LFs and label the resulting superstructure nodes with the `infer-rel` predicate. As noted in Section 4, the initial right-branching structure is subsequently rebracketed to better match the rhetorical structure in the of the text plan LF (TPLF).

5.2 Dev, Training, and Test Splits

We limit our attention to realizations in the SRC containing 5 or fewer sentences and only one subject per sentence.[7] Of the 1,760 sparky pairs in the SRC, we used a set of 73 sparky pairs for development, defining a sparky pair as the TPLF–SENTLF pair corresponding to a single sparky alternative. These pairs were used primarily for debugging and testing and are not used further in the evaluation.

[7]The only multi-subject sentences in the SRC are of the form, "Restaurant A, (Restaurant B, ...,) and Restaurant N offer exceptional value among the selected restaurants" and do not add to the variety of clause-combining operations of interest to us.

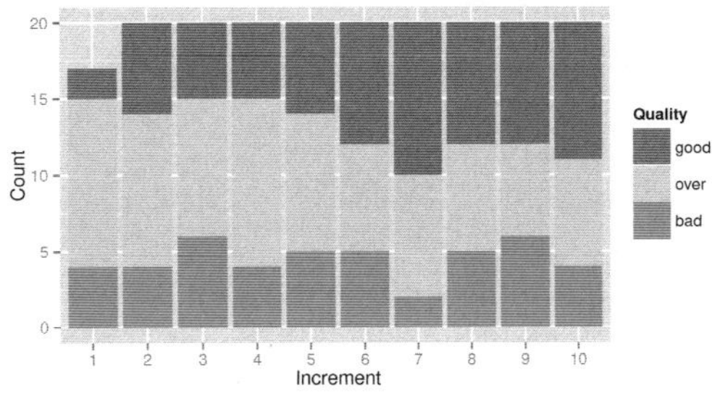

Figure 7: Manual evaluation of the quality of the top 20 rules as good, overspecified (but still valid) or bad, for training increments of increasing size

We use 700 sparky pairs for the training and test sets and reserve the remaining sparky pairs for future work. The training set consists of 200 sparky pairs used for rule induction, where we incrementally add 20 pairs at a time to the training set to evaluate how much training data is necessary for our approach to work. The test set consists of 500 sparky pairs for use in evaluating the coverage of the rules inferred during training.

5.3 Quality of Learned Rules

In our first evaluation we evaluate the rate of rule acquisition. We present the algorithm first with 20 sparky pairs and then add an additional 20 sparky pairs in each iteration, resulting in 10 sets of learned rules to compare to each other. This allows us to see how well new data allows the algorithm to generalize the induced rules.

To evaluate the quality of the learned rules, we conducted a manual evaluation of the top 20 rules as ranked by the perceptron model. We report the proportion of these rules rated as good, overspecified (more specific than desired, but still valid) or bad in Figure 7. As the figure shows, the proportion of good rules increases relative to the overspecified ones, with the proportion of bad rules remaining low. With the full training set, a total of 46 rules are learned, almost equally split between good, overspecified and bad (15/17/14, resp.).

In examining the learned rules, we observe that the learning algorithm manages to diminish the number of highly-ranked bad rules with spurious content changes, as these only infrequently contribute towards deriving a target LF. However, the presence of bad rules owing to parse errors persists, as certain parse errors occur with some regularity. As such, in future work we plan to investigate whether learning from n-best parses can manage to better work around erroneous parses.

5.4 Coverage

The first question of coverage is straighforward: do the rules we learn recover all of the types of clause-combining operations used by SPaRKy? Manual evaluation reveals good coverage for all five kinds of clause-combining operations in the top 20 rules of the final model. WITH-REDUCTION, MERGE, CUE-WORD-INSERTION, and CUE-WORD-CONJUNCTION (for all connectives in the corpus) are covered by good rules, i.e. ones that are comparable in quality to the kind we might write by hand. In addition to these good rules, WITH-REDUCTION and CUE-WORD-CONJUNCTION are also represented in several overspecified rules. RELATIVE-CLAUSE is only represented by overspecified rules.[8]

Additionally, in order to assess the extent to which the learned rules cover the contexts where the SPaRKy clause-combining operations can be applied in the SRC, we also applied the final set of learned rules to all of the input TPLFs in the test set. The test set contained 453 usable input pairs,[9] of which we were able to exactly reproduce 229 using the inferred rules. Naturally, we do not expect 100% coverage here as the test set will also contain some LFs suffering from parse errors, though this coverage level suggests our method would benefit from a larger training set. Importantly, applying the learned rules to the test set input generated 19,058 possible sentLFs (or 40 output LFs per input LF, on average), a sufficiently large number for a sentence plan ranker to learn from.

5.5 Experimenting with other clause-combining operations

Using a single-stage version of the algorithm, we also examined its capabilities with respect to learning clause-combining operations not present in the SRC. To create training examples, we created 167 input pairs based on TPLFS from the SRC using set of 16 hand-crafted rules including all the clause-combining operations pictured in Table 2. From these 167 pairs the algorithm induced 22 clause-combining operations, fully covering the 16 hand-crafted rules with some overspecification. Importantly, this preliminary finding suggests that developers can use this system to acquire a larger variety of clause-combining operations than those represented in the SRC with less need for extensive knowledge engineering.

6 Conclusions and Future Work

We have presented a clause-combining rule induction method that learns how to rewrite lexico-semantic dependency graphs in ways that go beyond current end-to-end NLG learning methods (Angeli et al., 2010; Konstas and Lapata, 2013), an important step towards ameliorating the knowledge acquisition bottleneck for NLG systems that produce texts with rich discourse structures. Future work will evaluate the system on multiple domains and push into the realm of robust, simultaneous induction of lexicalization, clause-combining and referring expression rules.

Acknowledgments

We thank the anonymous reviewers and the OSU Clippers Group for their helpful feedback and discussion. Supported in part by NSF grants IIS-1143635 and IIS-1319318 and by DFG SFB 1102.

References

Gabor Angeli, Percy Liang, and Dan Klein. 2010. A simple domain-independent probabilistic approach to generation. In *Proc. of the 2010 Conference on Empirical Methods in Natural Language Processing*, pages 502–512, Cambridge, MA, October.

Mandya Angrosh and Advaith Siddharthan. 2014. Text simplification using synchronous dependency grammars: Generalising automatically harvested rules. In *Proc. of the 8th International Natural Language Generation Conference*, pages 16–25, Philadelphia, Pennsylvania, USA, June.

Yoav Artzi and Luke Zettlemoyer. 2013. Weakly supervised learning of semantic parsers for mapping instructions to actions. *TACL*, 1:49–62.

Regina Barzilay and Mirella Lapata. 2005. Collective content selection for concept-to-text generation. In *Proc. of Human Language Technology Conference and Conference on Empirical Methods in Natural Language Processing (HLT/EMNLP)*, pages 331–338, Vancouver.

[8] Naturally elements of these rules are also present in some of the genuinely bad rules that remain in the final model. Even in these bad rules, however, the operations are appropriately constrained: WITH- REDUCTION is predicated on the use of *have* and CUE-WORD-INSERTION of *on the other hand* on the use of `contrast-rels` and of *since* on the use of `justify-rels`.

[9] Of the original 500 pairs, we excluded 29 pairs larger than the maximum size used in our staged learning, as well as 18 pairs where the target realization could not be parsed.

Trevor Cohn and Mirella Lapata. 2013. An abstractive approach to sentence compression. *ACM Transactions on Intelligent Systems and Technology*, 4(3):1–35.

Michael Collins. 2002. Discriminative training methods for hidden Markov models: theory and experiments with perceptron algorithms. In *Proc. of the 2002 Conference on Empirical Methods in Natural Language Processing*.

Nina Dethlefs, Helen Hastie, Heriberto Cuayáhuitl, and Oliver Lemon. 2013. Conditional random fields for responsive surface realisation using global features. In *Proc. of the 51st Annual Meeting of the Association for Computational Linguistics*, volume 1, pages 1254–1263, Sofia, Bulgaria.

Pablo A. Duboue and Kathleen R. McKeown. 2001. Empirically estimating order constraints for content planning in generation. In *Proc. of 39th Annual Meeting of the Association for Computational Linguistics*, pages 172–179, Toulouse, France, July.

Dominic Espinosa, Michael White, and Dennis Mehay. 2008. Hypertagging: Supertagging for surface realization with CCG. In *Proc. of the 46th Annual Meeting of the Association for Computational Linguistics: Human Language Technologies*, pages 183–191, Columbus, Ohio, June.

David M Howcroft, Crystal Nakatsu, and Michael White. 2013. Enhancing the expression of contrast in the SPaRKy Restaurant Corpus. In *Proc. of the 14th European Workshop on Natural Language Generation*.

Ravi Kondadadi, Blake Howald, and Frank Schilder. 2013. A statistical nlg framework for aggregated planning and realization. In *Proc. of the 51st Annual Meeting of the Association for Computational Linguistics*, volume 1, pages 1406–1415, Sofia, Bulgaria.

Ioannis Konstas and Mirella Lapata. 2013. A global model for concept-to-text generation. *Journal of Artificial Intelligence Research*, 48:305–346.

Tom Kwiatkowksi, Luke Zettlemoyer, Sharon Goldwater, and Mark Steedman. 2010. Inducing probabilistic CCG grammars from logical form with higher-order unification. In *Proc. of the 2010 Conference on Empirical Methods in Natural Language Processing*.

Wei Lu, Hwee Tou Ng, and Wee Sun Lee. 2009. Natural language generation with tree conditional random fields. In *Proc. of the 2009 Conference on Empirical Methods in Natural Language Processing*, pages 400–409, Singapore.

François Mairesse and Steve Young. 2014. Stochastic language generation in dialogue using factored language models. *Computational Linguistics*, 40(4):763–799.

Crystal Nakatsu and Michael White. 2010. Generating with discourse combinatory categorial grammar. *Language Issues in Language Technology*, 4(1):1–62.

Shimei Pan and James Shaw. 2004. Segue: A hybrid case-based surface natural language generator. In *Proc. of the 3rd International Conference of Natural Language Generation*, pages 130–140, Brockenhurst, UK.

Rajakrishnan Rajkumar and Michael White. 2014. Better surface realization through psycholinguistics. *Language and Linguistics Compass*, 8(10):428–448.

Ehud Reiter and Robert Dale. 2000. *Building natural generation systems*. Studies in Natural Language Processing. Cambridge University Press.

Ehud Reiter. 2010. Natural language generation. In Alexander Clark, Chris Fox, and Shalom Lappin, editors, *The Handbook of Computational Linguistics and Natural Language Processing*, Blackwell Handbooks in Linguistics, chapter 20. Wiley-Blackwell.

Amanda Stent and Martin Molina. 2009. Evaluating automatic extraction of rules for sentence plan construction. In *Proc. of the SIGDIAL 2009 Conference*, pages 290–297, London, UK.

Marilyn A. Walker, S. Whittaker, Amanda Stent, P. Maloor, J. Moore, M. Johnston, and G. Vasireddy. 2004. Generation and evaluation of user tailored responses in multimodal dialogue. *Cognitive Science*, 28(5):811–840, October.

Marilyn Walker, Amanda Stent, François Mairesse, and Rashmi Prasad. 2007. Individual and domain adaptation in sentence planning for dialogue. *Journal of Artificial Intelligence Research*, 30:413–456.

Michael White and Rajakrishnan Rajkumar. 2009. Perceptron reranking for CCG realization. In *Proc. of the 2009 Conference on Empirical Methods in Natural Language Processing*, pages 410–419, Singapore, August.

Michael White and Rajakrishnan Rajkumar. 2012. Minimal dependency length in realization ranking. In *Proc. of the 2012 Joint Conference on Empirical Methods in Natural Language Processing and Computational Natural Language Learning*, pages 244–255, Jeju Island, Korea, July.

Michael White, Robert AJ Clark, and Johanna D Moore. 2010. Generating tailored, comparative descriptions with contextually appropriate intonation. *Computational Linguistics*, 36(2):159–201.

Kristian Woodsend and Mirella Lapata. 2011. Learning to simplify sentences with quasi-synchronous grammar and integer programming. In *Proc. of the 2011 Conference on Empirical Methods in Natural Language Processing*, pages 409–420, Edinburgh, Scotland, UK.

Reading Times Predict the Quality of Generated Text Above and Beyond Human Ratings

Sina Zarrieß **Sebastian Loth** **David Schlangen**
Bielefeld University
Universitätsstraße 25
33615 Bielefeld, Germany
{sina.zarriess,sebastian.loth,david.schlangen}@uni-bielefeld.de

Abstract

Typically, human evaluation of NLG output is based on user ratings. We collected ratings and reading time data in a simple, low-cost experimental paradigm for text generation. Participants were presented corpus texts, automatically linearised texts, and texts containing predicted referring expressions and automatic linearisation. We demonstrate that the reading time metrics outperform the ratings in classifying texts according to their quality. Regression analyses showed that self-reported ratings discriminated poorly between the kinds of manipulation, especially between defects in word order and text coherence. In contrast, a combination of objective measures from the low-cost mouse contingent reading paradigm provided very high classification accuracy and thus, greater insight into the actual quality of an automatically generated text.

1 Introduction

Evaluating and comparing systems that produce natural language text as output, such as natural language generation (NLG) systems, is notoriously difficult. Many aspects of linguistic well-formedness and naturalness play a role for assessing the quality of an automatically generated text. On the sentence-level, this includes grammatical and morpho-syntactic correctness, lexical meaning, fluency, and stylistic appropriateness. On the text-level, further criteria related to coherence, text structure, and content should be considered. One of the most widely applied and least controversial NLG evaluation methods is to collect human ratings. Human ratings have been used for system comparison in a number of NLG shared tasks (Gatt and Belz, 2010; Belz et al., 2011), for validating other automatic evaluation methods in NLG (Reiter and Belz, 2009; Cahill, 2009; Elliott and Keller, 2014), and for training statistical components of NLG systems (Stent et al., 2004; Mairesse and Walker, 2011; Howcroft et al., 2013).

When no extrinsic tasks or factors for evaluating an NLG system are available, human judges are typically asked to rate the quality of texts or sentences according to several linguistic criteria, such as 'A: how fluent is the text?' and 'B: how clear and understandable is the text?' (e.g. (Belz et al., 2011)). This is a hard and unnatural task for most naive users, and can be non-trivial even for experts: raters have to reflect on and differentiate between detailed, linguistic aspects of text quality, and assign scores precisely and systematically across a set of generated outputs that potentially contain various types of linguistic defects. The rating task turns increasingly difficult if they have to compare texts with multiple sentences and multiple types of linguistic defects, e.g. fluency on the sentence level, clarity and coherence on the text level. Consequently, low agreement between raters, and even inconsistencies between ratings of the same human judge have been found in previous studies (Belz and Kow, 2010; Cahill and Forst, 2010; Dethlefs et al., 2014). Standard evaluation methods for, e.g. text summarisation tend to avoid possible interactions between local sentence-level and global text-level defects. Instead, they focus on coherence and content (Nenkova, 2006; Owczarzak et al., 2012). In particular, this is due to the fact that independently rating coherence and clarity locally for each sentence and globally for an entire text is tedious, unnatural, tiring and hardly achievable for human judges.

In other disciplines of linguistic research, a range of experimental paradigms have been established that provide more systematic and objective means to assess human text reading. In particular, psycholinguistic approaches typically use objective measures such as reading times and eye movements to quantify how well human readers can process a sentence. The advantage of these measures is that humans typically focus on reading the text. Importantly, they do not consciously control their eye movements. Longer reading times or certain patterns of eye movements have been well associated with difficulties that humans encounter when reading text, e.g. apparent inconsistencies as garden path sentences (Christianson et al., 2001), and complex grammatical constructs (Traxler et al., 2002).

This paper investigates whether more objective reading measures can be exploited for evaluating NLG systems and systematically measuring text quality. However, using eye tracking for evaluation purposes is more costly than relying on ratings. Furthermore, most eye tracking studies used carefully designed stimuli to test a specific effect at a particular known position in a sentence. In sum, eye tracking is highly sensitive to pro-

Proceedings of the 15th European Workshop on Natural Language Generation (ENLG), pages 38–47,
Brighton, September 2015.

cessing difficulties. But due the costly devices and experiments, it was - to the best of our knowledge - not applied for evaluating comparably uncontrolled texts that are typical in NLG.

Thus, we have developed and tested mouse contingent reading (MCR) for evaluating generated texts. This method combines the sensitivity of eye tracking with the cost effectiveness of a rating study. The automatically generated texts are presented to human raters in a sentence-by-sentence, mouse-contingent way such that a number of parameters of the reading process are recorded, e.g. the time that people spent looking at single sentences and an entire text. We hypothesized that these parameters are more informative for the quality of a text than the user ratings of clarity and fluency.

As objective criteria for text quality are hardly available in NLG (Dale and Mellish, 1998; Hardcastle and Scott, 2008), we did not compare reading times and ratings on manual, potentially flawed annotations of text quality. Instead, we selected experimental material from a corpus-based generation framework that combines sentence-level linearisation and text-level referring expression generation (Zarrieß and Kuhn, 2013). We based our study on a set of texts that were available in 3 versions: (i) the "gold standard" corpus text, (ii) automatically linearised texts where word order deviated from the original corpus and contained potential fluency-related defects, (iii) texts with potential defects in referring expressions and linearisation which are likely to deteriorate clarity or coherence on the discourse level. We controlled the broad type of linguistic defects but not the details of each sentence or text. We argue that an objective evaluation method for NLG should clearly distinguish coherence and surface-related aspects of text quality.

In our data, there is a single human-authored version of each text which is free of errors. We do not know whether a deviation of the other versions is an error or an acceptable alternative realisation. Thus, in contrast to typical eye tracking studies we do not aim at detecting the effect of a particular type of error. Our assumption is more conservative: we expect that a set of automatically generated texts that deviates significantly from a set of corpus texts on several levels of linguistic realisation (referring expressions and linearisation) has lower quality than texts that only deviate from the corpus on a single level (linearisation). To further accommodate for the fact that we do not control the exact degree of acceptability of the potential defects, we add a set of filler texts that we manually manipulated to contain severe errors in coherence.

Based on the human ratings and MCR data collected for a set of automatically generated texts, we investigated whether a regression model can predict which types of linguistic defects were present in the text read by the participant, i.e. which generation components were used to generate it. We find that it is possible to achieve a good prediction accuracy for text quality, despite the fact that there is uncertainty with respect to the exact number and types of errors in the texts. However, the accuracy of the regression models varies considerably according to the type of predictors: Human ratings can hardly discriminate incoherent automatically generated texts from original corpus texts and texts containing defects in word order. A regression model based on reading time predictors achieved a very good fit and largely outperformed the rating model in separating different levels of quality in NLG output. This suggests that some effects were not reliably reflected in the subjective ratings that are consciously controlled and calculated by the participants. However, these effects were accounted for by the objective reading measures that are (mostly) outside of conscious control.

Section 2 provides background on research in NLG evaluation. Section 3 introduces our MCR paradigm. The generation framework we used to collect our experimental material is presented in Section 4. Section 5 describes the experimental design. The models are discussed in Section 6.

2 Background on NLG Evaluation

In recent years, the NLG community has become increasingly interested in comparative evaluation between NLG systems (Gatt and Belz, 2010; Koller et al., 2010; Belz et al., 2011; Banik et al., 2013; Hastie and Belz, 2014). Generally, evaluation methods for assessing NLG systems fall into three main categories: 1) automatic evaluation methods that compare system output against one or multiple reference texts, 2) human evaluation methods where human readers are asked to judge a text, typically with respect to several criteria. If the NLG component is embedded in an end-to-end system, such as a dialogue system, 3) extrinsic factors of task success and usefulness of the NLG output can be measured. For corpus-based NLG components such as surface realisers or referring expression generators, extrinsic factors cannot be assessed, but in this case, reference or gold text outputs are often available. Langkilde (2002) first suggested to use automatic evaluation measures inspired from methods in machine translation, such as BLEU (Papineni et al., 2002) or NIST (Doddington, 2002), that measure the n-gram overlap between the system and some reference text, sentence or phrase. The advantage of such automatic and cheap evaluation methods can be enormous. If tightly integrated in the development cycle of an NLG system, they allow fast and empirically optimised implementation decisions. In turn, a lot of research on NLG evaluation focussed on defining and validating automatic evaluation measures. Such a metric is typically considered valid if it correlates well with human judgements of text quality (Stent et al., 2005; Foster, 2008; Reiter and Belz, 2009; Cahill, 2009; Elliott and Keller, 2014). However, automatic evaluation measures in NLG still have a range of known conceptual deficits, i.e. they do not reflect appropriateness of content (Reiter and Belz,

2009), or meaning (Stent et al., 2005). Thus, many studies and evaluation challenges in NLG additionally collect human ratings to assess the quality.

Compared to the large body of work on automatic evaluation measures, there has been little research that assessed the validity of human evaluation methods. Hardcastle and Scott (2008) provided an extensive discussion of human and automatic evaluation for text quality. They proposed a Turing-style test where participants are asked to judge whether a text was generated by a computer or written by a human. Belz and Kow (2010) showed that higher agreement between human raters can be obtained if they compare two automatically generated texts, instead of assigning scores to texts in isolation. Belz and Kow (2011) found that human judges preferred to use continuous rating scales over discrete rating scales. Siddharthan and Katsos (2012) investigated two offline measures inspired from psycholinguistic studies of sentence processing for assessing text readability, namely magnitude estimation and sentence recall. They demonstrate that the sentence recall method did not discriminate well between sentences of differing fluency if sentences were short. On the other hand, human judgements, did not discriminate well between surface level disfluencies and breakdowns in comprehension.

3 Mouse Contingent Reading

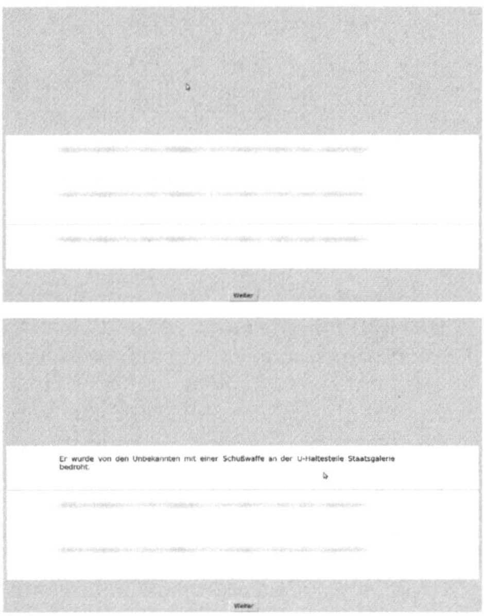

Figure 1: Screenshots of the mouse-contingent reading GUI. Top panel: at the start of each trial, all sentences are masked and the mouse cursor is positioned above them. Bottom panel: the participant has moved the mouse to the first sentence and unmasked it.

In mouse contingent reading (MCR), the reader is presented a text on a computer screen. The entire text is covered by a mask or masking pattern. Only if the reader moves the mouse cursor over a particular section of text, the mask is removed and the text is shown in clear font (see Figure 1). This paradigm is equivalent to gaze contingent reading (McConkie and Rayner, 1975; Reder, 1973) and self-guided reading (Hatfield, 2014) but it does not require an eye tracking device or touch sensitive device. However, the same metrics can be collected, i.e. the time spent on each area of interest and the scan path. Figure 2 shows an example of how the reader transits forth and back between areas of interest and how much time is spent on each area.

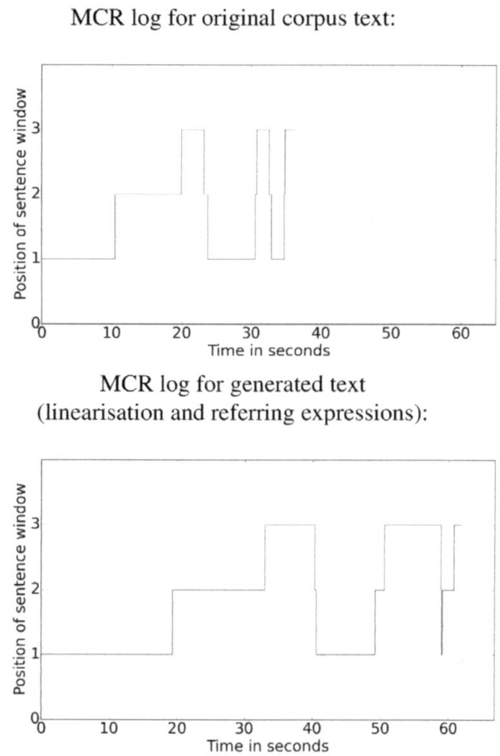

Figure 2: Visualisation of reading times recorded with MCR for a text in two different quality conditions

In reading studies, eye tracking and gaze contingent designs are the most popular paradigms. The words or phrases that a reader is currently processing and attending are indicated by fixations on them (Rayner, 1998; Rayner, 2009). However, hand motions are also highly informative to cognitive processes in general (Freeman et al., 2011). Importantly, a hand oriented paradigm requires much less technical efforts and allows a precise data acquisition. In case of MCR, the collected data approximate the comparable eye tracking data as they indicate which part of the text was attended.

4 Generation Framework

Zarrieß and Kuhn (2013) present a combined, corpus-based generation framework for two well-studied NLG

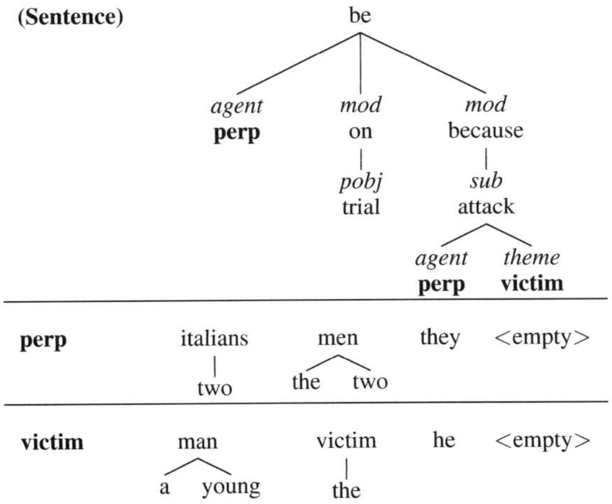

Figure 3: Example NLG input from (Zarrieß and Kuhn, 2013): a non-linearised dependency structure with slots for REs and lists for candidate RE realisations

sub-tasks: referring expression generation in context (REG) and surface realisation (linearisation). Their system generates texts from dependency-based inputs that can be more or less specified. Figure 3 illustrates an example for a dependency-based input with underspecified referring expressions. The linearisation component of the system predicts the order of words, i.e. nodes in the dependency tree. The REG component computes a ranking over candidate realisations for each RE slot and inserts the top-ranked expression into the tree. Additionally, these NLG inputs are available in a more specified version, i.e. as non-linearised dependency trees containing the referring expressions from the original corpus text. In this case, the NLG task consists of linearisation only.

Compared to other text generation tasks, such as e.g. text summarisation, this NLG framework is more restricted. The order of sentences, lexical choice and basic sentence structure are defined by the corpus-based input annotations. Our setting has two NLG components that can be switched on and off on demand. We exploit this for obtaining automatically generated text that differ in their quality. Thus, we use texts that have been generated from different components of the system. This approach is very similar to the idea of evaluating an NLG system in a architectural ablation mode, demonstrated in Callaway and Lester (2001).

The NLG inputs in Zarrieß and Kuhn (2013) were obtained from manual RE annotations and automatic dependency annotations for a corpus of 200 German newspaper articles. The texts are short reports on robberies as they can be found in the local newspaper. Thus, they all describe similar events between two referents (a victim and a perpetrator). The RE annotations also contain implicit mentions of victim and perpetrator referents in particular syntactic contexts (such as passives, or coordinations). Therefore, the RE component can delete REs that were realised in the original text, or introduce REs that were originally implicit.

Table 1 shows an example from the original corpus text and an automatically generated version by the system. Please note that neither gold nor generated texts contain punctuation. Since the system does not predict punctuation, this was removed from the original texts. Furthermore, the automatically generated text deviates from the original corpus text in a range of linearisation and REG decisions. These deviations are not necessarily ungrammatical or incoherent (as e.g. the predicted RE in the second sentence which is still understandable and does not degrade coherence). On the other hand, there can be sentences that are clearly misconstrued such as the third sentence where ungrammatical word order and incoherent or superfluous REs result in an unclear meaning of the sentence.

Thus, we controlled for the broad, expected level of text quality, rather than applying a costly manual annotation of error types present in the generated texts. As the focus of our study is on predicting defects in text quality that are due to clarity and fluency, we selected texts from Zarrieß and Kuhn (2013)'s data set where the linearisation and REs deviated from the original corpus texts. As a sanity check for our evaluation metrics, we included the original corpus texts and further manipulated some of the generated texts such that their referring expressions would be very hard to resolve and obscure the relation between two sentences. These texts were treated as *fillers*. Each generated text is available in two versions: a) generated by the linearisation and referring expression component containing defects in the realisation of reference and word order, and b) generated by the linearisation component containing perfect referring expressions and potential defects in word order. This provided us a hierarchy of levels of text quality. Linearisation mostly affects the fluency (and sometimes the grammaticality) on the sentence level, whereas wrong predictions of referring expressions can result in incoherent transitions between sentences which affects clarity on the text level.

5 Experiment

This study tested human evaluation methods for text generation. We focussed on the problem of evaluating NLG output formed of multiple sentences and detecting whether the user experienced difficulties in reading and understanding the text.

5.1 Hypothesis

In evaluations of text generation, the quality of a text has to be assessed on different levels of linguistic well-formedness including grammatical correctness, fluency, and intelligibility or clarity. Cases of misconstrued texts are not just right or wrong but they vary on a scale from well-formed through understandable but yet difficult to read to unintelligible. Often, it is difficult to pinpoint which components and decisions of

Original corpus text	Automatically generated text
Auf dem Weg von der U-Bahn-Haltestelle Dornbusch zu seiner Wohnung in Ginnheim ist ein 27jähriger in der Nacht zum Samstag überfallen und ausgeraubt worden	Auf dem Weg von der U-Bahn-Haltestelle Dornbusch zu seiner Wohnung in Ginnheim in der Nacht zu Samstag überfallen und ausgeraubt worden ist ein 27jähriger
On the way from the metro station Dornbusch to his apartment in Ginnheim, a 27-year-old has been attacked and robbed Saturday's night	
Der Täter hatte sein Opfer gegen 1.30 Uhr zunächst scheinbar harmlos nach der nächsten Telefonzelle gefragt	Der Täter hatte **den 27jährigen** gegen 1.30 Uhr zunächst scheinbar harmlos nach der nächsten Telefonzelle gefragt
*Around 1:30 o'clock, the perpetrator had asked his victim (***the 27-year-old***) for the next phone box in a seemingly harmless way*	
Nachdem ihm diese an der Ecke Ernst-Schwendler-Straße Platenstraße gezeigt worden war machte er kehrt und verfolgte den 27jährigen	Nachdem Platenstraße diese an der Ecke Ernst-Schwendler-Straße gezeigt ihm worden war er machte kehrt und verfolgte **der Täter sein Opfer**
*After it had been shown to him on the corner Ernst-Schwendler street Platen street, he returned and (***the perpetrator***) followed the 27-year-old (***the victim***)*	

Table 1: Example corpus text and corresponding NLG output. Word order defects are underlined, generated REs that differ from corpus REs are in bold face. The English translations do not show word order problems, but predicted REs are given in brackets and bold face.

the NLG contributed to the well-formedness. In particular, a single component can affect all levels of well-formedness, e.g. the realisation of word order can impair the readability and intelligibility of a text.

We expected that naïve participants would have difficulties in independently rating different aspects of text quality, e.g. clarity and fluency. We assumed that the rating task would be even more tedious on the sentence-level such that we collected global user ratings for fluency and clarity. We hypothesised that the parameters of the reading process such as the time spent on individual sentences, and the transitions between sentences would be more objective, local measures and can at least complement ratings of perceived quality. Thus, we recorded the reading parameters in our study and aimed to identify the links between ratings, reading parameters and levels of text quality.

Suboptimal NLG decisions affect an entire sentence or text. Thus, the MCR study was designed to assess the well-formedness of larger units. We used three comparably large areas of interest formed by each sentence of the texts. In contrast to typical reading studies at the level of single sentence processing, the cursor motions were selectively recorded for transitions between sentences. These transitions are most likely related to measures at the text level that we were interested in, i.e. clarity and fluency. Furthermore, the ratings of clarity and fluency were collected with regards to the entire text.

5.2 Experimental Setting

Participants Thirty-three participants were recruited from the department's participant pool (including students and staff). They received €5 as well as candy sweets in exchange for their time and effort.

Apparatus The participants were seated in front of a typical office computer screen. A dedicated Python programme controlled the presentation of the stimuli, recorded the reading times[1] and mouse transitions, and collected the ratings. The participants interacted with the programme through a standard mouse and keyboard.

Materials and Conditions From the set of NLG outputs with potential defects in clarity and fluency, as described in Section 4, we randomly selected 16 texts. A subset of twelve texts were presented in three conditions: a) the original corpus text without any defects (*gold*), b) automatically linearised texts that could include defects in word order (*lin*), and c) automatically linearised texts with automatically generated referring expressions, i.e. these texts could include defects in word order and referring expressions (*sem*). The remaining four sentences were hand manipulated such they would be clearly distorted in terms of syntax, reference and intelligibility (*filler*).

The critical texts were assigned to one of three lists such that all lists contained four texts per condition and each text occurred once per list. Additionally, all lists included the four filler items.

Procedure The participants were welcomed to the lab and handed a written consent form. If they agreed to take part in the study, the participants were handed written instructions asking them to read the texts displayed on screen using the mouse and to rate them for clarity and fluency afterwards.

The session started with an additionally selected practice item to familiarise the participants with the design of the study. In the experimental session, the 16 items were presented in random order. Each trial started as soon as the participant confirmed the ratings to the previous item. The mouse cursor was positioned

[1]The reading times were approximated by measuring the dwell time of the mouse cursor on a sentence. This is equivalent to measuring the dwell time of the point of gaze in gaze contingent reading.

above the three sentences such that the entire text was masked. The participants initiated the clock by moving the cursor to the first sentence. The sentences unmasked as soon as the mouse cursor entered the white space surrounding the script and was masked again as soon as the mouse left this area (see Figure 1). Thus, at any point in time either one or no sentence was presented without the masking pattern. Once the participant had completed reading the text, they clicked a confirmation button below all sentences.

This button click triggered the display of two rating questions. First, a fluency rating was elicited by asking "How well does the text read? Is it formulated in a linguistically correct way?" Secondly, "How clear and understandable is the meaning and content of the text?" asked for a clarity rating. Instead of a discrete Likert-scale, we adopted the magnitude estimation paradigm, i.e. the participants were instructed to score sentences relative to each other by assigning them a number (Siddharthan and Katsos, 2012). The entire session including instruction and debriefing lasted about half an hour.

6 Results

In total, we collected reading and rating data of 528 experimental trials from thirty-three participants. In the following, we analyse the subjective ratings and the objective reading parameters with respect to our experimental conditions and investigate whether they can separate texts with different types of linguistic defects. Table 2 provides an overview of the measures we calculated and used as predictors for regression models.

6.1 Ratings

In the magnitude estimation paradigm, each participant uses their own numerical scale for assigning fluency and clarity scores. The raw scores were standardised with a z-transformation such that 0 is the mean rating for each participant. The variables **fluency-z** and **clarity-z** indicate to which extent a participant's rating of a text is better or worse than their mean rating.

As shown in Table 2, the overall tendency for fluency and clarity z-scores was as expected: on average, participants assigned the highest scores to *gold* texts, followed by *lin*, *sem* and *filler* texts. This suggests that on average the participants rated the evaluation criteria as intended and that the hierarchy of perceived text quality corresponds to our assumptions. Furthermore, the relatively low standard deviation between the means of the participants' ratings indicates that z-scores obtained from magnitude estimation ratings are relatively consistent.

6.2 Reading Measures

Using the MCR design, we recorded the time spent for reading single sentences and the text also the scan-path, i.e. the number and order of transitions and regressions between sentences. For identifying the most informative predictors, we derived a number of measures from the raw data that are described in the following.

Reading Time Using the dwell times (the time span that a particular sentence was not masked) and number of words per sentence, we computed the **speed**[2] and the **pace**[3] as first order derivatives. Nine predictors at sentence level and three at text level were computed. In addition, we computed the time required to read the entire text for the first time. Normalising this time span by the total reading time of the text provides a measure for how much time was spent on regressions within the text compared to the first pass.

Scan-path Next to dwell times, the scan-path can inform about the quality of a text. This could be reflected in how often particular sentences were visited and how often the participant transited between sentences. However, our regression analyses showed that reading time measures are generally more effective than scan-path predictors (see Section 6.3 below). In Table 2, we show the means for **path-log** as a log-normalised measure for the total number of transitions between sentences.

Standardising The individual differences in reading times and scan-paths between individual participants were pronounced. Additionally, they were also differences between texts, e.g. their content and lengths. As with the ratings, we added a standardised (z-score) measure of the reading parameters to the list of predictors (e.g., pace-total-z). This z-score is based on the mean and standard deviation of one parameter of one participant. For accommodating the variance in between the texts, we computed a second z-score (termed 'z2' in the following) based on the mean and SD of an items' reading times for all sentence-level predictors. This score reflects how a text or sentence compares to the other items.

As shown in Table 2, the means of the reading time measures do not comply with the expected quality hierarchy in the same way as ratings. Thus, it was not the case that lower quality texts are generally read more slowly than more coherent or gold texts. For instance, *sem* texts were read slowest (total time) whereas fillers can be identified by a high pace and large number of transitions, i.e. a long scan-path. *Sem* and *lin* texts can be distinguished in terms of the local, sentence-based reading times, e.g. 'speed_sent_z2' or 'time_sent3_z2'. Thus, the ratings and the MCR data appear to provide disjoint information such that one cannot substitute the other, e.g. a low clarity rating does not imply a prolonged reading time and vice-versa.

6.3 Regression Models

For testing whether and to what extent the user ratings and the reading times discriminate between the types of generated texts, the measures were used as predictors in regression models. This provides insight into

[2]Number of words in a sentence or text divided by the summed reading times

[3]Summed dwell time divided by length of text or sentence

		Filler		Sem		Lin		Gold	
		mean	sd	mean	sd	mean	sd	mean	sd
Ratings	fluency_z	-0.41	0.38	-0.32	0.50	-0.04	0.36	0.77	0.47
	clarity_z	-0.53	0.40	-0.18	0.49	0.17	0.36	0.54	0.51
Text RTs	pace_total_z	0.79	0.33	-0.22	0.64	-0.17	0.59	-0.40	0.65
	path_log	2.29	0.42	2.04	0.41	2.10	0.37	2.14	0.43
	speed_total_z	-0.44	0.12	0.22	0.79	0.07	0.81	0.15	0.87
	time_total_z	0.04	0.37	0.15	0.46	-0.09	0.49	-0.10	0.62
	time_1stpass_z	-0.29	0.36	0.30	0.49	0.09	0.48	-0.11	0.47
Sentence RTs	pace_1sent_z2	0.00	0.79	-0.04	0.83	-0.02	0.75	0.06	0.75
	pace_2sent_z2	-0.00	0.70	0.02	0.74	-0.01	0.64	-0.00	0.71
	pace_3sent_z2	0.00	0.72	0.08	0.65	0.07	0.78	-0.15	0.60
	speed_1sent_z2	-0.00	0.79	0.12	0.86	-0.10	0.71	-0.02	0.72
	speed_2sent_z2	0.00	0.70	0.21	0.79	-0.10	0.64	-0.11	0.62
	speed_3sent_z2	-0.00	0.72	0.19	0.63	0.01	0.72	-0.20	0.55
	time_1sent_z2	-0.00	0.79	0.04	0.85	-0.06	0.73	0.02	0.74
	time_2sent_z2	-0.00	0.70	0.12	0.77	-0.06	0.64	-0.06	0.67
	time_3sent_z2	-0.00	0.72	0.15	0.65	0.03	0.76	-0.18	0.58

Table 2: Means and SD for ratings, text-based and sentence-based reading times. SD is computed on mean values per participant and indicates agreement/consistency between participants.

the type of relation between the text quality conditions on the one hand, and multiple evaluation metrics on the other hand. The dependent variable of our models was the text condition, with four possible values - *filler*, *sem*, *lin* or *gold*. We used hierarchical binary regression[4] and we fitted three binary regression models that iteratively distinguish a particular text type from a set of remaining texts. The hierarchy of the models corresponds to the types of errors and to the level of text quality: First, we applied a *filler* model that should separate *filler* texts (25%) from all other texts. These items were manually distorted and thus, contained a greatest number of defects. In the next step, we excluded the fillers items and build a model that separates *sem* texts (33%) from the remaining *lin* and *gold* texts. The *sem* texts were automatically linearised and included generated referring expressions, thus the remaining items were expected to entertain less defects. Finally, we designed a model that separates *lin* (50%) from *gold* texts.

We were interested in how well different sets of predictors perform in the regression analysis. For each step (*filler, sem, lin*) of the text quality hierarchy, we evaluated the following models: a) **Ratings** based on fluency and clarity z-scores, b) **Text RTs** based on text-level time, space, speed, time-1stpass and their z-scores, c) **All RTs** based on Text RTs and sentence-level time, pace, speed and corresponding z-scores (computed over texts), d) **Combined** based on a combination of Ratings and All RTs.

We excluded non-significant predictors using stepwise backward regression. Therefore, each model in-

Predictors	% Fit	% Acc.	# Coef.	R^2
	Filler vs. other (Sem, Lin ,Gold)			
	Majority BL: 75%			
Ratings	76.33	76.14	1	0.133
Text RTs	81.06	81.06	2	0.359
All RTs	100.0	96.78	11	0.885
Combined	100.0	96.02	11	0.905
	Sem vs. other (Lin, Gold)			
	Majority BL: 66.66%			
Ratings	67.91	67.93	2	0.143
Text RTs	66.92	64.89	5	0.113
All RTs	100.0	94.19	14	0.926
Combined	100.0	94.94	15	0.943
	Lin vs. other (Gold)			
	Majority BL: 50%			
Ratings	66.66	66.29	2	0.26
Text RTs	68.18	65.15	9	0.23
All RTs	75.75	67.42	18	0.412
Combined	77.65	74.62	17	0.521

Table 3: Hierarchical binary regression for text quality conditions, using different sets of predictors ('RTs' stands for reading times, 'All RTs' include text and sentence reading measures).

[4]Ordinal or multinomial regression can handle multiple values in the dependent variable, but uses more complex statistics and the resulting models are harder to interpret.

cludes a different number of coefficients. In Table 3, we report the performance of the final models obtained from backward regression in terms of the goodness of fit (% Fit), the prediction accuracy in ten-fold cross validation (% Acc.), the number of significant predictors (# Coef.) and Nagelkerke's R^2.

Table 2 shows that that the clarity and fluency ratings of *filler* and *sem* texts are lower on average. But the data in Table 3 indicate these ratings hardly achieved any error reduction compared to the majority baseline, i.e. these ratings were not informative with regards to identifying these texts. This is particularly remarkable in the case of *fillers* as they are clearly erroneous and should be identified by any reliable metric. The rating model performs slightly better in the last step of the hierarchical regression, i.e. for distinguishing linearised texts and original corpus texts. We attribute this effect to the pronounced difference between fluency ratings of gold texts as compared to other texts (see Table 2).

The global text-level predictors **Text RTs** perform slightly better in the case of *fillers*, and comparably worse in the *sem* and *lin* conditions. However, when we add sentence-level reading times to the set of predictors, the model achieves an accuracy of 96% for discriminating *sem* texts and 94% for fillers which is above and beyond the rating model. The high accuracy shows that mouse contingent reading data are very informative with regards to the quality of automatically generated texts.

We note that combining the reading parameters and the ratings in the *filler* and *sem* model did not improve the accuracy compared to only using the reading parameters (see Table 3). Thus, we attribute most of the predictive power of the combined model to the reading measures. In the *filler* model, the clarity rating score was statistically significant, but did not add to the prediction accuracy of the model. In the *sem* model, the fluency rating is significant. When distinguishing *gold* and *lin* texts, the reading parameters were less effective predictors compared to the *filler* and *sem* models. This affected the model's accuracy such that the fluency ratings contributed significantly to the model. However, including the reading parameters still improved the model's accuracy substantially. This suggests that the measures we recorded with sentence-by-sentence reading are especially informative for predicting quality defects on the level of text clarity and coherence.

6.4 Predictors

In Table 4, we present the plain coefficients for the final *filler*, *sem* and *lin* models that we obtained from combining sentence-level and text-level reading measures and ratings. The stepwise backward regression procedure excludes different subsets of predictors from the initial models. For instance, the text-level reading times, such as total speed and pace, are not significant for identifying *filler* and *sem* texts. On the other hand, they discriminate between *lin* and *gold* texts. The *filler* and *sem* models used sentence-level predictors for time, pace and speed of particular sentences. This pattern suggests that defects in referring expression realistion, which are present in *filler* and *sem* texts but not in *lin* and *gold* texts, deteriorate the clarity and coherence of NLG output which is reflected in longer reading times on particular sentences in a text.

Predictor	**Filler**	**Sem**	**Lin**
(Intercept)	-13.457	8.704	0.271
pace-1sent-z2	8.122	-52.90	-
pace-2sent	22.033	-21.38	9.188
pace-3sent	-	76.32	8.067
pace-3sent-z2	-	-66.76	-
speed-1sent-z2	-	213.2	-
speed-2sent	0.035	0.023	0.021
speed-2sent-z2	9.683	12.65	-
speed-3sent	-0.084	0.097	0.009
speed-3sent-z2	-	-	0.732
time-1sent	-1.17	-0.7345	0.607
time-1sent-z2	-	-259.4	-
time-2sent-z2	-21.5	-120.5	-1.223
time-3sent	2.047	-5.399	-
time-3sent-z2	-2.55	62.61	-
pace-total	-	-	-31.852
pace-total-z	-	-	4.298
display-3sent-log	-	-	1.331
time-1stpass-z	-	-	2.04
speed-total	-	-	-0.003
speed-total-z	-	-	3.062
time-1stpass-z	-	-	-1.23
time-total-z	-	-	-2.283
fluency-z	-	-1.629	-1.068
clarity-z	-1.352	-	-

Table 4: Sentence-level, text-level, rating-based predictors and their coefficients in final *filler*, *sem* and *lin* models from Table 3

6.5 Discussion

Generally, our results corroborate the common claim that quality of generated text is a multi-faceted and graded phenomenon which cannot be reduced to a small number of quality criteria that can be easily assessed in a rating task. Despite the fact that averaged ratings seem to correspond roughly to the expected hierarchy of text quality, a regression analysis of individual ratings for text instances shows a more detailed picture. A combination of reading time metrics identifies generated texts that contain defects in word order and referring expressions with high accuracy, while the rating predictors could hardly discriminate between instances of different text quality conditions. We found that objective sentence-level and text-level reading time measures can complement each other and account for complex interactions between aspects of text quality. This result has implications for standard human evaluation set-ups in NLG, summarization and possibly Machine Translation which are often based on several self-reported rating criteria.

We showed that an experimental paradigm such as MCR provides low-cost and natural means for recording objective reading measures while sidestepping the technical and practical requirements of an eye-tracking study. Our MCR set-up is based on a simple GUI that presents pieces of text in a mouse-contigent way and can be deployed on crowd-sourcing platforms.

Further research is needed to understand how predictors generalise and how the metrics can be applied to a reliable comparison of NLG systems. The fact that standardising across participants and across texts was effective, implies that prior knowledge about individual reading behavior of a participant is needed to accurately identify texts where understanding and reading difficulties occurred. Such parameters could be collected by introducing additional error-free and clearly erroneous texts into the experiment. The acquired data would reflect a burn-in phase for the predictors and provide the data for standardising the metrics.

A surprising result is that is that (error-free) gold texts were not associated with faster reading times. It is possible that the fact that users had to rate each text after reading it might have impaired their natural reading behavior. On the other hand, users might spend less time on clearly deficitive texts as they were unable to integrate them syntactically and/or semantically. This effect will be investigated in future work.

7 Conclusion

Evaluating automatically generated texts is a complex task and involves dealing with a range of interacting levels of linguistic realisation. While many users can easily and naturally read texts, they cannot be expected to provide detailed, objective and systematic assessments of the linguistic quality of a text. This study suggests that there is a lot to be gained from exploring psycholinguistically plausible methods and paradigms for human evaluation in NLG. We adopted a simple and low-cost mouse contingent reading paradigm for an evaluation study in text generation. We showed that parameters of the reading process recorded with MCR, such as reading time for texts and sentences, provide very effective predictors for discriminating between generated texts of different quality levels, whereas self-reported quality ratings do not.

References

Eva Banik, Claire Gardent, and Eric Kow. 2013. The KBGen challenge. In *Proceedings of the 14th European Workshop on Natural Language Generation (ENLG)*, pages 94–97.

Anja Belz and Eric Kow. 2010. Comparing rating scales and preference judgements in language evaluation. In *Proceedings of the 6th International Natural Language Generation Conference*, INLG '10, pages 7–15, Stroudsburg, PA, USA. Association for Computational Linguistics.

Anja Belz and Eric Kow. 2011. Discrete vs. continuous rating scales for language evaluation in nlp. In *Proceedings of the 49th Annual Meeting of the Association for Computational Linguistics: Human Language Technologies: short papers-Volume 2*, pages 230–235. Association for Computational Linguistics.

Anja Belz, Michael White, Dominic Espinosa, Eric Kow, Deirdre Hogan, and Amanda Stent. 2011. The first surface realisation shared task: Overview and evaluation results. In *Proceedings of the 13th European workshop on natural language generation*, pages 217–226. Association for Computational Linguistics.

Aoife Cahill and Martin Forst. 2010. Human evaluation of a german surface realisation ranker. In *Empirical methods in natural language generation*, pages 201–221. Springer.

Aoife Cahill. 2009. Correlating human and automatic evaluation of a german surface realiser. In *Proceedings of the ACL-IJCNLP 2009 Conference Short Papers*, pages 97–100. Association for Computational Linguistics.

Charles Callaway and James Lester. 2001. Evaluating the effects of natural language generation techniques on reader satisfaction. In *Proceedings of the 23rd Annual Conference of the Cognitive Science Society*, pages 164–169.

Kiel Christianson, Andrew Hollingworth, John F Halliwell, and Fernanda Ferreira. 2001. Thematic Roles Assigned along the Garden Path Linger. *Cognitive Psychology*, 42(4):368–407, June.

Robert Dale and Chris Mellish. 1998. Towards evaluation in natural language generation. In *Proceedings of the First International Conference on Language Resources and Evaluation*, volume 562.

Nina Dethlefs, Heriberto Cuayáhuitl, Helen Hastie, Verena Rieser, and Oliver Lemon. 2014. Cluster-based prediction of user ratings for stylistic surface realisation. In *Proceedings of EACL 2014*.

George Doddington. 2002. Automatic evaluation of machine translation quality using n-gram co-occurrence statistics. In *Proceedings of the second international conference on Human Language Technology Research*, pages 138–145. Morgan Kaufmann Publishers Inc.

Desmond Elliott and Frank Keller. 2014. Comparing automatic evaluation measures for image description. In *Proceedings of the 52nd Annual Meeting of the Association for Computational Linguistics: Short Papers*, volume 452, page 457.

Mary Ellen Foster. 2008. Automated metrics that agree with human judgements on generated output for an embodied conversational agent. In *Proceedings of the Fifth International Natural Language Generation Conference*, pages 95–103. Association for Computational Linguistics.

Jonathan B. Freeman, Rick Dale, and Thomas A. Farmer. 2011. Hand in Motion Reveals Mind in Motion. *Frontiers in Psychology*, 2.

Albert Gatt and Anja Belz. 2010. Introducing shared tasks to nlg: The tuna shared task evaluation challenges. In *Empirical methods in natural language generation*, pages 264–293. Springer.

David Hardcastle and Donia Scott. 2008. Can we evaluate the quality of generated text? In *Proceedings of LREC*.

Helen Hastie and Anja Belz. 2014. A comparative evaluation methodology for nlg in interactive systems. In *Proceedings of LREC'14*.

Hunter Hatfield. 2014. Self-Guided Reading: Touch-Based Measures of Syntactic Processing. *Journal of Psycholinguistic Research*, October.

David Howcroft, Crystal Nakatsu, and Michael White. 2013. Enhancing the expression of contrast in the sparky restaurant corpus. In *Proceedings of the 14th European Workshop on Natural Language Generation*, pages 30–39, Sofia, Bulgaria, August. Association for Computational Linguistics.

Alexander Koller, Kristina Striegnitz, Donna Byron, Justine Cassell, Robert Dale, Johanna Moore, and Jon Oberlander. 2010. The first challenge on generating instructions in virtual environments. In *Empirical Methods in Natural Language Generation*, pages 328–352. Springer.

Irene Langkilde-Geary. 2002. An empirical verification of coverage and correctness for a general-purpose sentence generator. In *Proceedings of the 12th International Natural Language Generation Workshop*, pages 17–24.

François Mairesse and Marilyn A Walker. 2011. Controlling user perceptions of linguistic style: Trainable generation of personality traits. *Computational Linguistics*, 37(3):455–488.

George W. McConkie and Keith Rayner. 1975. The span of the effective stimulus during a fixation in reading. *Perception & Psychophysics*, 17(6):578–586, November.

Ani Nenkova. 2006. Summarization evaluation for text and speech: issues and approaches. In *Proceedings of INTERSPEECH*.

Karolina Owczarzak, John M Conroy, Hoa Trang Dang, and Ani Nenkova. 2012. An assessment of the accuracy of automatic evaluation in summarization. In *Proceedings of Workshop on Evaluation Metrics and System Comparison for Automatic Summarization*, pages 1–9. Association for Computational Linguistics.

Kishore Papineni, Salim Roukos, Todd Ward, and Wei-Jing Zhu. 2002. Bleu: a method for automatic evaluation of machine translation. In *Proceedings of the 40th annual meeting on association for computational linguistics*, pages 311–318. Association for Computational Linguistics.

Keith Rayner. 1998. Eye movements in reading and information processing: 20 years of research. *Psychological Bulletin*, 124(3):372–422.

Keith Rayner. 2009. Eye movements in reading: Models and data. *Journal of Eye Movement Research*, 2(5):1–10.

Stephen M. Reder. 1973. On-line monitoring of eye-position signals in contingent and noncontingent paradigms. *Behavior Research Methods & Instrumentation*, 5(2):218–228, March.

Ehud Reiter and Anja Belz. 2009. An investigation into the validity of some metrics for automatically evaluating natural language generation systems. *Computational Linguistics*, 35(4):529–558.

Advaith Siddharthan and Napoleon Katsos. 2012. Offline sentence processing measures for testing readability with users. In *Proceedings of the First Workshop on Predicting and Improving Text Readability for target reader populations*, pages 17–24. Association for Computational Linguistics.

Amanda Stent, Rashmi Prasad, and Marilyn Walker. 2004. Trainable sentence planning for complex information presentation in spoken dialog systems. In *Proceedings of the 42Nd Annual Meeting on Association for Computational Linguistics*, ACL '04, Stroudsburg, PA, USA. Association for Computational Linguistics.

Amanda Stent, Matthew Marge, and Mohit Singhai. 2005. Evaluating evaluation methods for generation in the presence of variation. In *Computational Linguistics and Intelligent Text Processing*, pages 341–351. Springer.

Matthew J Traxler, Robin K Morris, and Rachel E Seely. 2002. Processing Subject and Object Relative Clauses: Evidence from Eye Movements. *Journal of Memory and Language*, 47(1):69–90, July.

Sina Zarrieß and Jonas Kuhn. 2013. Combining referring expression generation and surface realization: A corpus-based investigation of architectures. In *ACL (1)*, pages 1547–1557.

Moving targets: human references to unstable landmarks

Adriana Baltaretu
TiCC
Tilburg Univeristy
a.a.baltaretu@uvt.nl

Emiel Krahmer
TiCC
Tilburg University
e.j.krahmer@uvt.nl

Alfons Maes
TiCC
Tilburg University
maes@uvt.nl

Abstract

In the present study, we investigate if speakers refer to moving entities in route directions (RDs) and how listeners evaluate these references. There is a general agreement that landmarks should be perceptually salient and stable objects. Animated movement attracts visual attention, making entities salient. We ask speakers to watch videos of crossroads and give RDs to listeners, who in turn have to choose a street on which to continue (Experiment 1) or choose the best instruction among three RDs (Experiment 2). Our results show that speakers mention moving entities, especially when their movement is informative for the navigation task (Experiment 1). Listeners understand and use moving landmarks (Experiment 1), yet appreciate stable landmarks more (Experiment 2).

1 Introduction

One of the applications of Natural Language Generation (Reiter et al., 2000) is the automatic generation of route directions, e.g., Roth and Frank (2009); Dale et al., (2005). These instruction typically involve Referring Expressions Generation (REG), (Krahmer and Van Deemter, 2012), for the generation of references to landmarks. Until recently, REG for landmarks and studies on human navigation have focussed exclusively on references to stable entities; in fact, to the best of our knowledge moving targets have never been studied before. Emerging technology (e.g., Google Glass) allows systems to include all relevant visual information in RDs. This raises the question whether references to moving landmarks actually occur.

With support from wearable technology, navigation systems could become spatially aware. For example, navigation systems could produce more human-like instructions by making use of the visual information captured by devices that incorporate video cameras. A navigation system could ground actions in space by referring to both stable ("the tall building") and moving ("the cyclist going left") information. However, we know little about how the dynamic character of the environment influences referential behaviour. We address this issue by analysing if moving entities in the environment affect route direction (RD) production and evaluation.

RDs are instructions guiding a user on how to incrementally go from one location to another (Richter and Klippel, 2005). These instructions contain numerous references to entities in the environment (henceforth landmarks). Traditionally, landmarks have been defined as route-relevant stable entities (such as buildings) that function as points of reference (Allen, 2000). One likely reason for which unstable entities are underrepresented in most standard navigation studies, is that the set-up of these studies often implies some kind of (temporal and / or spatial) asymmetry between the speaker and addressee perspectives, which makes moving entities unreliable reference points. For example, instructions are communicated over distance (e.g., telephone) or asynchronously (e.g., after travelling the route or on the basis of maps). In contrast, in this study we synchronize the two perspectives and focus on in-situ turn-by-turn RDs, where the request for assistance is formulated and followed on the spot. While having access to a shared dynamic environment, speakers can refer to any entity that could improve the instruction. We analyse if speakers refer to moving entities in RDs and asses listeners preference for such references.

Among other aspects, perceptual salience has been theorized to be an important quality of landmarks (Sorrows and Hirtle, 1999) and movement is known to contribute to the perceptual salience

Proceedings of the 15th European Workshop on Natural Language Generation (ENLG), pages 48–51,
Brighton, September 2015. ©2015 Association for Computational Linguistics

of objects. Movement is processed effortlessly by the visual system and attracts attention when informative about the location of a target (Hillstrom and Yantis, 1994). In this study, we focus on animated motion. In general, animate entities influence visual attention and reference production (Downing et al., 2004); (Prat-Sala and Branigan, 2000). Moreover, animated movement in itself (automatically) captures visual attention (Pratt et al., 2010). We hypothesize that if entities grab attention, then speakers would mention them and that listeners would prefer these RDs positively, especially when their motion is task-informative.

2 Experiment 1 - Production

2.1 Methods

2.1.1 Participants

56 dyads of native Dutch-speaking students of Tilburg University (50 women, 21.2 mean age) participated in exchange for partial course credits. Participants were randomly assigned to the speaker role (35 women). All participants gave consent to the use of their data.

2.1.2 Materials

144 street view HD videos were recorded in 72 intersections of Rotterdam. The experimental videos depicted 36 low traffic, +- shaped intersections. Each intersection was recorded three times illustrating a different movement manipulation (see Figure1): (a) no pedestrians / cyclists moving in the intersection (no movement condition (NM), 36 videos); (b) a person walking / cycling towards the intersection (irrelevant movement condition (IM), 36 videos); (c) the same person recorded some seconds later, while taking a turn in the required direction (relevant movement condition (RM), 36 videos). The people recorded were naive pedestrians casually walking / cycling down the street, without paying attention to the camera. In addition, each intersection had other stable object that could be referred to. The filler videos (36 videos) depict a different set of crowded and complex shaped intersections. In addition, two paper booklets with line drawing maps of the intersections were prepared (the speaker booklet included an arrow showing the direction to be taken).

2.1.3 Procedure

The speaker's task was to provide route instructions based on the map and on the video. The

Figure 1: Experimental trials: an intersection with no movement, with a cyclist going towards the intersection, and with a cyclist taking a turn.

listener had to mark in his booklet the indicated street. The listener was allowed to ask questions only if the instructions were unclear. Each video lasted about three seconds and was projected on a white wall (size: 170 x 120 cm). The videos could not be replayed, but the last frame was displayed until the listener announced he is finished. Pointing was discouraged by installing a screen between participants up to shoulder level. Each intersection was shown only once to each dyad. Participants were randomly assigned to one of the three presentation lists. The task started with two warm-up trials followed by 72 video trials (36 experimental trials). There were no time constraints.

2.1.4 Design and statistical analysis

This study had Movement Type (levels: no movement, irrelevant movement, relevant movement) as within participants factor and Presentation List (levels: 1, 2 and 3) as between participants factor. We analysed the type of landmark mentioned by the producer in the first instruction (moving man / stable objects) using logit mixed model analysis with Movement Type and Presentation List as fixed factors; participants and item pictures as ran-

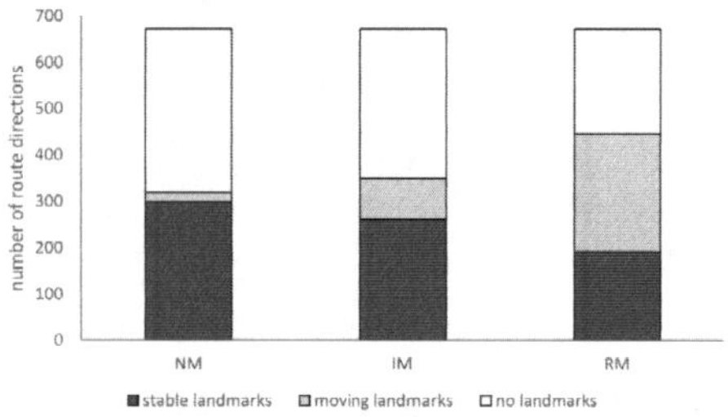

Figure 2: For each condition, number of route directions with different types of landmarks

dom factors; p–values were estimated via parametric bootstrapping. The factors were centred to reduce colinearity. The first converging model is reported. This included random intercepts for participants and videos and random slope for Movement Type in videos. Only significant results are reported. Next we analysed if moving entities are mentioned together with stable ones, clarification questions and listener error rates.

3 Results

2016 RDs (56 speakers * 36 videos) were produced in this experiment. Across the three conditions, participants mentioned both stable (N = 752) and moving entities (N = 361) (see Figure2).

In the NM condition, participants rarely referred to moving people (M = 0.03). Statistical analysis was performed only on the data from the IM and RM conditions. There was no significant effect of Presentation List ($p > .05$). There was a main effect of Movement Type ($\beta = 1.913$; SE = 0.27; $p < .001$). In the RM condition participants referred more often to the moving person taking a turn (M = 0.37), than in the IM condition (M = 0.13).

Few cases (0.02 %) of RDs included both the moving and the stable landmarks (3 cases in NM; 18 cases in IM, and 22 cases in RM).

In general, the task was easy: there were 80 questions asked by listeners and no signals of major communication breakdowns. The questions were asked when the speaker did not refer to landmarks in his initial instruction (55%), when the speaker referred to a stable landmark (31.25%), when the speaker referred to a moving landmark (13.75%). The most frequent type of question was the one in which listeners introduced (new) stable landmarks.

When choosing the street, listeners made few errors (11 cases of incorrectly marked streets and 8 cases in which the first choice was corrected).

4 Experiment 2 - RD evaluation

4.1 Participants

32 native Dutch-speaking students of Tilburg University (12 women, 20.7 mean age) participated in exchange for partial course credits. All participants gave consent to the use of their data.

4.2 Materials

The materials consisted of 72 videos (the experimental trials from the IM and RM condition used in Experiment 1). Overlaid on the videos, a semi-transparent red arrow depicted the route and the direction to be followed.

Based on the production data, for each video a set of three route directions was created as follows: a route direction without landmarks (e.g., turn left); a route direction with a stable landmark (e.g., turn left at Hema); a route direction with a moving landmark (e.g., turn left where that man / woman / cyclist is going). The stable landmarks used in these RDs were the most often mentioned objects in Experiment 1. The moving landmarks were referred to as *the man / woman / cyclist*.

4.3 Procedure

The participants' task was to watch the videos, read the RDs and choose the one that they liked most. Participants saw 36 trials as follows: first a fixation cross was displayed for 500ms, followed by the video and the three instructions placed below the video. The position on screen of the RDs was counterbalanced. Each intersection was shown only once, and participants were randomly assigned to one of the two presentation lists.

4.4 Design and statistical analysis

This study had Movement Type (levels: irrelevant movement, relevant movement) as within participants factor and Presentation List (levels: 1, 2) as between participants factor. The dependent variable was the type of RD chosen. Statistical analysis was performed as in Experiment 1. The model had Movement Type and Presentation List as fixed factors; subjects and videos as random factors.

5 Results

Out of 1152 cases (36 scenes x 32 participants), RDs with landmarks were chosen more often

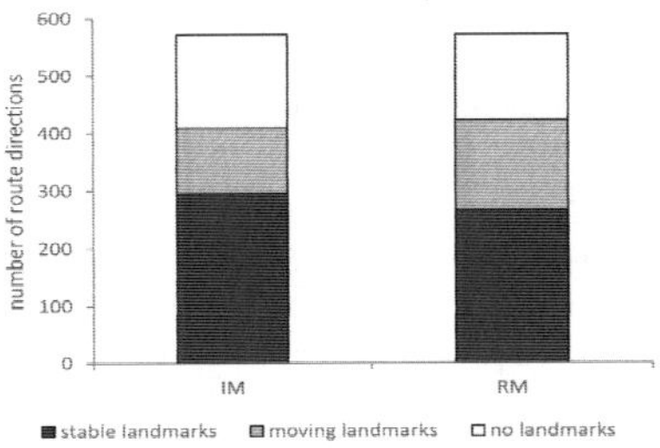

Figure 3: For each condition, types of landmarks chosen

(73% of the cases) than RDs without landmarks (see Figure3). To see if movement influenced the choice for a specific type of landmark, the statistical analysis was done on a data set consisting of the RDs with landmarks.

In general, participants chose more often stable landmarks (77.06% of the cases) than moving landmarks. There was a main effect of Movement Type ($\beta = 1.211$; SE = .265; $p < .001$). This model included random intercepts for subjects and for videos.

For videos depicting irrelevant movement, participants chose more often instructions with stable landmarks (M = 0.85) than with moving landmarks (M = 0.15). For videos depicting relevant movement, the same pattern is observed though there was a slight increase in the preference for moving landmarks (stable landmarks M = 0.75; moving landmarks M = 0.25). There was no significant effect of Presentation List ($p > .05$).

6 Conclusions

In conclusion, human speakers do use references to moving landmarks. Speakers referred to moving objects especially when their movement was informative. Listeners did not encounter difficulties understanding these instructions. Yet, they preferred instructions with stable landmarks. In the light of technological developments our results highlight that navigation systems should not only add landmarks to the instructions, but also adjust the type of landmarks. Speakers naturally refer to items with a relevant movement trajectory. Further work is needed to investigate if moving entities were mentioned because they were more salient than their stable counterparts and second, to validate the efficiency of such RDs for listeners. In future research, we hope to address the question how current REG algorithms can be adapted to generate references to moving targets.

References

Gary L Allen. 2000. Principles and practices for communicating route knowledge. *Applied Cognitive Psychology*, 14(4):333–359.

Robert Dale, Sabine Geldof, and Jean-Philippe Prost. 2005. Using natural language generation in automatic route. *Journal of Research and practice in Information Technology*, 37(1):89.

Paul E Downing, David Bray, Jack Rogers, and Claire Childs. 2004. Bodies capture attention when nothing is expected. *Cognition*, 93(1):27–38.

Anne P Hillstrom and Steven Yantis. 1994. Visual motion and attentional capture. *Perception & Psychophysics*, 55(4):399–411.

Emiel Krahmer and Kees Van Deemter. 2012. Computational generation of referring expressions: A survey. *Computational Linguistics*, 38(1):173–218.

Mercè Prat-Sala and Holly P Branigan. 2000. Discourse constraints on syntactic processing in language production: A cross-linguistic study in english and spanish. *Journal of Memory and Language*, 42(2):168–182.

Jay Pratt, Petre V Radulescu, Ruo Mu Guo, and Richard A Abrams. 2010. Its alive! animate motion captures visual attention. *Psychological Science*, 21(11):1724–1730.

Ehud Reiter, Robert Dale, and Zhiwei Feng. 2000. *Building natural language generation systems*, volume 33. Cambridge University Press, Cambridge.

Kai-Florian Richter and Alexander Klippel. 2005. A model for context-specific route directions. In *Spatial cognition IV. Reasoning, action, interaction*, pages 58–78. Springer, Berlin.

Michael Roth and Anette Frank. 2009. A NLG-based application for walking directions. In *Proceedings of the 47th Annual Meeting of the Association for Computational Linguistics*, pages 37–40, Singapore.

Molly E Sorrows and Stephen C Hirtle. 1999. The nature of landmarks for real and electronic spaces. In *Spatial information theory. Cognitive and computational foundations of geographic information science*, pages 37–50. Springer, Berlin.

Acknowledgements

The first author received financial support from the Netherlands Organization for Scientific Research, via NWO Promoties in de Geesteswetenschappen (322-89-008), which is greatly acknowledged. Partial results of this study have been presented in CogSci 2015.

A Framework for the Generation of Computer System Diagnostics in Natural Language using Finite State Methods

Rachel Farrell
Dept Computer Science
University of Malta
rachelannefarrell@gmail.com

Gordon Pace
Dept Computer Science
University of Malta
gordon.pace@um.edu.mt

Michael Rosner
Dept Intelligent Computer Systems
University of Malta
mike.rosner@um.edu.mt

Abstract

Understanding what has led to a failure is crucial for addressing problems with computer systems. We present a meta-NLG system that can be configured to generate natural explanations from error trace data originating in an external computational system. Distinguishing features are the generic nature of the system, and the underlying finite-state technology. Results of a two-pronged evaluation dealing with naturalness and ease of use are described.

1 Introduction

As computer systems grow in size and complexity, so does the need for their verification. Whilst system diagnostics produced by automated program analysis techniques are understandable to developers, they may be largely opaque to less technical domain experts typically involved in scripting parts of the system, using domain-specific languages (Hudak, 1996) or controlled natural languages (CNLs) (Kuhn, 2014). Such individuals require higher level, less technical explanations of certain classes of program misbehaviour.

The problem boils down to an NLG challenge, starting from the trace (representing a history of the system) and yielding a narrative of the behaviour at an effective level of abstraction. The choice of an appropriate level of abstraction is particularly challenging since it is very dependent on the specification being matched or verified.

Pace and Rosner (Pace and Rosner, 2014), showed how a finite-state (FS) system can be used to generate effective natural language descriptions of behavioural traces. Starting from a particular property, they show how more natural and abstract explanations can be extracted from a system trace violating that property. However, the approach is manual and thus not very feasible for a quality assurance engineer. We show how their approach can be generalised to explain violations of general specifications. Since the explanation needs to be tailored for each particular property, we develop a general system, fitting as part of a verification flow as shown in Fig. 1. Typically, a quality assurance engineer is responsible for the top part of the diagram — giving a property specification which will be used by an analysis tool (testing, runtime verification, static analysis, etc) to try to identify violation traces. With our approach, another artefact is required, the *explanation specification*, which embodies the domain-specific natural language information for the property in question. From this, a generic NLG tool produces a specialised generation tool (embodying the domain-specific information and general information implicit in the traces) which can produce explanations for violations of that property. Our techniques have been implemented in a generic NLG tool, for which we show that the cost of adding user explanations for a property at an appropriate level of abstraction and naturalness is very low especially when compared to the cost of extending the system to identify such behaviours (e.g. developing test oracles or expressing a property using a formal language). The main novelty has been to develop a framework for generalising the approach developed earlier. We also further substantiate the claim that there is a place for FS methods in NLG.

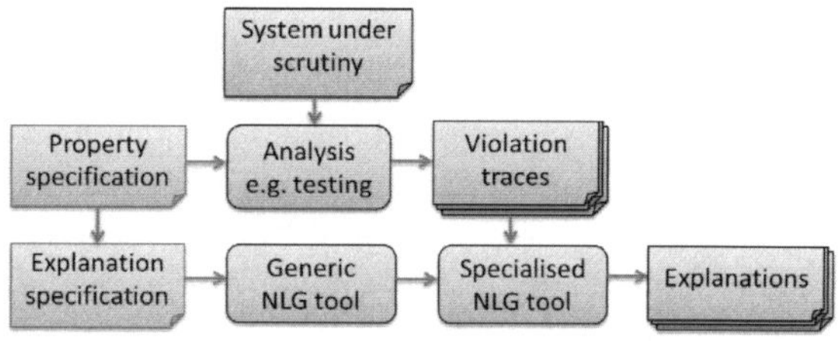

Figure 1: The architecture for general system diagnostics

2 Trace Explanation Styles

For explanations we adopted a CNL approach. The target language comprises (i) domain-specific terms and notions particular to the property being violated by the traces; and (ii) terms specific to the notions inherent to traces — such as the notions of events (as occurrences at points in time) and temporal sequentiality (the trace contains events ordered as they occurred over time). Following Pace and Rosner, we identify a sequence of progressively more sophisticated explanations of a particular violation trace. To illustrate this, consider an elevator system which upon receiving a request for the lift from a particular floor (`<r1>`–`<r4>`), services that floor by moving up or down (`<u>`, `<d>`). Once the lift arrives at a particular floor (`<a1>`–`<a4>`), the doors open (`<o>`). The

Proceedings of the 15th European Workshop on Natural Language Generation (ENLG), pages 52–56,
Brighton, September 2015. ©2015 Association for Computational Linguistics

doors can then either close (<c>) automatically, or after a floor request. Monitoring the property that the lift should not move with an open door, we will illustrate explanations with different degrees of sophistication of the violation trace: `<a4,o,r4,a4,r2,c,d,a3,d,a2,o,r3,u>`.

The simplest explanation is achieved in CNL0, where every symbol is transformed into a separate sentence, with an additional sentence at the end giving the reason why a violation occurred.

CNL0
The lift arrived at floor 4. The doors opened. A user requested to go to floor 4. The lift arrived at floor 4. A user requested to go to floor 2. The doors closed. The lift moved down. The lift arrived at floor 3. The lift moved down. The lift arrived at floor 2. The doors opened. A user requested to go to floor 3. The lift moved up. However this last action should not have been allowed because the lift cannot move with open doors.

In CNL1, the text is split into paragraphs consisting of sequences of sentence:

CNL1

1. The lift arrived at floor 4.
2. The doors opened. A user requested to go to floor 4. The lift arrived at floor 4.
3. A user requested to go to floor 2. The doors closed. The lift moved down. The lift arrived at floor 3. The lift moved down. The lift arrived at floor 2.
4. The doors opened. A user requested to go to floor 3. The lift moved up. However this last action should not have been allowed because the lift cannot move with open doors.

In CNL2, aggregation (Dalianis, 1999) techniques combine the single clause sentences from the previous two realisations to build multi-clause sentences, thus eliminating redundancy achieved through (i) the use of commas and words such as 'and', 'then', 'but' or 'yet', and (ii) the grouping of similar events, for example by stating the number of occurrences (e.g. 'moved down two floors').

CNL2

1. The lift arrived at floor 4.
2. The doors opened and a user requested to go to floor 4, yet the lift was already at floor 4.
3. A user requested to go to floor 2, then the doors closed. The lift moved down two floors and arrived at floor 2.
4. The doors opened, a user requested to go to floor 3, and the lift moved up. However this last action should not have been allowed because the lift cannot move with open doors.

Since the explanation contains detail which may be unnecessary or can be expressed more concisely, CNL3 uses summarisation — for instance, the first sentence in the explanation below summarises the contents of what were previously paragraphs 1–3. The last paragraph is left unchanged, since every sentence included there is required to properly understand the cause of the error.

CNL3

1. The lift arrived at floor 4, serviced floor 4, then serviced floor 2.
2. The doors opened, a user requested to go to floor 3, and the lift moved up. However this last action should not have been allowed because the lift cannot move with open doors.

For Pace and Rosner the explanation language is a CNL, whose basis, described in the Xerox Finite State Toolkit (XFST) (Beesley and Karttunen, 2003) by a human author, states how system trace actions should be expressed. The natural language explanation is obtained by composing FS transducers in a pipeline. FS technologies are best-known for the representation of certain kinds of linguistic knowledge, most notably morphology (Wintner, 2008). In contrast, we used XFST to implement linguistic techniques such as structuring the text into paragraphs, aggregation, contextuality — as previously illustrated.

3 Generalised Explanations

Given a particular property, one can design a NLG tool capable of explaining its violation traces. Some of the explanation improvements presented in the previous section are common to most properties. We thus chose to address the more general problem of trace violation explanations, such that, although domain-specific concepts (e.g. the meaning of individual events and ways of summarising them) need to be specified, much of the underlying machinery pertaining to the implied semantics of the event traces (e.g. the fact that a trace is a temporally ordered sequence of events, and that the events are independent of each other) will be derived automatically. The resulting approach, as shown in Fig. 1, in which we focus on the *Generic NLG* component uses the domain-specific information about a particular property (the *Explanation Specification* script provided by a QA engineer) to produce an explanation generator for a whole class of traces (all those violating that property). A specification language was created to facilitate the creation of a specification by non-specialist users. A script in the general trace-explanation language is used to automatically construct a specific explanation generator in XFST, going beyond a NLG system by developing a generator of trace explanation generators.

4 Specifying Trace Explanations

Scripts for our framework allow the user to specify the domain-specific parts of the explanations for a particular property, leaving other generic language features to be deduced automatically. The core features of the scripting language are:

Explaining events: Rather than give a complete sentence for each event represented by a symbol, we split the information into the *subject* and *predicate*, enabling us to derive automatically when sequential actions share a subject (thus allowing their combination in a more readable form). For example, the `EXPLAIN` section of the script is used to supply such event definitions:

```
EXPLAIN {
 <a4>: {
    subject:   "the lift";
    predicate: "arrived at level four";
 }
 ...
}
```

Events in context: Certain events may be better explained in a different way in a different context. For instance, the event `a4` would typically be described as 'The lift arrived at floor four', except for when the lift is already on the fourth floor, when one may say that 'The lift remained at floor four'. Regular expressions can be used to check the part of the trace that precedes or follows a particular event to check for context:

```
<a4>: {
   subject:    "the lift";
   predicate {
     context: {
       default: "arrived at level four";
       <r4>_ :  "remained at floor four";
     }
   }
}
```

Compound explanations: Sometimes, groups of symbols would be better explained together rather than separately. Using regular expressions, the `EXPLAIN` section of the script allows for such terms to be explained more succinctly:

```
<r2><c><d><a3><d><a2>: {
  subject:    "the lift";
  predicate: "serviced floor 2";
}
```

Errors and blame: Errors in a violation trace typically are the final event in the trace. We allow not only for the description of the symbol in this context, but also an explanation of what went wrong and, if relevant, where the responsibility lies:

```
ERROR_EXPLAIN {
  [<u>|<d>]: {
    blame: "due to a lift controller malfunction";
    error_reason:
      context: {
        default: "";
        [<o>[<r1>|<r2>|<r3>|<r4>]]_:
           "the lift cannot move with open doors";
      }
  }
}
```

Document structure: A way is needed to know how to structure the document by stating how sentences should be formed and structured into paragraphs. Using CNL1 as an example, we can add a newline after the lift arrives at a floor. Similarly, based on the example for CNL2, we specify that the event sequence `<o><r4><4>` should be aggregated into a (enumerated) paragraph:

```
SENTENCE_AGGREGATION{
  [<1>|<2>|<3>|<4>]: { newline: after; }
  <o><r4><4>;
}
```

5 Evaluation

Two aspects of our approach were evaluated: (i) How much effort is required to achieve an acceptable degree of naturalness, and (ii) How difficult it is for first time users to write specifications.

5.1 Effort In-Naturalness Out

Since, using our framework a degree of naturalness can be achieved depending on the complexity of the logic encoded in our script, unsatisfactory explanations may be caused by limitations of our approach or just a badly written script. The framework was first evaluated to assess how effort put into writing the script for a particular property correlates with naturalness of the explanations.

To measure this, we considered properties for an elevator controller, a file system and a coffee vending machine. We then built a series of scripts, starting with a basic one and progressively adding more complex features. For each property, we thus had a sequence of scripts of increasing complexity, where the time taken to develop each was known. These scripts were then executed in our framework on a number of traces, producing a corpus of natural language explanations each with the corresponding trace and associated script development time. The sentences together with the corresponding trace (but not the script or time taken to develop it) were then presented using an online questionnaire to human judges who were asked to assess the naturalness, readability and understandability of the generated explanations.

Explanations were rated on a scale from 1–6[1]. Evaluators were presented with a fraction of the generated explanations, shown in a random order, to prevent them from making note of certain patterns, which might have incurred a bias. Over 477 responses from around 64 different people.

The results of this analysis can be found in Table 1, which shows the scores given to explanations for the different systems and for traces produced by the scripts with different complexity. The results show that the naturalness of the generated explanations was proportional to the time taken to write the scripts — the best-faring explanations having a high rate of aggregation and summarisation. Interestingly, even with scripts written quickly e.g. 15–20 minutes[2] many evaluators still found the explanations satisfactory.

Figure 2 shows the results of plotting time taken to write the script (x-axis) against naturalness of the explanation (y-axis). For the coffee machine and elevator controller traces, the graphs begin to stabilise after a relatively short time, converging to a limit 80% of which is roughly achieved during the first 20–30% of the total time taken to create the most comprehensive script we wrote. The graph for the file system traces gives a somewhat different view; a higher overall score is obtained, yet we do not get the same initial gradient steepness[3]. A reason for the discrepancy in the graph shape could be that traces obtained for this system contained many repeated symbols in succession, hence until a script handled this repetition, the explanations received low scores. This shows that there may exist a relation between the kind of system being considered and the effort and linguistic techniques required to generate natural sounding explanations for its traces.

[1]From 1–6: unnatural and difficult to follow, unnatural but somewhat easy to follow, unnatural but very easy to follow, contains some natural elements, fairly natural, very natural and easy to follow.

[2]Recall that one script can be used to explain any counterexample trace for that property, and would thus be repeatedly and extensively used during system verification or analysis.

[3]It is worth noting that, for example, the first data point in all graphs occurs at the time after which similar linguistic techniques were included in the script.

Table 1: Overall scores given to generated explanations

System	Time /mins	Score 1	2	3	4	5	6	Mean	Mode	Median
Elevator system	10	1	8	10	9	2	10	3.83	3,6	4
	16	2	4	4	9	15	9	4.35	5	5
	24	1	2	2	4	15	6	4.6	5	5
	39	1	0	3	8	8	11	4.77	6	5
File system	12	5	7	11	3	3	1	2.83	3	3
	19	5	8	7	7	8	7	3.62	2,5	4
	22	2	5	13	5	6	3	3.5	3	3
	32	0	2	4	5	14	18	4.98	6	5
Coffee machine	10	3	4	4	12	5	8	4	4	4
	15	3	6	4	8	14	4	3.92	5	4
	25	1	3	5	3	9	8	4.38	5	5
	28	1	1	3	10	10	11	4.67	6	5
	38	2	1	2	4	18	17	4.95	5	5

We can thus conclude that whilst a certain inherent limit exists, natural-sounding explanations can be well achieved using this system. Effort however is rather important, and usually, the more time invested in building a script, the better the quality of the output. Nevertheless, even with minimal effort, a script author highly familiar with the input language can obtain a rather satisfactory output.

5.2 User Acceptance Test

To assess the framework's accessibility, we ran a four-hour experiment with four new users familiar with concepts such as regular expressions. They were requested to produce scripts to explain different properties unaided and were then asked to rate the ease of use and expressivity of the input language, their satisfaction with the output generated, and whether it matched their expectations. Given the low number of participants, the results are only indicative, and assessing the quality of the scripts they produced would not have given statistically meaningful results.

Overall, these users characterised the scripting language between *somewhat difficult* to *easy to use*. Dealing with contextual explanation of events presented the greatest challenges, although all managed to produce an error explanation which required using this concept. Apart from simply explaining every symbol as a complete sentence, the users also managed to create scripts involving aggregation and summarisation. The users expressed satisfaction with the explanations produced, although one of the subjects commented that scripts sometimes had to be executed to understand exactly the effect of a particular line of code.

The fact that all users managed to produce successful scripts within four hours indicates that it is not excessively difficult to use. That the overall idea was easily understood and the input language quickly learnt suggests that this kind of system could minimise the overheads associated with the task of automated explanation generation for systems more complex than those illustrated here.

6 Related Work

BabyTalk BT-45 (Reiter et al., 2008) generates textual summaries of low-level clinical data from a Neonatal Intensive Care Unit. Summaries are created for different audiences, such as doctors and nurses, to help them in making treatment decisions. Generated summaries were found to be useful, but lacking in narrative structure compared to those created by humans. Further investigation is needed to determine where the trade-offs lie between acceptable explanations, underlying data complexity, and computational efficiency. Power (Power, 2012) describes OWL-Simplified English, a CNL for non-specialists used to edit semantic web ontologies in OWL, notably employing FS techniques for the definition of a user-oriented communication language. See also (Galley et al., 2001) whose NLG system combines FS) grammars with corpus-based language models. These works are limited to producing generators for any trace, rather than creating a higher-order framework which is used to write scripts which produce the generators.

7 Conclusions

Understanding why a violation occurred has many benefits for end-users of verification techniques and can save time when designing complex systems. The solution presented has the advantage of not being difficult to use by people with a computer science background, and can generate natural, easily understandable explanations despite inherent limitations of FS technologies. Should the constraints of regular languages prove to be such that this system would not be applicable in many areas, there is the possibility of *not* using FS techniques without any major changes in the framework's general architecture. Another possibility would be examining how the techniques discussed could be applied to provide dynamic explanations of online systems.

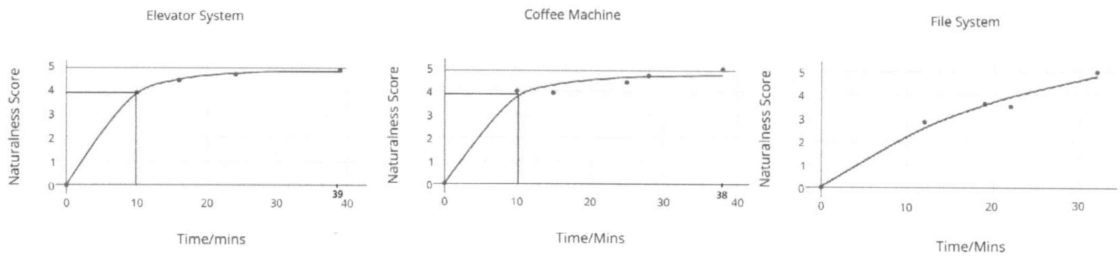

Figure 2: Graphs of the naturalness score given against the time after which the corresponding input script was created

References

Kenneth R Beesley and Lauri Karttunen. 2003. *Finite-state morphology*, volume 3 of *Studies in computational linguistics*. CSLI Publications.

Hercules Dalianis. 1999. Aggregation in naltural language generation. *Computational Intelligence*, 15(04).

Michel Galley, Eric Fosler-lussier, and Ros Potamianos. 2001. Hybrid natural language generation for spoken dialogue systems. In *In Proceedings of the 7th European Conference on Speech Communication and Technology*, pages 1735–1738.

Paul Hudak. 1996. Building domain-specific embedded languages. *ACM Computing Surveys*, 28:196.

Tobias Kuhn. 2014. A survey and classification of controlled natural languages. *Computational Linguistics*, 40(1):121–170, March.

Gordon J. Pace and Michael Rosner. 2014. Explaining violation traces with finite state natural language generation models. In Brian Davis, Kaarel Kaljurand, and Tobias Kuhn, editors, *Controlled Natural Language*, volume 8625 of *Lecture Notes in Computer Science*, pages 179–189. Springer International Publishing.

Richard Power. 2012. Owl simplified english: A finite-state language for ontology editing. In Tobias Kuhn and Norbert E. Fuchs, editors, *Controlled Natural Language*, volume 7427 of *Lecture Notes in Computer Science*, pages 44–60. Springer Berlin Heidelberg.

Ehud Reiter, Albert Gatt, François Portet, and Marian van der Meulen. 2008. The importance of narrative and other lessons from an evaluation of an nlg system that summarises clinical data. In *Proceedings of the Fifth International Natural Language Generation Conference*, INLG '08, pages 147–156, Stroudsburg, PA, USA. Association for Computational Linguistics.

Shuly Wintner. 2008. Strengths and weaknesses of finite-state technology: a case study in morphological grammar development. *Natural Language Engineering*, 14(04):457–469.

A Snapshot of NLG Evaluation Practices 2005 - 2014

Dimitra Gkatzia
Department of Computer Science
Heriot-Watt University
EH14 4AS Edinburgh, UK
d.gkatzia@hw.ac.uk

Saad Mahamood
Department of Computing Science
University of Aberdeen
Scotland, United Kingdom
s.mahamood@abdn.ac.uk

Abstract

In this paper we present a snapshot of end-to-end NLG system evaluations as presented in conference and journal papers[1] over the last ten years in order to better understand the nature and type of evaluations that have been undertaken. We find that researchers tend to favour specific evaluation methods, and that their evaluation approaches are also correlated with the publication venue. We further discuss what factors may influence the types of evaluation used for a given NLG system.

1 Introduction

Evaluation plays a crucial role in helping to understand whether a given approach for a text generating Natural Language Generation (NLG) system has expressed particular properties (such as quality, speed, etc.) or whether it has met a particular potential (domain utility). Past work within the NLG community has looked at the issues of evaluating NLG techniques and systems, the challenges unique to the NLG context in comparison to Natural Language Analysis (Dale and Mellish, 1998), and the comparisons between evaluation approaches (Belz and Reiter, 2006). Whilst there has been a better understanding of the types of evaluations that can be conducted for a given NLG technique or system (Hastie and Belz, 2014) there is little understanding on the frequency or types of evaluation that is typically conducted for a given system within the NLG community.

In this paper, we shed some light on the frequency of the types of evaluations conducted for NLG systems. In particular, we have focused only on end-to-end complete NLG system as opposed to NLG components (referring expression generation, surface realisers, etc.) in our meta-analysis of published NLG systems from a variety of conferences, workshops, and journals for the last ten years since 2005. For the purpose of this research, we created a corpus consisting of these papers (Section 3). We then investigated three questions 4: (1) which is the most preferred evaluation method; (2) how does the method use change over time; and (3) whether the publication venue influences the evaluation type. In Section 5, we discuss the results of the meta analysis and finally in Section 6 we conclude the paper and we discuss directions for future work.

[1] Dataset available from here: https://github.com/Saad-Mahamood/ENLG2015

2 Background

NLG evaluation methodology has developed considerably over the last several years. Work by Dale and Mellish (1998) initially focused on the role that evaluation methods should play for a given NLG system and how they are different from the kind of evaluations undertaken by the natural language understanding community.

Traditional NLG evaluations have typically fell into one of two types: *intrinsic* or *extrinsic* (Belz and Reiter, 2006). Intrinsic evaluations of NLG systems seek to evaluate properties of the system. Past NLG systems have typically been evaluated using human subjects (Dale and Mellish, 1998). Humans have been involved in either reading and rating texts and comparing the ratings for NLG generated texts against human written texts for metrics such as quality, correctness, naturalness, understandability, etc. Extrinsic evaluations, on the other hand, have typically consisted of evaluating the impact of a given system such as its effectiveness for a given application (Belz and Reiter, 2006). These can include measuring correctness of decisions made in a task based evaluation, measuring the number of post-edits by experts, or measuring usage/utility of a given system.

The intrinsic evaluation of text output quality for NLG systems has seen different evaluation approaches. Recently, NLG systems have evaluated

Proceedings of the 15th European Workshop on Natural Language Generation (ENLG), pages 57–60,
Brighton, September 2015.

this particular property using comparisons to corpus text through the use of automatic metrics (Reiter and Belz, 2009). The use of automatic metrics, such as BLEU and ROUGE, have been shown to correlate with human judgements for text quality and are an attractive way of performing evaluations for NLG applications due to being fast, cheap, and repeatable (Reiter and Belz, 2009). Nevertheless, questions remain with regards to the quality and representativeness of corpora (Reiter and Sripada, 2002) used for these metrics and whether these metrics are appropriate for measuring other factors such as content selection, information structure, appropriateness, etc. (Scott and Moore, 2007).

Whilst there is an understanding of the types of evaluations that can be conducted, other unresolved issues remain. Issues such as having realistic input, having an objective criterion for assessing the quality of the NLG output, deciding on what aspects to measure for a given NLG system, what controls to use, acquiring adequate training and test data, and finally, handling disagreements between human judges (Dale and Mellish, 1998). These unresolved issues of evaluating NLG systems could be related to the fact that language is inherently context dependant. What is relevant for on NLG application task in a given domain may not be relevant to another system in a different domain (Paris et al., 2007). Thus, making direct quantitative NLG system or component evaluation comparisons is difficult outside of shared task evaluations. Additionally, whilst there has been speculation that evaluations based on human ratings and judgements are the most popular way of evaluating NLG systems (Reiter and Belz, 2009) we are not aware of any quantitative measures that supports this supposition.

3 Corpus Creation

To better understand the current nature of NLG system evaluations we performed a meta-analysis. We started by assembling a corpus consisting of as many peer reviewed papers as they could be retrieved which described end-to-end systems published at a variety of NLG conferences and workshops (ENLG, INLG, ACL, NAACL, EACL, EMNLP and COLING) and some journals (e.g. JAIR). We specifically chose a period of the last 10 years of publications to limit the scope of the corpus collection. In total, a corpus of 79 papers was assembled (consisting of: ENLG - 17, INLG - 12, ACL - 20, NAACL - 5, EACL - 7, EMNLP - 10, COLING - 3, Journals - 5). Each paper within the collected corpus was annotated using the intrinsic and extrinsic evaluation classification categories of Hastie and Belz (2014). Hastie and Belz broke down intrinsic and extrinsic evaluation methods into the following types:

Intrinsic Methods

1. *Output Quality Measures*: These assess the similarity of the systems' output to a reference model or assess quality criteria using BLUE, NIST, ROUGE, etc.
2. *User Like Measures*: For this type of evaluation, users/participants are asked questions such as "How useful did you find the generated text?" and they usually use Likert or rating scales.

Extrinsic Methods

1. *User Task Success Metrics*: A form of evaluation that measures anything that has to do with what the user gains from the systems' output, such as decision making, comprehension accuracy etc.
2. *System Purpose Success Metrics*: An evaluation type where a given system is evaluated by measuring whether it can fulfil its initial purpose.

The collected 79 papers were annotated by two annotators. To agree on the annotation procedure a set of 5 papers was annotated by both annotators. Thereafter, each annotated 33 and 49 papers including an overlapping set of 22 papers. From this overlapping set the Cohen's kappa agreement score of $\kappa = .824$ ($p < .001$) was computed.

4 Meta-analysis

Using the collected corpus of papers we investigated whether there were significant differences between the evaluation methods used. In particular we focused on the following three qualitative aspects: (1) proportionally of evaluation methods, (2) method use over time, and (3) with regard to the publication venue.

4.1 Proportions of Evaluation Methods

It was found that the majority of papers report an intrinsic evaluation method (74.7%), whereas a very small proportion of the papers report an extrinsic (15.1%) or both types of evaluation (10.1%), see also Table 1.

Regarding intrinsic evaluation, we further observed that papers report *User like measures* significantly more often than *Output Quality measures* (see also Table 2). With regard to extrinsic

Intrinsic	Extrinsic	Both
59	12	8
74.7*%	15.2*%	10.1*%

Table 1: High level descriptive statistics. * denotes significance at $p < .016$, using Z-test (after Bonferroni correction).

evaluation, most papers report a *User Task Success* evaluation setup as opposed to *System Purpose Success* methods (Table 2).

Intrinsic		Extrinsic	
Output Quality	User Like	User Task Success	System purpose success
42 38.2*%	50 **45.4*%**	13 11.8*%	5 4.6*%

Table 2: Detailed descriptive statistics. * denotes significance at $p < .008$, using Z-test (after Bonferroni correction).

We speculate that intrinsic methods are inherently easier, cheaper and quicker to be performed than extrinsic evaluations (Belz and Reiter, 2006), and therefore researchers opt for these significantly more often than extrinsic methods. In addition, intrinsic methods can be domain-independent which allows comparisons between methods. Finally, not all systems can be assessed for user task or system purpose success, e.g. commercial weather forecast systems.

4.2 Evaluation Trends over Time

Next, we investigated whether there was a change in the selection of evaluation metrics between the present and the past. For this analysis, the data was separated into three groups. The first group consisted of papers published between 2005 - 2008 (25 papers), the second group consists of publications between 2009 - 2011 (24 papers) and the last one contains papers published from 2012 to 2015 (30 papers). We used only the first and the last group in order to identify whether there are differences in the application of evaluation methods.

We observed that papers published after 2012 are significantly ($p < 0.04$) more likely to include *System Purpose* evaluations. We can also observe a trend towards intrinsic evaluations, as well as a reduction in using *User Task Success* evaluations, however the differences are not statistically significant (see also Table 3).

	2005-2008	2012-2015
Output Quality	44%	60%
User Like	56%	70%
User Task Success	24%	6.6%
System Purpose	0%	**13.4*%**

Table 3: Proportions of evaluation metrics in papers. Note that some papers contain more than one type of evaluation. * denotes significance at $p < .05$, using T-test in pair-wise comparisons.

We assume that this shift in evaluation metrics is correlated with the system design - more specific systems with well defined end users. In addition, more general purpose systems such as adult humour generation systems (Valitutti et al., 2013) have been recently developed which can be evaluated with a *System Purpose* metric in a straightforward way.

4.3 Correlations between Evaluation Methods and Publication Venue

Finally, we looked into whether papers published in specific venues "prefer" specific types of evaluation. We used Pearson's χ^2 to identify relations between the publication venues and the evaluation methods. Table 4 presents for each conference the percentages of papers that use specific evaluation metrics.

	Output Quality	User Like	User Task Success	System Purpose
ACL	70*%	65%	15%	5%
COLING	66*%	33%	33%	0%
EACL	43*%	71%	14%	0%
EMNLP	80*%	40%	20%	0%
NAACL	80*%	60%	0%	0%
ENLG	35*%	64%	12%	12%
INLG	25*%	75%	17%	17%

Table 4: Proportions of papers that report specific evaluation metrics. Note that some papers contain more than one type of evaluation. * denotes significance at $p < .05$, using Pearson's χ^2 test.

We found that more than half of the papers published at ACL, COLING, EMNLP and NAACL contain an *Output Quality* study, whereas for EACL, ENLG and INLG these percentages are below 50%. Most papers published at ACL, EACL, NAACL, ENLG and INLG also contain a "User Like" study. Extrinsic evaluation seems not to be popular across all venues (see also Table 4).

We further investigated whether there was a difference between ACL (including EACL, COLING, NAACL and EMNLP) publications and NLG publications (including ENLG and INLG). Table 5 shows the results obtained. From this analysis, journal papers have been omitted due to their low frequency.

Possible speculation for this significant difference in the use of the *Output Quality* evaluation type between the two sets of conference venues could be related to the fact that the ACL venues are patronised by a majority NLU audience. Therefore, NLG papers submitted to these conferences would be more likely to use automatic metrics

	Output Quality	User Like	User Task Success	System Purpose
ACL	68*%	57%	15%	2%
NLG	31*%	68%	13%	13%

Table 5: Proportions of ACL vs NLG papers that report specific evaluation metrics. Note that some papers contain more than one type of evaluation. * denotes significance at $p < .05$, using Pearson's χ^2 test.

(such as BLEU or ROUGE) as these measures are widely used by the NLU community as well.

5 Discussion

Output quality evaluations using automatic metrics can be repeatable (Belz and Reiter, 2006). However, automatic evaluations require large aligned corpora (input and output data), which are not always available for NLG. In such cases, other types of evaluations are preferred. In addition, Reiter and Sripada (2002) argue that the information presented in aligned corpora might not be always true, due to the fact that text from experts can be erroneous. *Output quality* metrics are sensitive to this, therefore, the research community often uses automatic metrics paired with other types of evaluations (55%) in order to overcome this barrier.

User like metrics are straightforward and easily applicable, therefore it is not surprising that these are the most popular measures among researchers. These metrics can evaluate an NLG system quickly and thus can be incorporated in any stage of a system's design. User likeness is one indication of whether a system is going to be used, as users will not use a system that they do not like. However, success on user like metrics does not equate with *system purpose success* and *user task success*. Although there are studies discussing the relation between *output quality metrics* and *user like metrics* e.g. (Foster, 2008; Belz and Reiter, 2006), to our knowledge there are not any studies discussing the relation between *user like metrics* and extrinsic metrics.

Finally, extrinsic metrics have been the least popular among researchers, due to their time-consuming nature and their complication to be organised. In addition, extrinsic metrics can be also expensive. For instance, the STOP evaluation cost £75,000 over 20 months; the SKILLSUM and BT45 evaluations cost about £20,000 over six months (Reiter and Belz, 2009).

6 Conclusion

At present NLG evaluation does not include a standardised approach for evaluating systems. Although papers tend to use automatic methods to overcome this limitation (especially papers at ACL conferences), extrinsic methods are more thorough than intrinsic and they can provide useful insights of the domains' needs, and thus they provide better indications of the systems' usefulness and utility. However, quicker and less resource intensive means are needed to allow for more systems to be evaluated with extrinsic methods.

In future, we will expand the scope of the survey by adding a greater number of journal papers for analysis and secondly and by looking at the quantitative evaluation differences between NLG systems and components. In addition, we will look into whether specific organisation and/or groups of researchers have influenced the evaluation approaches. Finally, it would be interesting to investigate whether the influential papers (for instance papers with high number of citations) have played a role in the selection of the evaluation methods.

References

Anja Belz and Ehud Reiter. 2006. Comparing automatic and human evaluation of nlg systems. In *EACL*.

Robert Dale and Chris Mellish. 1998. Towards the Evaluation of Natural Language Generation. In *Proceedings of the First International Conference on Language Resources and Evaluation*, volume 562.

Mary Ellen Foster. 2008. Automated Metrics That Agree With Human Judgements On Generated Output for an Embodied Conversational Agent. In *Proceedings of the Fifth International Natural Language Generation Conference*, pages 95–103.

Helen Hastie and Anja Belz. 2014. A Comparative Evaluation Methodology for NLG in Interactive Systems. In *Proceedings of the Language Resources and Evaluation Conference*.

Cécile Paris, Donia Scott, Nancy Green, Kathy McCoy, and David McDonald. 2007. Desiderata for Evaluation of Natural Language Generation. In *Shared Tasks and Comparative Evaluation on Natural Language Generation - Workshop Report*, pages 9–15.

Ehud Reiter and Anja Belz. 2009. An Investigation into the Validity of Some Metrics for Automatically Evaluating Natural Language Generation Systems. *Computational Linguistics*, 35(4):529–558.

Ehud Reiter and Somayajulu Sripada. 2002. Should corpora texts be gold standards for NLG? In *INLG*, pages 97–104, Harriman, NY.

Donia Scott and Johanna Moore. 2007. An NLG evaluation competition? Eight reasons to be cautious. In *Workshop on Shared Tasks and Comparative Evaluation in Natural Language Generation*, pages 22–23, Arlington, VA.

Alessandro Valitutti, Hannu Toivonen, Antoine Doucet, and Jukka M. Toivanen. 2013. "Let Everything Turn Well in Your Wife": Generation of Adult Humor Using Lexical Constraints. In *ACL*.

Japanese Word Reordering Executed Concurrently with Dependency Parsing and Its Evaluation

Tomohiro Ohno[1,a) **Kazushi Yoshida**[2)] **Yoshihide Kato**[3,b)] **Shigeki Matsubara**[2,c)]
[1]Information Technology Center, Nagoya University, Japan
[2]Graduate School of Information Science, Nagoya University, Japan
[3]Information & Communications, Nagoya University, Japan
[a)]ohno@nagoya-u.jp [b)]yoshihide@icts.nagoya-u.ac.jp
[c)]matubara@nagoya-u.jp

Abstract

This paper proposes a method for reordering words in a Japanese sentence based on concurrent execution with dependency parsing so that the sentence becomes more readable. Our contributions are summarized as follows: (1) we extend a probablistic model used in the previous work which concurrently performs word reordering and dependency parsing; (2) we conducted an evaluation experiment using our semi-automatically constructed evaluation data so that sentences in the data are more likely to be spontaneously written by natives than the automatically constructed evaluation data in the previous work.

1 Introduction

Although Japanese has relatively free word order, Japanese word order is not completely arbitrary and has some sort of preference. Since such preference is incompletely understood, even Japanese natives often write Japanese sentences which are grammatically well-formed but not easy to read. For example, in Figure 1, the word order of S1 is less readable than that of S2 because the distance between the bunsetsu "*Suzuki-san-ga* (Mr. Suzuki)" and its modified bunsetsu "*toi-te-shimat-ta* (solved)" is large and thus the loads on working memory become large (Nihongo Kijutsu Bunpo Kenkyukai, 2009; Uchimoto et al., 2000)

There have been some conventional researches for reordering words in a sentence so that the sentence becomes easier to read (Belz et al., 2011; Filippova and Strube, 2007; Harbusch et al., 2006; Kruijff et al., 2001; Ringger et al., 2004; Shaw and Hatzivassiloglou, 1999; Uchimoto et al., 2000; Yokobayashi et al., 2004). Most of the conventional researches used syntactic information by assuming that an input sentence for word reordering

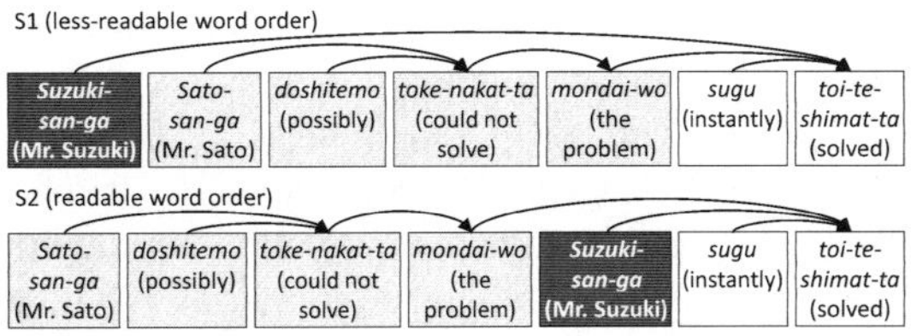

Note: A box and an arrow express a *bunsetsu*[1] and a dependency relation, respectively. Both the sentences S1 and S2 have the same meaning which is translated as "Mr. Suzuki instantly solved the problem that Mr. Sato could not possibly solve." in English. The difference between S1 and S2 is just in their word orders in Japanese.

Figure 1: Example of less-readable/readable word order

has been already parsed. There is a problem that the errors of dependency parsing increase when an input sentence is less-readable, and the parsing errors cause negative effects on word reordering. To solve the problem, we previously proposed a method for concurrently performing word reordering and dependency parsing and confirmed the effectiveness of their proposed method using evaluation data created by randomly changing the word order in newspaper article sentences (Yoshida et al., 2014). However, since some of the just automatically created sentences are unlikely to be spontaneously written by a native, the evaluation is thought to be not enough. In addition, the probablistic model has room for improvement in targeting at sentences which a native is likely to spontaneously write.

This paper proposes a new method on Japanese word reordering based on concurrent execution with dependency parsing by extending the probablistic model proposed by Yoshida et al. (2014), and describes an evaluation experiment using our

[1]*Bunsetsu* is a linguistic unit in Japanese that roughly corresponds to a basic phrase in English. A bunsetsu consists of one independent word and zero or more ancillary words. A dependency relation in Japanese is a modification relation in which a modifier bunsetsu depends on a modified bunsetsu. That is, the modifier bunsetsu and the modified bunsetsu work as modifier and modifyee, respectively.

Proceedings of the 15th European Workshop on Natural Language Generation (ENLG), pages 61–65,
Brighton, September 2015. ©2015 Association for Computational Linguistics

evaluation data semi-automatically constructed by adding human judgement after automatically changing word order in newspaper article sentences. The experimental results showed the effectiveness of our method.

2 Word Order and Dependency

In this section, we discuss the relation between word order and dependency in a Japanese sentence using the example shown in Figure 1.

On the ground that dependency is one of fundamental contributing factors which decide the appropriate word order (Nihongo Kijutsu Bunpo Kenkyukai, 2009), the conventional method (Uchimoto et al., 2000) reordered words using syntactic information obtained by dependency parsing which was assumed to be beforehand performed. However, the accuracy of dependency parsing decreases when an input sentence has less-readable word order such as S1 because dependency parsers are usually trained on syntactically annotated corpora in which sentences have the readable word order such as S2.

On the other hand, if word reordering is performed before dependency parsing, the accuracy of the word reordering is thought to decrease because syntactic information can not be utilized. In fact, to change the word order in S1 to the appropriate one such as S2, it is necessary to comprehend the dependency structure of S1.

The above discussion indicates that word reordering and dependency parsing depend on each other. Therefore, we can consider it is more desirable to concurrently perform the two processes than to sequentially perform them.

3 Word Reordering Method

In our method, a sentence, on which morphological analysis and bunsetsu segmentation have been performed, is considered as the input. We assume that the input sentence might have word order which is not easy to read but grammatically well-formed. Our method identifies the suitable word order which is easy to read by being executed concurrently with dependency parsing.

We realize the concurrent execution of dependency parsing and word reordering by searching for the maximum-likelihood pattern of word order and dependency structure for an input sentence. We use the same search algorithm as one proposed by Yoshida et al. (2014), which can efficiently find the approximate solution from a huge number of candidates of the pattern by extending CYK algorithm used in conventional dependency parsing. In this paper, we refine the probabilistic model proposed by Yoshida et al. (2014) to improve the accuracy. Note our method reorders bunsetsus in a sentence without paraphrasing and does not reorder morphemes within a bunsetsu. In addition, we assume there are not any inverted structures and commas in an input sentence.

3.1 Probabilistic Model for Word Reordering

When a sequence of bunsetsus in an input sentence $B = b_1 \cdots b_n$ is provided, our method identifies the structure S which maximizes $P(S|B)$. The structure S is defined as a tuple $S = \langle O, D \rangle$ where $O = \{o_{1,2}, o_{1,3}, \cdots, o_{1,n}, \cdots, o_{i,j}, \cdots, o_{n-2,n-1}, o_{n-2,n}, o_{n-1,n}\}$ is the word order pattern after reordering and $D = \{d_1, \cdots, d_{n-1}\}$ is dependency structure. Here, $o_{i,j}$ $(1 \leq i < j \leq n)$ expresses the order between b_i and b_j after reordering. $o_{i,j}$ is 1 if b_i is located before b_j, and is 0 otherwise. In addition, d_i expresses the dependency relation whose modifier bunsetsu is b_i.

In the probablistic model proposed by Yoshida et al. (2014), $P(S|B)$ was calculated as follows:

$$\begin{aligned} P(S|B) &= P(O, D|B) \\ &= \sqrt{P(O|B) \times P(D|O,B)} \\ &\quad \times \sqrt{P(D|B) \times P(O|D,B)} \end{aligned} \tag{1}$$

We extend the above model and calculate $P(S|B)$ as follows:

$$\begin{aligned} P(S|B) = &\{P(O|B) \times P(D|O,B)\}^{\alpha} \\ &\times \{P(D|B) \times P(O|D,B)\}^{1-\alpha} \end{aligned} \tag{2}$$

where α is a weight and $0 \leq \alpha \leq 1$. Formula (2) is obtained for the weighted geometric average[2] between the following two Formulas (3) and (4).

$$P(O,D|B) = P(O|B) \times P(D|O,B) \tag{3}$$

$$P(O,D|B) = P(D|B) \times P(O|D,B) \tag{4}$$

Here, Formulas (3) and (4) are derived by expanding $P(O,D|B)$ based on multiplication theorem. Formula (3) is thought to represent the processing flow in which dependency parsing is executed after word reordering, and Formula (4) is thought to

[2] We pre-experimentally confirmed that the calculated result of the weighted geometric average was better than that of the weighted arithmetic average.

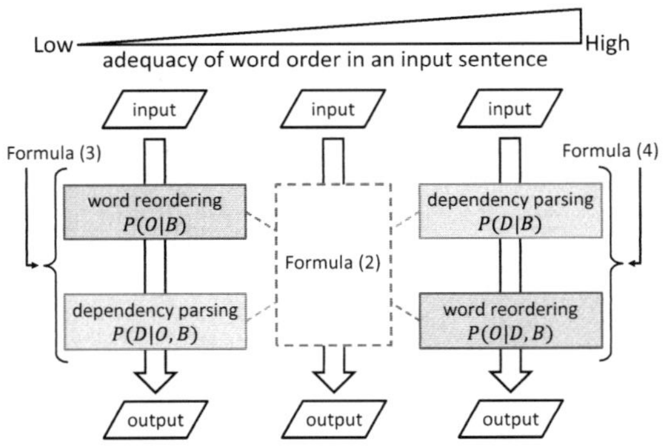

Figure 2: Relationships among Formulas (2) – (4).

represent the inverse flow. According to the probability theory, the calculated result of Formula (2) is equal to those of Formulas (3) and (4). However, in practice, since each factor in the formulas is estimated based on a training corpus, the results of these formulas are different from each other.

Figure 2 shows a conceptual diagram which represents relations among Fomulas (2) – (4). If an input sentence has low adequacy of word order, it is thought that performing word reordering before dependency parsing enables $S = \langle O, D \rangle$ to be identified with higher accuracy, and thus, we can conceive an idea of calculating $P(O, D|B)$ by Fomula (3). Conversely, if an input sentence has high adequacy of word order, it is probably better to perform word reordering after dependency parsing, and thus, we can think of calculating $P(O, D|B)$ by Fomula (4). Therefore, we mix Formulas (3) and (4) by adjusting the weight α depending on the adequacy of word order in an input sentence, instead of using the constant 0.5 in the previous model proposed by Yoshida et al. (2014).

Each factor in Formula (2) is estimated by the maximum entropy method in the same approximation procedure as that of Yoshida et al. (2014).

4 Experiment

To evaluate the effectiveness of our method, we applied our method to less-readable sentences artificially created by changing the word order of Japanese newspaper article sentences, and evaluated how much our method could reproduce the word order of the original sentences.

4.1 Construction of Evaluation Data

From a viewpoint of utilizing our method for support revision, it is desirable to use less-readable sentences spontaneously written by Japanese natives in the experiment. However, it is not easy to collect a large amount of pairs composed of such a sentence and the corresponding sentence which was modified by hand so that the word order becomes readable, and also, such data is unavailable. In addition, since spontaneously written sentences have many factors other than word order which decrease the readability, it is difficult to conduct the evaluation with a focus solely on word order.

Therefore, our previous work (Yoshida et al., 2014) artificially generated sentences which were not easy to read, by just automatically changing the word order of newspaper article sentences in Kyoto Text Corpus[3] based on the dependency structure. However, just automatically changing the word order may create sentences which are unlikely to be written by a native. To solve the problem, we semi-automatically constructed the evaluation data by adding human judgement. That is, if a subject judges that a sentence generated by automatically changing the word order in the same way as the previous work (Yoshida et al., 2014) may have spontaneously written by a native. Our constructed data has 552 sentences including 4,906 bunsetsus.

4.2 Outline of Experiment

Since our method needs to decide the weight α in Formula (2) in advance, we conducted 5-fold cross validation using the evaluation data constructed in Section 4.1. Concretely, we divided 552 sentences into 5 sets, and then, we repeated an experiment 5 times, in which we used one set from among 5 sets as the test data and the others as the held-out data to decide α. As the training data to estimate each probability in Formula (2), we used 7,976 sentences in Kyoto Text Corpus, which were different from the 552 sentences. Here, we used the Maximum Entropy Modeling Toolkit for Python and C++[4] with the default options except "-i (iteration) 1000."

In the evaluation of word reordering, we obtained the **complete agreement** (the percentage of the sentences in which all words' order completely agrees with that of the original sentence)

[3] http://nlp.ist.i.kyoto-u.ac.jp/EN/

[4] http://homepages.inf.ed.ac.uk/lzhang10/maxent_toolkit.html

Table 1: Experimental results (word reordering)

	pair agreement	complete agreement
our method	83.82% (19,474/23,232)	30.98% (171/552)
Yoshida	82.90% (19,259/23,232)*	30.25% (167/552)
sequential 1	82.39% (19,140/23,232)*	26.99% (149/552)*
sequential 2	83.35% (19,365/23,232)	26.63% (147/552)*
input order	76.78% (17,838/23,232)*	0% (0/552)*

Note: The agreements followed by * differ significantly from those of our method (McNemar's test; $p < 0.05$).

Table 2: Experimental results (dep. parsing)

	dependency accuracy	sentence accuracy
our method	83.39% (3,631/4,354)	40.04% (221/552)
Yoshida	82.75% (3,603/4,354)	39.49% (218/552)
sequential 1	84.75% (3,690/4,354)*	36.78% (203/552)
sequential 2	86.08% (3,748/4,354)*	37.50% (207/552)

Note: The accuracies followed by * differ significantly from those of our method (McNemar's test; $p < 0.05$).

and **pair agreement** (the percentage of the pairs of bunsetsus whose word order agrees with that in the original sentence), which are defined by Uchimoto et al. (2000). Here, when deciding α using the held-out data, we calculate the α to two places of decimals which maximizes the pair agreement. In the evaluation of dependency parsing, we obtained the **dependency accuracy** (the percentage of correctly analyzed dependencies out of all dependencies) and **sentency accuracy** (the percentage of the sentences in which all the dependencies are analyzed correctly), which were defined by Uchimoto et al. (1999).

We compared our method to Yoshida's method (Yoshida et al., 2014) and two conventional sequential methods. Both the sequential methods execute the dependency parsing primarily, and then, perform the word reordering by using the conventional word reordering method (Uchimoto et al., 1999). The difference between the two is the method of dependency parsing. The sequential methods 1 and 2 use the dependency parsing method proposed by Uchimoto et al. (2000) and the dependency parsing tool CaboCha[5], respectively. All of the methods used the same training features as those described in Yoshida et al. (2014).

4.3 Experimental Results

Table 1 shows the experimental results on word reordering of each method. Here, the last row shows the agreements measured by comparing the input word order with the correct word order. The agreements mean the values which can be achieved with no reordering. The both agreements of our method are micro averages for the agreements of each of the 5 sets. As the result of decision of α by using the held-out data, the α for 3 sets was 0.66, and the α for the other two sets was 0.75. The both agreements of our method were highest among all. We can confirm the effectiveness of our method.

Although the purpose of our method is reordering to improve readability, our method generates a dependency structure as a by-product. Here, for reference, we show the experimental results on dependency parsing in Table 2. The dependency accuracy of our method was significantly lower than that of the two sequential methods, and was higher than that of Yoshida's method although there was no significant difference. On the other hand, the sentence accuracy of our method was highest among all the methods although there were no significant differences in them. As a result of analysis, especially, our method and Yoshida's method tended to improve the sentence accuracy very well in case of short sentences. On the other hand, CaboCha, which is a dependency parser in sequential 2, tended not to depend very well on the length of sentences.

5 Conclusion

This paper proposed the method for reordering bunsetsus in a Japanese sentence based on executing concurrently with dependency parsing. Especially, we extended the probablistic model proposed by Yoshida et al. (2014) to deal with sentences spontaneously written by a native. In addition, we conducted the experiment using our semi-automatically constructed evaluation data so that the sentences are likely to be spontaneously written by a native. The experimental results showed the effectiveness of our method.

In the future, we would like to develop a word reordering method which can take account of comma positions by integrating our method with a method for identifying proper comma positions (for example, Murata et al., 2010).

Acknowledgments

This research was partially supported by the Grant-in-Aid for Young Scientists (B) (No.25730134) and Scientific Research (B) (No.26280082) of JSPS.

[5]http://taku910.github.io/cabocha/

References

Anja Belz, Michael White, Dominic Espinosa, Eric Kow, Deirdre Hogan, and Amanda Stent. 2011. The first surface realisation shared task: Overview and evaluation results. In *Proceedings of the 13th European Workshop on Natural Language Generation (ENLG2011)*, pages 217–226.

Katja Filippova and Michael Strube. 2007. Generating constituent order in German clauses. In *Proceedings of the 45th Annual Meeting of the Association for Computational Linguistics (ACL2007)*, pages 320–327.

Karin Harbusch, Gerard Kempen, Camiel van Breugel, and Ulrich Koch. 2006. A generation-oriented workbench for performance grammar: Capturing linear order variability in German and Dutch. In *Proceedings of the 4th International Natural Language Generation Conference (INLG2006)*, pages 9–11.

Geert-Jan M. Kruijff, Ivana Kruijff-Korbayová, John Bateman, and Elke Teich. 2001. Linear order as higher-level decision: Information structure in strategic and tactical generation. In *Proceedings of the 8th European Workshop on Natural Language Generation (ENLG2001)*, pages 74–83.

Nihongo Kijutsu Bunpo Kenkyukai, editor, 2009. *Gendai nihongo bunpo 7 (Contemporary Japanese Grammar 7)*, pages 165–182. Kuroshio Shuppan. (In Japanese).

Eric Ringger, Michael Gamon, Robert C. Moore, David Rojas, Martine Smets, and Simon Corston-Oliver. 2004. Linguistically informed statistical models of constituent structure for ordering in sentence realization. In *Proceedings of the 20th International Conference on Computational Linguistics (COLING2004)*, pages 673–679.

James Shaw and Vasileios Hatzivassiloglou. 1999. Ordering among premodifiers. In *Proceedings of the 37th Annual Meeting of the Association for Computational Linguistics (ACL '99)*, pages 135–143.

Kiyotaka Uchimoto, Satoshi Sekine, and Hitoshi Isahara. 1999. Japanese dependency structure analysis based on maximum entropy models. In *Proceedings of the 9th Conference of the European Chapter of the Association for Computational Linguistics (EACL '99)*, pages 196–203.

Kiyotaka Uchimoto, Masaki Murata, Qing Ma, Satoshi Sekine, and Hitoshi Isahara. 2000. Word order acquisition from corpora. In *Proceedings of the 18th International Conference on Computational Linguistics (COLING2000)*, volume 2, pages 871–877.

Hiroshi Yokobayashi, Akira Suganuma, and Rin-ichiro Taniguchi. 2004. Generating candidates for rewriting based on an indicator of complex dependency and it's application to a writing tool. *Journal of Information Processing Society of Japan*, 45(5):1451–1459. (In Japanese).

Kazushi Yoshida, Tomohiro Ohno, Yoshihide Kato, and Shigeki Matsubara. 2014. Japanese word reordering integrated with dependency parsing. In *Proceedings of the 25th International Conference on Computational Linguistics (COLING2014)*, pages 1186–1196.

Sentence Ordering in Electronic Navigational Chart Companion Text Generation

Julie Sauvage-Vincent
Institut Mines-Télécom
Télécom Bretagne
Technopôle Brest Iroise
CS 83818
29238 Brest Cedex 3, France
jsauva01@telecom-bretagne.eu

Yannis Haralambous
Institut Mines-Télécom
Télécom Bretagne
Technopôle Brest Iroise
CS 83818
29238 Brest Cedex 3, France
yannis.haralambous@telecom-bretagne.eu

John Puentes
Institut Mines-Télécom
Télécom Bretagne
Technopôle Brest Iroise
CS 83818
29238 Brest Cedex 3, France
john.puentes@telecom-bretagne.eu

Abstract

We present the sentence ordering part of a natural language generation module, used in the framework of a knowledge base of electronic navigation charts and sailing directions. The particularity of the knowledge base is that it is based on a controlled hybrid language, that is the combination of a controlled natural language and a controlled visual language. The sentence ordering process is able to take into account hybrid (textual and visual) information, involving cartographic data, as well as landscape "read" by the navigator.

1 Introduction

The French Marine Hydrographic and Oceanographic Service (SHOM, *Service Hydrographique et Océanographique de la Marine*) issues, on a quadrennial basis, *Instructions nautiques*, a series of nautical books providing navigators of coastal and intracoastal waters with useful information.

Instructions nautiques are intended as a complement to Electronic Navigational Charts (ENCs) and add a wide variety of essential information not provided in the ENCs for maritime navigation. In this sense they are considered as *companion texts* of ENCs.

Information found in *Instructions nautiques* are in some cases subject to real-time updates. To make this possible, an ongoing SHOM project is to build a knowledge base (KB) covering both ENCs and nautical instructions. This KB is intended to communicate with ENCs and more globally with any compatible Electronic Charts Display Information System.

Updates are planned to be operated mainly by SHOM domain experts, who may not be necessarily proficient in ontology formalism or in language technology. Therefore, it has been decided to use a *controlled natural language* for exchanges between experts and the KB (Haralambous et al., 2014). On the other hand, information contained in the KB covers not only (textual) *Instructions nautiques* but also (visual) ENCs. These two modalities are tightly bound, coreferential and complementary: each modality covers information that the other is unable to transmit.

In order to establish intermodal coreferentiality and complementarity, a new type of controlled language has been defined (Haralambous et al., 2015), called *controlled hybrid language* (CHL), which is intended to be based on hybrid sentences, like for instance:

[The wreck of Morania 130] lies at the bottom of [lake Erie].

In Fig. 1 (on the next page), the reader can see this (multimodal) sentence analyzed. On the bottom of the figure one can see the two visual and textual modalities; and above them, the corresponding syntactic trees: on the right, the usual constituency syntax tree of the textual sentence (georeferenced named entities, placed in brackets, are considered as indivisible noun phrases); on the left, the syntax tree of a small part of the map, considered as a sentence in a visual language, using the Symbol-Relation formalism (Ferrucci et al., 1996; Ferrucci et al., 1998). In both cases, the formal grammars have synthesized attributes (in the sense of Knuth (1968)) carrying semantics: using a bottom-up synthesis approach we obtain their semantics, represented as First-Order Logic graphs (predicates are hexagons, connectors are circles, functions are rounded rectangles, and constants are rectangles). Once the two graphs are established, and after a coreference resolution step, they are transformed and merged into the KB graph, at the top.

When starting from the KB, operators $\mathfrak{V}$ and $\mathfrak{T}$ filter their input into information that is represented visually and information that is represented

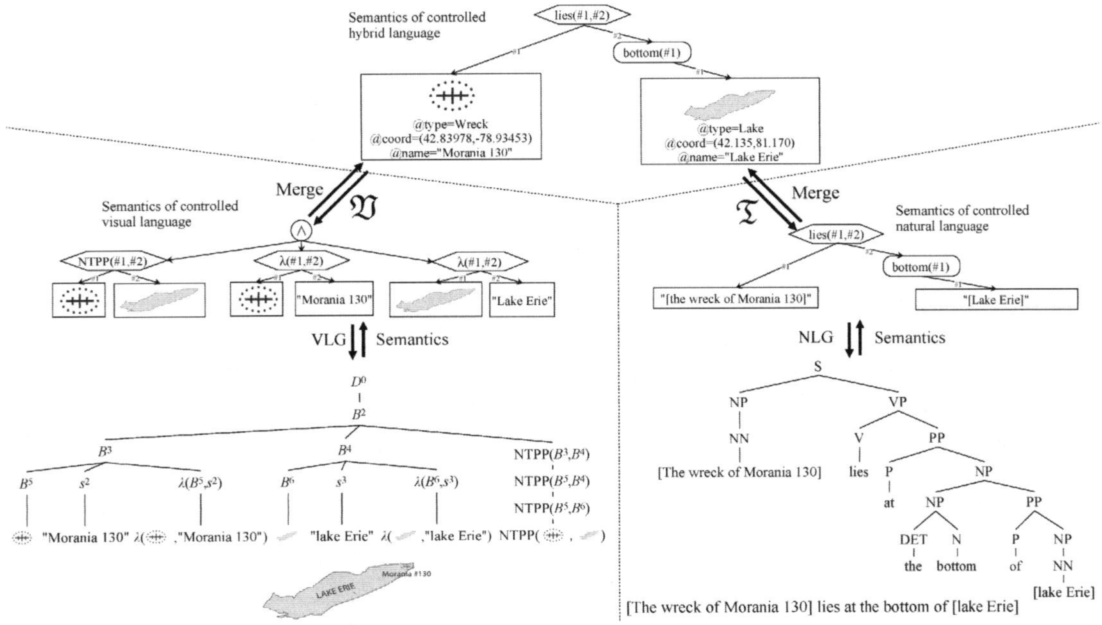

Figure 1: An example of sentence in the CHL INAUT (taken from Haralambous et al. (2015)).

textually (with some redundancy in order to establish coreferential entities). Their outputs are graphs corresponding to FOL formulas. To obtain text, we use NLG and VLG (visual language generation) to obtain a part of the map.

The goal of the INAUT NLG module—which we are currently developing—is to produce the most *fluent*[1] multi-sentence texts possible. This paper addresses the stage of *sentence ordering* (as part of discourse planning), which plays a central role in the achievement of this goal.

2 Related work

Ordering sentences to create a natural and understandable paragraph for the reader is part of what Reiter and Dale (2000) call *discourse planning*.

A widely used approach to discourse planning is based on rhetorical structure theory (Mann and Thompson, 1988), which requires writing a rule for each textual structure. Although this solution has been proved efficient in various contexts (cf. Taboada and Mann (2006)), this is not the case for the *Instructions nautiques* corpus, written by different authors who do not necessarily share the same rhetorical structures and processes.

The NaturalOWL (Androutsopoulos et al. (2013)) system per se could be used for INAUT automatic text generation, if there were not for some major differences. NaturalOWL is essentially based on Centering Theory, i.e., it respects thematic intersentential coherence. In our case there are some additional issues, related to the fact that INAUT is build upon a *hybrid* language: information contained in text is not the only input anymore, and we must guarantee conformance to the itinerary of a vessel, to the geographic "guiding path" of each *Instructions nautiques* volume and, last but not least, to the visual characteristics of the landscape. Indeed, *Instructions nautiques* are, inter alia, textual interpretations of the real world as seen by the navigator, and for this reason sentence order must respect the order navigators "read" the landscape. Another major difference in our system is real-time interaction with users. The latter necessarily has an impact on the structure of generated text: when content determination may be relaunched on different data every few milliseconds, the stability of generated text becomes a major issue.

3 Data and pre-processing

The corpus consists of 462 INAUT controlled hybrid language sentences manually translated from the legacy *Instructions nautiques*.

Let us consider the first step of NLG, namely content determination.

[1] In the sense of criteria S1–S5 of Androutsopoulos et al. (2013, p. 703).

3.1 Content determination

Among the attributes of nodes in the KB we have coordinates for all geolocalized objects. Therefore, hybrid language structure provides a link between geolocalization and (textual) sentence entities. Content determination can be initiated by both (1) textual criteria (selecting a paragraph in the document tree structure), and (2) visual criteria (selecting an area on an ENC).

In case (1), one obtains immediately a subgraph of the KB by taking the nodes hierarchically located under the chosen paragraph node. In case (2), a query sent to the KB server returns all georeferenced nodes located entirely or partially in the selected area of the map.In both cases one obtains a (not necessarily connected) subgraph of the KB.

By the nature of the data, two further steps are needed, both obtained by inference, but on different kinds of data, namely spatial data and temporal/meteorological context.

The first inference step concerns cases where information about a geolocalized object can be inferred from the map. More generally, one can extract knowledge from the map data, which will complement, enhance, or contradict the textual data.

As for temporal and meteorological context, tide and weather conditions obviously have an impact on navigation. This is also the case for regulations based on a schedule. Inference based on these data may act as a filter on the subgraph obtained either hierarchically or by area selection.

Finally, an important feature of the INAUT system is to inform navigators on potentially dangerous situations. By attaching—either manually or by applying inference to geography and context—a *dangerousness coefficient* to specific nodes under given conditions, the system may introduce specific warnings in the generated text.

4 Modelling the domain experts sentence ordering process

We consider the discourse planner as a multicriteria decision process based on frequent patterns of the writing process. Therefore, our main task is to model the implicit knowledge of authors concerning the description of a maritime environment.

4.1 Domain experts sentence ordering process

We detected common patterns in the way authors describe the maritime environment, and will try to discuss them from a cognitive and linguistic point of view.

These patterns are constrained by several criteria: our approach is to assign score to each criterion found in a sentence, in order to calculate the global sentence score in our "bag" of sentences, and reorganize the latter by sorting it in decreasing order of score. The greater the score, the greater the likelihood for the sentence to appear at the beginning of a paragraph. The computation of the score is done by the sum $f(s) = \sum_{i=1}^{n} c_i \cdot w_i$ where s is a sentence, c_i is a criterion value and w_i is the corresponding score. Given a set S of n sentences s_i, if $f(s_1) > f(s_2)$, then the sentence s_1 is more likely to precede s_2.

To assign score to objects, we must understand which features domain experts use to describe a natural environment in general.

Let us consider the different features used in our ordering sentences module.

Landmarks When dealing with (a) authors tend to use *landmarks* as much as possible. Selection of elements useful in assisting human navigation in an open space has been addressed in the context of urban orientation. Michon and Denis (2001) attest the landmark usage preference in order to identify areas where difficulties in term of way finding are likely to occur.

We find this preference in our corpus as well: *Instructions nautiques* authors often prefer man-made landmarks —that facilitate the environment reading— over natural objects.

Geometric primitives Objects occurring in the description of a map or of a landscape can be of three different topological natures: *areas*, *lines* and *points*. We observed that SHOM domain experts describe objects in this order: *polygonal shapes* before *lines*, before *points*. According to Brosset et al. (2008) this can be explained by the fact that, from the point of view of observers, natural environment is seen as a *spatial network*: linear objects structure the network with edges and links, polygonal shapes act as a partition of the space, and finally points act as visual landmarks.

Name and size Two other features are directly connected to individual objects: their *size* and *name*. Indeed, named objects appear more frequently in the corpus than unnamed ones and larger objects more frequently than smaller ones.

Proximity spaces Another feature taking part in the multicriteria decision process is *geographic position relative to the vessel.*

When receiving directions, users tend to create by anticipation a mental representation of the route —whether they are standard or problematic routes. Unlike pedestrian navigation, maritime navigation requires a most precise representation of the surrounding and forthcoming environment.

According to Tversky (2003) humans structure environment in various mental spaces. Le Yaouanc et al. (2010) extended Tversky's spaces to *proximity spaces*. These structure the visual perception of the landscape and therefore, logically, also its description. Proximity spaces are defined by actions users are able to perform within them. We distinguish four different proximity spaces (from the closest to the observer to the furthest away): (a) the *space of the body*, (b) the *experienced space*, (c) the *distant space* (d) and, finally, the *space at the horizon*. In their paper, Le Yaouanc et al. (2010) state that the different subjects of their study have used an order following these proximity spaces when describing an environmental scene.

It is interesting to note that in the SHOM corpus the order assigned by domain experts is the reverse of the one stated above in 93% of the cases. This difference relates to the fact that Le Yaouanc et al. (2010) used terrestrial environmental scene descriptions while the SHOM corpus deals exclusively with offshore environmental scene descriptions.

Thus, the further away objects are, the greater the score assigned to them. *Proximity spaces* are a typical example of an *hybrid feature*: the textual part alone would be clearly insufficient in providing information about size and position of objects.

Cardinal directions In the same spirit, we add yet another feature, namely *cardinal directions*. Indeed the latter provide an additional hint on the order of sentences in a paragraph since an environmental scene is usually observed in the reading direction of the observer (Nachson and Hatta, 2001; Fuhrman and Boroditsky, 2010), in our case from left to right for 84.8% of the paragraphs where the description of objects is done in a longitudinal way.

Using the various features mentioned in this section, we have built a SVM classifier for ranking sentences. The classifier provides a lattice structure of ranked sentence pairs. Out of this lattice we obtain a best possible global order of sentences by a standard lattice-traversal algorithm.

4.2 The Stability Issue

Content determination, as part of the NLG process, depends on several parameters (the area selection, the temporal and meteorological context, etc.) which operate on three different temporal scales affecting NLG: slow landscape changes imply very few KB updates but temporal and meteorological context changes may need to be updated several times daily. Finally, selection updates done on the GUI with a mouse may be only milliseconds apart.

All three temporal scales, and the last one at the highest degree, raise the problem of *NLG stability*: a text should not change while the user is reading it or while the reader is using the mouse to change the selection area.

The issue of stability is a general NLG issue, and as such also affects sentence ordering. Changing the sentence order of a paragraph can be extremely disturbing for the reader.

In fact, user interaction with the GUI causes not only visual changes, but also simultaneous multi-level linguistic structure changes. To overcome this issue we introduce the method of *smooth text generation*, as follows:

We consider the function T that maps the values of the various text generation parameters to the text generated. This discrete function is "smoothed" in the following way:

1. When the mouse crosses a boundary between two areas covering the same nodes but different sentence orders, then the same sentence order is kept, until some nodes disappear or new nodes appear.
2. When the mouse enters a zone covering new nodes, then the sentences generated out of these nodes are—as much as possible—added at the end of the generated paragraph.
3. Generated text updates are slightly delayed so that a quick mouse move will not alter the gen-

erated text until the mouse is still for a time duration longer than a given threshold.

5 Conclusion and Future Work

We presented in this paper the sentence ordering part of the natural language generation module of the INAUT system. The particularity of this system is that it is based on a controlled hybrid language and hence covers simultaneously textual and visual knowledge.

We have shown that hybrid features (textual and visual) can be used to build a classifier that orders sentences in a paragraph.

Future work in the project involves a two-parts evaluation —(1) an automatic method based on comparison with the legacy corpus, and (2) a human-centered evaluation— and the exploration of other hybrid features impacting on sentence order, in particular by using the domain experts feedback of the second evaluation phase.

Furthermore, we will also consider hybrid language generation, i.e., having the system choose which information will be represented in visual or in textual modality, and insure coreferential redundancy among the modalities.

References

Ion Androutsopoulos, Gerasimos Lampouras, and Dimitrios Galanis. 2013. Generating natural language descriptions from OWL ontologies: the NaturalOWL system. *J. Artif. Int. Res.*, 48:671–715.

David Brosset, Christophe Claramunt, and Éric Saux. 2008. Wayfinding in natural and urban environments: a comparative study. *Cartographica*, 43(1):21–30.

Filomena Ferrucci, Giuliano Pacini, Giorgio Satta, Maria I. Sessa, Genoveffa Tortora, Maurizio Tucci, and Giuliana Vitiello. 1996. Symbol-Relation Grammars: A Formalism for Graphical Languages. *Information and Computation*, 131:1–46.

Filomena Ferrucci, Genny Tortora, Maurizio Tucci, and Giuliana Vitiello. 1998. Relation Grammars: A Formalism for Syntactic and Semantic Analysis of Visual Languages. In Kim Marriott and Bernd Meyer, editors, *Visual Language Theory*, pages 219–243. Springer.

Orly Fuhrman and Lera Boroditsky. 2010. Cross-cultural differences in mental representations of time: Evidence from an implicit nonlinguistic task. *Cognitive Science*, 34(8):1430–1451.

Yannis Haralambous, Julie Sauvage-Vincent, and John Puentes. 2014. INAUT, a Controlled Language for the French Coast Pilot Books *Instructions nautiques*. In Brian Davis, Kaarel Kaljurand, and Tobias Kuhn, editors, *Controlled Natural Language*, volume 8625 of *Lecture Notes in Computer Science*, pages 102–111. Springer.

Yannis Haralambous, Julie Sauvage-Vincent, and John Puentes. 2015. A hybrid (visual/natural) controlled language. Submitted.

Donald E. Knuth. 1968. Semantics of context-free languages. *Math. Syst. Theor.*, 2:127–145.

Jean-Marie Le Yaouanc, Éric Saux, and Christophe Claramunt. 2010. A semantic and language-based representation of an environmental scene. *Geoinformatica*, 14(3):333–352.

William C. Mann and Sandra A. Thompson. 1988. Rhetorical structure theory: Toward a functional theory of text organization. *Text*, 8(3):243–281.

Pierre-Emmanuel Michon and Michel Denis. 2001. When and why are visual landmarks used in giving directions? In Daniel R. Montello, editor, *Spatial Information Theory*, volume 2205 of *Lecture Notes in Computer Science*, pages 292–305. Springer.

Israel Nachson and Takeshi Hatta. 2001. Directional tendencies of Hebrew, Japanese, and English readers. *Perceptual and Motor Skills*, 93:178–180.

Ehud Reiter and Robert Dale. 2000. *Building Natural Language Generation Systems*. Studies in Natural Language Processing. Cambridge University Press, Cambridge, U.K.

Maite Taboada and William C. Mann. 2006. Applications of rhetorical structure theory. *Discourse studies*, 8(4):567–588.

Barbara Tversky. 2003. Structures of mental spaces. how people think about space. *Environment and behavior*, 35(1):66–80.

Natural Language Generation from Pictographs

Leen Sevens, Vincent Vandeghinste, Ineke Schuurman, Frank Van Eynde
Centre for Computational Linguistics
KU Leuven, Belgium
firstname@ccl.kuleuven.be

Abstract

We present a Pictograph-to-Text translation system for people with Intellectual or Developmental Disabilities (IDD). The system translates pictograph messages, consisting of one or more pictographs, into Dutch text using WordNet links and an n-gram language model. We also provide several pictograph input methods assisting the users in selecting the appropriate pictographs.

1 Introduction

Being unable to access ICT is a major form of social exclusion. For people with IDD, the use of social media or applications that require the user to be able to read or write, such as email clients, is a huge stumbling block if no personal assistance is given. There is a need for digital communication interfaces that enable written contact for people with IDD.

Augmentative and Alternative Communication (AAC) assists people with communication disabilities to be socially active in the digital world. Pictographically augmented text is a specific form of AAC that is often used in schools, institutions, and sheltered workshops to allow accessible communication. Between two and five million people in the European Union could benefit from symbols or symbol-related text as a means of written communication (Keskinen et al., 2012).

Within the Able to Include framework,[1] a EU project aiming to improve the living conditions of people with IDD, we developed a Pictograph-to-Text translation system. It provides help in constructing Dutch textual messages by allowing the user to input a series of pictographs and translates these messages into NL. English and Spanish versions of the tool are currently in development. It can be considered as the inverse translation engine of the Text-to-Pictograph system as described by Vandeghinste et al. (Accepted), which is primarily conceived to improve *comprehension* of textual content.

The system converts Sclera[2] and Beta[3] input messages into Dutch text, using WordNet synsets and a trigram language model. After a discussion of related work (section 2), we describe some characteristics of pictograph languages (section 3), followed by an overview of the different pictograph input methods (section 4). The next part (section 5) is dedicated to the architecture. We present our preliminary results for Pictograph-to-Dutch translation in section 6. Finally, we conclude and discuss future work in section 7.

2 Related work

Our task shares elements with regular machine translation between natural languages and with Natural Language Generation (NLG). Jing (1998) retrieves the semantic concepts from WordNet and maps them to appropriate words to produce large amounts of lexical paraphrases for a specific application domain. Similar to our approach, Liu (2003) uses statistical language models as a solution to the word inflection problem, as there may exist multiple forms for a concept constituent. The language model re-scores all inflection forms in order to generate the best hypothesis in the output. Our solution is specifically tailored towards translation from pictographs into text.

A number of pictograph-based input interfaces can be found in the literature. Finch et al. (2011) developed picoTrans, a mobile application which allows users to build a source text by combining pictures or common phrases, but their application is not intended for people with cognitive disabilities. The Prothèse Vocale Intelligente (PVI) sys-

[1] http://abletoinclude.eu/

[2] http://www.sclera.be/

[3] https://www.betasymbols.com/

Proceedings of the 15th European Workshop on Natural Language Generation (ENLG), pages 71–75,
Brighton, September 2015. ©2015 Association for Computational Linguistics

tem by Vaillant (1998) offers a limited vocabulary of pictographs, each one corresponding to a single word. PVI searches for predicative elements, such as verbs, and attempts to fill its semantic slots, after which a tree structure is created and a grammatical sentence is generated. Fitrianie and Rothkrantz (2009) apply a similar method, requiring the user to first select the pictograph representation of a verb and fill in the role slots that are made available by that verb. Their system does not take into account people with cognitive disabilities. Various pictograph chat applications, such as Messenger Visual (Tuset et al., 1995) and Pictograph Chat Communicator III (Munemori et al., 2010), allow the user to insert pictographs, but they do not generate NL.

The Pictograph-to-Text translation engine differs from these applications in that it is specifically designed for people with cognitive disabilities, does not impose any limits on the way in which pictograph messages are composed and generates NL output where possible. Furthermore, the system's architecture is as language-independent as possible, making it very easy to add new target languages.

3 Pictograph languages

Many pictograph systems are in place. Although differences exist across pictograph sets, some features are shared among them. A pictograph of an entity (noun) can stand for one or multiple instances of that entity. Pictographs depicting actions (verbs) are deprived of aspect, tense, and inflection information. Auxiliaries and articles usually have no pictograph counterpart. Pictograph languages are simplified languages, often specifically designed for people with IDD. The Pictograph-to-Text translation system currently gives access to two pictograph sets, Sclera and Beta (see Figure 1).

Sclera pictographs[4] are mainly black-and-white pictographs. They often represent *complex* concepts, such as a verb and its object (such as *to feed the dog*) or compound words (such as *carrot soup*). There are hardly any pictographs for adverbs or prepositions.

The *Beta* set[5] is characterized by its overall consistency. Beta hardly contains any complex pictographs. Most of the pictographs represent *simplex* concepts.

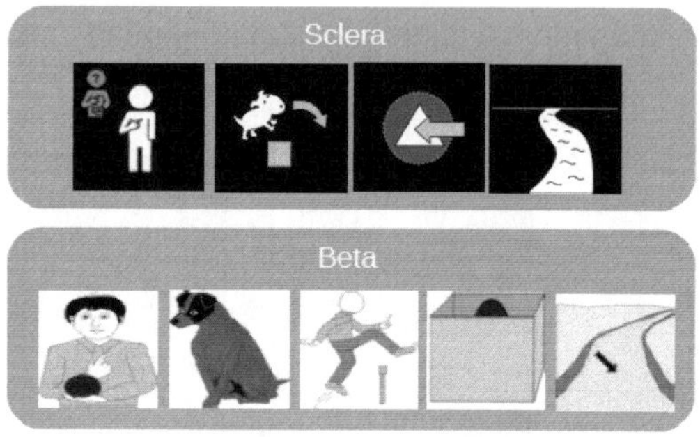

"My dog jumped in the river."
"My dogs jump in a stream."
"My dogs leaped into the river."
Etc.

Figure 1: Example of a Beta and a Sclera sequence. Pictographs can correspond to different words and word forms in a NL, as shown for English in this example. The Sclera sequence contains a complex pictograph, namely the jumping dog.

4 Pictograph input methods

The Pictograph-to-Text translation engine relies on pictograph input and the user should be able to efficiently select the desired pictographs. We have developed two different input methods. The first approach offers a static hierarchy of pictographs, while the second option scans the user input and dynamically adapts itself in order to suggest appropriate pictographs. Usability tests will have to be performed with the target audience.

The *static hierarchy of pictographs* consists of three levels. The structure of the hierarchy is based on topic detection and frequency counts applied to 69,636 email messages sent by users of the WAI-NOT communication platform.[6]

The second method is a *dynamic pictograph prediction tool*, the first of its kind. Two different prototypes have been developed, which will eventually be merged. The first model relies on *n-gram information*. The WAI-NOT email corpus was translated into pictographs (285,372 Sclera pictographs and 284,658 Beta pictographs) in order to enable building a language model using the

[4]Freely available under Creative Commons License 2.0.

[5]The coloured pictographs can be obtained at reasonable prices. Their black-and-white equivalents are available for free.

[6]http://www.wai-not.be/ uses the Text-to-Pictograph engine to augment emails with sequences of Sclera or Beta pictographs, allowing people with communicative disabilities to familiarize themselves with information technology.

SRILM toolkit (Stolcke, 2002). The second model relies on *word associations* within a broader context: The system identifies the most frequent lemmas in the synset (see section 5.1) of each entered pictograph and retrieves a list of semantically similar words from DISCO,[7] an application that allows to retrieve the semantic similarity between arbitrary words and phrases, along with their similarity scores. Pictographs that are connected to these words are presented to the user.

5 Natural Language Generation from Pictographs

The main challenge in translating from pictograph languages to NL is the fact that a pictograph-for-word correspondence will almost never provide an acceptable output. Pictograph languages often lack pictographs for function words. A single pictograph often encodes information corresponding to multiple words with multiple inflected word forms in NL.

Section 5.1 describes how the bridge between Sclera and Beta pictographs and natural language text was built. The system's general architecture is outlined in section 5.2. It introduces a set of parameters, which were tuned on a training corpus (section 5.3). Finally, as explained in section 5.4, an optimal NL string is selected.

5.1 Linking pictographs to natural language text

Pictographs are connected to NL words through a semantic route and a direct route.

The *semantic route* concerns the use of WordNets, which are a core component of both the Text-to-Pictograph and the Pictograph-to-Text translation systems. For Dutch, we used the Cornetto (Vossen et al., 2008) database. Vandeghinste and Schuurman (2014) manually linked 5710 Sclera and 2746 Beta pictographs to Dutch synsets (groupings of synonymous words) in Cornetto.

The *direct route* contains specific rules for appropriately dealing with pronouns (as pictographs for pronouns exist in Sclera and Beta) and contains one-on-one mappings between pictographs and individual lemmas in a dictionary.

5.2 Architecture of the system

When a pictograph is selected, its synset is retrieved, and from this synset we retrieve all the synonyms it contains. For each of these synonyms, we apply *reverse lemmatization*, i.e. we retrieve the full linguistic paradigm of the lemma, together with its part-of-speech tags. For Dutch, we created a reverse lemmatizer based on the SoNaR corpus.[8]

Each of these surface forms is a hypothesis for the language model, as described in section 5.4. For nouns, we generate additional alternative hypotheses which include an article, based on part-of-speech information.

5.3 Tuning the parameters

The Pictograph-to-Text translation system contains a number of decoding parameters. *Threshold pruning* determines whether a new path should be added to the existing beam, based on the probability of that path compared to the best path. *Histogram pruning* sets the beam width. The *Cost* parameter estimates the cost of the pictographs that still need processing (based on the amount of pictographs that still needs processing). Eventually, *Reverse lemmatizer minimum frequency* sets a threshold on the frequency of a token/part-of-speech/lemma combination in the corpus, limiting the amount of possible linguistic realizations for a particular pictograph. For Dutch, frequencies are based on occurrence within the SoNaR corpus.

These parameters have to be tuned for every pictograph language/NL pair. For Dutch, our tuning set consists of 50 manually translated messages from the WAI-NOT corpus. We ran five trials of local hill climbing on the parameter search space, with random initialization values, in order to maximize BLEU (Papineni et al., 2002). BLEU is a commonly used metric in Statistical Machine Translation. We did this until BLEU converged onto a fixed score. From these trials, we took the optimal parameter settings.

5.4 Decoding

We performed Viterbi-decoding based on a trigram language model, trained with the SRILM toolkit on a very large corpus. The Dutch training corpus consists of Europarl (Koehn, 2005), CGN (Oostdijk et al., 2003), CLEF (Peters and Braschler, 2001), DGT-TM (Steinberger et al., 2012) and Wikipedia.[9]

[7]http://www.linguatools.de/disco/

[8]http://tst-centrale.org/producten/corpora/sonar-corpus/

[9]http://en.wikipedia.org/wiki/

6 Preliminary results

We present results for Sclera-to-Dutch and Beta-to-Dutch. The test set consists of 50 Dutch messages (975 words) that have been sent with the WAI-NOT email system and which were manually translated into pictographs (724 Sclera pictographs and 746 Beta pictographs).[10] We have evaluated several experimental conditions, progressively activating more features of the system.

The first condition is the *baseline*, in which the system output equals the Dutch pictograph names.[11] The next condition applies *reverse lemmatization*, allowing the system to generate alternative forms of the Dutch pictograph names.[12] We then added the *direct route*, which mostly influences pronoun treatment. The following condition adds the *semantic route*, using Cornetto synsets, allowing us to retrieve all word forms that are connected to the same synset as the pictograph. Finally, we let the system generate alternative hypotheses which also include *articles*.

Table 1 shows the respective BLEU, NIST (Doddington, 2002), and Word Error Rate (WER) scores for the translation of messages into Sclera and into Beta. We use these metrics to present improvements over the baseline. As the system translates from a poor pictograph language (with one pictograph corresponding to multiple words and word forms) into a rich NL, these scores are not absolute.[13] Future work will consist of evaluating the system with human ratings by our target group.

7 Conclusion

These first evaluations show that a trigram language model for finding the most likely combination of every pictograph's alternative textual representations is already an improvement over the initial baseline, but there is ample room for improvement in future work.

Condition	BLEU	NIST	WER
Sclera			
Baseline	0.0175	1.5934	76.4535
Rev. lem.	0.0178	1.6852	76.8411
Direct	0.0420	2.2564	66.9574
Synsets	0.0535	2.5426	65.9884
Articles	0.0593	2.8001	67.4419
Beta			
Baseline	0.0518	2.767	70.4457
Rev. lem.	0.0653	3.0553	70.3488
Direct	0.0814	3.3365	63.0814
Synsets	0.0682	3.1417	61.4341
Articles	0.0739	3.4418	63.1783

Table 1: Evaluation of Pictograph-to-Dutch conversion.

The Pictograph-to-English and Pictograph-to-Spanish translation systems are currently in development.

It is important to note that we assume that the grammatical structure of pictograph languages resembles and simplifies that of a particular NL. Nevertheless, the users of pictograph languages do not always need to introduce pictographs in the canonical order or could omit some of them. Future work will look into generation-heavy and transfer approaches for Pictograph-to-Text translation. In the generation-heavy approach, the words conveyed by the input pictographs will be considered as a bag of words. All their possible permutations will be evaluated against a language model (Vandeghinste, 2008). In the transfer system, the input sentence will be (semantically) analyzed by a rule-based parser. A number of transfer rules convert the source language sentence structure into the sentence structure of the target language, from which the target language sentence is generated, using language generation rules. Both methods can be combined into a hybrid system.

User tests will reveal how both the static hierarchy of pictographs and the dynamic prediction tools can be improved.

References

G. Doddington. 2002. Automatic Evaluation of Machine Translation Quality Using N-gram Co-occurrence Statistics. In *HLT-02*, pages 138–145.

A. Finch, K. Tanaka-Ishii, W. Song, and E. Sumita. 2011. picoTrans: Using Pictures as Input for Machine Translation on Mobile Devices. In *IJCAI-11*, pages 2614–2619.

S. Fitrianie and L. Rothkrantz. 2009. Two-Dimensional Visual Language Grammar. In *TSD-09*, pages 573–580.

[10] In future work, we will also evaluate pictograph messages that are created by real users. We thank one of the anynomous reviewers for this suggestion.

[11] Note that Beta file names often correspond to Dutch lemmas, while Sclera pictographs usually have more complex names, including numbers to distinguish between alternative pictographs for depicting the same concept. This explains why the Sclera baseline is lower.

[12] The Sclera file names are often too complex to generate variants for the language model.

[13] For instance, the system has no means of knowing whether the user is talking about a *chicken* or a *hen*, or whether the user *eats* or *ate* a pizza.

H. Jing. 1998. Usage of WordNet in Natural Language Generation. In *COLING-ACL-98*.

T. Keskinen, T. Heimonen, M. Turunen, J.P. Rajaniemi, and S. Kauppinen. 2012. SymbolChat: A Flexible Picture-based Communication Platform for Users with Intellectual Disabilities. *Interacting with Computers*, 24(5):374–386.

P. Koehn. 2005. Europarl: A Parallel Corpus for Statistical Machine Translation. In *MT Summit-05*, pages 79–86.

F.-H. Liu, L. Gu, Y. Gao, and M. Picheny. 2003. Use of statistical N-gram models in Natural Language Generation for Machine Translation. In *ICASSP-03*, pages 636–639.

J. Munemori, T. Fukada, M. Yatid, T. Nishide, and J. Itou. 2010. Pictograph Chat Communicator III: a Chat System that Embodies Cross-Cultural Communication. In *KES-10*, pages 473–482.

N. Oostdijk, W. Goedertier, F. Van Eynde, L. Boves, J. P. Martens, M. Moortgat, and H. Baayen. 2003. Experiences from the Spoken Dutch Corpus Project. In *LREC-02*, pages 340–347.

K. Papineni, S. Roukos, T. Ward, and W. Zhu. 2002. Evaluation of Machine Translation. In *ACL-02*, pages 311–318.

C. Peters and M. Braschler. 2001. European Research letter: Cross-language System Evaluation: the CLEF Campaigns. *Journal of the American Society for Information Science and Technology*, 52(12):1067–1072.

R. Steinberger, A. Eisele, S. Klocek, S. Pilos, and P. Schlüter. 2012. DGT-TM: A Freely Available Translation Memory in 22 Languages. In *LREC-12*, pages 454–459.

A. Stolcke. 2002. SRIL: An Extensible Language Modeling Toolkit. In *ICSLP-02*.

P. Tuset, J.M. Barbern, P. Cervell-Pastor, and C. Janer. 1995. Designing Messenger Visual, an Instant Messenging Service for Individuals with Cognitive Disability. In *IWAAL-95*, pages 57–64.

P. Vaillant. 1998. Interpretation of Iconic Utterances Based on Contents Representation: Semantic Analysis in the PVI System. *Natural Language Engineering*, 4(1):17–40.

V. Vandeghinste and I. Schuurman. 2014. Linking Pictographs to Synsets: Sclera2Cornetto. In *LREC-14*, pages 3404–3410.

V. Vandeghinste, I. Schuurman, L. Sevens, and F. Van Eynde. Accepted. Translating Text into Pictographs. *Natural Language Engineering*.

V. Vandeghinste. 2008. *A Hybrid Modular Machine Translation System. LoRe-MT: Low Resources Machine Translation*. LOT, Utrecht.

P. Vossen, I. Maks, R. Segers, and H. van der Vliet. 2008. Integrating Lexical Units, Synsets, and Ontology in the Cornetto Database. In *LREC-08*.

Translating Italian to LIS in the rail stations

Alessandro Mazzei
Dipartimento di Informatica, Università degli Studi di Torino
Via Pessinetto 12, 10149, Torino, Italy
mazzei@di.unito.it

Abstract

This paper presents an ongoing project about the symbolic translation from Italian to Italian Signed Language (LIS) in the rail stations domain. We describe some technical issues in the generation side of the translation, i.e. the use of XML templates for microplanning, the implementation of some LIS linguistic features in the grammar.

1 Introduction

Several commercial and research projects use avatars for automatic translation into signed languages (SLs) and most of these projects investigate on relatively small domains in which translation may perform quite well. Among them: post office announcements (Cox et al., 2002), weather forecasting (Verlinden et al., 2001; Mazzei et al., 2013), driver's license renewal (San-Segundo et al., 2012), and train announcements (Segouat and Braffort, 2009; Ebling, 2013). However, SLs still pose many challenges related to the specific linguistic features (e.g. no function words and articles) as well as to the specific communication channels (e.g. the characteristic use of the space).

LIS4ALL is a project for the automatic translation from Italian to LIS in the Italian rail stations domain. The domain is completely specified by the Rete Ferroviaria Italiana (RFI), which produced the manual *MAS* (Manuale degli Annunci Sonori), that describes the details of each specific message (RFI, 2011). MAS specifies 39 classes: 13 for arriving trains, 15 for leaving trains, 11 for special situations (e.g. strikes). The classes have been designed by a group of linguists to produce concise Italian messages. Full relative clauses, coordination and complex structures are avoided. As a consequence, the Italian rail stations domain is a controlled plain language. Note that the vocal rail station messages are produced in real-time by using text-to-speech, and the textual input message is produced by a proprietary closed source software that uses raw data extracted from a database. In the project we had access only to the textual messages but we do not have access to raw data. As a consequence, LIS4ALL concerns automatic translation with NLG rather than uniquely NLG.

An initial study of the domain (5014 messages form 24 hours messages produced at the Torino Porta Nuova Station) has showed that four classes account for $\sim$85% of total messages: these are A1: *simple arrive*, P1: *simple leave*, A2: *arrive on a different rail*, A3: *delayed arrive*. In this paper we discuss a symbolic translator designed to account for these four classes of messages.[1]

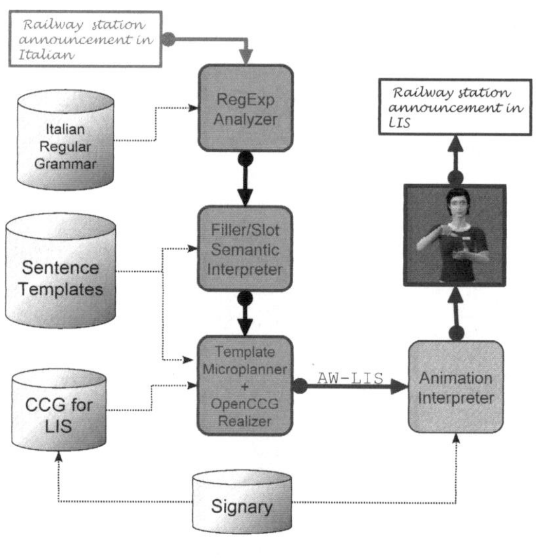

Figure 1: The architecture of the Italian to LIS traslator.

Figure 1 illustrates the current architecture, thus a pipeline which includes five modules: (1) a regular expression parser for Italian; (2) a filler/slot

[1] We plan to account for the remaining classes in the future.

Proceedings of the 15th European Workshop on Natural Language Generation (ENLG), pages 76–80,
Brighton, September 2015. ©2015 Association for Computational Linguistics

based semantic interpreter; (3) a generator; (4) a spatial planner; (5) an avatar that performs the synthesis of the sequence of signs. On the basis of this architecture, our translator can be classified as semantic transfer based system (Hutchins and Somer, 1992). Indeed, since the source language is controlled, the translation is a deterministic process that poses a number of challenges just related to the target language, thus in the generation process.

Indeed, the LIS4ALL translator adopts the architecture designed in the ATLAS project (Mazzei et al., 2013) with two essential changes. The first change is related to the analysis of the Italian sentences: the domain corpus shows that typical railway station messages have several prepositional phrases which pose hard problems to conventional natural language parsers. As a consequence, we developed a domain specific regular expressions parser. The second change is related to the semantic representation. In ATLAS a logic semantics was adopted, that was the input of an expert system micro-planner. In contrast, in LIS4ALL we adopt a simpler non-recursive filler/slot semantics. For parsing, we have built four regular expressions corresponding to the four most frequent classes in the domain corpus. For each class, we designed a set of semantic slots that can be filled by domain lexical items (time, rail number, station names, etc.). So, the role of the semantic interpreter is just to extract the semantics of these Italian domain lexical items, and to convert them into a format that can be realized in LIS domain lexical items. The translation consists essentially in converting the filler/slot semantics produced by the semantic interpreter into a logic format that can be exploited in generation. In Table 1 we reported an Italian message, its translation into LIS, and the filler/slot semantics produced by the semantic interpreter.

In Section 2 we give some details about the transfer process to transform the filler/slot semantics in hybrid logic semantics; in Section 3 we describe the implementation in a Combinatory Categorial Grammar (CCG) of a number of specific LIS linguistic phenomena. Finally, Section 4 closes the paper with some considerations.

ITA: Il treno Regionale 10220 di Trenitalia delle ore 05:35 proveniente da Cuneo arrivera con un ritardo previsto di 10 minuti .

LIS: TRENO REGIONALE NUMERO 1 0 2 2 0 TRENITALIA POSS ORE 5 35 MATTINA CUNEO VENIRE , RITARDO 10 MINUTI PREVISTO ARRIVARE FUT_DEVE

sem:
```
:type :A3
:numero "10220"
:impresa_ferroviaria "trainitaly"
:categoria "REGIONAL"
:località_di_provenienza "cuneo"
:ampm "morning"
:ora_arrivo "05:35"
:hh "5"
:mm "35"
:tempo_ritardo "10"
```

Table 1: An ITA/LIS sentence of the class A3 and its filler/slot semantics. GLOSSES are used to denote LIS signs. The underlined texts correspond to variable lexical items. Rough translation: *The regional train 10220 of Trenitalia arriving at 05:35am from Cuneo, will arrive with an expected delay of 10 minutes.*

2 Microplanning with XML transformations

Previous work on the symbolic translation of SL in rail stations domains adopted “video templates” for the generation side (Segouat and Braffort, 2009; Ebling, 2013). In contrast, our generator is more complex and adopts the standard pipeline architecture of the NLG (Reiter and Dale, 2000). The generator is composed by two elements: a template based microplanner and the OpenCCG realizer.

Following (Foster and White, 2004), we implemented a transformation based microplanner that is able to exploit the filler/slot structure produced by the semantic interpreter. The main idea is to recursively rewrite the semantics elements by using a number predefined XML templates. Four templates are used at the first stage to specify the main structures of the sentences plans, while seven templates are used at the second stage to specify the specific structures of a number of specific linguistic constructions, e.g. the rail number.

For the implementation of the microplanner we exploited the bidirectional nature of OpenCCG by adopting a bottom-up approach to build the XML templates. For each MAS class we choose an Italian sentence belonging to the class and we produce, with the help of a bilingual signer, the LIS translation of the sentence. In Table 1 we report the translation of a sentence belonging to the class A3 (delayed arrive).

By starting from the Italian/LIS translation of the sentence, we have followed four steps:

1. We have implemented the fragment of the grammar necessary to realize/parse the LIS sentence, i.e. to account the linguistic phenomena contained in the sentence (see Section 3).

2. We have obtained the hybrid logic formula expressing the linguistic meaning of the sentence by parsing the sentence.

3. We have modified the XML file containing the hybrid logic formula by introducing a number of *holes*. Each hole, implemented as a XML attribute, corresponds to a LIS lexical item. For instance, in the XML fragment

```
<diamond mode="SYN-NOUN-RMOD">
 <nom name="n4:number"/>
 <prop id="delay-amount" name="10"/>
</diamond>
```

   that is the linguistic meaning of the number 10 and that corresponds to the delay amount, we have introduced the hole "delay-amount". In this way, the XML processor will be able to rewrite the exact delay for all the sentences of the class A3.

4. We have designed a number of XML transformations in order to convert the filler/slot semantics produced by the interpreter to the corresponding logical formula. A single filler/slot semantic element will substitute the XML fragment corresponding to a single hole in the final logical formula.

So, in total we have designed a total amount of 11 XML transformations to account for all the filler/slot semantic elements of the four MAS classes. Note that some of these transformations are recursive. This is the case, for instance, of the train code: LIS signers realize the code with a sequence of digits rather than with a single number, as in Italian (see Table 1).

3 A CCG for LIS in rail stations

We have designed a new CCG for LIS in the rail stations domain starting from the CCG for LIS devised in ATLAS project (Mazzei et al., 2013).

SLs do not have adpositions and articles, and use pronouns and conjunctions in very specific ways (Brentani, 2010). As a consequence, a very challenging topic is the grammatical design of the modifiers. In contrast to vocal languages, where the modification of a noun with another noun is usually marked by adpositions, in SLs the proximity in the sentence is the only possible indicator of the modification[2]. Indeed, noun modifications occurs often in the the rail station domain: in the LIS sentence of Table 1 there are five noun $\leftarrow$ noun modifications, which are used to indicate train code (TRENO $\leftarrow$ NUMERO), train company (TRENO $\leftarrow$ TRENITALIA), scheduled time (TRENO $\leftarrow$ ORE), delay amount (TRENO $\leftarrow$ RITARDO). Our CCG design uses type-change for promoting a standard noun category (N) into a noun modifier category ($N\backslash N$). However, this design increases the ambiguity of the grammar, since a noun could be the modifier of all previous nouns. In order to mitigate the grammar ambiguity, we have enriched the noun category with a *type-change count* feature. The idea is to allow the modification of a noun only if this noun has not been obtained with another type-change. Formally:

$TC_1 : N_{tc_1} \rightarrow N_{tc_0}$
$TC_2 : N_{tc_1} \rightarrow N_{tc_0}\backslash N_{tc_0}$

In this way, the noun NUMERO cannot (1) be modified by the noun RITARDO, and in the same derivation (2) modify the noun TRENO. From another point of view, the introduction of the type-change count feature constrains the hybrid logic dependency structure to be flat.

Another well known problem related to modifiers is their realization order. Similar to vocal languages, SLs have strong pragmatic preferences for specific modifiers order. The symbolic and statistical nature of OpenCCG allows to manage this issue by using a probabilistic approach. Indeed, it is possible to associate probabilities over logically equivalent derivations by using a language model (White, 2005). In order to use this feature, we have built an "artificial" corpus of 50 LIS sentences by using the four most frequent MAS templates. By using this corpus, we have built a trigrams based model language that derives the most natural modifiers sequence.

[2]Spatial agreement is another indication of syntactic agreement (Wright, 2008; Mazzei et al., 2013), but we did not yet model this feature in the actual CCG for LIS.

Another grammar issue concerns the lexical semantics. OpenCCG organizes the lexical items in an ontological structure. In the implementation of the LIS grammar we have used the backbone of the DOLCE ontology (Masolo et al., 2002), i.e. the LIS lexical items ($\sim$120 signs) have been classified under the top level categories of DOLCE. For instance, the semantic category *rail* has been collocated as a child of the DOLCE category *non agentive physical object*.

Another specific feature of the LIS CCG lexicon concerns the lexicalization of some station names. Previous approaches to SL translation in the rail station domain propose to fingerspell the names of the secondary stations (Segouat and Braffort, 2009; Ebling, 2013), i.e. the station which do not have a well known name in the national Deaf community. In contrast, we propose to exploit the virtual nature of the avatar by producing a classifier sign that generate dynamically new lexical items. We distinguish two kinds of rail stations: (1) In the case of a well-known station, the avatar uses the sign adopted by the Deaf community; (2) In contrast, in the case of less known station, the avatar realizes a classifier sign indicating a wide board while the name of the station will appear in written Italian "centered on the board" (Figure 2). Note that we had to modify the lexicalization mechanism of OpenCCG with a workaround in order to implement this feature. Indeed OpenCCG assumes a "closed lexicon", i.e. assumes that the lexicon is a closed set completely specified in the grammar. We have introduced a post-processing lexical substitution procedure that replaces a generic sign for less known stations with the board sign, modified in real time with the name of the station. More details on the linguistic impact of the board sign are reported in (Geraci and Mazzei, 2013).

4 Summary and future work

We have described some issues related to the generation module of the symbolic translator from Italian to LIS designed in the LIS4ALL project. The main contribution of this paper is to show that the combination of a filler/slot semantics with a XML transformation-based microplanner is adequate to generate controlled domain languages.

A prototype of the translator has been implemented in *Clojure*[3], that is a functional programming language that works on the Java virtual machine. Clojure exploits the the widespread use of Java by allowing (1) to call efficiently external Java libraries, and (2) to deploy software on different machines. Indeed, in order to implement the template based microplanner, we have used the *Enlive* library[4], i.e. a selector based system primary designed for web templating. Moreover, the OpenCCG realizer has been natively called from the Clojure code.

[3]http://clojure.org

Figure 2: The sign for *Rebaudengo Fossata*, a less known station in Turin.

In the next future we plan to introduce in the generator the linguistic management of signing space since previous work have showed that CCG can compactly model this linguist feature (Wright, 2008; Mazzei et al., 2013).

Finally, we intend to evaluate the quality of our translator by using both task-based human evaluation (Mazzei et al., 2013) as well as metric-based automatic evaluation (Battaglino et al., 2015).

Acknowledgments

This work has been partially supported by the project LIS4ALL, partially funded by Regione Piemonte, Innovation Hub for ICT, 2011-2014, POR-FESR 07-13.

This work is dedicated to Leonardo Lesmo who substantially contributed to its realization.

References

Cristina Battaglino, Carlo Geraci, Vincenzo Lombardo, and Alessandro Mazzei. 2015. Prototyping and preliminary evaluation of sign language translation system in the railway domain. In *Universal Access in*

[4]https://github.com/cgrand/enlive

Human-Computer Interaction. Access to Interaction - 9th International Conference, UAHCI 2015, Held as Part of HCI International 2015, Los Angeles, CA, USA, August 2-7, 2015, Proceedings, Part II, pages 339–350.

Dana Brentani, editor. 2010. *Sign Languages*. Cambridge University Press.

Stephen Cox, Michael Lincoln, Judy Tryggvason, Melanie Nakisa, Mark Wells, Marcus Tutt, and Sanja Abbott. 2002. Tessa, a system to aid communication with deaf people. In *Proceedings of the fifth international ACM conference on Assistive technologies*, pages 205–212. ACM.

Sara Ebling. 2013. Evaluating a swiss german sign language avatar among the deaf community. In *Third International Symposium on Sign Language Translation and Avatar Technology*, October.

Mary Ellen Foster and Michael White. 2004. Techniques for text planning with XSLT. In *Proceedings of the Workshop on NLP and XML (NLPXML-2004): RDF/RDFS and OWL in Language Technology*, pages 1–8. Association for Computational Linguistics.

Carlo Geraci and Alessandro Mazzei. 2013. Last train to "rebaudengo fossano": The case of some names in avatar translation. In *Proceedings of the 6th Workshop on the Representation and Processing of Sign Languages*, pages 63–66.

W.John Hutchins and Harold L. Somer. 1992. *An Introduction to Machine Translation*. London: Academic Press.

Carlo Masolo, Stefano Borgo, Aldo Gangemi, Nicola Guarino, Alessandro Oltramari, and Luc Schneider. 2002. Wonder Web deliverable D17. The Wonder Web Library of Foundational Ontologies and the DOLCE Ontology. Technical Report D17, ISTC-CNR.

Alessandro Mazzei, Leonardo Lesmo, Cristina Battaglino, Mara Vendrame, and Monica Bucciarelli. 2013. Deep natural language processing for italian sign language translation. In *AI*IA 2013: Advances in Artificial Intelligence - XIIIth International Conference of the Italian Association for Artificial Intelligence, Turin, Italy, December 4-6, 2013. Proceedings*, pages 193–204.

E. Reiter and R. Dale. 2000. *Building Natural Language Generation Systems*. Studies in Natural Language Processing. Cambridge University Press.

Rete Ferroviaria Italiana RFI. 2011. *Manuale Annunci Sonori - MAS (http://www.rfi.it/cms-file/allegati/rfi/MAS.pdf)*. Rete Ferroviaria Italiana (RFI).

Rubén San-Segundo, Juan Manuel Montero, R Córdoba, Valentin Sama, F Fernández, LF D'Haro, Verónica López-Ludeña, D Sánchez, and A García. 2012. Design, development and field evaluation of a spanish into sign language translation system. *Pattern Analysis and Applications*, 15(2):203–224.

Jérémie Segouat and Annelies Braffort. 2009. Toward modeling sign language coarticulation. In *Gesture in Embodied Communication and Human-Computer Interaction, 8th International Gesture Workshop, GW 2009, Bielefeld, Germany, February 25-27, 2009, Revised Selected Papers*, pages 325–336.

Margriet Verlinden, Corrie Tijsseling, and Han Frowein. 2001. A signing avatar on the WWW. In *Gesture and Sign Languages in Human-Computer Interaction, International Gesture Workshop, GW 2001, London, UK, April 18-20, 2001, Revised Papers*, pages 169–172.

Michael White. 2005. Designing an Extensible API for Integrating Language Modeling and Realization. In *Proceedings of the Workshop on Software*, Software '05, pages 47–64, Stroudsburg, PA, USA. Association for Computational Linguistics.

Tony Wright. 2008. A combinatory categorial grammar of a fragment of american sign language. In *Proc. of the Texas Linguistics Society X Conference*. CSLI Publications.

Response Generation in Dialogue using a Tailored PCFG Parser

Caixia Yuan Xiaojie Wang Qianhui He
School of Computer Science
Beijing University of Posts and Telecommunications
{yuancx, xjwang}@bupt.edu.cn
alisonchinabupt@gmail.com

Abstract

This paper presents a parsing paradigm for natural language generation task, which learns a tailored probabilistic context-free grammar for encoding meaning representation (MR) and its corresponding natural language (NL) expression, then decodes and yields natural language sentences at the leaves of the optimal parsing tree for a target meaning representation. The major advantage of our method is that it does not require any prior knowledge of the MR syntax for training. We deployed our method in response generation for a Chinese spoken dialogue system, obtaining results comparable to a strong baseline both in terms of BLEU scores and human evaluation.

1 Introduction

Grammar based natural language generation (NLG) have received considerable attention over the past decade. Prior work has mainly focused on hand-crafted generation grammar (Reiter et al., 2005; Belz, 2008), which is extensive, but also expensive. Recent work automatically learns a probabilistic regular grammar describing Markov dependency among fields and word strings (Konstas and Lapata, 2012a, Konstas and Lapata, 2013), or extracts a tree adjoining grammar provided an alignment lexicon is available which projects the input semantic variables up the syntactic tree of their natural language expression (Gyawali and Gardent, 2014). Although it is a consensus that at a rather abstract level natural language generation can benefit a lot from its counterpart natural language understanding (NLU), the problem of leveraging NLU resources for NLG still leaves much room for investigation.

In this paper, we propose a purely data-driven natural language generation model which exploits a probabilistic context-free grammar (PCFG) parser to assist natural language generation. The basic idea underlying our method is that the generated sentence is licensed by a context-free-grammar, and thus can be deduced from a parsing tree which encodes hidden structural associations between meaning representation and its sentence expression. A tailored PCFG, i.e., a PCFG easily tailored to application-specific concepts, is learned from pairs of structured meaning representation and its natural language sentence and then used to guide generation processes for other previously unseen meaning representations. Table 1 exemplifies a record from the application under consideration.

Our model is closest to (Konstas and Lapata, 2012a) and (Konstas and Lapata, 2013) who reformulate the Markov structure between a meaning representation and a string of text depicted in (Liang, et al., 2009) into a set of CFG rewrite rules, and then deduce the best derivation tree for a database record. Although this Markov structure can capture a few elements of rudimentary syntax, it is essentially not linguistic grammars. Thus the sentences produced by this model are usually ungrammatically informed (for instance, its 1-BEST model produces grammatically illegal sentences like "Milwaukee Phoenix on Saturday on Saturday on Saturday on Saturday"). (Konstas and Lapata, 2013) claims that long range dependency is an efficient complementary to CFG grammar, and incorporates syntactic dependency between words into the reranking procedure to enhance the performance. Although conceptually similar, our model directly learns more grammatical rewrite rules from hybrid syntactic trees whose nonterminal nodes are comprised of phrasal nodes inheriting from a common syntactic parser, and conceptual nodes designed for encoding target meaning representation. Therefore, the learning aspect of two models is fundamentally different. We have a single CFG grammar that applies throughout, where-

Proceedings of the 15th European Workshop on Natural Language Generation (ENLG), pages 81–85,
Brighton, September 2015.

Table 1: Examples of meaning representation input as a structured database and its corresponding natural language expression. Each meaning representation has several fields, each field has a value.

Meaning representation	action1	object1	value11	value12	action2	object2	value21	value22
	confirm	person	100	120	request	date	null	null
Text	与会人数在100人到200人之间，请问您在哪天开会？(The number of participants is between 100 and 200. When is the meeting scheduled?)							

as they train different CFG grammar and dependency grammar respectively.

The major advantage of our approach is that it learns a tailored PCFGs directly from MR and NL pairs, without the need to manually define CFG derivations, which is one of the most important prerequisites in (Belz and Kow, 2009) and (Konstas and Lapata, 2013), and thus porting our method to another applications is relatively easy. We demonstrate the versatility and effectiveness of our method on response generation for a Chinese spoken dialogue system (SDS)[1].

2 Problem Formulation

2.1 The grammar

Following most previous works in this area (Liang, et al., 2009; Konstas and Lapata, 2013), we use the term record r to refer to a $(m,\ w)$ pair. Each meaning representation m is described as several fields f, each field has a value $f.v$. As exemplified in Table 1, each m in the referred SDS system has eight fields (e.g., action, object1, value11), each field has a specific value. The value can be a string (e.g., confirm, person), or a numeric quantity (e.g., 100, 120), or null. The text is simply a sequence of words $w = (w_1, ..., w_{|w|})$.

Our goal is to learn a PCFG for interpreting a MR using NL expression. In order to generate more coherent sentence, the established grammar should capture recursive structure of phrases. Meanwhile, in order to generate sentence expressing target meanings, the grammar should also capture concept embeddings corresponding to desired meaning fields. Under this framework, a tailored PCFG grammar we used for generation can be described as a 6-tuple:

$$G = \langle N_p, N_c, T, S, L, \lambda \rangle \quad (1)$$

where N_p is a finite set of non-terminal symbols produced by a common parser, N_c is a finite set of concept symbols related to specific record fields, T is a finite set of NL terminal symbols (words), $S \in N_p$ is a distinguished start symbol, L is a lexicon which consists of a finite set of production rules, and λ is a set of parameters that defines a probability distribution over derivations under G.

2.2 Grammar Induction

In this section, we present a learning procedure for the grammar described above. The input to the learning algorithm is a set of training sentences paired with their correct meaning representations (as illustrated in Table 1). The output from the learning algorithm is a PCFG describing both phrase and concept embeddings. The learning algorithm assumes that a common phrase structure parser is available, but it does not require any prior knowledge of the MR syntax.

As a concrete example, consider the record in Table 1. We first analyze its sentence expression using the Stanford parser (Chen and Manning, 2014) whose nonterminals are syntactic categories (e.g., NP, VP, JJ, NN). Figure 1(a) outlines the partial parser tree of sentence in Table 1. The meaning of the sentence is then integrated by adding conceptual symbols of its subparts into the parser tree. Figure 1(b) shows a hybrid parse tree of Figure 1(a). Here the nonterminal symbols in bold, PERSON, VAL1 and VAL2, represent domain-specific concepts corresponding to fields person, value1 and value2.

To get the hybrid parse tree, we first align phrases in the NL with the actual MR fields mentioned using the model of (Liang, et al., 2009) which is learned in an unsupervised manner using EM to produce which words in the text were spanned by the fields. The aligned pairs are recorded in a temporary table. Then for each phrase in the table, we find the minimal subtree spanning it, and modify its ancestor node attached directly below the subtree's root node to the conceptual symbol of its aligned field. All ancestor nodes keep unchanged for phrases not in the alignment table. The cen-

[1] A demo can be found at http://www.aidc.org.cn:8008/WebContent/

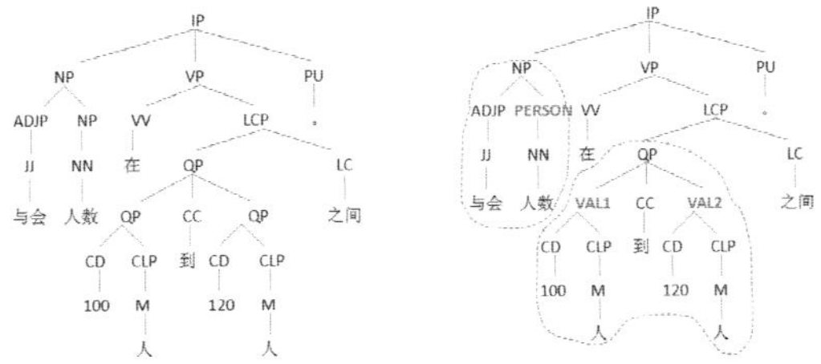

(a) (b)

Figure 1: Example of (a) a syntactic tree and (b) its corresponding hybrid tree from which the tailored PCFG defined in Formula (1) is constructed. The subtree circled by dotted line contains conceptual node and its terminal derivations.

tral characteristic of a tree structured representation is that component concept appears as a node in a tree, with its word realizations as terminal nodes derived by it. For example, the concept PERSON has a terminal node "人数", and VALUE1 "100人", these could then form part of the representation for the sentence "与会人数在100 人到200 人之间。(The number of participants is between 100 and 200.)" The use of a recursive hybrid syntactic and conceptual structure is one characteristic that distinguishes the proposed grammar from earlier work in which meaning is represented by logical forms or regular grammars (Lu and Ng, 2011; and Konstas and Lapata, 2013).

Given hybrid trees, N_p, N_c, T, S and the set of derivations that are possible are fixed, we only need to learn a probabilistic model parameterized by λ. Since the "correct" correspondence between NL words and MR fields is fully accessible, i.e., there is a single deterministic derivation associated with each training instance, model parameter λ can be directly estimated from the training corpus by counting. Because the derived trees output by parser can be noisy, we need to process them to obtain cleaner PCFG rules. We compare the 3-best trees produced by the Stanford Parser, and prune off the inconsistent components voted by majorities when extracting and counting rules.

2.3 Decoding

Our goal in decoding is to find the most probable sentence $\hat{s}$ for a given meaning expression m:

$$\hat{s} = g(\underset{D\ s.t.\ m(D)=m}{\operatorname{argmax}} P(D|G) \cdot \ln(|D|+1)) \quad (2)$$

where g is a function that takes as input a derivation tree D and returns $\hat{s}$, $m(D)$ refers to the meaning representation of a derivation D, and $P(D|G)$ is product of weights of the PCFG rules used in a derivation D, the factor $\ln(|D|+1)$, offers a way to compensate the output sentence length $|D|$. We use a decoding paradigm introduced in (Konstas and Lapata, 2013) which is essentially a bottom-up chart-parsing algorithm without forcing the input to exhibit linear structure. It first fills the diagonal cell of the chart with terminal words with the top scoring words emitted by the unary rules of the type $A \rightarrow \alpha$, where A is a non-terminal symbol, and α is a terminal word.

In order to search among exponentially many possible tree structures for a given MR, a k-best decoder is achieved by adding to the chart a list of the top k words and production rules, then an external language model is used to rerank the derived partial trees in a timely manner with cube pruning (Huang and Chiang, 2005).

3 Empirical Evaluation

We conducted experiments on a Chinese spoken dialogue system (SDS) for booking meeting room. Our NLG module receives structured input from dialogue management (DM) module and generates natural language response to user. The structured input includes dialogue actions (e.g., greet, request, confirm), objects (e.g., date, budget, location) and object values which can be a null. The SDS corpus consists of 1,406 formal meaning representations, along with their Chinese NL expressions written by 3 Chinese native speakers. The average sentence length for the example data is 15.7 Chinese words. We randomly select 1,000 record pairs as training data, and the remaining 406 is used as testing data.

To evaluate the quality of the generated sentences, the BLEU score (Papineni et al., 2002) is computed by comparing system-generated sentences with human-written sentences. In addition, we evaluated the generated text via a human judgment as designed in (Angeli et al., 2010). The subjects were presented with a MR and were asked to rate its corresponding NL expression along two dimensions: grammatical fluency and semantic correctness. A five point rating scale is designed where a higher number indicates better performance. The averaged score of three human evaluators was computed.

In order to compare our work with previous related work, Table 2 summarizes results achieved

Table 2: BLEU scores, and human ratings for syntactic fluency (SF) and semantic correctness (SC) of different systems.

system	BLEU	SF	SC
1-BEST-Konstas	9.32	2.29	1.94
k-BEST-Konstas	21.85	3.91	3.12
1-BEST-Our	30.88	4.36	3.95
k-BEST-Our	31.96	4.34	4.33
HUMAN	–	4.76	4.89

	action1	object1	vlue11	other fields
	confirm	place	北京	null
1-BEST-Konstas	会议在北京在北京(The meeing is in Beijing in Beijing)			
k-BEST-Konstas	地点在北京，在北京召开(The place is in beijing, take place in Beijing)			
1-BEST-Our	初步定在北京，好的(Scheduled in Beijing, alright)			
k-BEST-Our	会议将在北京召开，对吗(The meeting will be held in Beijing, right?)			

Figure 2: An example of generations produced by each of the four models.

using the proposed tailored PCFGs with that using the grammar described in (Konstas and Lapata, 2013). 1-BEST signifies results obtained from the basic decoder described in Section 2.3, and k-BEST is results of the k-best decoder reranked with a bigram language model. Here we set $k = 20$ without more fine-tuning work.

To make intensive comparisons, the length of the generated sentence is not restricted as a fixed number, while varying from 1 to a length of the longest sentence in the training data. The sentences with different length are overall sorted to obtain the 1-BEST and the k-BEST.

From Table 2, we find that differences in BLEU scores between 1-BEST-Konstas and 1-BEST-Our are statistically significant (9.32 vs. 30.88). Since the only difference between these two results is the grammar used, we have reason to justify that the tailored grammar learnt from the hybrid phrase-concept trees is superior for modeling NL and MR correspondence to that used in (Konstas and Lapata, 2013). It is interesting to notice that k-BEST-Konstas observes substantial increase in performance compared to 1-BEST-Konstas, while k-BEST-Our only achieves a slight increase compared to 1-BEST-Our. Statistical language model offers potentially significant advantages for the sequential Markov grammar as reported in (Konstas and Lapata, 2013), but it contributes little to the tailored PCFGs. This also verifies the robustness of the proposed method.

Table 2 also summarizes the human ratings for each system and the gold-standard human-authored sentences. From Table 2 we can observe that our method consistently produce good Chinese sentences in terms of both grammatical coherence and semantic soundness, which is consistent with the results of automatic evaluation. Another major advantage of our method over method of (Konstas and Lapata, 2013) is that it does not require any prior knowledge of the MR syntax for training. Therefore, transplanting our method to other NLG application is relatively easy.

Figure 2 shows the generations of the four models on an example. 1-BEST-Konstas is only able to form Markov but not grammatical associations. k-BEST-Konstas improves it by accounting for more possible associations, but errors are still made due to the lack of syntactic structure. 1-BEST-Our and k-BEST-Our remedies this. However, unexpected sentences are still produced in the cases of long rang correlation. For example, k-BEST-Our produced a sentence " 会议日期什么时候举行呢？(When is the meeting date held?)" which is a grammatically well-formed sentence but has poor fluency and meaning. As perceived in the work of syntactic parsing, PCFG is very difficult to capture long range dependency of word strings.

4 Conclusions

We have presented a PCFG-based natural language generation method. In particular, the method learns tailored PCFG rules from hybrid phrase-concept trees automatically augmented from the output of a common syntactic parser. A compelling advantage of the proposed method is that it does not rely on prior knowledge of the MR syntax for training. We have shown the competitive results in a Chinese spoken dialogue system. Future extensions include deploying more efficient decoding algorithms, and richer structural features to rerank the derivations.

Acknowledgments

This work was partially supported by Natural Science Foundation of China (No. 61202248, No. 61273365), Discipline Building Planing 111 Base Fund (No. B08004).

References

Gabor Angeli, Percy Liang, and Dan Klein. 2010. A Simple Domain-Independent Probabilistic Approach to Generation. In *Proceedings of the Conference on Empirical Methods in Natural Language Processing*, pp. 502-512, Cambridge, MA.

Ioannis Konstas and Mirella Lapata. 2013. A Global Model for Concept-to-Text Generation. *Journal of Artificial Intelligence Research*, 48(2013): 305-346.

Ioannis Konstas and Mirella Lapata. 2012a. Concept-to-Text Generation via Discriminative Reranking. In *Proceedings of the 50th Annual Meeting of the Association for Computational Linguistics: Human Language Technologies*, pp. 369-378, Jeju, South Korea.

Ioannis Konstas and Mirella Lapata. 2012b. Unsupervised Concept-to-text Generation with Hypergraphs. In *Proceedings of 2012 Conference of the North American Chapter of the of the ACL: Human Language Technologies*, pp.752-761, Montreal, Canada.

Liang Huang and David Chiang. 2005. Better K-best Parsing. In *Proceedings of the 9th Interna-tional Workshop on Parsing Technology*, pp. 53-64, Vancouver, British Columbia.

David Chiang. 2007. Hierarchical Phrase-Based Translation. *Computational Linguistics*, 33(2): 201-228.

Percy Liang, Michael I. Jordan, and Dan Klein. 2009. Learning Semantic Correspondences with Less Supervision. In *Proceedings of the Joint Conference of the 47th Annual Meeting of the ACL and the 4th International Joint Conference on Natural Language Processing of the AFNLP*, pp. 91-99, Suntec, Singapore.

Wei Lu and Hwee Tou Ng. 2011. A Probabilistic Forest-to-String Model for Language Generation from Typed Lambda Calculus Expressions. In *Proceedings of the 2011 Conference on Empirical Methods in Natural Language Processing*, pp. 1611-1622, Edinburgh, Scotland, UK.

Anja Belz. 2008. Automatic Generation of Weather Forecast Texts Using Comprehensive Probabilistic Generation-space Models. *Natural Language Engineering*, 14(4):431-455.

Anja Belz and Eric Kow. 2009. System Building Cost vs. Output Quality in Data-to-text Generation. In *Proceedings of the 12th European Workshop on Natural Language Generation*, pp. 16-24, Athens, Greece.

Danqi Chen and Christopher D. Manning. 2014. A Fast and Accurate Dependency Parser using Neural Networks. In *Proceedings of the 2014 Conference on Empirical Methods in Natural Language Processing*, pp. 740-750, Doha, Qatar.

Nathan McKinley and Soumya Ray. 2014. A Decision-Theoretic Approach to Natural Language Generation. In *Proceedings of the 52nd Annual Meeting of the Association for Computational Linguistics*, pp. 552-561, Baltimore, Maryland, USA.

Kishore Papineni, Salim Roukos, Todd Ward, and Wei-Jing Zhu 2002. BLEU: a Method for Automatic Evaluation of Machine Translation In *Proceedings of the 40th Annual Meeting of the Association for Computational Linguistics*, pp. 311-318. Philadelphia, PA.

Bikash Gyawali and Claire Gardent 2014. Surface Realisation from Knowledge-base. In *Proceedings of the 52nd Annual Meeting of the Association for Computational Linguistics*, pp. 424-434. Baltimore, Maryland.

Miguel Ballesteros, Bernd Bohnet, Simon Mille, and Leo Wanner. 2015. Data-driven Sentence Generation with Non-isomorphic Trees. In *Proceedings of the 2015 Annual Conference of the North American Chapter of the ACL*, pp. 387-397, Denver, Colorado.

Verena Rieser and Oliver Lemon. 2009. Natural Language Generation as Planning Under Uncertainty for Spoken Dialogue Systems. In *Proceedings of the 12th Conference of the European Chapter of the A-CL*, pp. 683-691, Athens, Greece

Yuk Wah Wong and Raymond J. Mooney. 2007. Generation by Inverting a Semantic Parser That Uses Statistical Machine Translation. In *Proceedings of the Human Language Technology and the Conference of the North American Chapter of the Association for Computational Linguis-tics*, pp. 172-179, Rochester, NY.

Ondrej Dusek and Filip Jurcicek. 2015. Training a Natural Language Generator from Unaligned Data. In *Proceedings of the 53rd Annual Meeting of the Association for Computational Linguistics and the 7th International Joint Conference on Natural Language Processing*, pp.410-419, Beijing, China.

Michael White and Rajakrishnan Rajkumar. 2009. Perceptron Reranking for CCG Realization. In *Proceedings of the 2009 Conference on EmpiricalMethods in Natural Language Processing*, pp.451-461, Suntec, Singapore.

Generating récit from sensor data: evaluation of a task model for story planning and preliminary experiments with GPS data

Belén A. Baez Miranda **Sybille Caffiau** **Catherine Garbay** **François Portet**
Univ. Grenoble Alpes, LIG, F-38000 Grenoble, France
FirstName.LastName@imag.fr

Abstract

Automatic story generation is the subject of a growing research effort which has mainly focused on fictional stories. In this paper, we present some preliminary work to generate récits (stories) from sensors data acquired during a ski sortie. In this approach, the story planning is performed using a task model that represents domain knowledge and sequential constraints between ski activities. To test the validity of the task model, a small-scale user evaluation was performed to compare the human perception of récit plans from hand written or automatically generated récits. This evaluation showed no difference in story plan identification adding credence to the eligibility of the task model for representing story plan in NLG. To go a step further, a basic NLG system to generate narrative from activities extracted from GPS data is also reported.

1 Introduction

Stories are a common construct used by humans to share their experience (with physicians, friends, relatives...) by which they tell what happened. In this paper, we focus on human activity stories that we call "activity récits" with the aim of generating these from real ambient data. According to (Adam, 2011), a *récit* is a set of events related to facts that have been effectively experienced, observed or captured. Our problem statement lays onto the narrative structure, the récit plan.

Computational Narratology (CN) is the study of narratives from the point of view of computation and information processing (Mani, 2013). Most of the current researches in CN are related to creativity, where the stories emerge from a set of predefined parameters, trying to imitate literary genres like fairy tales (Riedl and Young, 2010). However, we are interested in stories depicting human activity from real ambient data for which we have no control and little knowledge. In this paper, we focus on a ski touring application. Figure 1 shows an

10.00. awful weather, we went to Chamechaude, a usual destination in case of bad weather. In order to add some more climbing, we start 100 m below the Col de Porte, down the lift. The weather is not beautiful, objectively not very cold but we slip under a fine rain that freezes a bit. We climb quickly and we warm up quickly. Above the rain stopped and I even have the feeling it was too hot in the humid atmosphere! We took only a few breaks, and I do not remember having eaten or drunk anything [...] [Translated from French]

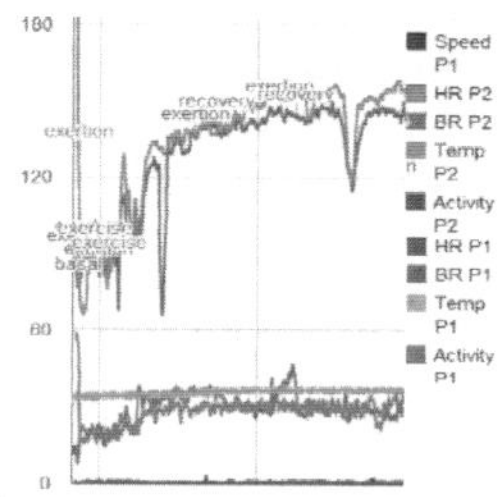

Figure 1: Example narrative and its corresponding raw data captured along a ski touring activity (two persons involved P1 and P2)

application to ski touring where skiers, alone or in groups, use special devices such as GPS (Global Positioning System), heart rate monitor, temperature etc. After their journey, they may share their experience, observations, and other evaluative elements (weather conditions, terrain and key places to visit) on websites such as www.skitour.fr.

The final goal of the research is to be able to generate a coherent and faithful story from the sensor raw data. In this paper, we present work about two research questions (among many others) linked to this final goal:

1. *What kind of model can ensure story representation and coherence? How can we evaluate it?*

2. *Is GPS data sufficient to generate initial stories?*

The first question has been partially studied in (Baez Miranda et al., 2014) where a task model approach was chosen to abstract and structure knowledge about a ski activity. However, this model was not evaluated. This paper thus reports an experiment in which the validity of the task model for récit plan, is evaluated by comparing the perception of the story plan using texts automatically generated from predefined task model instances (hand made) with human textual productions. This experiment is described in Section 2.

Proceedings of the 15th European Workshop on Natural Language Generation (ENLG), pages 86–89,
Brighton, September 2015. ©2015 Association for Computational Linguistics

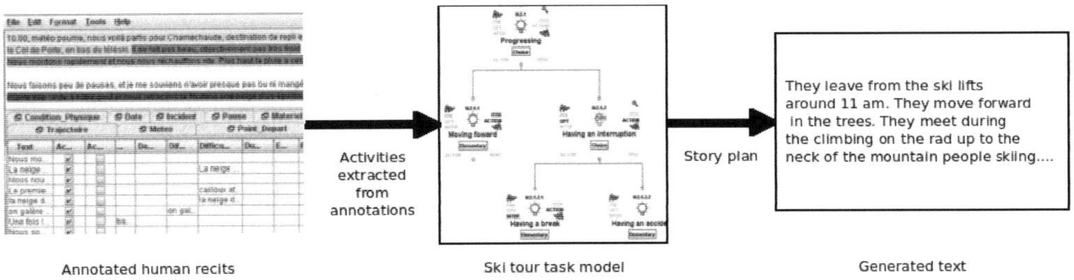

Figure 2: Steps for the récit generation for the task model evaluation.

The second question, though on a completely different aspect than the first one, is linked to an inherent problem in any system based on sensors. What kind of information can be inferred from them? Is this information sufficient? Since, ski touring corpus texts are mainly structured by the route, we report an initial basic data-to-text system that generates texts from GPS data in Section 3.

2 Evaluation of récit plan

To represent the story plan and cope with the precise case of human activity, we propose to use the notion of task model (Caffiau et al., 2010), which has been used previously by (Cavazza et al., 2002) for fictional but interactive stories. As presented in (Baez Miranda et al., 2014), this task model is core to our approach to story generation. In the approach, raw data is firstly captured and interpreted. The resulting interpretations are structured and linked together in a second step, according to the task model. One sequence of the task model is then identified as the story plan and used to drive the generation stage. This aim to result in an activity récit that emerges directly from the sensor data but is organised according to the task model expressing the human activity.

To evaluate the temporal perception of the récit, we followed the steps depicted in Figure 2. Several ski tour récits from www.skitour.fr were collected and annotated by the authors using a schema based on the task model. Then, the annotations were used as input to the task model. This story plan was then linearised into text using chronological order. Note, that to evaluate only the task model and to avoid side effect due to data processing, no raw data was used in this process. For more detail about the process, the reader is referred to (Baez Miranda et al., 2014).

18 French speakers (12 men and 6 women) aged between 19 and 38 were asked to rebuild chronological sequences of ski touring activities after reading separately three récits. The text selection was performed based on the text size, complexity of the ski touring sortie; clarity of the description of the sortie, linguistic quality, and finally the number of protagonists of the sortie and the level of expertise shown in the narration of the sortie. The duration of the experiment was 25 min in average. Each text was presented to each participant (within participants design) in either two versions, (i) the original human written one from the collected corpus of ski touring récits and (ii) the generated text based on the task model. The experiment consisted in sorting cards of basic activity into the sequence of the actual sortie using adhesive tape and a paper-made timeline. Once the reading was finished, the reader choose the cards corresponding to the events encountered in the text. Then, all the cards were arranged on the timeline according to the chronological order perceived during the lecture. The participants did not know whether the text presented was generated automatically or not.

The distance between the participant's answers and the reference story plan was computed using an edit distance similar to the Word Error Rate (WER). An ANOVA performed on the distance value showed a significant effect of text (human vs. computer) ($F(1,18) = 7.583$, $p=0.0131$). A participant effect was also found ($F(17,18)=2.281$, $p=0.0457$). Regarding the size of the participant's sequences, a difference between the human texts and the generated ones was found ($F(1,48) = 5.604$, $p = 0.022$) and a text effect ($F(1,18)=3.666$, $p=0.033$), that appears significant when the text is taken as factor. It seems thus that the generated texts induce significantly less errors during the activity identification than the original ones ($F(1,18)=8.993$, $p=0.00771$).

Regarding the distance, the generated texts present a chronological order more explicit and that may explain why participants were able to perceive easier the structure of the events sequence and to reconstruct the path. In human texts, the chronological order is more implicit because of the text configuration, which can include many satellite details or events omissions, like ellipses.

However, it could be possible to find that some activities were identified in the human texts but not

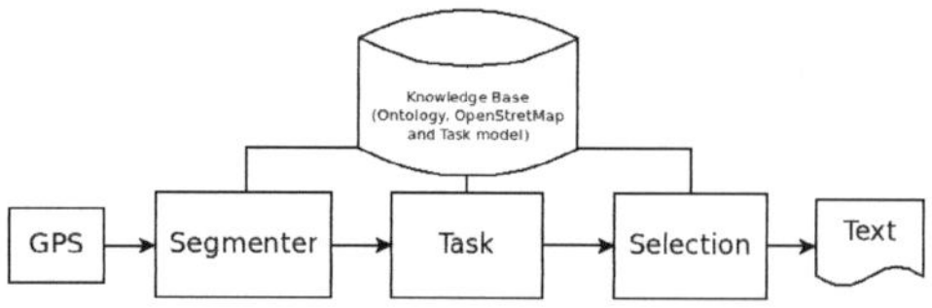

Figure 3: The basic GPS-to-récit system.

in the generated ones. This could be explained by many reasons, such as a possible lack of coverage during the task model construction; activities not identified during the corpus analysis or the fact that, due to the presence of ambiguity in human texts, the participants did not distinguish the activities correctly. Improvements in the task model and in the collection and analysis of the corpus would thus be needed in order to make the approach more robust.

These results show that task model is an eligible support to abstract activity events and structure then. In our approach, instances of task model (récit plan) emerge from ambient sensor data, in the next section, we present a preliminary experiment to extract human activities events (concrete tasks in task model) from GPS data.

3 Generating Récits from real data: The case of the GPS traces

In ski touring, the most important component of the story is the progress of the tour in the followed track. As a matter of fact, the goal of the sortie (e.g., peak, lake, col, etc.) is very often also the goal of the story, although other goals can be found in the human authored corpus (e.g., doing the sortie in the shortest time). The first step is thus to extract the movement and break activities.

To do so, a basic system sketched in Figure 3, has been designed to process the successive geographic localisations provided by a GPS device. First, GPS data from one sortie is temporally segmented based on the altitude. Then, these segments are abstracted into activities. The selection of activities is then performed using the task model so as to obtain a sequence of activities which is valid with respect to the model[1]. Then each activity of the sequence is lexicalised and a simple GRE is performed. Sentence planning is performed using rigid syntactic patterns which are unified with the lexicalised tasks and then realised as text.

3.1 Corpus collection

A small "parallel corpus" was formed through voluntary skiers, involving (i) acquired numerical data and (ii) narratives written by the skiers after their sortie. Physiological and actimetric data were specifically collected for this sortie using a smartphone running the RecordMe application (Blachon et al., 2014) and physiological sensors. These data involve time, location, altitude, heart and breath rate, etc. Extracts of numerical and textual data are shown in Figure 1. This corpus is composed of 5 records (three of which are of couple of skiers) but will grow in the near future.

3.2 Processing

The GPS segmentation consists in aggregating altitude points into segments of points that can be approximated by a straight line with a low amount of error. The Douglas-Peucker algorithm (Douglas and Peucker, 1973) was used for its simplicity. At the end of the process, a list of segments is obtained each of them being labelled as having either a `positive, null or negative` dénivelée[2]. All successive segments with the same dénivelée label are then merged.

Then, the segments are classified based on the average speed of the segment into 'ascending', 'moving forward', 'descending' or 'break'[3]. These segments populate an ontology (Baez Miranda et al., 2014) and are then enriched with links to the next and previous activities, the start and end time, the dénivelée, the average speed as well as the set of participants performing them.

Other important information is Point of Interest. These are encountered along the way (e.g., the Achard lake, the chairlift). These provide: first, an alternative description since ski tour sortie are rarely described by latitude and longitude but by using natural geographical description (See (Turner et al., 2010) for reference) ; second, subgoals to the récit structure since some POIs are main steps to reach the final goal. POI can be extracted using services such as OpenStreetMap which collects information about POI all over the world. For instance a query about the area of the 'Croix de Chamrousse' [4] gives the results presented in Figure 4. From this, every natural elements can be retrieved and associated to the tasks through co-occurrence links.

The abstraction of segments into tasks is for the moment very crude as it consists only of classification based on speed and slope (e.g., a speed of 15km/h in a descending segment is a 'descent' ski activity). Activity selection is then performed following the chronological order and the task model.

[1] Note that this selection is very crude at the moment since not all types of activity can be retrieved from the GPS data.

[2] a dénivelée is a difference in altitude between the starting point and the ending point

[3] 'ascending', 'moving forward', 'descending' are specific cases of the task 'moving forward'

[4] Chamrousse is a famous ski resort in the French Alps

```
<osm version="0.6" >
<node lat="45.1258501" lon="5.9025905">
 <tag k="ele" v="2253"/>
 <tag k="name" v="Croix de Chamrousse"/>
 <tag k="natural" v="peak"/></node>
<node lat="45.1255687" lon="5.9001744">
 <tag k="aerialway" v="pylon"/></node>
 ...
```

```
cat s
actor {P1,P2}
activity descent
locomotion_mode ski
goal {station}
source {Chamrousse_Peak}
time {10:21}
duration {22:32}
```

Figure 4: OpenStreetMap description and semantic representation

For each activity, if the addition of this activity to the set of selected activities makes a valid scenario wrt the model, the activity is added. In any case, the segments containing the main goal of the sortie and the start and end ones should be included into the set of selected activities.

Each activity is translated into a semantic frame. For instance, a descending activity for participant P1 can be represented by the structure in Figure 4. This structure is then matched to predefined set of syntactic structures which constrain lexical choices. The sentence could then be realised as "Departing from Chamrousse. At 08:16 P1 mounts to Col des 3 Fontaines during 1:52. At 10:08 he has a break to Croix de Chamrousse during 0:13 [...]". The realisation is performed using simpleNLG (Gatt and Reiter, 2009).

4 Future work

The project is at its initial phase and there are many improvements to perform. One of the most important task for the text generation part is to adopt a more structured approach to microplannification. We are working on re-implementing the micro-planner used in the BabyTalk project (Portet et al., 2009). On the macro-planner side, the reasoning must be more integrated so that a dynamic planning is performed and missing data is taken into account. An important challenge is to handle several narrative threads since several skiers can participate to the sortie. Regarding the data processing, the next step will be to include more signals such as physiological ones that can inform about the physiological state of the skier along the track (tired, resting, etc.). This will permit more adaptation of the output toward either sport-like récit (focusing on performance) or leisure one (focusing on where skiers have been).

On the coherence side, to improve and to produce a more natural text, we need to explore other aspects such as temporality. Currently, the story plan from the task model can produce a sequence of events linked in causal way by establishing preconditions and effects during the task model construction. However, this is not reflected in the generated texts. So, we need to add discourse connectors that indicate this causal links. Rendering simultaneous tasks is also an important feature to add to the model. The task model can express this, but it is not yet reflected in the generated text.

Finally, generating an activity récit from sensor data raises specific issues, in particular regarding the paucity of data. Inferencing and reasoning processes are then needed to cope with this lack of information and keep the récit consistent.

References

Jean-Michel Adam. 2011. *Genre de récits. Narrativité et généricité des textes*. Academia.

Belén A. Baez Miranda, Sybille Caffiau, Catherine Garbay, and François Portet. 2014. Task based model for récit generation from sensor data: an early experiment. In *5th International Workshop on Computational Models of Narrative*, pages 1–10.

David Blachon, François Portet, Laurent Besacier, and Stéphan Tassart. 2014. RecordMe: A Smartphone Application for Experimental Collections of Large Amount of Data Respecting Volunteer's Privacy. In *UCAmI 2014*, pages 345–348, Belfast, UK.

S Caffiau, D L Scapin, P Girard, M Baron, and F Jambon. 2010. Increasing the expressive power of task analysis: Systematic comparison and empirical assessment of tool-supported task models. *Interacting with Computers*, 22(6):569–593.

Marc Cavazza, Fred Charles, and Steven J. Mead. 2002. Character-based interactive storytelling. *IEEE Intelligent Systems*, 17(4):17–24.

David H Douglas and Thomas K Peucker. 1973. Algorithms for the reduction of the number of points required to represent a digitized line or its caricature. *Cartographica*, 10(2):112–122.

Albert Gatt and Ehud Reiter. 2009. Simplenlg: A realisation engine for practical applications. In *Proceedings of ENLG-2009*.

Inderjeet Mani. 2013. *Computational Modeling of Narrative*, volume 18. Morgan & Claypool.

François Portet, Ehud Reiter, Albert Gatt, Jim Hunter, Somayajulu Sripada, Yvonne Freer, and Cindy Sykes. 2009. Automatic generation of textual summaries from neonatal intensive care data. *Artificial Intelligence*, 173(7-8):789–816.

M. O. Riedl and R. M. Young. 2010. Narrative planning: Balancing plot and character. *Journal of Artificial Intelligence Research*, 39:217–268.

Ross Turner, Somayajulu Sripada, and Ehud Reiter. 2010. Generating approximate geographic descriptions. In *Empirical Methods in Natural Language Generation: Data-oriented Methods and Empirical Evaluation*, pages 121–140.

Generating and Evaluating Landmark-based Navigation Instructions in Virtual Environments

Amanda Cercas Curry
School of Mathematical and Computer Sciences
Heriot-Watt University
Edinburgh
ac293@hw.ac.uk

Dimitra Gkatzia
School of Mathematical and Computer Sciences
Heriot-Watt University
Edinburgh
d.gkatzia@hw.ac.uk

Verena Rieser
School of Mathematical and Computer Sciences
Heriot-Watt University
Edinburgh
v.t.rieser@hw.ac.uk

Abstract

Referring to landmarks has been identified to lead to improved navigation instructions. However, a previous corpus study suggests that human "wizards" also choose to refer to street names and generate user-centric instructions. In this paper, we conduct a task-based evaluation of two systems reflecting the wizards' behaviours and compare them against an improved version of previous landmark-based systems, which resorts to user-centric descriptions if the landmark is estimated to be invisible. We use the GRUVE virtual interactive environment for evaluation. We find that the improved system, which takes visibility into account, outperforms the corpus-based wizard strategies, however not significantly. We also show a significant effect of prior user knowledge, which suggests the usefulness of a user modelling approach.

1 Introduction

The task of generating successful navigation instructions has recently attracted increased attention from the dialogue and Natural Language Generation (NLG) communities, e.g. (Byron et al., 2007; Dethlefs and Cuayáhuitl, 2011; Janarthanam et al., 2012; Dräger and Koller, 2012) etc. Previous research suggests that landmark-based route instructions (e.g. "*Walk towards the Castle*") are in general preferable because they are easy to understand, e.g. (Millonig and Schechtner, 2007; Chan et al., 2012; Elias and Brenner, 2004; Hansen et al., 2006; Dräger and Koller, 2012). However, landmarks might not always be visible to the user. A recent corpus study by Cercas and Rieser (2014) on the MapTask and two Wizard-of-Oz corpora, Spacebook1 and Spacebook2,[1] empirically investigated the type of reference objects human instruction givers tend to choose under different viewpoints. It was found that human "wizards" do not always generate instructions based on landmarks, but also choose to refer to street names or generate user-centric instructions, such as "*Continue straight*".

This paper compares three alternative generation strategies for choosing possible reference objects: one system reflecting an improved version of a landmark-based policy, which will resort to a user-centric description if the landmark is not visible; and two systems reflecting the wizards' behaviours in Spacebook1 and Spacebook2. We hypothesise the first system will outperform the other two in terms of human-likeness and naturalness, as defined in Section 3. We use the GRUVE (Giving Route Instructions in Uncertain Virtual Environments) system (Janarthanam et al., 2012) to evaluate these alternatives.

2 Methodology

We designed two corpus-based strategies (System **B**, **C**) and one rule-based system based on a heuristic landmark selection algorithm (**A**). Also see examples in Table 1. Strategies for systems B and C aim to emulate the wizards' strategies dependent on different viewpoints: System B uses data from Spacebook1, where the wizard follows the user around, and thus, shares the viewpoint of the user. System C uses data from Spacebook2, where the wizard follows the user remotely on GoogleMaps via GPS tracking, and thus, street names are visible to the wizard, but only the approximate location is known.

- **System A: Landmark and User-centric** strategy reflects an improved version over

[1]The Spacebook data is freely available here: `http://www.macs.hw.ac.uk/ilabarchive/spacebook/login.php`

Proceedings of the 15th European Workshop on Natural Language Generation (ENLG), pages 90–94,
Brighton, September 2015.

Systems	Output
System A	"Keep going straight towards Farmfoods Ltd." (***landmark***)
System B	"Continue straight" (***user-centric***)
System C	"Keep walking along Nicholson Street"(***street name***)

Table 1: Example of user view on GoogleStreetMaps (left) and system outputs (right).

previous work, in that it mainly produces landmark-based instructions, but resorts to user-centric instructions when no landmarks are available (also see our landmark selection algorithm as described below). We also call this the *visibility* strategy.

- **System B: Spacebook1-based** strategy produces instructions using street names, landmarks and user-centric references in the same proportions as the wizards in Spacebook1. We also call this the *shared viewpoint* strategy.
- **System C: Spacebook2-based** strategy produces landmark-based and street name-based instructions as in Spacebook2. A landmark or a street name is selected based on a threshold on the landmark's salience (determined through trial and error). We also call this the *birds-eye* strategy.

All three strategies select landmarks based on landmark salience, following Götze and Boye (2013), using a heuristic based on (also see Figure 1): the distance between the landmark and the user, the distance between the user and the target, the angle formed by these two lines, the type of landmark and whether the landmark has a name. We adjusted this heuristic to match our system.

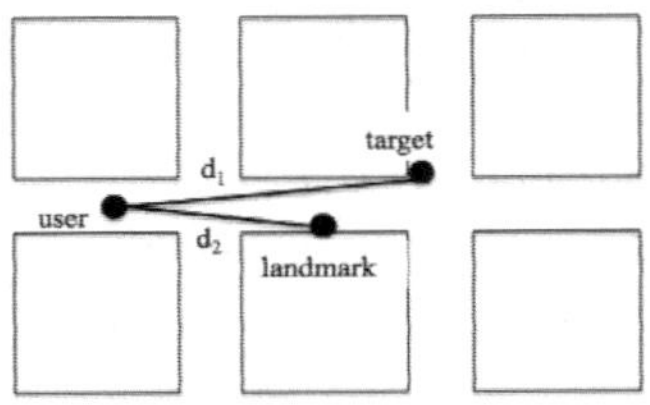

Figure 1: Spatial features used by landmark heuristic.

Note that GRUVE only provides information on static landmarks, e.g. shops, restaurants, banks, etc., available from GoogleMaps and Open Street Map. It does not identify moving objects, such as cars, as potential landmarks. In current work (Gkatzia et al., 2015), we investigate how to generate landmarks based on noisy output from object recognition systems.

3 Evaluation

3.1 Experimental Setup

We used the GRUVE virtual environment for evaluation. GRUVE uses Google StreetView to simulate instruction giving and following in an interactive, virtual environment, also see Table 1. We recruited 16 subjects, with an even split amongst males and females and age ranges between 20 and 56. Six users were not native English speakers.

Before the experiment, users were asked about their previous experience. After the experiment we asked them to rate all systems on a 4-point Likert scale regarding human-likeness and naturalness (where 1 was "Agree" and 4 was "Disagree"). *Human-likeness* is defined as an instruction that could have been produced by a human. *Naturalness* is defined as being easily understood by a human. The order of systems was randomised.

4 Results

In total we gathered 1071 navigation instructions. For evaluation, we compared a number of objective and subjective measures. The results are summarised below (also see Table 2) :

- **Task Completion:** The overall task completion rate (binary encoding) was 68.1%. System A was slightly more successful with a task completion rate of 80% compared to 62.5% for systems B and C, but this difference was not statistically significant (χ^2 test, p=.574).[2] However, a planned comparison for task completion time showed that users take longer when using System A compared to the two other systems, but again the difference between the systems was not found to be statistically significant (Mann-Whitney U-Test[3], p=.739 for System A vs. B, p=.283 for A vs. C, and p=.159 for C vs. B).

- **Human-likeness and Naturalness:** Furthermore, users tend to rate System A higher for human-likeness (χ^2, p=.185) and for naturalness (χ^2, p=.093) than system B and C, but again the difference was not statistically significant. We also observed the following mixed effects: Users tend to report the system to be more natural and human-like if they had managed to complete the task (χ^2, p=.002 and p=.000, respectively). This could be a reflection of user frustration, where users report the system to be less human-like if they are dissatisfied with the instructions provided.
- **Familiarity Effects:** We also observed the following effects of prior user knowledge: Ten users reported they were familiar with the location before the experiment. These users were significantly more likely to report that the instructions were accurate and of the correct length (χ^2, p=.037).

  In addition, users familiar with Google StreetView found the instructions to be significantly easier to follow (χ^2, p=.003), more accurate and more natural and human (χ^2, p=.021) compared to those with little or no experience. Only two users reported having no experience with Google StreetView, eight reported having a little experience and six reported being very familiar with it. These familiarity effects of prior knowledge suggest a user-modelling approach.

4.1 Discussion

The data shows an indication that System A is able to better support task completion, while being perceived more natural than Systems B and C. However, this trend is not significant. Table 3 shows an analysis of how often each system chose a reference object in our experiments. System A produces significantly more landmark-based descriptions than B and C (Mann-Whitney U-test for nonparametric data, p=.003 and p=.041 respectively). These results seem to confirm claims by prior work that landmark-based route instructions are in general preferable. In future work, we will compare our improved version, which also uses user-centric descriptions, with a vanilla landmark-based strategy in order to determine the added value of taking visibility into account.

Measure	objective		subjective	
Metric	compl. rate	compl. time	naturalness	human-likeness
Scale	binary	seconds	4-point Likert	
A	0.80	900.06	1.0	1.0
B	0.63	799.75	2.0	2.0
C	0.63	883.31	1.0	2.0

Table 2: Average results for objective (mean) and subjective (mode) measures.

System	landmark	user-centric	street name
System A	66.22	33.78	0
System B	61.54	23.50	14.96
System C	56.05	0	43.95

Table 3: Frequencies of reference objects chosen by each system.

4.2 User Comments and Qualitative Data

Users were asked to provide some additional comments at the end of the questionnaire. Overall, the subjects reported liking the use of landmarks like shops and restaurants. Users not familiar with the location found this less useful, particularly when the system referred to buildings that were not labelled on StreetView. For example, the location natives can easily identify the Surgeon's Hall in Edinburgh, but for those who are unfamiliar with the neighbourhood, the building is not so easily identifiable. Users also reported liking user-centric instructions as they are simple and concise, such as "Turn left". Some users reported they would like to know how far away they are from their destination. A few users also commented that the instructions could be repetitive along long routes.

Users reported the system used landmarks that

[2]Although the percentage difference seems large it is equivalent to only two subjects.

[3]We used the non-paramentric version of a t-test since the data was not normally distributed.

were not visible, whether because they were too far away or they were hidden by another building. There was no difference in the number of users reporting this for each system. This suggests the landmark-selection heuristic will require further adjustments, e.g adjusting the weights or limiting the search area. Users that were familiar with the location reported that although some of the landmarks presented were not visible, they were still helpful as the users knew where these landmarks were and could make their way to them. The use of landmarks that are not necessarily visible but are known to the instruction follower is common amongst human direction givers, using these landmarks as a starting point for further directions (Golledge, 1999). Again, these findings suggest the usefulness of a user modelling approach to landmark selection.

5 Conclusions and Future Work

This paper presented a task-driven evaluation of context-adaptive navigation instructions based on Wizard-of-Oz data. We found that a heuristic-based system, which uses landmarks and user-centric instructions dependent on estimated visibility, outperforms two corpus-based systems in terms of naturalness and task completion, however, these results were not significant. In future work, we hope to recruit more subjects in order to show statistical significance of this trend. Our results also show that there are significant familiarity effects based on prior user knowledge. This suggests a user modelling approach will be useful when it comes generating navigation instructions, e.g. following previous work on user modelling for NLG in interactive systems (Janarthanam and Lemon, 2014; Dethlefs et al., 2014). Finally, we hope to repeat this experiment under real-world conditions, rather than in a virtual setup in order to eliminate artefacts, such as the influence of technical problems.

Acknowledgements

This research received funding from the EPSRC GUI project - "Generation for Uncertain Information" (EP/L026775/1) and EPSRC DILiGENt - "Domain-Independent Language Generation" (EP/M005429/1).

We would like to thank Oliver Lemon for his helpful comments.

References

Donna Byron, Alexander Koller, Jon Oberlander, Laura Stoia, and Kristina Striegnitz. 2007. Generating Instructions in Virtual Environments (GIVE): A Challenge and an Evaluation Testbed for NLG. In *Workshop on Shared Tasks and Comparative Evaluation in Natural Language Generation.*

Edgar Chan, Oliver Baumann, Mark a Bellgrove, and Jason B Mattingley. 2012. From objects to landmarks: the function of visual location information in spatial navigation. *Frontiers in psychology*, 3:304, January.

Nina Dethlefs and Heriberto Cuayáhuitl. 2011. Combining hierarchical reinforcement learning and bayesian networks for natural language generation in situated dialogue. In *Proceedings of the 13th European Workshop on Natural Language Generation (ENLG).*

Nina Dethlefs, Heriberto Cuayáhuitl, Helen Hastie, Verena Rieser, and Oliver Lemon. 2014. Cluster-based prediction of user ratings for stylistic surface realisation. In *Proceedings of the 14th Conference of the European Chapter of the Association for Computational Linguistics*, pages 702–711. Association for Computational Linguistics.

Markus Dräger and Alexander Koller. 2012. Generation of landmark-based navigation instructions from open-source data. In *Proceedings of the Thirteenth Conference of the European Chapter of the ACL (EACL)*, Avignon.

Birgit Elias and Claus Brenner. 2004. Automatic Generation and Application of Landmarks in Navigation Data Sets. *Developments in Spatial Data Handling*, pages 469–480.

Dimitra Gkatzia, Verena Rieser, Phil Bartie, and William Mackaness. 2015. From the virtual to the real world: Referring to objects in spatial real-world images. In *Conference on Empirical Methods in Natural Language Processing (EMNLP)*, Lisbon. Forthcoming.

Reginald G Golledge. 1999. *Wayfinding behavior: cognitive mapping and other spatial processes*, volume 41.

Jana Götze and Johan Boye. 2013. Deriving Salience Models from Human Route Directions. In *Proceedings of the IWCS 2013 Workshop on Computational Models of Spatial Language Interpretation and Generation (CoSLI-3)*, pages 7–12, Potsdam, Germany. Association for Computational Linguistics.

Stefan Hansen, Kai-florian Richter, and Alexander Klippel. 2006. Landmarks in OpenLS - A Data Structure for Cognitive Ergonomic Route Directions. In *GIScience*, pages 128–144. Springer-Verlag, Berlin Heidelberg.

Srinivasan Janarthanam and Oliver Lemon. 2014. Adaptive Generation in Dialogue Systems Using Dynamic User Modeling. *Computational Linguistics*, 40(4):883–920.

Srinivasan Janarthanam, Oliver Lemon, and Xingkun Liu. 2012. A web-based evaluation framework for spatial instruction-giving systems. In *50th Annual Meeting of the Association for Computational Linguistics (ACL)*.

Alexandra Millonig and Katja Schechtner. 2007. Developing Landmark-Based Pedestrian-Navigation Systems. *IEEE Transactions on Intelligent Transportation Systems*, 8(1):43–49, March.

Verena Rieser and Amanda Cercas Curry. 2014. Towards Generating Route Instructions Uncer Uncertainty: A Corpus Study. In *SemDial'14*, Edinburgh.

Summarising Unreliable Data

Stephanie Inglis
Department of Computing Science
University of Aberdeen
r01si14@abdn.ac.uk

Abstract

Unreliable data is present in datasets, and is either ignored, acknowledged ad hoc, or undetected. This paper discusses data quality issues with a potential framework in mind to deal with them. Such a framework should be applied within data-to-text systems at the generation of text rather than being an afterthought. This paper also shows ways to express uncertainty through language and World Health Organisation (WHO) corpus studies, and an experiment which analyses how subjects approached summarising data with data quality issues. This work is still ongoing.

1 Introduction

Databases are used in multiple fields for various purposes. While gathering and using this data, issues arise regarding the quality of the data. These problems take multiple forms, and identifying them within a dataset can sometimes prove challenging or impossible (Daniel et al. 2008). Once identified, action needs to be taken. In a large database, amending all problem entries could be a costly task prone to human error, potentially creating more issues. Alternatively, it may not be possible to resolve the error. Either way, the user of the data must be informed of these errors if they are to use this data accurately.

Currently when companies use data to generate text, data quality issues are resolved ad hoc rather than during the generation phase. Instead, a framework should be created to deal with these issues at the point of generation, rather than amending the document if required.

First, we cover a discussion of related work followed by a corpus study of Ebola and Global Road Traffic reports provided by the WHO. An experiment is used to investigate further in Section 4. Finally we outline future steps.

2 Related Work

2.1 Data Quality

The quality of data impacts the amount of confidence we can have in our conclusions. By being aware of the issues within the data, we can begin to attempt resolution.

Daniel et al. (2008) discusses a system which aggregates reports in an attempt to improve the quality of reports hampered by poor quality data (see Figure 1). The data is acquired after summer from various sources such as hospitals, laboratories and emergency rooms. These reports are for the Italian Department of Health to predict the number drugs required over a winter period to treat flu, to prepare for outbreaks or to negotiate prices with manufacturers. Incorrect conclusions could result in overspending and the health department losing money, or not having enough drugs readily available for those who require them. The key problems are categorised as completeness, consistency and confidence issues. These are some issues likely to be missed by data cleaning tools.

Completeness covers missing data, which includes empty cells as well as entirely lost entries. This system ignores rows with the diagnosis field missing as these could result in false drug quantity estimations.

Consistency covers data that is not classified together but has the same meaning. The example entries in the paper show "influenza" and "flu" to be different diagnoses however they should be represented as the same. This can also occur through human error by mistypes which will also create a new, unwanted diagnosis e.g. "flu" being mistyped as "flyu". The precision of the diagnosis may result in additional entries such as including the type of flu of a patient. When ordering "influenza" drugs, underestimation may occur as "flu", "flyu" and "flu type A" may not be included in the count.

Thirdly, **confidence** shows how accurate data is. Rows may be fraudulent or erroneous leading to more incorrect estimations. Misinterpretations

Proceedings of the 15th European Workshop on Natural Language Generation (ENLG), pages 95–99,
Brighton, September 2015.

ID	Diagnosis	Hospital	Province	...	Problem	Action
1	Flu	San Raffaele	Milano	...	Refers to same therapy	Treat similarly
2	Influenza	Santa Clara	Trento	...		
3	Flyu	San Raffaele	Milano	...	Mistyped	Interpret as "Flu"

Figure 1 – Examples of poor data quality and the action taken to deal with it.

of variable meanings also present issues. The example shown in the paper is "cost" of the drug differing for the same diagnosis. This could be interpreted by some as with tax added, while others omitted it.

While this is more of a consistency issue, its interpretation impacts the confidence of the data. A proposed solution is to replace an ambiguous variable with a more general variable, such as adjusting cost to become maximum cost.

2.2 Vague Language

Another aspect to investigate is the language used when conveying unreliable data, such as numerical data. When the author is writing a report and is unsure of the data, language becomes vague to allow for uncertainty. The reader will see these words and intuitively know that the author is not certain about their conclusion.

Van Deemter (2010) claims something to be vague if "it allows borderline cases", and subsequently defined categories of vague language. Adjectives themselves are vague as they allow borderline. Vague quantifiers such as "many", "most" or "few also allow borderline cases. For lack of specificity, the term is not vague by definition but a concrete value is not provided, such as "more than 5". Comparatives use degrees of adjectives such as "30 is greater than 28". Finally, hedges express uncertainties by using words such as "appears", "suggests" or "may". This allows the author to make statements without committing to them as fact such as "numbers appear to be increasing".

This work looks at vagueness in the context of data quality issues as described above. For example, different vague language is used for missing data and inconsistent data.

2.3 Real World Applications

The use of vague language in low data quality situations is present in industry applications.

BT-Nurse is one application, generating handovers for nurses caring for pre-term neonates and sick babies (Hunter et al, 2012). The handover is generated at the end of a shift so the next nurse on the ward knows the babies current conditions. High data quality is important as the health of the babies depend on it. An example of incomplete data is when a baby is intubated, but an accurate time is not recorded. To try to correct this, the ventilator mode data is checked. When an estimation is present in the text, phrases such as "around 19:45" and "by about 06:15" were used.

Sripada et al. (2014) discuss a system able to generate 50,000 high quality weather reports in less than two minutes. This system is used by the Met Office to generate reports for public use. As these are predictions, the further away the forecast, the greater the uncertainty in the data. Therefore the reports on day 3 have different language compared to those reports on day 1. The paper shows this on practise where on day 3 the word "expected" is included, whereas this would be omitted if the forecast was for day 1. The use of vague language helps to convey this uncertainty.

3 WHO Ebola Reports

Information can be communicated through various mediums, ranging from visual graphs to sentences. The WHO[1] has followed the Ebola virus disease outbreak and provided detailed weekly reports and frequent updates on the situation. The reports used span from 29th August 2014 to 4th February 2015, containing 24 main weekly reports and 12 additional update reports. These reports contain a variety of tables, maps, graphs and sentences describing the number of suspected, probable and confirmed cases and deaths that have occurred in various countries as a result of the outbreak. The focus was primarily on the three most affected countries – Guinea, Liberia and Sierra Leone. An attempt was made to use the figures given in the tables to replicate sentences using the SimpleNLG (Gatt and Reiter, 2009) library. While doing so, the issues mentioned in section 2.1 arose.

[1] World Health Organisation, *Situation reports with epidemiological data: archive,* http://www.who.int/csr/disease/ebola/situation-reports/archive/en/ . Last accessed 23rd June 2015.

Country	Case definition	Cases	Deaths
Liberia	Confirmed	950	*
	Probable	1923	*
	Suspected	1376	*
	All	4249	2458

"Data acquisition continues to be a challenge in Liberia. Evidence obtained from responders and laboratory staff in the country suggests that the situation in Liberia is getting worse"

Figure 2- A data and textual example taken from the Situation Report on the 15th October 2014. This shows an instance of missing data in deaths reported in Liberia.

3.1 Data Quality

Incompleteness was largely evident in Liberia's data (see Figure 2). No data was given from report 4 to 20, covering almost 2 months. Throughout these reports, phrases such as "data acquisition continues to be a challenge" in report 14 can be found to describe Liberia's situation. Eventually, the data reached a quality so low that the same report quotes "problems with data gathering make it hard to draw any firm conclusions from recent data" whereas previously, WHO had at least speculated on trends in the data.

Inconsistencies exist between the numbers in the table and the text. Numbers were not mentioned explicitly in the text until around report 20. However, some vague statements appeared beforehand, such as "with over 200 new cases reported" on the 18th September. When numerical data was mentioned, it almost exclusively referred to the confirmed deaths. Data on Guinea was mostly inconsistent, with only 5 of the 26 reports being consistent between the tabular data and the textual data. One explanation is that reports were updated after publishing when late lab results were produced, but only for one layout.

Finally, there is evidence of lack of **confidence**. Data is incorrect in some situations, such as when the number of deaths exceeded the number of cases. This can be seen in report 12 on the 8th October, occurring in both Liberia and Sierra Leone. Identifying data that is inaccurate will lower the confidence.

3.2 Vague Language

The reports on Ebola have numerous examples of vague language being used.

Phrases such as "this is a genuine decline", "there may not yet be full agreement", and "based on the best information available" appeared frequently. The adjectives "genuine", "full" and "best" allow borderline cases, and so are vague. Therefore the phrases themselves are vague, and suggest this is more an opinion of the writer rather than fact. Vague quantifiers such as "many of the suspected cases", "there appears to be some evidence", and "very few confirmed cases were reported" also appeared often. Lack of specificity is rare but it does exist, for example "countries report that more than 80%". The main comparative phrase in these reports is "it is too soon to say". Finally, examples of hedges include phrases that include the words "appears", "suggests" or "may". These words are used in the majority of the reports such as "appears to have stabilised", "which suggests that many of the suspected cases", and "which may lead to a revision of the numbers of cases and deaths".

Vague language was strongly used to describe the data in the Ebola reports. To investigate this further, an experiment was done using data from a different report, described in the next section.

4 Pilot Study

4.1 Set Up

To investigate human language in describing unreliable data, subjects were asked to summarise tables of data (see Figure 3). The experiment makes use of the Global Road Traffic reports for 2009[2] and 2013[3] provided by the WHO. A new domain was selected to observe differences between this corpus and the Ebola corpus, though none are identified yet (see Future Work).

Subjects were asked to assume the role of a news reporter on Twitter and report information to followers. Due to Twitter constraints, subjects were restricted to only 140 characters per country. This forced subjects to be concise and to prioritise the information given to them.

For 6 of the 183 possible countries, the number of deaths reported by the police, the number of estimated deaths, and a 95% confidence interval

[2] World Health Organisation. (2009). Global status report on road safety 2009. Available: http://www.who.int/violence_injury_prevention/road_safety_status/2009/en/. Last accessed 23rd June 2015.

[3] World Health Organisation. (2013). Global status report on road safety 2013. Available: http://www.who.int/violence_injury_prevention/road_safety_status/2013/en/. Last accessed 4th June 2015.

were given. While the reported figures were provided by police data, the estimated deaths were produced by a model by the WHO, which applies negative binomial regression if the police data is less than 85% complete.

While the data was for real countries, they were renamed Country A to F to avoid bias. 22 subjects successfully completed the experiment, providing 132 tweets for analysis.

Country C

2007 Reported Deaths	2007 Estimated Deaths	95% Confidence Interval
105,725	196,445	155,727 - 266,999
2010 Reported Deaths	**2010 Estimated Deaths**	**95% Confidence Interval**
130,037	231,027	*Not reported*

Subject 1

In 2010, there were 130,037 deaths reported of an estimated 231,027, up from 2007, when 105,725 deaths were reported out of 196,445.

Figure 3- An example of stimulus used in the experiment taken from the reports, and an example of a tweet given.

4.2 Findings

To evaluate the tweets, they were annotated by the first author to identify the different techniques subjects used to report information. These were:

- If the exact police or WHO numbers were used
- If a description of the numbers was used i.e. "around 300 deaths"
- If a trend in the data was mentioned
- If data quality was mentioned
- If opinions were given

No second annotator was present. The example in Figure 3 was annotated as police numbers, WHO numbers and a trend ("up from 2007").

As this is a pilot study, further study is needed to improve confidence in these findings. It was found that different subjects used different techniques ($p<0.001$ for police numbers, WHO numbers, Descriptions and Opinions, $p=0.007$ for trends using Pearson Chi-Squared). The only instance this did not apply to was data quality indicating subjects used this technique in a similar way. If data quality was mentioned by subjects, they were likely to add an opinion ($p=0.02$, Pearson Chi-Squared).

If data was **incomplete**, the quality of data was more significantly likely to be mentioned ($p<0.001$, Pearson Chi-Squared), as well as more specifically that missing data was the quality issue ($p<0.001$, Pearson Chi-Squared).

Unlike incomplete data, subjects were not significantly more likely to mention data quality if data was **inconsistent** ($p=0.157$, Pearson Chi-Squared). However, when data was consistent, subjects were likely to acknowledge this ($p<0.001$, Pearson Chi-Squared). Subjects were also significantly likely to mention trends when the data was consistent ($p=0.01$, Pearson Chi-Squared).

As there was no indication of how **confident** we could be in the data, there was no way to investigate if subjects' tweets correlated with the actual accuracy of the data. An observation however was that only one of the 16 mentions of confidence was positive. The remaining 15 were unconfident in the data.

Another notable result was trends and descriptions were correlated, and were used as a pairing in 53 of the 75 instances that either trends or descriptions appeared ($p<0.001$, Pearson Chi-Squared).

Of the 132 tweets, only one directly mentioned the confidence interval, so this element of the experiment was discarded.

5 Future Work

Analysis of the vague language used in the experiment tweets will be done, as well as language comparisons between the two WHO corpuses used in this paper. Further experiments will be conducted using mechanical turk. One will use 20 countries and 150 subjects while another will give 75 subjects only reported figures and a further 75 subjects only estimated figures to provide a base line for the first experiment. These will concentrate on the findings from the initial experiment. Another potential experiment will give subjects text and investigate if they can identify present data quality issues. The increase in results should allow a deeper analysis. After analysing the results and undertaking further research into more low quality datasets, a framework will be developed and generated text will be evaluated by human subjects. Improvements will be made to the framework based on the feedback of subjects.

References

Daniel, F., Casati, F., Palpanas, T., Chayka, O. and Cappiello, C. (2008). Enabling Better Decisions Through Quality-Aware Reports In Business Intelligence Applications.

Gatt, A. and Reiter, E. (2009). SimpleNLG: A realisation engine for practical applications. Proceedings of ENLG-2009

Hunter, J., Freer, Y., Gatt, A., Reiter, E., Sripada, S. and Sykes, C. (2012). Automatic generation of natural language nursing shift summaries in neonatal intensive care: BT-Nurse. Artificial Intelligence in Medicine, 56(3), pp.157–172.

Sripada, S.G., Burnett, N., Turner, R., Mastin, J., and Evans, D. (2014). A Case Study: NLG meeting Weather Industry Demand for Quality and Quantity of Textual Weather Forecasts. INLG 2014.p1-5.

Van Deemter, K. (2010), Not Exactly: In Praise of Vagueness, Oxford University Press, Oxford, GBR.

Generating Descriptions of Spatial Relations between Objects in Images

Adrian Muscat
Communications & Computer Engineering
University of Malta
Msida MSD 2080, Malta
adrian.muscat@um.edu.mt

Anja Belz
Computing, Engineering & Maths
University of Brighton
Lewes Road, Brighton BN2 4GJ, UK
a.s.belz@brighton.ac.uk

Abstract

We investigate the task of predicting prepositions that can be used to describe the spatial relationships between pairs of objects depicted in images. We explore the extent to which such spatial prepositions can be predicted from (a) language information, (b) visual information, and (c) combinations of the two. In this paper we describe the dataset of object pairs and prepositions we have created, and report first results for predicting prepositions for object pairs, using a Naive Bayes framework. The features we use include object class labels and geometrical features computed from object bounding boxes. We evaluate the results in terms of accuracy against human-selected prepositions.

1 Introduction

The task we investigate is predicting the prepositions that can be used to describe the spatial relationships between pairs of objects in images. This is not the same as inferring the actual 3-D real-world spatial relationships between objects, but has some similarities with that task. This is an important subtask in automatic image description (which is important not just for assistive technology, but also for applications such as text-based querying of image databases), but it is rarely addressed as a subtask in its own right. If an image description method produces spatial prepositions it tends to be as a side-effect of the overall method (Mitchell et al., 2012; Kulkarni et al., 2013), or else relationships are not between objects, but e.g. between objects and the 'scene' (Yang et al., 2011). An example of preposition selection as a separate sub-task is Elliott & Keller (2013) where the mapping is hard-wired manually.

Our main data source is a corpus of images (Everingham et al., 2010) in which objects have been annotated with rectangular bounding boxes and object class labels. For a subset of 1,000 of the images we also have five human-created descriptions of the whole image (Rashtchian et al., 2010).

We collected additional annotations for the images (Section 2.3) which list, for each object pair, a set of prepositions that have been selected by human annotators as correctly describing the spatial relationship between the given object pair.

The aim is to create models for the mapping from image, bounding boxes and labels to spatial prepositions as indicated in Figure 1. In this we use a range of features to represent object pairs, computed from image, bounding boxes and labels. We investigate the predictive power of different types of features within a Naive Bayes framework (Section 3), and report first results in terms of two measures of accuracy (Section 4).

2 Data

2.1 VOC'08

The PASCAL VOC 2008 Shared Task Competition (VOC'08) data consists of 8,776 images and 20,739 objects in 20 object classes (Everingham et al., 2010). In each image, every object belonging to one of the 20 VOC'08 object classes is annotated with its object class label and a bounding box (among other annotations):

1. *class*: one of: aeroplane, bird, bicycle, boat, bottle, bus, car, cat, chair, cow, dining table, dog, horse, motorbike, person, potted plant, sheep, sofa, train, tv/monitor.
2. *bounding box*: an axis-aligned bounding box surrounding the extent of the object visible in the image.

2.2 VOC'08 1K

Using Mechanical Turk, Rashtchian et al. (2010) collected five descriptions each for 1,000 VOC'08 images selected randomly but ensuring there were

Proceedings of the 15th European Workshop on Natural Language Generation (ENLG), pages 100–104,
Brighton, September 2015. ©2015 Association for Computational Linguistics

$\longrightarrow$ beside(person(Obj_1), person(Obj_2));
beside(person(Obj_2), dog(Obj_3));
in_front_of(dog(Obj_3), person(Obj_1))

Figure 1: Image from PASCAL VOC 2008 with annotations, and prepositions representing spatial relationships (objects numbered in descending order of size of area of bounding box).

50 images in each of the 20 VOC'08 object classes. Turkers had to have high hit rates and pass a language competence test before creating descriptions, leading to relatively high quality.

We obtained a set of candidate prepositions from the VOC'08 1K dataset as follows. We parsed the 5,000 descriptions with the Stanford Parser version 3.5.2[1] with the PCFG model, extracted the nmod:*prep* prepositional modifier relations, and manually removed the non-spatial ones. This gave us the following set of 38 prepositions:

$\mathbf{V}$ = { *about, above, across, against, along, alongside, around, at, atop, behind, below, beneath, beside, beyond, by, close_to, far_from, in, in_front_of, inside, inside_of, near, next_to, on, on_top_of, opposite, outside, outside_of, over, past, through, toward, towards, under, underneath, up, upon, within* }

2.3 Human-Selected Spatial Prepositions

We are in the process of extending the VOC'08 annotations with human-selected spatial prepositions associated with pairs of objects in images. So far we have collected spatial prepositions for object pairs in images that have exactly two objects annotated (1,020). Annotators were presented with images from the dataset where in each image presentation the two objects, Obj_1 and Obj_2, were shown with their bounding boxes and labels. If there was more than one object of the same class, then the labels were shown with subscript indices (where objects are numbered in order of decreasing size of area of bounding box).

Next to the image was shown the template sentence "The Obj_1 is ___ the Obj_2", and the list of possible prepositions extracted from VOC 1K (see preceding section). The option 'NONE' was also available in case none of the prepositions was suitable (participants were discouraged from using it).

Each template sentence was presented twice, with the objects once in each order, "The Obj_1 is ___ the Obj_2" and "The Obj_2 is ___ the Obj_1".[2] Participants were asked to select all correct prepositions for each pair.

The following table shows occurrence counts for the 10 most frequent object labels:

person	dog	car	chair	horse	cat	bird	bicycle	motorbike	tv/monitor
783	123	112	92	92	88	86	79	77	63

Some prepositions were selected far more frequently than others; the top nine are:

next_to	beside	near	close_to	in_front_of	behind	on	on_top_of	underneath
304	211	156	149	141	129	115	103	90

3 Predicting Prepositions

When looking at a 2-D image, people infer all kinds of information not present in the pixel grid on the basis of their practice mapping 2-D information to 3-D spaces, and their real-world knowledge about the properties of different types of objects. In our research we are interested in the extent to which prepositions can be predicted without any real-world knowledge, using just features that can be computed from the objects' bounding boxes and labels. In this section we explore the predictive power of language and visual features within a Naive Bayes framework:

[1]http://nlp.stanford.edu/software/lex-parser.shtml

[2]Showing objects in both orders is necessary to capture non-reflexive prepositions such as *under, in, on* etc.

$$P(v_j|\mathbf{F}) \propto P(v_j)P(\mathbf{F}|v_j) \quad (1)$$

where $v_j \in \mathbf{V}$ are the possible prepositions, and $\mathbf{F}$ is the feature vector. Below we look at the predictive power of the prior model and the likelihood model as well as the complete model.

3.1 Prior Model

The prior model captures the probabilities of prepositions given ordered pairs of object labels L_s, L_o, where the normalised probabilities are obtained through a frequency count on the training set, using add-one smoothing. We then simply construe the model as a classifier to give us the most likely preposition v_{OL}:

$$v_{OL} = \underset{v \in \mathbf{V}}{argmax} \; P(v_j|L_s, L_o) \quad (2)$$

where v_j is a preposition in the set of prepositions $\mathbf{V}$, and L_s and L_o are the object class labels of the first and second objects.

3.2 Likelihood Model

The likelihood model is based on a set of six geometric features computed from the image size and bounding boxes:

- F_1: Area of Obj_1 (Bounding Box 1) normalized by Image size.
- F_2: Area of Obj_2 (Bounding Box 2) normalized by Image Size.
- F_3: Ratio of area of Obj_1 to area of Obj_2.
- F_4: Distance between bounding box centroids normalized by object sizes.
- F_5: Area of overlap of bounding boxes normalized by the smaller bounding box.
- F_6: Position of Obj_1 relative to Obj_2.

F_1 to F_5 are real valued features, whereas F_6 is a categorical variable over four values (N, S, E, W). For each preposition, the probability distributions for each feature is estimated from the training set. The distributions for F_1 to F_4 are modelled with a Gaussian function, F_5 with a clipped polynomial function, and F_6 with a discrete distribution. The maximum likelihood model, which can also be derived from the naive Bayes model described in the next section by choosing a uniform $P(v)$ function, is given by:

$$v_{ML} = \underset{v \in \mathbf{V}}{argmax} \; \prod_{i=1}^{6} P(F_i|v_j) \quad (3)$$

3.3 Naive Bayes Model

The naive Bayes classifier is derived from the maximum-a-posteriori Bayesian model, with the assumption that the features are conditionally independent. A direct application of Bayes' rule gives the classifier based on the posterior probability distribution as follows:

$$\begin{aligned} v_{NB} &= \underset{v \in \mathbf{V}}{argmax} \; P(v_j|F_1, ...F_6, L_s, L_o) \\ &= \underset{v \in \mathbf{V}}{argmax} \; P(v_j|L_s, L_o) \prod_{i=1}^{6} P(F_i|v_j) \end{aligned} \quad (4)$$

Intuitively, $P(v_j|L_s, L_o)$ weights the likelihood with the prior or *state of nature* probabilities.

4 Results

The current data set comprises 1,000 images, each labelled with one or more prepositions. The average prepositions per image over the whole dataset is 2.01. For training purposes, we create a separate training instance (Obj_s, Obj_o, v) for each preposition v selected by our human annotators for the given object pair Obj_s, Obj_o.

The models are evaluated with leave-one-out cross-validation, and two methods (Acc_A and Acc_B) of calculating accuracy (the percentage of instances for which a correct output is returned). The notation e.g. $Acc_A(1..n)$ is used to indicate that in this version of the evaluation method at least one of the top n most likely outputs (prepositions) returned by the model needs to match the (set of) human-selected reference preposition(s) for the model output to count as correct.

4.1 Accuracy method A

$Acc_A(1..n)$ returns the proportion of times that at least one of the top n prepositions returned by a model for an ordered object pair is in the complete set of human-selected prepositions for the same object pair. Acc_A can be seen as a system-level Precision measure. The table below shows $Acc_A(1)$ and $Acc_A(1..2)$ results for the three models:

Model	$Acc_A(1)$	$Acc_A^{Syn}(1)$	$Acc_A(1..2)$
v_{OL}	34.4%	43.9%	46.1%
v_{ML}	30.9%	35.6%	46.2%
v_{NB}	51.0%	57.2%	64.5%

Table 1: $Acc_B(1..n)$ for v_{NB} model and $n \leq 4$.

Preposition	$n=1$	$n=2$	$n=3$	$n=4$
next to	23.0%	77.0%	89.8%	93.1%
beside	58.3%	81.5%	85.8%	91.9%
near	43.6%	55.1%	74.4%	82.7%
close to	4.7%	14.8%	51.7%	87.9%
in front of	29.1%	39.7%	48.2%	52.5%
behind	31.0%	38.0%	50.4%	73.6%
on	72.2%	83.5%	85.2%	86.1%
on top of	10.7%	76.7%	81.6%	82.5%
underneath	53.3%	68.9%	84.4%	86.7%
beneath	15.5%	73.8%	79.8%	85.7%
far from	44.6%	62.2%	66.2%	68.9%
under	22.1%	27.9%	82.4%	83.8%
NONE	34.4%	53.1%	67.2%	73.4%
Mean	34.0%	57.9%	72.8%	80.7%
Mean Acc_B^{Syn}	50.9%	66.4%	77.9%	83.1%

In addition, the middle column above shows $Acc_A(1)$ results when sets of synonymous prepositions are considered identical. The synonym sets we chose for this purpose are: {*above, over*}, {*along, alongside*}, {*atop, upon, on, on_top_of*}, {*below, beneath*}, {*beside, by, next_to*}, {*beyond, past*}, {*close_to, near*}, {*in, inside, inside_of, within*} {*outside, outside_of*}, {*toward, towards*}, {*under, underneath*}.

4.2 Accuracy method B

$Acc_B(1..n)$ computes the mean of preposition-level accuracies. Accuracy for each preposition v is the proportion of times that v is returned as one of the top n prepositions out of those cases when v is in the human-selected set of reference prepositions. Acc_B can be seen as a preposition-level Recall measure.

Table 1 lists the $Acc_B(1..n)$ values for the v_{NB} model for each n up to 4; values are shown for the 13 most frequent prepositions (in order of frequency) and for the mean of all preposition-level accuracies. The last row shows the means for a version of Acc_B that takes synonyms into account as described in the last section.

5 Discussion

Looking at the naive Bayes results in Table 1, accuracy for some prepositions (e.g. *close to*) improves dramatically from $Acc_B(1)$ to $Acc_B(1..4)$. This implies that where the target preposition is not ranked first, it is often ranked second, third or fourth. There are synonym effects at work as shown by the Acc^{Syn} results; but there also is competition between prepositions that are not near synonyms, as shown by the fact that $Acc_A(1..2)$ results are better than $Acc_A^{Syn}(1)$ results.

For some prepositions, accuracy remains low even at n=4. This may reflect the general issue that human annotators use two different perspectives in selecting prepositions: (i) that of a viewer looking at the image, and (ii) that of one or both of the objects involved in the spatial relationship being described. Regarding (i), e.g. in the image in Figure 1, the dog is 'in front of' the person because it is between the viewer and the person. Regarding (ii), in other examples, a person can be 'in front of' a monitor, or one chair 'opposite' another, even when the viewer sees them both from the side.

The naive Bayes framework we have investigated here is a simple approach which is likely to be outperformed by more sophisticated ML methods. E.g. in calculating the likelihood term $P(F|v)$, our approach assumes the features to be independent; feature weighting per preposition was not carried out; and the data set is small relative to what we are using it for.

6 Conclusion

We have described (i) a dataset we are developing in which object pairs are annotated with prepositions that describe their spatial relationship, and (ii) methods for automatically predicting such prepositions on the basis of features computed from image and object geometry and object class labels. We have found that on the basis of language information (object class labels) alone we can predict prepositions with 34.4% accuracy, rising to 43.9% if we count near synonyms as correct. Using both language and visual information we can predict prepositions with 51% accuracy, rising to 57.2% with near synonyms. We have also found that where the target preposition is not ranked top, it is often ranked very near the top, as can be seen from the Acc_B results.

The next step in this research will be to increase our dataset and to apply machine learning methods such as support vector machines and neural networks to our learning task.

References

Desmond Elliott and Frank Keller. 2013. Image description using visual dependency representations. In *EMNLP'13*, pages 1292–1302.

Mark Everingham, Luc Van Gool, Christopher KI Williams, John Winn, and Andrew Zisserman. 2010. The pascal visual object classes (voc) challenge. *International journal of computer vision*, 88(2):303–338.

Gaurav Kulkarni, Visruth Premraj, Vicente Ordonez, Sudipta Dhar, Siming Li, Yejin Choi, Alexander C Berg, and Tamara Berg. 2013. Babytalk: Understanding and generating simple image descriptions. *Pattern Analysis and Machine Intelligence, IEEE Transactions on*, 35(12):2891–2903.

Margaret Mitchell, Xufeng Han, Jesse Dodge, Alyssa Mensch, Amit Goyal, Alex Berg, Kota Yamaguchi, Tamara Berg, Karl Stratos, and Hal Daum Iii. 2012. Midge: Generating image descriptions from computer vision detections. In *Proceedings of EACL'12*.

Cyrus Rashtchian, Peter Young, Micah Hodosh, and Julia Hockenmaier. 2010. Collecting image annotations using amazon's mechanical turk. In *Proceedings of the NAACL HLT 2010 Workshop on Creating Speech and Language Data with Amazon's Mechanical Turk*, pages 139–147. Association for Computational Linguistics.

Yezhou Yang, Ching Lik Teo, Hal Daumé III, and Yiannis Aloimonos. 2011. Corpus-guided sentence generation of natural images. In *Proceedings of the Conference on Empirical Methods in Natural Language Processing*, pages 444–454. Association for Computational Linguistics.

Towards Flexible, Small-Domain Surface Generation: Combining Data-Driven and Grammatical Approaches

Andrea Fischer, †Vera Demberg, and Dietrich Klakow
Spoken Language Systems / † MMCI Cluster of Excellence
Saarland University
Saarbrücken, Germany
afischer@lsv.uni-saarland.de / vera@coli.uni-saarland.de
dietrich.klakow@lsv.uni-saarland.de

Abstract

As dialog systems are getting more and more ubiquitous, there is an increasing number of application domains for natural language generation, and generation objectives are getting more diverse (e.g., generating informationally dense vs. less complex utterances, as a function of target user and usage situation). Flexible generation is difficult and labour-intensive with traditional template-based generation systems, while fully data-driven approaches may lead to less grammatical output, particularly if the measures used for generation objectives are correlated with measures of grammaticality. We here explore the combination of a data-driven approach with two very simple automatic grammar induction methods, basing its implementation on OpenCCG.

1 Introduction & Related Work

As language-operated interactive devices become increasingly ubiquitous, there is an increasing need for not only generating utterances that are comprehensible and convey the intended meaning, but language that is adaptive to different users as well as situations (see also (Dethlefs, 2014) for an overview). Adaptation can happen at different levels, concerning content as well as the formulation of generated sentences. We here focus only on sentence formulation with the goal of being able to automatically generate a large variety of different realisations of a given semantic representation. Our study explores the combination of a data-driven approach (Mairesse et al., 2010) with a grammar-based approach using OpenCCG (White et al., 2007).

The use of templates is a common and well-performing approach to natural language generation. Usually, either the generation process consists of selecting appropriate fillers for manually-built patterns, or the semantic specification constrains the allowable surface constructions so strongly that it effectively constitutes a form of template as well. While such approaches do guarantee grammaticality when templates (or grammars, respectively) are well-designed, the amount of formulation variation that can be generated based on templates is either very low, or requires a huge manual effort in template creation.

One relevant objective in adapting to a user and a situation is utterance complexity. (Demberg et al., 2011) show that a dialog system that generates more concise (but also more complex) utterances is preferred in a setting where the user can fully concentrate on the interaction, while a system that generates less complex utterances is preferred in a dual tasking setting while the user has to steer a car (in a simulator) at the same time. But how do we know which utterance is a "complex" one? We can draw on psycholinguistic models of human sentence processing difficulty, such as dependency locality theory (measuring dependency lengths within the sentence; longer dependencies are more difficult), information density (measuring surprisal – the amount of information conveyed in a certain time unit; a higher rate of information per time unit is more difficult) or words-per-concept (how many words are used to convey a concept).

In this paper, we focus on the measure of *information density*, which uses the information-theoretic measure of surprisal (Hale, 2001; Levy, 2008), as well as the ratio of concepts per words. Our aim is to flexibly generate utterances that differ in information density, producing high-density and low-density formulations for the same underlying semantic representation. We evaluate different parametrisations of our approach by evaluating how many different high vs. low density utterances can be generated. We additionally present judgments from human evaluators rating both grammaticality and meaningfulness.

We collect a small corpus of utterances from the target domain and have them annotated by naive participants with a very shallow notion of semantics, inspired by (Mairesse et al., 2010). We then parse the sentences and automatically create typed templates. During generation, these typed templates are then combined into new unseen sentences, covering also previously unobserved semantic combinations. Generation flexibility in this approach depends entirely on the crowd-sourced domain corpus. Our approach is related to (DeVault et al., 2008), who automatically induce a tree-adjoining-grammar for the Doctor Perez domain.

Our system is realised using OpenCCG. Currently, we disallow cross composition and type raising and thus employ Categorial Grammar as the underlying model.

Proceedings of the 15th European Workshop on Natural Language Generation (ENLG), pages 105–108,
Brighton, September 2015.

2 Data

Our data consists of 247 German-language utterances informing about movie screenings. Each utterance may inform about the aspects: movie title, director, actor, genre, screen date and time, cinema, ticket price, and the screened version. They were collected from native speakers of German via crowd-sourcing. For this, we generated random semantic requests and elicited realisations for them from native speakers. The obtained surfaces were then annotated by different persons. Annotation follows (Mairesse et al., 2010)'s semantic stack scheme with a slight modification: instead of allowing multiple instances of one semantic value stack, we explicitly mark alternatives as shown.

Am	4.	und am	5. Juli	wird
date inform	07-04-2015 date inform	alternative date inform	07-05-2015 alternative date inform	inform

Titanic	mit	Leonardo DiCaprio	gezeigt .
titanic title inform	actor inform	Leonardo DiCaprio actor inform	inform

Figure 1: Data example from our domain.

We focus on the 117 unique requests with only positive (”inform”) stacks, disregarding negative (”reject”) data for now. We have a total of 158 sentences realising these 117 entries. We use 75% of our data as training set and 25% as development set. As test set, we construct 200 additional requests for which we do not elicit example sentences. All sets contain roughly equal amounts of each semantic aspect.

3 Our Approach

Based on the annotated sentences, our goal is to automatically populate a lexicon of multi-word units such that these units express a specific attribute from our domain and can be combined with other lexicon entries into a grammatically correct structure. We cannot solely rely on shallow language models for grammaticality (as Mairesse does) as the language model scores may be correlated with output from other objective measures. Specifically, one of our measures of grammatical complexity, surprisal, is often estimated based on n-gram models. Hence, when seeking to optimise for short utterances with high surprisal, we might end up only selecting highly ungrammatical utterances.
To avoid issues, we decided to explore whether the data-driven approach can be combined with a grammar-based approach. We automatically parse all training data with a dependency parser (we use the dependency parser from the *mate-tools* toolkit, based on (Bohnet, 2010)), and build a categorial grammar based on these parses. The resulting automatically-learned domain-specific lexicon can then be used for generation with OpenCCG. Our approach can hence be thought of as a very naive way of grammar induction.
The dependency parse gives us information about heads and their dependents, which allows us to construct categorial grammar categories. However, we do not know from the automatic parse which dependents are arguments vs. modifiers. We here explore two simple approaches:

In the **all-arguments (arg)** style, we build a CG type that produces exactly the encountered configuration of immediate dominance and linear precedence. This means that we assume all dependents to be arguments of their governing head. We arbitrarily choose to consume the arguments on the *right* of heads first, followed by those on the left.

In the **all-modifiers (mod)** style, we treat all dependents D as modifiers of their head H. Thus, we construct a CG type modifying H's type from each pair (H, d) where $d \in D$.

For both flavours, we use part-of-speech tags as basic types. For now, we forego any additional constraints. Clearly this means that our grammars overgenerate. Our goal here in this paper is to explore the extent to which we are able to generate a large amount of linguistic variants and the extent to which these are considered "good" by human comprehenders.
The modifier-only approach is less constrained than the argument-only variant, which should lead to more variety and lower grammaticality.

3.1 Request Semantics

In our approach, each word is considered to be either semantically informative or semantically void. It is semantically informative if it is a word or placeholder for a certain information type. For instance, "ACTOR" is the placeholder for an actor's name, and the noun "Originalversion" indicates that a movie is shown in its original version. All other words are considered to be semantically void and called *padding*.
In this setting, a request specifies only the semantic stacks to be conveyed plus the amount of *padding* to use. Note that using more *padding* biases the generation process towards more verbose formulations.
Additionally we assign a special semantic representation (”VERB”) to verb types. This is done to focus the search on full sentences instead of accepting arbitrarily complex noun phrases as complete answers to requests.

3.2 Sub-Tree Merging

As our requests are structure-agnostic, the search space always contains all words potentially usable for a request irrespective of compatibility with each other.
In order to alleviate the arising problem of search space size, we merge words that often co-occur into larger entries in the lexicon. We do this as follows: adjacent heads and dependents are merged if they do not both contain semantic information. As an example, a semantically informative adjective (such as "untertitelte"="subtitled") cannot merge with a noun head if the latter contains semantic information it-

self (as "Abenteuerfilm"="adventure movie" does). However, if the head is semantically void (such as "Film"="movie"), the two words are combined into one lexicon entry "untertitelte_Film" with the semantic assignment "version=subtitled". This reduces the search space and speeds up search greatly.

We implement two slightly different versions of this. In the first, verbs are exempt from merging. In the second, verbs may be merged with *padding* words, resulting in longer "VERB" chunks. One may expect this to result in slightly increased grammaticality.

4 Experimental Setup

We build four grammars from data: two argument-only (A1, A2) and two modifier-only grammars (M1, M2). In A1 and M1, verbs are exempt from merging, in A2 and M2, verbs are merged with surrounding padding words as described in 3.2.

4.1 Manually-Constructed Grammar

Additionally, we construct a small grammar G manually. In G, we also do not make use of type raising nor cross composition, but we employ features to enforce both congruence on linguistic features and thematic fit between e.g. verbs and nouns (e.g. only a price or a movie may be assigned a cost, but not a director). G models the most common structures used in the original data and contains most of the vocabulary used therein.

4.2 Search Timeout

We determine the search timeout to use in each generation request from the development set. Figure 2 shows achieved development set coverages in dependency of OpenCCG search timeouts. In this experiment, we use a *padding* of 5, as this is the maximal *padding* encountered in data. Our search is thus calibrated on the most complex utterance(s) in the data.

After roughly three hours, most of the grammars have achieved saturation satisfactorily well. We set the timeout to three and a half hours for our main experiments.

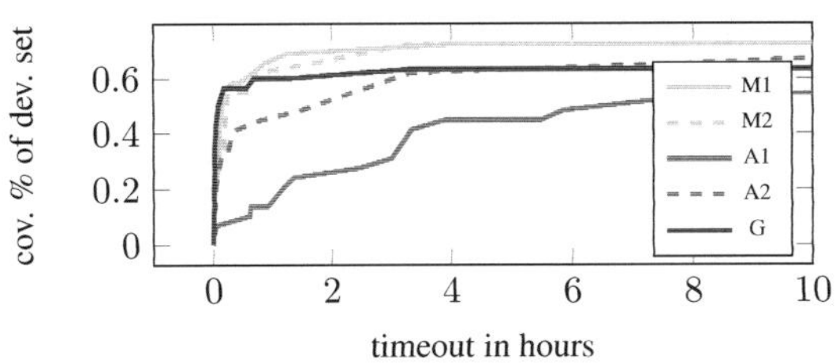

Figure 2: Dev. set coverage vs. search timeout in hours.

4.3 Language Model for Perplexity Evaluation

We train a simple Kneser-Ney smoothed trigram on our training data, which we use in order to pre-select candidates for further evaluation.

4.4 Main Generation Experiment

After training and timeout selection, we automatically generated 200 semantic requests, each consisting of 2 to 8 semantic stacks, and generated realisations for each semantic request by each of our grammars. We do this six times in total, varying the number of padding semantics P between 0 and 5.

We then select one short and one long sentence per semantic request from each grammar's output. We pick the sentence with the lowest language model perplexity from the 25% longest and 25% shortest sentences, respectively, selecting 1540 sentences.

5 Results

5.1 Test Set Coverage

Table 1 below shows the number of test semantics that each grammar is able to produce results for, grouped by the *padding* they contain (cf. 4.4).

Every other row indicates cumulative coverages, i.e., the number of covered semantics when using up to that many *padding* words, giving an impression of the coverage increments when using more *padding* words.

P	0	1	2	3	4	5
A1	89%	0%	**84%**	71%	51%	18%
$\sum$A1	90%	90%	90%	90%	90%	90%
A2	**89%**	0%	78%	52%	26%	12%
$\sum$A2	89%	89%	89%	89%	89%	89%
M1	44%	13%	73%	67%	52%	14%
$\sum$M1	44%	57%	76%	77%	79%	79%
M2	44%	14%	77%	**75%**	**68%**	**78%**
$\sum$M2	44%	58%	78%	79%	81%	81%
G	11%	**25%**	45%	44%	44%	44%
$\sum$G	11%	36%	45%	45%	45%	45%

Table 1: Test set coverage depending on request *padding* amount P. A1: arg/POS/verbmerge, A2: arg/POS/fullmerge, M1, M2: mod grammars. G: manually-created CCG. Coverages listed with *padding* $= P$ and *padding* $\leq P$ ($\sum$). Best indiv. cov. in bold.

The argument-only grammars achieve highest overall coverage, while the manual grammar achieves the worst coverage. In the arg grammars, using more *padding* deteriorates coverage. This is likely due to search space size increasing. The mod grammars fail to piece together short sentences.

5.2 Grammar Evaluation

In Table 2 we report language model perplexities (PP), parse scores from Stanford Parser, percentages of selected sentences parseable by the German Grammar HPSG, and average human ratings (1=worst, 5=best) of grammaticality and meaningfulness. Annotators agreed exactly in 44%, and differed by no more than 1 in 75.8% of cases. PCFG scores are inconclusive. G performs best except for in perplexity, which we believe is due to G overrepresenting unusual formulations

	misc			grammat.		meaning.	
	PP	PCFG	HP	mean	std	mean	std
A1	**12.69**	-113.57	0.36	3.62	1.24	3.52	1.38
A2	15.00	-128.11	0.45	3.14	1.38	3.11	1.48
M1	19.57	**-111.74**	0.07	1.97	0.94	2.04	**1.03**
M2	25.78	-113.99	0.02	1.80	0.91	2.03	1.13
G	51.79	-124.17	**0.66**	**4.34**	**0.87**	**4.30**	**1.03**

Table 2: Average values rounded to two decimal points. "S": avg. sentence surprisal. "PCFG": mean PCFG parse score. "HP": fraction parseable with HPSG.

as well as the fact that correct use of long-range dependencies leads to local increases in perplexity when the trigram horizon fails to adequately capture the dependency. G has consistently high output quality as evidenced by its small standard deviation of human ratings. The modifier-only grammars consistently perform worst. Both their fraction of HPSG-parseable sentences and human-perceived grammaticality are very low. The argument-only grammars perform fairly well, but do not quite reach up to the manually-written grammar. Their high standard deviation points towards a mix of high-quality and low-quality outputs. Notet that higher HPSG parseability does not necessarily imply higher human ratings. We believe this is due to correct, but confusing or unnatural stacking of attributions.

5.3 Information Density Variation

We plot the distributions of trigram perplexity at sentence level and those of the concepts-per-words ID measure. On both metrics, G is the most variable grammar. We positively note that A1 and A2's CPW range is comparable to that of G. The mod grammars construct more verbose, less informative formulations as evidenced by their lower CPW mean. Perplexity-wise, the arg grammars and mod grammars are very similar. The mod grammars have slightly higher mean perplexities, which – as the CPW plot evidences – does not necessarily indicate a lower ID variability. Rather, we believe this to be a simple reflection of lower local coherence which also diminishes the mod grammars' human ratings. G's extreme perplexity range can be explained by a tendency to overrepresent unlikely formulations. Given the human ratings of the grammars, we interpret the discrepancy between the arg grammars and G to point to a slightly narrower range of correct formulations in A1 and A2.

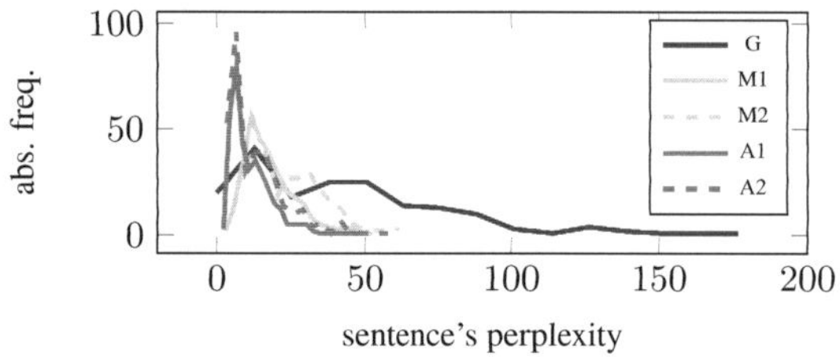

Figure 3: Perplexity distributions for grammars.

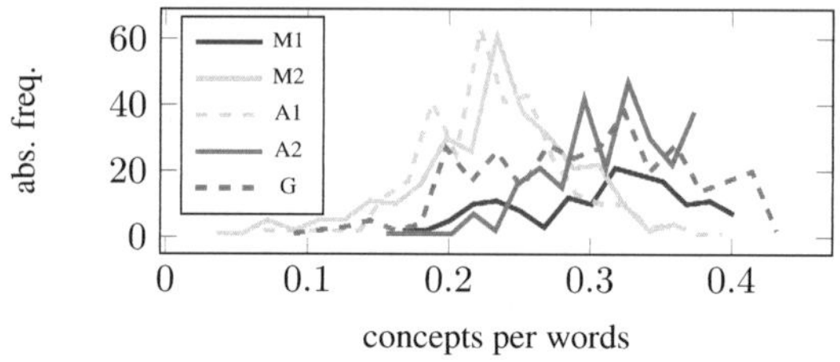

Figure 4: Concepts-per-words distributions for grammars.

6 Conclusion & Future Work

We have presented a simple, effective approach to grammar-based generation using Categorial Grammar as underlying formalism. The argument grammars in particular are able to reproduce the hand-written grammar's range of output variability well while achieving drastically better coverage.
Further work should concentrate on search efficiency, improving the quality of output, and further broadening the coverage of the induced grammars. The first point might be addressed by applying search heuristics which e.g. include the compatibility of elements with each other. We expect coverage, correctness, and variability to greatly benefit from constructing both argument and modifier types within the same grammar.

References

Bernd Bohnet. 2010. Very high accuracy and fast dependency parsing is not a contradiction. In *COLING '10*.

Vera Demberg, Andi Winterboer, and Johanna D. Moore. 2011. A strategy for information presentation in spoken dialog systems.

Nina Dethlefs. 2014. Context-sensitive natural language generation: From knowledge-driven to data-driven techniques.

David DeVault, David Traum, and Ron Artstein. 2008. Making Grammar-Based Generation Easier to Deploy in Dialogue Systems. In *SIGdial 2008*.

John Hale. 2001. A probabilistic earley parser as a psycholinguistic model. In *NAACL HLT 2001*.

Roger Levy. 2008. Expectation-based syntactic comprehension.

François Mairesse, Milica Gašić, Filip Jurčíček, Simon Keizer, Blaise Thomson, Kai Yu, and Steve Young. 2010. Phrase-based statistical language generation using graphical models and active learning. In *ACL 2010*.

Michael White, Rajakrishnan Rajkumar, and Scott Martin. 2007. Towards broad coverage surface realization with ccg. In *UCNLG+MT 2007*.

JSrealB: A bilingual text realizer for web programming

Paul Molins, Guy Lapalme
RALI
Informatique et recherche opérationnelle
Université de Montréal
CP 6128, Succ. Centre-Ville
Montréal, Québec, Canada H3C 3J7
udem@paul-molins.fr, lapalme@iro.umontreal.ca

Abstract

JSrealB is an English and French text realizer written in JavaScript to ease its integration in web applications. The realization engine is mainly rule-based. Table driven rules are defined for inflection and algorithmic propagation rules, for agreements. It allows its user to build a variety of French and English expressions and sentences from a single specification to produce dynamic output depending on the content of a web page.

Natural language generation can automate a significant part of textual production, only requiring a human to supply some important aspects and thus saving considerable time for producing consistent grammatically correct output. In recent years, tools such as SimpleNLG (Gatt and Reiter, 2009) facilitated text realization by a programmer provided they program their application in Java. This system was then extended with SimpleNLG-EnFr (Vaudry and Lapalme, 2013), a English-French version of SimpleNLG.

Another approach to text realization is JSreal (Daoust and Lapalme, 2014), a French Web realizer written in JavaScript. This paper describes an attempt at combining the ideas of SimpleNLG-EnFr and JSreal to produce a bilingual realizer for French and English from a single specification. JSrealB generates well-formed expressions and sentences. It can be used standalone for linguistic demonstrations or be integrated into complex text generation projects. But like JSreal, it is aimed at web developers, from taking care of morphology, declension and conjugation to creating well-formed texts. A web programmer who wishes to use JSrealB to produce flexible English and/or French textual or HTML output only needs to add two lines in the page: one for importing program and one for calling JSrealB loader to load the resources (i.e. lexicon and rules).

The principles underlying JSrealB are similar to those of SimpleNLG: programming language instructions create data structures corresponding to the constituents of the sentence to be produced. Once the data structure (a tree) is built in memory, it is traversed to produce the list of tokens of the sentence. This data structure is built by function calls whose names are the same as the symbols usually used for classical syntax trees: for example, `N` to create a *noun* structure, `NP` for a *Noun Phrase*, `V` for a *Verb*, `D` for a *determiner*, `S` for a *Sentence* and so on. Features added to the structures using the dot notation can modify the values according to what is intended.

JSrealB syntactic representation is patterned after classical constituent grammar notations. For example,

```
S(NP(D("a"),N("woman")).n("p"),
  VP("eat").t("ps"))
```

is the JSrealB specification for *The women ate*. Plural is indicated with feature `n("p")` where `n` indicates *number* and `p` *plural*. The verb is conjugated to past tense indicated by the feature tense `t` and value `ps`. Agreement between `NP` and `VP` is performed automatically.

French and English are languages whose structures are similar. Both languages use the same alphabet, they are both fusional languages sharing a similar conjugation system and their word order follows the same basic Subject-Verb-Object paradigm (Shoebottom, 1996). But structural differences do exist: e.g. the position of adjectives differs and rules for gender and number agreement differ for nouns and pronoun between these languages.

These differences must be taken into account at many levels. First, syntactic differences and agreements (i.e. features propagation), must be handled at the phrase or sentence level by

Proceedings of the 15th European Workshop on Natural Language Generation (ENLG), pages 109–111,
Brighton, September 2015. ©2015 Association for Computational Linguistics

algorithms. For French complex rules, we followed "Le bon usage, grammaire française" (Grevisse, 1980). For English, we relied on various sources from the web.

JSrealB lexicons are based on the ones found in SimpleNLG-EnFr (Vaudry and Lapalme, 2013). These lexicons can be completed by the user to add domain-specific vocabularies. In lexicons, words have grammatical properties (e.g. category, gender, etc.) and a link to an inflection table. Tables are defined for nouns, adjectives, verbs, determiners and pronouns in both English and French. These inflection rules are language specific and correspond to the information found in (Bescherelle, 2012) and (Delaunay and Laurent, 2013). These conjugation, declension or transformation tables are included with the lexicon in JSrealB, they are defined declaratively for each language and interpreted by a rule engine common to both languages. There are also rules for the proper localization of dates, numbers and punctuation in each language.

Our goal was to develop an English and French text realizer with minimal specific adaptations to each language. We have promoted the systematic application of rules hoping it is possible to support other languages at limited cost. This is contrast with SimpleNLG-EnFr and JSreal in which many irregular forms were included in the lexicon.

Text realization uses a syntactic hierarchical tree representation that creates a sentence by combining phrases and terminals. The relations between these lexical units determine the propagation of features between words for determining proper agreements. For example, in

```
S(NP(D("le"),
     N("monsieur").n("p")),
  VP(V("avoir").t("i"),
     NP(D("un"),N("souris"))))
```

grammatical categories of words are already specified in the syntactic representation. Word order usually follows the left to right order of the terminals in the tree except in some coordinated sentences where position of coordinate must be determined.

The relations between non-terminals specified in the input determine the grammatical functions of each element, which are roughly similar between French and English. We can then compute the agreement between elements of the sentence in order to propagate appropriate features to the words according to the rules of the language.

Orthographic realization is performed after morphological realization. Sentence relays features, especially HTML tags, capitalization and full stop, to its children elements with the aim of formatting each phrase with proper elision.

JSrealB implements French and English grammatical categories: noun, pronoun, determiner, adjective, preposition, conjunction, and complement; the implemented phrases are: noun, verbal, adjectival, adverbial, prepositional, subordinate, and coordinate. The sentence combines all these phrases.

Supported inflections are conjugation for simple tenses, and declension in gender and number for every grammatical category. Noun phrase agrees in gender and number, while verbal phrase agrees with every type of subject (i.e. common or proper noun, or pronoun).

JSrealB currently realize sentences structured in the Subject-Verb-Object paradigm (e.g. *It will rain tomorrow.*), or noun phrases (e.g. *Heavy snowfalls this night!*).

But there is still much work in order to obtain a more complete coverage. For example negation is not yet handled: in French, negation is realized with two adverbs *ne* and *pas* (e.g. *il ne parle pas*), while in English there is only one: *not* (e.g. *he does not speak*). Moreover, the proper placement of the adverb is quite intricate.

There are also contractions (e.g. *can not* sometimes contracts in *cannot* in English) and elision (e.g. *it is* become *it's*) which has only partial support in French.

We will proceed to add new rules and types of sentences. Nevertheless, the core of the program is well developed and tested, and various extension mechanisms have been designed so that we can quickly achieve a better coverage.

Availability

Examples of the use of JSrealB, and a web-based development environment are available at:

`http://rali.iro.umontreal.ca/rali/?q=en/jsrealb-bilingual-text-realiser`

The javascript code of the realizer, the lexicon and tables are made available to the NLG community at:

`https://github.com/rali-udem/JSrealB`

References

Bescherelle, *Bescherelle La conjugaison pour tous*, Hatier, 2012.

N. Daoust and G. Lapalme, "JSreal: A Text Realizer for Web Programming", *Language Production, Cognition, and the Lexicon,* Springer, 2014, pp. 363-378.

B. Delaunay and N. Laurent, *Bescherelle La grammaire pour tous*, Hatier, France, 2013.

B. Garner, *Garner's Modern American Usage*, Oxford University Press, 2009.

A. Gatt and E. Reiter, "SimpleNLG: A realisation engine for practical applications", in *12th European Workshop on Natural Language Generation*, Athens, Greece, 2009, pp. 90-93.

M. Grevisse, *Le bon usage, grammaire française,* 11e édition, Duculot, Louvain-la-Neuve, Belgique, 1980.

P.-L. Vaudry and G. Lapalme, Adapting SimpleNLG for bilingual English - French realisation, *14th European Workshop on Natural Language Generation*, Sofia, Bulgaria, 2013, pp. 183-187.

A game-based setup for data collection and task-based evaluation of uncertain information presentation

Dimitra Gkatzia, Amanda Cercas Curry, Verena Rieser and Oliver Lemon
Interaction Lab
Heriot-Watt University
EH14 4AS, Edinburgh
{d.gkatzia,ac293,v.t.rieser,o.lemon}@hw.ac.uk

Abstract

Decision-making is often dependent on uncertain data, e.g. data associated with confidence scores, such as probabilities. A concrete example of such data is weather data. We will demo a game-based setup for exploring the effectiveness of different approaches (graphics vs NLG) to communicating uncertainty in rainfall and temperature predictions (www.macs.hw.ac.uk/InteractionLab/weathergame/). The game incorporates a natural language extension of the MetOffice Weather game[1]. The extended version of the game can be used in three ways: (1) to compare the effectiveness of different information presentations of uncertain data; (2) to collect data for the development of effective data-driven approaches; and (3) to serve as a task-based evaluation setup for Natural Language Generation (NLG).

1 Introduction

NLG technology achieves comparable results to commonly used data visualisation techniques in terms of supporting accurate human decision-making (Gatt et al., 2009). In this paper, we present a task-based setup to explore whether NLG technology can also be used to support decision-making when the underlying data is uncertain. The Intergovernmental Panel on Climate Change (IPCC) (Manning et al., 2004) and the World Meteorological Organisation (WMO) (Kootval, 2008) list the following advantages of communicating risk and uncertainty: information on uncertainty has been shown to improve decision making; helps to manage user expectations; promotes user confidence; and is reflective of the state of science. Results by Stephens (2011) further show that, although people prefer reports us-

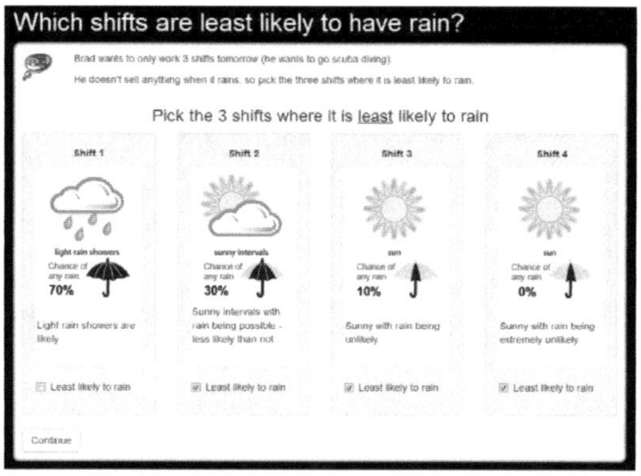

Figure 1: Screenshot of the Extended Weather Game (graphs and text version).

ing percentages (e.g. 10% chance of rain), this does not necessarily equate with *understanding*, i.e. making the right decision based on this information. One possible explanation is low "risk literacy" (Cokely et al., 2012), i.e. a reduced ability to accurately interpret and act on numerical information about risk and uncertainty.

In this research, we aim for a better understanding of how to effectively translate numerical risk and uncertainty measures into "laymen's" terms using natural language, following the recommendations of the WMO (Kootval, 2008). For example, the relative risk of 1 in 1000 could be described as *exceptionally unlikely*. We expect that through the use of language we will improve understanding and thus decision-making for users with low risk literacy (as measured by the Berlin literacy test[2]).

2 The Weather Game

Recruiting users to perform evaluations is a laborious task and many studies suffer from underpowered evaluations. Therefore, we use a crowdsourcing technique known as "game with a purpose", which has been shown to assist in recruit-

[1] http://www.metoffice.gov.uk/news/releases/archive/2011/weather-game

[2] http://www.riskliteracy.org/researchers/

Proceedings of the 15th European Workshop on Natural Language Generation (ENLG), pages 112–113, Brighton, September 2015. ©2015 Association for Computational Linguistics

ing more participants and collecting more accurate results (Venhuizen et al., 2013).

We build upon a previous study by Stephens (2011) called the Weather Game, which was conducted in collaboration with the MetOffice. The game starts by asking demographic questions such as age, gender and educational level. Then, the game introduces the "ice-cream seller" scenario, where given the temperature and rainfall forecasts for four weeks for two locations, users have to choose where to send the ice-cream seller in order to maximise sales. These forecasts describe predicted rainfall and temperature levels in three ways: (a) through graphical representations (original game), (b) through textual forecasts and (c) through combined graphical and textual forecasts. The textual format is generated with NLG technology as described in the next section. Users are asked to initially choose the location to send the seller and then they are asked to state how confident they are with their decision. Based on their decisions, the participants are finally presented with their "monetary gains", i.e. the higher likelihood of sunshine, the higher the monetary gains.

3 NLG Extension for the Weather Game

We developed two NLG systems (WMO-based and NATURAL) using SimpleNLG (Gatt and Reiter, 2009), which generate textual descriptions of rainfall and temperature data addressing the uncertain nature of forecasts in two ways:

1. WMO-based: uses the guidelines recommended by the WMO (Kootval, 2008) for reporting uncertainty. Consider for instance a forecast of sunny intervals with 30% probability of rain. This WMO-based system will generate the following forecast: "Sunny intervals with rain being possible - less likely than not." (Figure 1).
2. NATURAL: imitates forecasters and their natural way of reporting weather. For the previous example, this system will generate the following forecast: "Mainly dry with sunny spells".

4 Future Work

The Extended Weather Game is used in two ways:

- Firstly, to explore what type of information presentation can assist in decision making under uncertainty. The participants are presented with three main categories of information presentation: (1) graphical representations, (2) textual representations and (3) both.
- Secondly, we plan to use the information derived from the previous step, to develop an optimisation system, that is able to choose the right format of uncertain information presentation dependent on the data. We will then use the same setup to evaluate our optimisation approach.

5 Conclusions

This demo paper describes an NLG extension of the MetOffice Weather Game to be used for task-based evaluation and data collection for uncertain information presentation. At ENLG, we will demo the Extended Weather Game and we will discuss initial findings.

Acknowledgements

This research received funding from the EPSRC GUI project "Generation for Uncertain Information" (EP/L026775/1) and EPSRC DILiGENt - "Domain-Independent Language Generation" (EP/M005429/1).

References

Edward T. Cokely, Mirta Galesic, Eric Schulz, Saima Ghazal, and Rocio Garcia-Retamero. 2012. Measuring risk literacy: The berlin numeracy test. *Judgment and Decision Making*, 7(1):25–47.

Albert Gatt and Ehud Reiter. 2009. SimpleNLG: A realisation engine for practical applications. In *ENLG*.

Albert Gatt, Francois Portet, Ehud Reiter, James Hunter, Saad Mahamood, Wendy Moncur, and Somayajulu Sripada. 2009. From Data to Text in the Neonatal Intensive Care Unit: Using NLG Technology for Decision Support and Information Management. *AI Communications*, 22: 153-186.

Haleh Kootval, editor. 2008. *Guidelines on Communicating Forecast Uncertainty*. World Meteorological Organsation.

Martin Manning, Michel Petit, David Easterling, James Murphy, Anand Patwardhan, Hans-Holger Rogner, Rob Swart, and Gary Yohe. 2004. IPCC Workshop on Describing Scientific Uncertainties in Climate Change to Support Analysis of Risk and of Options.

Liz Stephens, Ken Mylne, and David Spiegelhalter. 2011. Using an online game to evaluate effective methods of communicating esemble model output to different audiences. In *American Geophysical Union, Fall Meeting*.

Noortje Venhuizen, Valerio Basile, Kilian Evang, and Johan Bos. 2013. Gamification for word sense labeling. In *Proceedings of the 10th International Conference on Computational Semantics (IWCS 2013) – Short Papers*, pages 397–403.

Generating Referential Descriptions Involving Relations by a Best-First Searching Procedure – A System Demo

Florin Haque
Saarland University
P.O. Box 151150
66041 Saarbrücken, GERMANY
s9flhaqu@stud.uni-saarland.de

Helmut Horacek
German Research Center for AI
Stuhlsatzenhausweg 3
66123 Saarbrücken, GERMANY
helmut.horacek@dfki.de

Abstract

Despite considerable research invested in the generation of referring expressions (GRE), there still exists no adequate generic procedure for GRE involving relations. In this paper, we present a system for GRE that combines attributes and relations, using best-first search technique. Preliminary evaluations show its effectiveness; the design enables the use of heuristics that meet linguistic preferences.

1 Motivation

Empirical evidence shows that humans use relations in GRE more often than necessary [Viethen, Dale 2008]. Nevertheless, algorithms involving relations, starting with [Dale, Haddock 1991] still have not reached a significant level of rigour and coverage (the method by [Krahmer, van Erk, Verleg 2003] does, to a certain extent). In particular, the incremental algorithm [Dale, Reiter 1995] constitutes a severe commitment for GRE involving relations, because the choice among alternate referents related to the intended one leads to substantial differences at early phases.

In order to remedy this problem, we have applied best-first searching (A*) to the issue at hand, as already explored for references to sets of objects involving boolean combinations of attributes [Horacek 2003]. This method yields the expression considered best according to the evaluation function used, with a guarantee of optimality, provided an *admissible* heuristic is built on the basis of the evaluation function.

2 General Approach and Some Specificities

Our approach applies the best-first search paradigm (as in [Horacek 2003]) to the conceptual algorithm described in [Horacek 1996], so that known unwanted effects (endless loops, unnecessary identification of objects) are avoided. Motivations, conceptualization and details of the implementation are described in [Haque 2015].

When searching for components of an adequate referring expression, a tree consisting of partial expressions describing the intended referent, also in terms of the objects related to it, is successively built. Tree expansion is geared by the A*-specific function f, which is composed of the cost of a partial expression built so far (g) and the most optimistic estimate of reaching a goal state (h), i.e., in a single step. This process terminates once an identifying and provably best description has been found. It is speeded up by A* specific and local similarity-based cut-offs.

The sum of g and h reflects the relative quality of competing partial descriptions. To impose a more fine-grained ordering over the candidates for the next descriptor to be tried out, we have used discriminatory power to resolve the ties.

1. Attributes and relations are treated in a uniform way. Relations are tried out after attributes by assigning lower costs to attributes, as relations require a description of the object related (attributes may suffice alone).
2. A relation may be chosen even if it applies to all potential distractors, but only if all the objects possessing this relation are not related with the same object via this relation.

Proceedings of the 15th European Workshop on Natural Language Generation (ENLG), pages 114–116,
Brighton, September 2015.

Object	Property with cost			
	type (1)	color (2)	in (3)	on (3)
c1, c2	cup	white	b1/b2	-
c3	cup	white	-	f1
b1	cup	white	-	f1
b2	bowl	white	t1	
t1, t2	table	grey	-	f1
f1	floor	dark grey	-	-

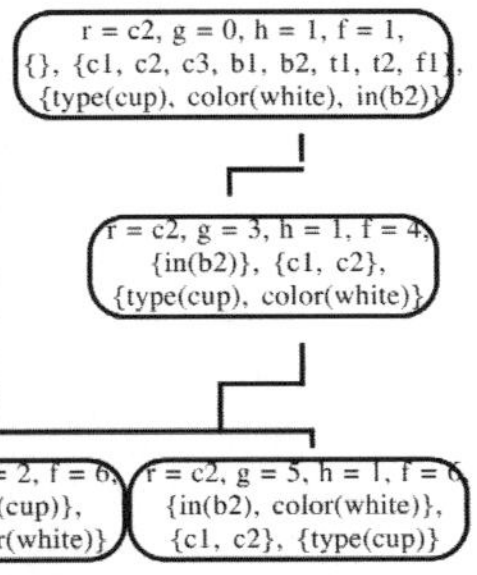

Figure 1. A small scenario and a fragment of the search tree

3 Implementation

The algorithm is implemented in C++, running on an Intel Core i5 processor with 1.6 GHz.

The functions *g* and *h* can be parameterized context-independently. For the test scenatios, we have used simple counts for each part, such as 1 for type, 2 for other attributes, and 3 for relations, so that the shortest expression results.

At first, we have tested the system with a few scenarios similar to those discussed in the literature – a room with tables, bowls, cups, etc., with some attributes (e.g., *type*, *color*) and relations (e.g., spatial containment – '*in*', spatial support – '*on*', left-of, and right-of). Figure 1 (top left) shows such a scenario (*cup c2* being the intended referent), and a portion of the search tree that illustrates the expansion of a node via a relation (in the node structure '*r*' is the local referent, and the last three sets include accumulated descriptors, context set, and available properties, respectively). It finally leads to the identifying expression "*the cup in the bowl on the table*". To check how the system handles relatively complex situations, we have designed a scenario composed of 40 entities with 10 well-defined descriptors (4 attributes and 6 relations).

Table 1 summarizes the results for some small scenarios (2nd line for the scenario from [Horacek 1996] and 3rd linr for the scenario from [Dale, Haddock 1991]) and for the extended one (last line), in terms of tree size and running time (ranging from smallest to largest). For the extended scenario, easy identification tasks do not require extra resources in comparison to the small scenarios. In contrast, identification of a specific bottle needed the largest tree (269 nodes) and longest run-time (298 msec) incorporating four chained relations in the generated expression which can be glossed as '*the bottle in the bowl which is in a plate on the table under which there is a glass*'.

The system is always able to find a reasonable expression without extra components, some including several attributes and relations. Since the evaluation functions used so far do not express subtle preferences, several ties may result. For example, "the metal bottle on the table", "the metal bottle right of a glass", "the white bottle right of a glass", "the bottle right of a glass with water" are produced as equivalent alternatives for identifying one specific bottle in the extended scenario.

4 Conclusion and Extensions

In this paper, we have presented an approach for generating referential descriptions involving relations by a best-first searching procedure. The system is able to find the best expression (or multiple equally good expressions if exist) according to the evaluation function used. For the examples we have tested so far, the resulting expressions are reasonable and the computation times needed are very convincing.

In further developing the system, we envision conceptual extensions, such as the use of negation ("the table on which there are no bottles", "the empty table"). Moreover, we need to make technical refinements, most importantly the use of context-sensitive evaluation functions for the resulting expressions, especially to cater for situation-dependent uses of descriptors redundant for identification purposes; the challenge here is to derive heuristic functions that are still admissible. In addition, we intend to test the system in larger and more diverse situations, preferably backed-up by corpus data.

no. of entities	*no. of tree nodes*	*time (msec)*
4	4 to 7	1 to 4
6	4 to 24	1 to 18
8	4 to 7	1 to 5
40	4 to 269	2 to 298

Table 1. Summary of searches for a few small scenarios and an extended one

References

Dale, R., and Haddock, N. 1991. Generating Referring Expressions Involving Relations. Proceedings of the *27th Annual Meeting of the European Chapter of the ACL (EACL'91)*, pp. 161-166, Berlin, Germany.

Dale, R., and Reiter, E. 1995. Computational Interpretations of the Gricean Maxims in the Generation of Referring Expressions. *Cognitive Science* 18, pp. 233-263.

Haque, F. 2015. Generating Referring Expressions Involving Relations by Best-First Searching. Master thesis, Saarland University, Department of Computer Science.

Horacek, H. 1996. A New Algorithm for Generating Referential Descriptions. In Proc. of *12th European Conference on Artificial Intelligence (ECAI-96)*, pp. 577-581, Budapest, Hungary.

Horacek, H. 2003. A Best-First Search Algorithm for Generating Referring Expressions. In Proc. of the *European Chapter of the ACL (EACL'2003)*, pp. 206-213, Budapest, Hungary.

Krahmer, E., v. Erk S., and Verleg, A. 2003. Graph-based Generation of Referring Expressions. *Computational Linguistics*, 29(1), pp. 53–72.

Viethen, J. and Dale, R. 2008. The Use of Spatial Relations in Referring Expressions. In Proceedings of the *5th International Natural Language Generation Conference* (INLG), pp. 59–67, Salt Fork, OH.

Generating Image Descriptions with Gold Standard Visual Inputs: Motivation, Evaluation and Baselines

Josiah Wang
Department of Computer Science
University of Sheffield
United Kingdom
j.k.wang@sheffield.ac.uk

Robert Gaizauskas
Department of Computer Science
University of Sheffield
United Kingdom
r.gaizauskas@sheffield.ac.uk

Abstract

In this paper, we present the task of generating image descriptions with gold standard visual detections as input, rather than directly from an image. This allows the Natural Language Generation community to focus on the text generation process, rather than dealing with the noise and complications arising from the visual detection process. We propose a fine-grained evaluation metric specifically for evaluating the *content selection* capabilities of image description generation systems. To demonstrate the evaluation metric on the task, several baselines are presented using bounding box information and textual information as priors for content selection. The baselines are evaluated using the proposed metric, showing that the fine-grained metric is useful for evaluating the content selection phase of an image description generation system.

1 Introduction

There has been increased interest in the task of automatically generating full-sentence natural language image descriptions in recent years. Compared to earlier work that annotates images with isolated concept labels (Duygulu et al., 2002), such detailed annotations are much more informative and discriminating, and are important for improved text and image retrieval. They also pose an interesting and difficult challenge for natural language generation.

Previous work on generating image descriptions concentrates on solving the problem 'end-to-end', that is to generate a description given an image as input (Yao et al., 2010; Kulkarni et al., 2011; Yang et al., 2011). Recent advances in large scale visual object recognition, especially in deep learning techniques, have reached a reasonably high level of accuracy in the last few years. For the task of classifying an image into one of 1,000 object categories (i.e. does the image contain an object of category X, yes or no?) on the ImageNet Large Scale Visual Recognition Challenge (ILSVRC'14) dataset (Russakovsky et al., 2014), the state-of-the-art currently performs at a 4.82% top-5 error rate (Ioffe and Szegedy, 2015) comparable to the 5.1% error rate of a human annotator who trained himself to recognise the object categories (Russakovsky et al., 2014). For the more challenging object category detection task (i.e. draw a bounding box around each instance of objects of the given categories), the state-of-the-art achieved a mean average precision of 43.9%. However, even at this level of performance, the errors from the visual output are still problematic when used as input to an image description generation system, especially when considering a large pool of candidate object categories to be mentioned in the description.

What if we were to assume that visual object recognisers have already achieved close to perfect detection rates, and that the object instances have already been identified and localised in an image? This then raises many interesting questions with regards to generating a description for an image, including: (i) how do we decide which objects are to be mentioned? (ii) how should these objects be ordered in the description? (iii) how do we infer and describe activities or actions? (iv) how to we describe spatial relations between objects? (v) how and when do we describe the object attributes? Many of these questions could be explored if we had a 'perfect' visual input to our image description generator.

To be able to begin to answer these questions, we proposed a pilot task, which has formed part of the ImageCLEF 2015 Scalable Image Annotation, Localization and Sentence Generation task bench-

Proceedings of the 15th European Workshop on Natural Language Generation (ENLG), pages 117–126,
Brighton, September 2015. ©2015 Association for Computational Linguistics

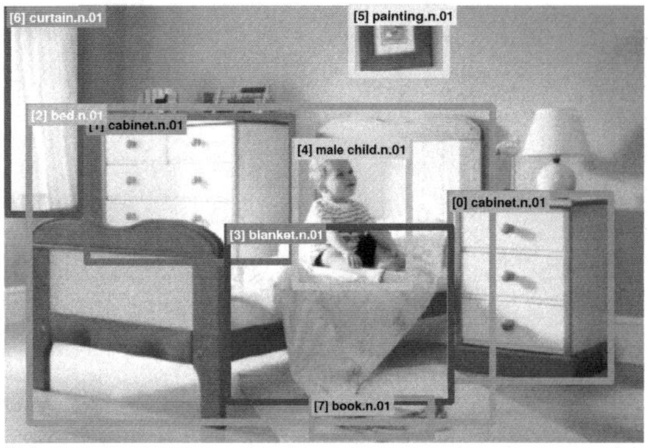

Figure 1: We present the task of generating textual descriptions given gold standard labelled bounding boxes as input. This allows researchers to focus on the text generation aspects of the image description generation task, rather than dealing with the noise arising from visual detection. This task also allows us to evaluate specific phases of the conventional generation pipeline, providing insights into which specific phases of the generation pipeline contribute to the performance of an image description generation system.

marking challenge (Villegas et al., 2015; Gilbert et al., 2015). More specifically, we assume that perfectly labelled object instances and their localisations are available to image description generation systems, as done in Elliott and Keller (2013) and Yatskar et al. (2014). Given this knowledge, we would like to evaluate how well image description generation systems perform through the various stages of Natural Language Generation (Reiter and Dale, 2000): content determination (what objects to describe), microplanning (how to describe objects) and realisation (generating the complete sentence). This pilot task is an attempt at encouraging fine-grained evaluation specifically for image descriptions, compared to general-purpose metrics like METEOR (Denkowski and Lavie, 2014) that evaluates text at a global, coarse-grained level. For our pilot, we concentrated on just one fine-grained metric: a content selection measure to evaluate how well a text generation system selects the correct object instances to be mentioned in the resulting image description.

A dataset has been introduced for this particular challenge. This paper will not discuss in great detail how the dataset has been collected and annotated; we instead refer readers to Gilbert et al. (2015) for more details about the challenge. The main purpose of this paper, instead, is to: (i) present and discuss the task of generating image descriptions with a *gold standard visual input*; (ii) propose a fine-grained metric specifically for evaluating the *content selection* capabilities of image description generation systems; (iii) introduce several *baselines* for this task and evaluate the baselines using the proposed fine-grained metric.

Overview. In section 2, we discuss the motivations for introducing the pilot task and the fine-grained metric in the ImageCLEF 2015 challenge, positioning them in relation to existing work. In section 3, we describe the task of generating image descriptions given gold standard visual inputs, along with a discussion on evaluating image description generation systems with regards to their content selection abilities. Section 4 presents several baselines for this task, while section 5 evaluates these baselines using the proposed content selection metric. Finally, we discuss further challenges with the proposed task, and introduce possible fine-grained metrics to be considered in the future.

2 Motivation and Related Work

There are currently three main groups of approaches to generating image descriptions. The most common and intuitive paradigm is the knowledge-based, generative approach that takes an image as input, detects instances of pre-defined object categories in the image using a visual recogniser, and then reasons about the detected objects to generate a novel textual description (Yao et al., 2010; Kulkarni et al., 2011; Yang et al., 2011; Li et al., 2011; Mitchell et al., 2012). However, these approaches are constrained to a limited number of categories, for example 20 in Kulkarni et al. (2011). We found that these approaches are generally sensitive to errors from visual input detection, as such errors tend to propagate and accumulate through the generation pipeline. The problem is accentuated when scaling up to a larger number of categories (e.g. 1000), where it becomes difficult to reason about what to describe amongst the candidate instances produced by the noisy visual detectors. Thus, generating image descriptions with gold standard visual input allows researchers to concentrate on the sentence generation aspects without being bogged down by the complications of the vision aspects of the task.

The second group of work revolves around de-

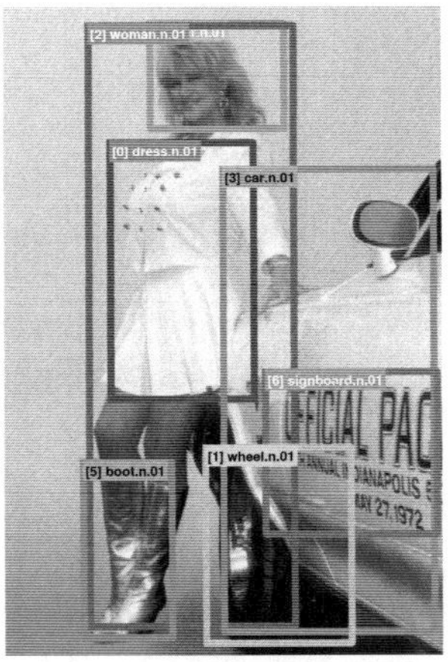

A [woman]^2 in a white [dress]^0 and gold [boots]^5 leaning on a [car]^3 .

A [woman]^2 poses along a [car]^3 .

[woman]^2 dressed in white with gold [boots]^5 poses next to a police [car]^3.

A [woman]^2 dressed in white leans against a white [car]^3 .

A [woman]^2 is leaning against a [car]^3.

A [woman]^2 with gold [boots]^5 leans against an Indy pace [car]^3 .

A blonde [woman]^2 wearing gold shiny [boots]^5 , a white [top]^0 and short white skirt is leaning on a [car]^3 .

Figure 2: An example image and its seven corresponding textual descriptions from the development dataset, with bounding box annotations labelled with WordNet concepts, and the correspondence of bounding boxes to entity mentions in the descriptions. For example, [woman]^2 in the first sentence refers to bounding box ID [2] in the image, and [dress]^0 corresponds to bounding box ID [0]. Correspondence is annotated at word level rather than at phrase level to avoid possible complications with multiple correspondences within the same phrase (*woman in a white dress*).

scription generation by retrieving existing textual descriptions from similar images. A common approach would be to map text and images to a common meaning space (Farhadi et al., 2010; Hodosh et al., 2013; Socher et al., 2014) or by using some similarity measure (Ordonez et al., 2011). Although such methods produce descriptions that are more expressive, they rely on a large amount of training data, and are unable to produce novel sentences. There have been attempts at retrieving only text fragments and combining them to generate novel descriptions (Kuznetsova et al., 2012; Kuznetsova et al., 2014) or by pruning irrelevant fragments for better generalisation (Kuznetsova et al., 2013). However, the resulting descriptions may still be pure 'guesswork' and may reference text fragments that are irrelevant to image content.

Most recently, work using deep learning approaches has produced state-of-the-art results (Karpathy and Fei-Fei, 2015; Donahue et al., 2015; Vinyals et al., 2015), by utilising Convolutional Neural Networks (CNN) (Krizhevsky et al., 2012; Razavian et al., 2014) as image features, and a Recurrent Neural Network (RNN) (Mikolov et al., 2010) for language modelling, and learning to generate descriptions jointly from images and their descriptions. The advantages of such models are that they cope better with noisy visual detections, and that the RNN language models are capable of modelling long range dependencies. The main disadvantages are (i) it is difficult to inspect what has been learnt by the model and hence to gain insight into what is working or not working in the system; (ii) these methods are dependent on image datasets aligned with sentences as learning is performed in a joint manner. The latter limitation means new datasets need to be produced even for small changes in the task, such as generating descriptions that are more or less detailed, or in more or less simplified language (e.g. for children) or have a specific information focus (say, focussing on buildings versus people in an image for a particular application). Thus, knowledge-based, generative approaches may have an advantage in this respect, as there is no need for aligned image-text datasets, since visual detection and sentence generation are independent, allowing the language model to be tuned at surface realisation stages.

Image description generation with gold standard input. As discussed, knowledge-based, generative approaches are sensitive to visual detection input errors. Therefore, previous work has proposed circumventing the problem by providing gold standard annotations as input to description generation systems. Elliott and Keller (2013) provide region annotations along with spatial relations between region instances. Yatskar et al. (2014) also provide gold standard region annotations, as well as fine-grained region properties such as attributes, parts, and activities. Zitnick and Parikh (2013) take a unique approach of generating scenes from clipart as an abstraction to real world images to address the issue of noisy input. Our work takes a similar direction as Elliott and Keller (2013) and Yatskar et al. (2014), but with bounding boxes as gold standard input, and with an emphasis on fine-grained evaluation of image description generation systems.

Evaluation of image description generation systems. Existing image description generation systems are most commonly evaluated using automatic evaluation metrics such as BLEU (Papineni et al., 2002), ROUGE (Lin, 2004), METEOR (Denkowski and Lavie, 2014) and most recently CIDEr (Vedantam et al., 2015). However, such global measures only allow evaluation of image description generation systems as a whole, without being able to ascertain which parts of the generation process, or components of the generation system, are responsible for performance gains or losses. Although evaluations based on human judgments could provide a more fine-grained metric (Yang et al., 2011; Mitchell et al., 2012; Kuznetsova et al., 2012), they are expensive and difficult to scale. We propose instead to exploit the pipeline of knowledge-based, generative approaches to generation, allowing us to inspect specific capabilities of image generation systems by means of evaluation with fine-grained metrics. Rather than just evaluating image description generation extrinsically with a global evaluation measure, we isolate evaluation of different phases of description generation, and treat each phase as a first-class citizen.

3 Task and Evaluation Measure

As mentioned above, we introduced as a benchmarking challenge the task of generating image descriptions for 450 test images given gold standard, labelled bounding box annotations as input (Figure 1). The category labels were restricted to 251 WordNet synsets selected specifically for the challenge. To enable evaluation with our proposed fine-grained metric, participants were also asked to annotate, within their generated descriptions, the bounding box ID to which a term in the description corresponds. A development dataset of 500 images was provided with labelled bounding box annotations and correspondence annotations between textual terms and bounding boxes. Figure 2 shows an example annotation of bounding boxes and the correspondences between bounding box instances and terms in the image descriptions. Note that correspondence was annotated at word level (unigram) rather than at phrase level (higher-order n-grams) to avoid possible complications with multiple correspondences within the same phrase (*woman in a white dress*).

3.1 Fine-grained Evaluation Metric

As a pilot, we propose a fine-grained metric to evaluate the content selection capabilities of an image description system. This *content selection* metric is the F_1 score averaged across all 450 test images, where each F_1 score is computed from the precision and recall averaged over all gold standard descriptions for the image.

Formally, let $I = \{I_1, I_2, ... I_N\}$ be the set of test images. Let $G^{I_i} = \{G_1^{I_i}, G_2^{I_i}, ..., G_M^{I_i}\}$ be the set of gold standard descriptions for image I_i, where each $G_m^{I_i}$ is the set of unique bounding box instances referenced in gold standard description m of image I_i. Let S^{I_i} be the set of unique bounding box instances referenced by the participant's generated sentence for image I_i. The precision P^{I_i} for test image I_i is computed as:

$$P^{I_i} = \frac{1}{M} \sum_{m}^{M} \frac{|G_m^{I_i} \cap S^{I_i}|}{|S^{I_i}|} \tag{1}$$

where $|G_m^{I_i} \cap S^{I_i}|$ is the number of unique bounding box instances referenced in both the gold standard description and the generated sentence, and M is the number of gold standard descriptions for image I_i.

Similarly, the recall R^{I_i} for test image I_i is computed as:

$$R^{I_i} = \frac{1}{M} \sum_{m}^{M} \frac{|G_m^{I_i} \cap S^{I_i}|}{|G_m^{I_i}|} \tag{2}$$

The content selection score for image I_i, F^{I_i}, is computed as the harmonic mean of P^{I_i} and R^{I_i}:

$$F^{I_i} = 2 \times \frac{P^{I_i} \times R^{I_i}}{P^{I_i} + R^{I_i}} \tag{3}$$

The final P, R and F scores are computed as the mean P, R and F scores across all test images.

The advantage of the macro-averaging process in equations (1) and (2) is that it implicitly captures the relative importance of the bounding box instances based on how frequently they occur across the gold standard descriptions. For example, in Figure 2, both *woman* and *car* are referenced in all seven gold standard descriptions, while *boot* is mentioned four times and *dress* twice. Thus, a generated description that references *woman* and *car* will naturally result in a higher score than one that references only *woman* and *dress*.

Note that for this metric, we are only concerned with evaluating the generation system's *content selection* capabilities, rather than its referring expression generation. As such, systems are free to generate any referring expression for each selected bounding box instance. We consider the evaluation of referring expressions as a potentially separate fine-grained evaluation task to be introduced in the future. In addition, we do not evaluate terms outside those that refer to bounding box instances, and as for the pilot task of the challenge use the global METEOR metric to cover evaluation of other aspects of image description generation.

4 Generating Descriptions: Baselines

We propose a set of baselines for the image description generation task, or more specifically the content selection task. These allow us to test the proposed fine-grained content selection metric (Section 3.1) and to gain some insights into what features might inform content selection. The baselines use visual and textual cues to select the bounding box instances to be described in the text to be generated.

4.1 Generation based on Visual Cues

Stratos et al. (2012) found that the size and position of visual entities in an image, to a certain extent, plays a part in determining what is mentioned in the corresponding description. As such, we consider two baselines based on different visual cues: (i) bounding box size (bigger objects have higher likelihood of being mentioned); (ii) distance of the centroid of the bounding box to the centre of the image (central objects have higher likelihood of being mentioned). For each test image, bounding boxes instances are sorted based on these visual cues, and a fixed threshold used to limit the number of instances to be selected for sentence generation. We will explore different thresholds in our experiments in Section 5.

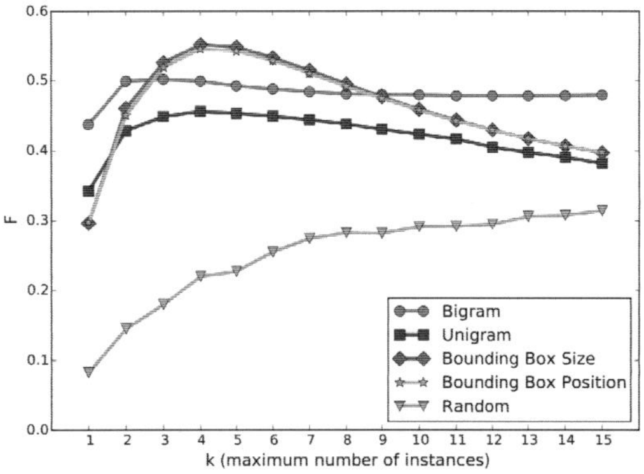

Figure 3: The content selection score, F, evaluated on the proposed baselines at varying levels of k (maximum number of instances per sentence). Standard deviations are omitted for clarity, but are included in Table 1.

4.2 Generation based on Textual Priors

We also consider baselines based on textual priors, as Stratos et al. (2012) also showed that the category of the object play a role in determining whether it will be mentioned in the corresponding textual description.

For the first baseline, we consider as a prior unigram counts of concepts that have been referenced to a bounding box in the gold standard descriptions from the development set. For each test image, bounding boxes are sorted by the frequency of their concept labels in the development set, i.e. frequently mentioned concepts have higher precedence.

We also consider a more sophisticated baseline based on bigram sequences, where a concept is selected based on how likely it is to be referenced *immediately after* another concept, i.e. there are no other terms referencing a bounding box in between. For instance, for the first sentence in Figure 2, we consider *woman* to be followed by *dress*, *dress* followed by *boot*, and *boot* followed by *car*, but not *woman* followed by *car* or *boot*. Concept selection is performed in a greedy fashion, by choosing from the pool of bounding boxes for each image, the concept that is most likely to occur first in a sentence, followed by the concept that is most likely to occur given the previously selected concept. The selection process terminates when no remaining concept from the candidate pool is likely to follow the previously selected concept.

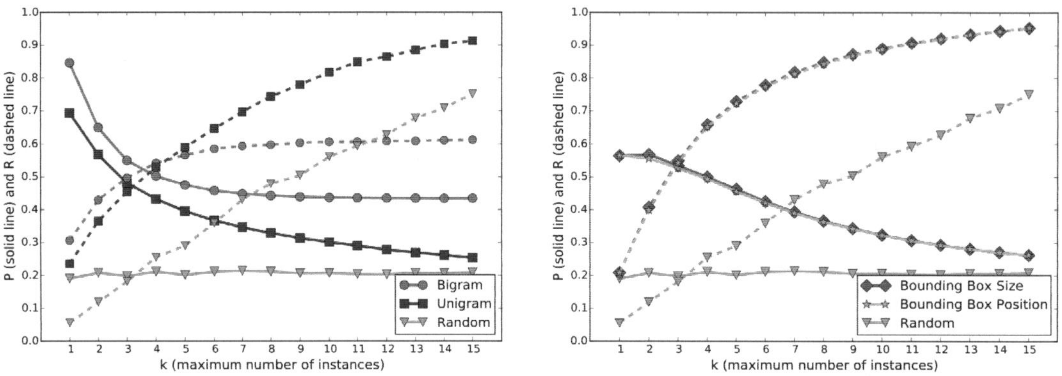

(a) Baselines based on textual priors

(b) Baselines based on visual cues

Figure 4: The precision P (solid lines) and recall R (dashed lines), as evaluated on the proposed baselines at varying levels of k. Again, error bars are omitted for clarity, but are included in Table 1.

For all baselines, we select the first term among the synonyms of the WordNet synset to generate the referring expression for each concept.

4.3 Function Words

Our metric only evaluates the content selection process and ignores everything else. However, for completeness and in the spirit of generating complete descriptions, we attempt to connect selected concept terms with randomly selected function words or phrases. The phrases are selected to be a random word from a predefined list of prepositions and conjunctions, followed by an optional article *the*.

5 Experimental Results

The generation systems described in Section 4 were evaluated using the proposed content selection metric (Section 3.1). We also compared the proposed systems to a baseline that selects bounding boxes at random, up to a pre-defined threshold k of the maximum allowed number of bounding boxes per image. We explore different values of this threshold by varying k from 1 to 15. We take $min(k, N_{box})$ for images with fewer than k bounding boxes, where N_{box} is the total number of bounding boxes for the image.

As an upper bound to how well humans perform content selection, we evaluated the gold standard descriptions by evaluating one description against the other descriptions of the image and repeating the process for all descriptions. The upper bound is computed to be $F = 0.74 \pm 0.12$, with $P = 0.77 \pm 0.11$ and $R = 0.77 \pm 0.11$.

Figure 3 shows the F-scores of our proposed generation systems. Firstly, we examine the effects of varying the threshold k on the number of instances to be selected. The F-score peaks at k between 3 and 4 across all systems except the random baseline, and then drops or remains stagnant beyond that. Figure 4 gives an insight about this observation when the precision P and recall R are examined separately. As expected, P decreases while R increases when k is increased. The two graphs intersect at about k between 3 to 4, suggesting that these values are an optimal tradeoff between precision and recall (the mean number of unique instances per description is 2.89 in the development dataset).

Comparing the baselines based on visual and textual cues, the F-score in Figure 3 suggests that baselines using textual cues perform better when k is small, and visual cues perform better with larger k's. However, Figure 4 gives a clearer picture, where the bigram-based system obtained the best precision regardless of k (Figure 4a), while the systems based on bounding box cues relied on the increased recall when increasing k to obtain a high F-score (Figure 4b). Note that the bigram-based generation system is less sensitive to larger k's as the model itself contains an internal stopping criterion when no suitable concept is likely to follow a selected concept, resulting in a lower but stable recall rate compared to other systems, when k is increased. Figure 5 shows some example sentences generated by our baseline systems, for k=3.

We can infer from the results that (i) using prior

knowledge on the ordering of concepts (i.e. bigrams) is helpful for concept selection; (ii) frequency of concepts (i.e. unigrams) are helpful when there are only one or two instances to be described, possibly because the remaining objects are not mentioned as frequently as the main actors; (iii) visual cues are helpful for concept selection, although the precision is reduced as k increases.

5.1 Combining Textual and Visual Priors

We also explored combining textual priors and visual cues, which could potentially produce a stronger baseline. This is done by re-ranking the bounding boxes, for each image, by the average rank from both systems. In the case of the bigram-based system, bounding boxes that are not selected are all assigned an equal rank: $0.5 \times ((N_{box} + 1) - N_s) + N_s$, where N_{box} is the number of all bounding boxes for the image and N_s the number of bounding boxes selected by the bigram-based system. For example, if only 3 out of 9 bounding boxes are selected (and assigned ranks 1, 2 and 3 respectively), then the remaining 6 bounding boxes are all assigned equal rank 6.5. Figure 6 compares the F-scores of systems combining textual priors (unigram or bigram) and visual cues (bounding box position) at k=3 and k=4; we omitted bounding box size as the results are similar to bounding box position. Combining unigram and bounding box position did not significantly improve the F-score compared to using bounding box position alone, at k=3 and k=4. As seen earlier, the performance of the unigram-based system at these k's is much lower than systems based on visual cues. The combination of bigram and bounding box position, however, seems to yield slightly improved performance at these k's. This is likely due to the bigram-based system providing higher precision and the system based on visual cues providing better recall. This shows that combining textual and visual priors may be beneficial when they complement each other.

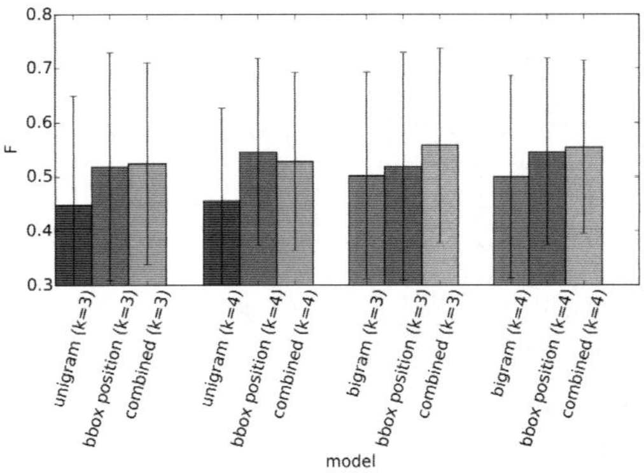

Figure 6: The content selection score, F, when combining textual priors and visual cues. For text priors, we compare both unigram and bigram priors. For visual cues, we show only the results for bounding box position as using bounding box size yields similar results. We compare the combined baselines at k=3 and k=4.

6 Discussion and Future Work

We presented the task of generating image descriptions from gold standard labelled bounding boxes as input to a text generation system. We also proposed a fine-grained evaluation metric specifically to evaluate the content selection capabilities of the image description generation system, which measures how well the system selects the concepts to be described compared against a set of human-authored reference descriptions. Several baselines were proposed to demonstrate the proposed metric on the task. We found that selecting a maximum of 3 to 4 instances is optimal for this dataset, and that both text and visual cues play a part in the content selection process.

Further challenges can be observed for the proposed generation task based solely on gold standard visual inputs:

Bounding boxes. Bounding boxes labelled with concepts may be a good starting point for a 'clean' input task, but may be somewhat uninformative as important visual information is discarded in the process that might prove useful for the generation process. A possible solution would be to enrich the bounding box inputs with more information, either as attributes (adjectives, verbs etc.) or directly using visual features. However, manually annotating such fine-grained information is an onerous task.

Suitability of metrics. Another possible issue with the proposed task is that it might be problematic to assume that all image description generation systems will be using a common pipeline. With the large variation in how image description generation systems are constructed, it may be difficult to constrain and expect systems to be using the same architecture that will enable us to evalu-

random:	[F=0.04]	[Wall]^{3} among [necktie]^{1} underneath [floor]^{2} .
bbox pos:	[F=0.00]	[Hallway]^{8} below the [wall]^{3} near the [floor]^{2} .
bbox size:	[F=0.39]	[Hallway]^{8} behind the [dog]^{0} underneath the [wall]^{3} .
unigram:	[F=0.05]	[Wall]^{3} near [floor]^{2} with the [dog]^{5} .
bigram:	[F=0.51]	[Dog]^{5} against [dog]^{0} beside the [dog]^{6} .
random:	[F=0.05]	[Park]^{9} behind [wheel]^{7} underneath the [window]^{6} .
bbox pos:	[F=0.59]	[Park]^{9} on the [car]^{1} below [river]^{5} .
bbox size:	[F=0.44]	[Park]^{9} behind the [car]^{1} against the [tree]^{3} .
unigram:	[F=0.42]	[Tree]^{3} beneath [car]^{1} by [window]^{6} .
bigram:	[F=0.71]	[Car]^{1} inside [flag]^{0} underneath the [flag]^{2} .
random:	[F=0.43]	[Wall]^{4} inside [door]^{3} around the [bicycle]^{0} .
bbox pos:	[F=0.79]	[Bicycle]^{0} in [floor]^{1} below [wall]^{2} .
bbox size:	[F=0.79]	[Bicycle]^{0} on [floor]^{1} with [wall]^{2} .
unigram:	[F=0.34]	[Table]^{7} in the [wall]^{4} around [wall]^{2} .
bigram:	[F=0.03]	[Table]^{7} near [door]^{3} .
random:	[F=0.66]	[Mouse]^{4} inside [field]^{3} against [helmet]^{0} .
bbox pos:	[F=0.75]	[Field]^{3} and [mouse]^{4} beside the [gun]^{1} .
bbox size:	[F=0.75]	[Field]^{3} along [mouse]^{4} underneath [gun]^{1} .
unigram:	[F=0.31]	[Field]^{3} inside [hand]^{2} below [helmet]^{0} .
bigram:	[F=0.00]	[Hand]^{2} .
random:	[F=0.39]	[Vest]^{6} at [hat]^{3} behind the [picture]^{7} .
bbox pos:	[F=0.49]	[Picture]^{7} on [man]^{2} beside the [train]^{4} .
bbox size:	[F=0.49]	[Picture]^{7} among [man]^{2} on the [train]^{4} .
unigram:	[F=0.77]	[Man]^{2} below the [hat]^{3} at [book]^{0} .
bigram:	[F=0.77]	[Man]^{2} around the [hat]^{3} along the [book]^{0} .

Figure 5: Example image descriptions generated by our baselines ($k = 3$).

ate them with such fine-grained metrics.

Future work with fine-grained metrics. Although we only consider one metric to evaluation the content selection capabilities of generation systems, further fine-grained metrics can be introduced to evaluate different components of the generation pipeline. Some examples include content ordering, lexicalisation or referring expression generation of concepts (and/or their attributes), evaluating the appropriateness of verbs, predicates and prepositions, and surface realisation.

Future work on image description generation. In this paper, we presented several baselines based on different textual and visual priors, and also explored combining cues from both text and vision. Future work on image description generation could involve stronger cues, for example from co-occurrences and spatial relationships between multiple objects.

We believe that the introduction of a fine-grained approach to evaluating image description generation tasks can encourage further growth in this area, linking further research between computer vision and natural language generation.

Acknowledgments

This work has been supported by the EU CHIST-ERA D2K 2011 Visual Sense project, EPSRC grant reference: EP/K019082/1.

References

Michael Denkowski and Alon Lavie. 2014. Meteor universal: Language specific translation evaluation for any target language. In *Proceedings of the EACL 2014 Workshop on Statistical Machine Translation.*

Jeffrey Donahue, Lisa Anne Hendricks, Sergio Guadarrama, Marcus Rohrbach, Subhashini Venugopalan, Kate Saenko, and Trevor Darrell. 2015. Long-term recurrent convolutional networks for visual recognition and description. In *Proceedings of the IEEE Conference on Computer Vision & Pattern Recognition.*

Pinar Duygulu, Kobus Barnard, Nando de Freitas, and David A. Forsyth. 2002. Object recognition as machine translation: Learning a lexicon for a fixed im-

		P	R	F
Upper bound		0.77 ± 0.11	0.77 ± 0.11	0.74 ± 0.12
Random	$k = 1$	0.19 ± 0.32	0.06 ± 0.12	0.08 ± 0.16
	$k = 2$	0.21 ± 0.24	0.12 ± 0.17	0.15 ± 0.19
	$k = 3$	0.20 ± 0.20	0.18 ± 0.22	0.18 ± 0.20
	$k = 4$	0.21 ± 0.18	0.26 ± 0.25	0.22 ± 0.20
	$k = 5$	0.20 ± 0.17	0.29 ± 0.27	0.23 ± 0.19
	$k = 6$	0.21 ± 0.17	0.36 ± 0.29	0.25 ± 0.19
	$k = 7$	0.21 ± 0.15	0.43 ± 0.31	0.27 ± 0.18
	$k = 8$	0.21 ± 0.15	0.48 ± 0.31	0.28 ± 0.18
	$k = 9$	0.21 ± 0.15	0.50 ± 0.32	0.28 ± 0.18
	$k = 10$	0.21 ± 0.14	0.56 ± 0.31	0.29 ± 0.17
Bounding Box Position	$k = 1$	0.57 ± 0.41	0.21 ± 0.19	0.30 ± 0.25
	$k = 2$	0.56 ± 0.27	0.40 ± 0.25	0.45 ± 0.25
	$k = 3$	0.53 ± 0.20	0.54 ± 0.26	0.52 ± 0.21
	$k = 4$	0.49 ± 0.16	0.65 ± 0.24	0.55 ± 0.17
	$k = 5$	0.46 ± 0.14	0.72 ± 0.23	0.54 ± 0.15
	$k = 6$	0.42 ± 0.13	0.77 ± 0.21	0.53 ± 0.14
	$k = 7$	0.39 ± 0.13	0.81 ± 0.19	0.51 ± 0.12
	$k = 8$	0.36 ± 0.12	0.84 ± 0.18	0.49 ± 0.12
	$k = 9$	0.34 ± 0.12	0.87 ± 0.16	0.47 ± 0.12
	$k = 10$	0.32 ± 0.12	0.89 ± 0.15	0.46 ± 0.12
Bounding Box Size	$k = 1$	0.56 ± 0.41	0.21 ± 0.19	0.30 ± 0.25
	$k = 2$	0.57 ± 0.27	0.41 ± 0.25	0.46 ± 0.25
	$k = 3$	0.53 ± 0.20	0.55 ± 0.26	0.53 ± 0.21
	$k = 4$	0.50 ± 0.16	0.66 ± 0.24	0.55 ± 0.17
	$k = 5$	0.46 ± 0.14	0.73 ± 0.22	0.55 ± 0.15
	$k = 6$	0.43 ± 0.14	0.78 ± 0.20	0.53 ± 0.13
	$k = 7$	0.39 ± 0.13	0.82 ± 0.19	0.51 ± 0.12
	$k = 8$	0.37 ± 0.13	0.85 ± 0.17	0.50 ± 0.12
	$k = 9$	0.34 ± 0.13	0.87 ± 0.16	0.48 ± 0.12
	$k = 10$	0.32 ± 0.12	0.89 ± 0.15	0.46 ± 0.12
Unigram	$k = 1$	0.69 ± 0.40	0.24 ± 0.18	0.34 ± 0.24
	$k = 2$	0.57 ± 0.29	0.36 ± 0.22	0.43 ± 0.23
	$k = 3$	0.48 ± 0.22	0.45 ± 0.23	0.45 ± 0.20
	$k = 4$	0.43 ± 0.19	0.53 ± 0.23	0.46 ± 0.17
	$k = 5$	0.40 ± 0.17	0.59 ± 0.22	0.45 ± 0.16
	$k = 6$	0.37 ± 0.16	0.65 ± 0.22	0.45 ± 0.15
	$k = 7$	0.35 ± 0.15	0.70 ± 0.22	0.44 ± 0.14
	$k = 8$	0.33 ± 0.14	0.74 ± 0.22	0.44 ± 0.14
	$k = 9$	0.31 ± 0.14	0.78 ± 0.21	0.43 ± 0.14
	$k = 10$	0.30 ± 0.13	0.82 ± 0.20	0.42 ± 0.13
Bigram	$k = 1$	0.85 ± 0.29	0.31 ± 0.17	0.44 ± 0.21
	$k = 2$	0.65 ± 0.24	0.43 ± 0.21	0.50 ± 0.21
	$k = 3$	0.55 ± 0.21	0.50 ± 0.22	0.50 ± 0.19
	$k = 4$	0.50 ± 0.21	0.54 ± 0.23	0.50 ± 0.19
	$k = 5$	0.47 ± 0.21	0.57 ± 0.23	0.49 ± 0.19
	$k = 6$	0.46 ± 0.20	0.59 ± 0.23	0.49 ± 0.18
	$k = 7$	0.45 ± 0.20	0.59 ± 0.23	0.48 ± 0.18
	$k = 8$	0.44 ± 0.20	0.60 ± 0.23	0.48 ± 0.18
	$k = 9$	0.44 ± 0.20	0.60 ± 0.24	0.48 ± 0.18
	$k = 10$	0.44 ± 0.20	0.61 ± 0.23	0.48 ± 0.18

Table 1: P, R and F scores (with standard deviations) of the content selection metric, as evaluated on different baselines at varying levels of k (1 to 10).

age vocabulary. In *Proceedings of the European Conference on Computer Vision*, pages 97–112.

Desmond Elliott and Frank Keller. 2013. Image description using visual dependency representations. In *Proceedings of the Conference on Empirical Methods in Natural Language Processing (EMNLP)*.

Ali Farhadi, Mohsen Hejrati, Amin Sadeghi, Peter Young, Cyrus Rashtchian, Julia Hockenmaier, and David Forsyth. 2010. Every picture tells a story: Generating sentences for images. In *Proceedings of the European Conference on Computer Vision*.

Andrew Gilbert, Luca Piras, Josiah Wang, Fei Yan, Emmanuel Dellandrea, Robert Gaizauskas, Mauricio Villegas, and Krystian Mikolajczyk. 2015. Overview of the ImageCLEF 2015 Scalable Image Annotation, Localization and Sentence Generation task. In *CLEF2015 Working Notes*, CEUR Workshop Proceedings, Toulouse, France, September 8-11. CEUR-WS.org.

Micah Hodosh, Peter Young, and Julia Hockenmaier. 2013. Framing image description as a ranking task: Data, models and evaluation metrics. *Journal of Artificial Intelligence Research (JAIR)*, 47(1):853–899, May.

Sergey Ioffe and Christian Szegedy. 2015. Batch normalization: Accelerating deep network training by reducing internal covariate shift. *CoRR*, abs/1502.03167.

Andrej Karpathy and Li Fei-Fei. 2015. Deep visual-semantic alignments for generating image descriptions. In *Proceedings of the IEEE Conference on Computer Vision & Pattern Recognition.*

Alex Krizhevsky, Ilya Sutskever, and Geoffrey E. Hinton. 2012. Imagenet classification with deep convolutional neural networks. In F. Pereira, C.J.C. Burges, L. Bottou, and K.Q. Weinberger, editors, *Advances in Neural Information Processing Systems 25*, pages 1097–1105. Curran Associates, Inc.

Girish Kulkarni, Visruth Premraj, Sagnik Dhar, Siming Li, Yejin Choi, Alexander C. Berg, and Tamara L. Berg. 2011. Baby talk: Understanding and generating image descriptions. In *Proceedings of the IEEE Conference on Computer Vision & Pattern Recognition.*

Polina Kuznetsova, Vicente Ordonez, Alexander Berg, Tamara Berg, and Yejin Choi. 2012. Collective generation of natural image descriptions. In *Proceedings of the 50th Annual Meeting of the Association for Computational Linguistics (Volume 1: Long Papers)*, pages 359–368, Jeju Island, Korea, July. Association for Computational Linguistics.

Polina Kuznetsova, Vicente Ordonez, Alexander Berg, Tamara Berg, and Yejin Choi. 2013. Generalizing image captions for image-text parallel corpus. In *The 51st Annual Meeting of the Association for Computational Linguistics - Short Papers*,

Sofia, Bulgaria, August. Association for Computational Linguistics.

Polina Kuznetsova, Vicente Ordonez, Tamara L. Berg, and Yejin Choi. 2014. Treetalk: Composition and compression of trees for image descriptions. In *Proceedings of the Conference on Empirical Methods in Natural Language Processing (EMNLP)*.

Siming Li, Girish Kulkarni, Tamara L. Berg, Alexander C. Berg, and Yejin Choi. 2011. Composing simple image descriptions using web-scale n-grams. In *Computational Natural Language Learning (CoNLL)*.

Chin-Yew Lin. 2004. Rouge: A package for automatic evaluation of summaries. In *Proc. ACL workshop on Text Summarization Branches Out*, page 10.

Tomas Mikolov, Martin Karafit, Luks Burget, Jan Cernock, and Sanjeev Khudanpur. 2010. Recurrent neural network based language model. In Takao Kobayashi, Keikichi Hirose, and Satoshi Nakamura, editors, *INTERSPEECH*, pages 1045–1048. ISCA.

Margaret Mitchell, Jesse Dodge, Amit Goyal, Kota Yamaguchi, Karl Stratos, Xufeng Han, Alyssa Mensch, Alex Berg, Tamara Berg, and Hal Daume III. 2012. Midge: Generating image descriptions from computer vision detections. In *Proceedings of the 13th Conference of the European Chapter of the Association for Computational Linguistics*, pages 747–756, Avignon, France, April. Association for Computational Linguistics.

Vicente Ordonez, Girish Kulkarni, and Tamara L. Berg. 2011. Im2text: Describing images using 1 million captioned photographs. In *Advances in Neural Information Processing Systems*.

Kishore Papineni, Salim Roukos, Todd Ward, and Wei-Jing Zhu. 2002. Bleu: a method for automatic evaluation of machine translation. In *Proceedings of 40th Annual Meeting of the Association for Computational Linguistics*, pages 311–318, Philadelphia, Pennsylvania, USA, July. Association for Computational Linguistics.

Ali Sharif Razavian, Hossein Azizpour, Josephine Sullivan, and Stefan Carlsson. 2014. CNN features off-the-shelf: An astounding baseline for recognition. In *IEEE Conference on Computer Vision and Pattern Recognition, CVPR Workshops 2014, Columbus, OH, USA, June 23-28, 2014*, pages 512–519.

Ehud Reiter and Robert Dale. 2000. *Building Natural Language Generation Systems*. Cambridge University Press, New York, NY, USA.

Olga Russakovsky, Jia Deng, Hao Su, Jonathan Krause, Sanjeev Satheesh, Sean Ma, Zhiheng Huang, Andrej Karpathy, Aditya Khosla, Michael S. Bernstein, Alexander C. Berg, and Fei-Fei Li. 2014. Imagenet large scale visual recognition challenge. *CoRR*, abs/1409.0575.

Richard Socher, Andrej Karpathy, Quoc Le, Christopher Manning, and Andrew Ng. 2014. Grounded compositional semantics for finding and describing images with sentences. *Transactions of the Association for Computational Linguistics*, 2:207–218.

Karl Stratos, Aneesh Sood, Alyssa Mensch, Xufeng Han, Margaret Mitchell, Kota Yamaguchi, Jesse Dodge, Amit Goyal, Hal Daumé III, Alexander C. Berg, and Tamara L. Berg. 2012. Understanding and predicting importance in images. In *Proceedings of the IEEE Conference on Computer Vision & Pattern Recognition*.

Ramakrishna Vedantam, C. Lawrence Zitnick, and Devi Parikh. 2015. Cider: Consensus-based image description evaluation. In *The IEEE Conference on Computer Vision and Pattern Recognition (CVPR)*, June.

Mauricio Villegas, Henning Müller, Andrew Gilbert, Luca Piras, Josiah Wang, Krystian Mikolajczyk, Alba García Seco de Herrera, Stefano Bromuri, M. Ashraful Amin, Mahmood Kazi Mohammed, Burak Acar, Suzan Uskudarli, Neda B. Marvasti, José F. Aldana, and María del Mar Roldán García. 2015. General Overview of ImageCLEF at the CLEF2015 Labs. Lecture Notes in Computer Science. Springer International Publishing.

Oriol Vinyals, Alexander Toshev, Samy Bengio, and Dumitru Erhan. 2015. Show and tell: A neural image caption generator. In *Proceedings of the IEEE Conference on Computer Vision & Pattern Recognition*.

Yezhou Yang, Ching Teo, Hal Daumé III, and Yiannis Aloimonos. 2011. Corpus-guided sentence generation of natural images. In *Proceedings of the Conference on Empirical Methods in Natural Language Processing (EMNLP)*, pages 444–454. Association for Computational Linguistics.

Benjamin Z. Yao, Xiong Yang, Liang Lin, Mun Wai Lee, and Song Chun Zhu. 2010. I2t: Image parsing to text description. *Proceedings of the IEEE*, 98(8):1485–1508.

Mark Yatskar, Michel Galley, Lucy Vanderwende, and Luke Zettlemoyer. 2014. See no evil, say no evil: Description generation from densely labeled images. In *Proceedings of the Third Joint Conference on Lexical and Computational Semantics (*SEM 2014)*, pages 110–120, Dublin, Ireland, August. Association for Computational Linguistics and Dublin City University.

C. Lawrence Zitnick and Devi Parikh. 2013. Bringing semantics into focus using visual abstraction. In *Proceedings of the IEEE Conference on Computer Vision & Pattern Recognition*.

Designing an Algorithm for Generating Named Spatial References

Rodrigo de Oliveira, Yaji Sripada, Ehud Reiter
Department of Computing Science
University of Aberdeen, Scotland
{rodrigodeoliveira,yaji.sripada,e.reiter}@abdn.ac.uk

Abstract

We describe an initial version of an algorithm for generating named references to locations of geographic scale. We base the algorithm design on evidence from corpora and experiments, which show that named entity usage is extremely frequent, even in less obvious scenes, and that names are normally used as the first focus on a global region. The current algorithm normally selects the Frames of Reference that humans also select, but it needs improvement to mix frames via a mereological mechanism.

1 Introduction

Geospatial data of public interest such as weather prediction data and river level data are increasingly made publicly available, e.g. DataPoint from the Met Office in the UK, River Level data from SEPA in Scotland and Global Forecast system data from NOAA in the US.

We are interested in developing computational techniques for expressing the information content extracted from these datasets in natural language using data-to-text natural language generation (Reiter et al., 2005) techniques. For example, from precipitation prediction data corresponding to several locations across Scotland, we are developing techniques to automatically generate the statement *Heavy rain likely to fall as snow on higher ground in the northeast of Scotland.*

An important subtask here is to automatically generate the spatial referring expression (SRE) *higher ground in the northeast of Scotland* to linguistically express the location of the snowing event found in the precipitation prediction data. This paper presents corpus analysis and experimental studies to guide the design of an algorithm for SRE generation. Studies of human written SREs (Turner et al., 2010) show a broad range of descriptors such as *north, east, coastal, inland, urban*, and *rural* to specify locations. Descriptors belong to one of many perspectives on the scene, or *Frames of Reference* (Levinson, 2003) or FoR for short, such as direction, coastal proximity, population density and altitude.

Our own corpus studies (Section 2) show that geographic names are the dominant descriptors in weather forecast texts, route descriptions and river level forecast reports. Our experiment to empirically understand the extent of usage of geographical names in SREs (Section 3) also shows that names are the most used descriptors, as well as the FoR that sets the first focus on a region. Using this empirical knowledge we propose an initial version of an algorithm (Section 4) that automatically generates SREs using names as well as other descriptors.

2 Corpus Analysis

The first stab at the problem was a corpus analysis study. We gathered a total of 36 texts in 3 domains (route descriptions, weather forecasts, river forecasts), in 3 languages (English, Portuguese and Spanish), for 3 target audiences (general public, fishing enthusiasts, kayaking enthusiasts).

We define an SRE as an adverbial (*inland*) or a noun phrase (*the north*), which ties non-spatial information to one location. Only sentences that contained at least 1 SRE were included in the corpus. For each SRE at least 1 FoR was annotated. Below are 3 examples from the corpus, all originally in English, where SREs are underlined:

1. (a) *<u>The Red River</u> is slowly rising* (b) *from <u>Emerson</u>* (c) *downstream to <u>Winnipeg</u>.*

2. (a) *From <u>the north</u>* (b) *<u>the A1</u>* (c) *<u>and M1</u> link* (d) *to <u>the A14 dual carriageway</u>* (e) *straight to <u>the city</u>.*

Proceedings of the 15th European Workshop on Natural Language Generation (ENLG), pages 127–135,
Brighton, September 2015.

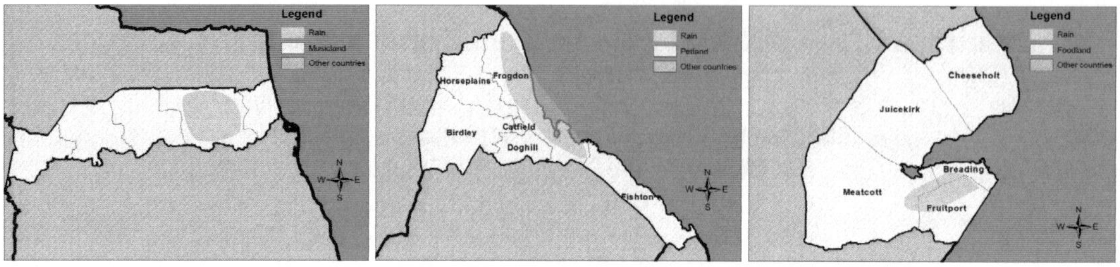

(a) Condition 0: no names (b) Condition 1: good fit (c) Condition 2: poor fit

Figure 1: Stimuli in the pilot experiment.

3. (a) *Dry with sunny spells on Saturday and Sunday these mainly inland* (b) *with Aberdeenshire coast becoming cloudy.*

Sentence 1 was extracted from a river level report for Manitoba, Canada, which seems to be aimed at the general public. In the instance, we identified 3 SREs, all of which using named entities as FoR. Sentence 2 is a route description for drivers to reach Cambridge, England, so it is also aimed at the general public. 2a uses a cardinal direction as FoR, 2e uses the entity's type, while 2b-c use named entities. Sentence 3 also seems to be intended for the general public; it is extracted from a weather forecast report for Aberdeenshire, Scotland. Both SREs use coastal proximity as FoR, while 3b also includes a named entity.

In total the corpus yielded 556 SREs, out of which 318 (57%) use named entities, either in isolation or combined with other FoR. It is important to remember that another 7 FoR appear in the corpus – cardinal direction, coastal proximity, population density, type, motion sequence, river segment and size – which means that names account for more than half of a total of 8 choices.

With the corpus in place, it became clear that names do not compete with other FoR in a balanced manner. Because of this expressive imbalance, we were lead to the suspicion that humans choose to refer to geographic regions by their names using a different strategy than when choosing other FoR. We suspect people may be more precise when they use FoR such as cardinal direction or coastal proximity, but they can be very imprecise when using names. This suspicion lead us to our first hypothesis:

Hypothesis 1: People mostly use named entities to refer to locations of geographic scale, even if the fit between the named location and the located entity/event is poor.

By the above hypothesis we mean that named entities are used as spatial references also in situations where using a name as reference is not so obvious. For instance, if the named location only covers a small portion of a located entity/event, or if the located entity/event is much smaller than the named location, we suspect that most people still use the named location as reference, hence the high frequency of named entities in the corpus.

3 Experiment

Even though the corpus analysis returned fruitful insights, we remained with a major shortfall to design a computational algorithm for an NLG system. We expect such an algorithm to be used in data-to-text systems – i.e. systems that write text from information stored in data bases – so a data-and-text parallel corpus is more suitable to inform us what our SREG algorithm must consider. Thus we resorted to experiments with human participants to collect spatial expressions, while having full access to the data underlying the text.

3.1 Pilot

To test hypothesis 1, we designed a pilot experiment (see Figure 1), where we showed 3 different maps (conditions) of fictitious countries to 14 human participants and asked them to describe where on those countries they could see a patch of rain. Both the no-name condition and the good-fit condition placed the rain patch very neatly on one specific region of the country, with the difference that the no-name condition did not have any names for the regions and the good-fit condition did. In the poor-fit condition, named regions were also present but the patch covered only a small portion of several regions. Participants were split into balanced groups and each group saw maps in a different order. The rationale behind the no-name con-

Condition	SRE Type						Σ
	name-only	other-only	name-1st	name-2nd	both-1st	none	
no-name	2	86	0	0	0	5	93
good-fit	43	3	41	5	1	0	93
poor-fit	12	2	72	5	2	0	93
Σ	57	91	113	10	3	5	279

Table 1: Experimental results showing types of SREs per condition. SREs can contain only names, only other FoR, none, or mix names with other FoR. When mixed, names can be the first or second focus, or both types can be first focus.

dition is to certify that people resort to other FoR when names are not available.

Curiously, names were not as dominant in the pilot experiment as they are in the corpus. The FoR used by all participants were names, cardinal direction (north, south, etc.) and some proximity (coast, border, etc.). In the vast majority of responses (94%), people used multiple FoR to refer to the location of the rain patch, which we believe helped balance the usage of FoR across responses. Names were used in 79% of responses in the good-fit condition – proximity 86% and direction 50% – and in the poor-fit condition names were used in 64% of responses – direction 79% and proximity 57%.

Even though names were not dominant, people still used names in most cases, even in a scenario where using a name was not so obvious (the poor-fit condition), speaking in favour of hypothesis 1. After results from the pilot experiment, we could see that most responses use a *first focus frame* (of reference) and a *a second focus frame*. Take the SRE *coastal areas of Frogdon* for instance. *Frogdon* (a name) indicates the first focus area, while *coastal areas* (proximity) sets a second focus on one particular portion of the first focus area. We suspect that most first-focus areas are named regions, which leads us to a second hypothesis:

Hypothesis 2: When mixing named entities with other FoR, people use named entities mostly for first-focus areas and other FoR for second-focus.

3.2 The main experiment

The above results were not formally verified with statistical tests because we believe our sample of 14 participants was not representative. In order to test our hypotheses with more statistical vigor, we ran a slightly modified version of the pilot experiment on Amazon Mechanical Turk, where 93 participants successfully completed the task. The difference from the pilot is that, instead of having only 1 image per condition, we prepared 2 images for the control condition, 4 for the good-fit condition and 4 for the poor-fit condition. As in the pilot, participants saw only 1 image per condition, so the system randomly chose a single map to display in each condition. With multiple images available in the experiment, we reduced the level of specificity between stimuli and responses.

Responses varied from single clauses to sentences containing 2 or more clauses, or even full paragraphs containing 2 or more sentences. We considered the entire response as 1 SRE, but since we are now interested in names versus non-names, we combined all other FoR that are not named entities. We marked SREs with 1 of the 5 following annotations:

name-only If the SRE only contained named entities as spatial references: *It will rain in Doghill.*

other-only If the SRE only contained non-named-entities as spatial references: *Rain can be expected in the south-most region of Musicland*[1]*. There is no other chance of rain.*

name-2nd If both names and other FoR were used, but named entities were used as second focus: *Throughout the far south of Foodland, going through Meatcott and Fruitport, rain is to be expected.*[2]

[1] Since we are interested in knowing *where in Musicland it is raining*, the descriptor *Musicland* is tautological, thus not counted as chosen descriptor to locate the event. Therefore, named entities are also ignored as contributing FoR in this description.

[2] Here it is not a lexical item that informs us that the named entities are used as second focus. It is the fact that the a direction (*the far south*) is used to select a larger sub-region of the global region (the country), within which the named regions (*Meatcott* and *Fruitport*) exist.

name-1st If both names and other FoR were used, but named entities were used as first focus.

both-1st If names and other FoR don't compete for first focus, but remain on the same level, so the resulting subregion is a union of multiple sub-regions. For example: *northwestern Fruitport... southwest of Breading... eastern part of Meatcott... not in the far northeast or southeast*. Fruitport, Breading and Meatcott are named regions but far north-east and south-east are directions. None is a part of the other, so the named areas and *not far north-east and south-east* complement each other at the same focus level.

none If no FoR, but only vague descriptors were used.

Finally we counted all possible combinations of FoR usage and aligned those with experimental conditions, as displayed in Table 1. The first intriguing observation is that 5 responses did not use any FoR, according to our annotation. 2 of them used only a quantifier (*much*, *most*), 2 only the name of the country (*Musicland*), and 1 used both (*some parts of Musicland*). Using only the name of the country does not successfully complete the task, because it does not answer the question "where *in the country* will it rain?". Quantifiers were also not annotated as other FoR because they are extremely vague. We were aiming at FoR that help a hearer more precisely identify referenced locations.

Even more interesting, 2 SREs created named entities in the no-name condition, i.e. where no name was available as per task. One participant decided to name an unnamed subregion of Musicland as *Drum County* and referred to it 'by its name'. Although odd, this suggests how people strongly feel the necessity for named entities when describing geographies. This is very similar to another response in the pilot experiment, where the participant described one unnamed subregion as *the penultimate state before reaching the coast*, and later stated in the comments that names should be on the map.

Hypothesis 1 states that people use names with a high frequency in any condition where names are available. If we exclude the no-name condition from the count, this hypothesis is supported with 97% (90/93) of name usage in the good-fit condition and 98% (91/93) in the poor-fit condition . We did *not* observe a significant difference in name usage between good-fit and poor-fit conditions, χ^2 (1,N=186) = 0.21, p = .65.

Hypothesis 2 was also supported, again excluding the no-name condition. People very often (113/126 or 90%) use names as the *first-focus area* and other FoR as the *second focus-area*.

After testing the above hypotheses, we observed the same phenomenon as identified by Turner and colleagues (2010): that people resort to other FoR more often when the fit between (rain) patch and region is poorer. In the good-fit condition 54% (50/93) of responses used other FoR, while 87% (81/93) of poor-fit responses contain other FoR. This means that there is a *significant* need for other FoR when moving from a good-fit to a poor-fit scenario, χ^2 (1,N=186) = 26.18, $p < .001$.

3.3 Preliminary conclusions

To date this project has shown evidence that:

- Humans use several FoR when referring to geographical locations.
- Regardless of scenario, named entities are almost always used.
- Named areas mostly function as a first focus area, wherein a descriptor of a second FoR can still be selected.

4 Algorithm

We used the knowledge described above to inform an algorithm that selects Frames of Reference. The procedure is basically the ContentSelector algorithm of the RoadSafe project (Turner, 2009), which looks at an event that takes place in a geography and selects one or more frames out of an array of frames. The input to the algorithm, as for many geographic information systems, is a set of points with latitude-longitude coordinates and some other value denoting the status of the point in some event. In Turner's sense, a Frame of Reference is a set of descriptors, and a descriptor is a non-overlapping partition of a geographic region where each descriptor can be used to refer to a specific partition. The frame contains all points of the dataset, but each descriptor encompasses a particular subset of points.

For instance, take the US as our global geography, which contains several thousands of points.

The Frame of Reference StateNames contains 50 descriptors, one for each US state, so each descriptor contains a couple of hundreds of points. Altogether StateNames contains all points that form the US. Another frame could be CoastalProximity, which is composed of only 2 descriptors, Coastal and Inland, where most points belong to the Inland descriptor and the rest to Coastal. Note that in this example, all points that belong to the descriptor Kansas of the frame StateNames also belong to the descriptor Inland of the frame CoastalProximity, but such overlaps are not always true. Out of the points that form the descriptor Texas, some belong to Inland and others to Coastal.

Following the US example, the high-level goal of the algorithm is to select one or more descriptors that *best* locate a target subset of all the points in the US. For instance if our dataset contains a binary variable for "rain" for each point, and we are interested in describing the location of the "raining points" – or simply answering the question "where in the US is it raining?" – the algorithm's task is to return a set of descriptors that encompasses the majority of points with rain=true values. If the result is {Colorado, Coast}, the NLG system where the algorithm lives should be able to produce the sentence "it will rain on the Coast and in Colorado".

Turner describes the ContentSelection algorithm in detail (p. 122), so below we highlight its main steps:

1. Take as input a set of points representing an event, along with meta-data for Frames of Reference.
2. Count the density of target points for each descriptor of each frame.
3. Remove a frame if all its descriptors have non-zero densities.
4. Of the remaining frames, rank them by a predefined preference order.
5. Use the first frame with non-zero densities.
6. Try adding each subsequent frame, if this reduces the number of false positives.
7. Use the descriptors with non-zero densities of the chosen frames.

We take the algorithm and include, first of all, a NamedAreas frame. This however is currently done in the same fashion as all other frames in the RoadSafe project. The true conceptual modification to the original algorithm was the threshold of density (step 3). RoadSafe fixes this value at 0, which means that if all descriptors of a Frame of Reference have at least 1 target point, then this frame cannot be chosen. We suspect that humans are more lenient when computing density. We believe that humans can choose frames where all descriptors have non-zero densities, by focussing on descriptors with high densities and ignoring descriptors with low (yet non-zero) densities. Therefore our version of the algorithm selects a descriptor as candidate if it reaches a density threshold, and it ignores a FoR if all its descriptors are candidates.

4.1 A small-scaled quantitative evaluation

To test how the algorithm currently performs, we ran it using 7 weather forecast datasets provided by the UK's meteorology agency: MetOffice. The data contained numerical predictions for a region in the UK (Grampian), and each dataset also accompanies a textual summary, against which we used to compare our algorithm. We chose DICE to evaluate how comparable each output was. This metrics has been widely used by the Referring Expression community (Gatt et al., 2008; Belz and Gatt, 2008). The results are displayed in Table 2.

To compare MetOffice's FoR choices with those by our algorithm, we ran it using 6 different density thresholds: 0.0, 0.2, 0.4, 0.6, 0.8 and 1.0. A density threshold is in this sense the minimum event density a descriptor can have to be accepted as a candidate. If you recall the explanation of the algorithm above, a Frame of Reference is rejected if all its descriptors are rejected, but equally if all its descriptors cannot be rejected. For example, it only makes sense to select Inland as a descriptor if Coastal is not a candidate; if both Inland and Coastal are equally valid, then we can say the event (e.g. rain) is taking place in the entire region, as far as coastal proximity is concerned. As explained above, the fixed density threshold in the original algorithm was 0.0, which means that 1 single point was enough to make a descriptor invalid. By running the algorithm with different density thresholds, we are able to have an idea of some optimal threshold, where non-zero-density descriptors still get rejected.

From this initial evaluation, we could verify

Dataset	MO	BL	D	DT=.0	D	DT=.2	D	DT=.4	D	DT=.6	D	DT=.8	D	DT=1	D
May 21	nam, cst	nam	0.7	*	0	dir	0	nam	0.7	nam	0.7	nam	0.7	nam	0.7
May 25		nam	0	nam	0	nam	0	-	1	-	1	-	1	-	1
May 27	nam	nam	1	*	0	*	0	dir	0	dir	0	nam, dir	0.7	nam	1
May 28	nam	nam	1	*	0	*	0	nam	1	nam, dir	0.7	-	0	-	0
Jun 01	nam, dir	nam	0.7	*	0	dir	0.7	nam, dir	1	nam	0.7	nam	0.7	nam	0.7
Jun 02	nam	nam	1	nam	1	nam	1	nam	1	nam, dir	0.7	dir	0	-	0
Jun 04	dir	nam	0	nam	0	nam, dir	0.7	nam	0	nam, dir	0.7	-	0	-	0
		Average	0.6		0.1		0.3		0.7		0.6		0.4		0.5

Table 2: Comparison of 1st-focus FoR choice between MetOffice texts and the algorithm running with different density thresholds. Assigning 2 (or more) 1st-focus FoR to a dataset is very similar to assigning "both-1st" to experimental responses. Please refer to Section 3.2 for a more detailed discussion on multiple 1st-focus FoR. Abbreviations: nam = NamedArea; dir = Directions; cst = CoastalProximity; MO = MetOffice; BL = Baseline; DT = Density Threshold; D = DICE score; * = all descriptors reach the threshold, so no FoR is discriminative enough to be chosen; - = no descriptor reaches the threshold, so no FoR qualifies as candidate to be chosen.

that, at its current state, the algorithm is performing relatively well in choosing the 'favourite' frame, which is NamedAreas. Another important observation is that the algorithm reached, at this relatively small evaluation, its optimal density threshold at 0.4, as indicated by the DICE value of 0.7, which is higher than the baseline of 0.6. The baseline is simply the most common FoR in the dataset, which is named entities. Surely a more substantial evaluation with a larger dataset will be required before we are safe to make stronger claims about thresholds and performance.

It is important to highlight how we annotated our corpus texts. Frames were considered chosen if they were the first-focus FoR in the description (see 3.1 for a discussion on first vs. second-focus FoR). For instance, if "in Aberdeen and in the west" was the expression, both names and direction were annotated as first-focus frames; if "in western Aberdeen" was the case, then only name was considered first-focus, with direction annotated as second-focus and therefore outside the comparison with the algorithm. This is necessary because, although we gained valuable knowledge about first and second-focus with previous studies, the functionality for focus is not yet present in the algorithm, thus we are not yet ready to evaluate it for this mechanism.

4.2 An example

Below we provide an example of how the algorithm decides for Frames of Reference and descriptors. We take a dataset used in the evaluation exercise, which contains rain forecast data for the Grampian region, in Scotland. The region has a coastal line at the North Sea and is composed of 3 authority areas, namely: Aberdeen, Aberdeenshire and Moray.

As explained above, the data is provided by MetOffice, who also provides textual summaries for the data. From an analysis of the summaries we identified 3 Frames of Reference used with a frequency higher than 5% to describe rain events. These frames, their descriptors and frequencies are:

NamedAreas (83%): Aberdeen, Aberdeenshire and Moray.

Directions (33%): NorthEast, SouthEast, SouthWest, NorthWest.

CoastalProximity (17%): Coastal, Inland.

In the Directions frame, we coded only the inter-cardinal directions as descriptors. This is necessary because the algorithm needs to compute each descriptor as a non-overlapping atomic partition. A North descriptor would overlap with an East descriptor, forming exactly the partition North-East. For this reason, a description such as "the North" is achieved if the algorithm selects the descriptors North-West and North-East, but not South-West and South-East.

The frequencies become the weights of each frame in the algorithm, and the decision for a descriptor is based on the utility score of a descriptor. Utility is computed by multiplying the event density within a descriptor and its Frame of Reference weight. The event density is the percentage of points of a given descriptor that are also within the event. For example, if the descriptor NorthEast has 32 points in total and 18 are marked with <rain,true>, while 14 are marked with <rain,false>, the rain-event density of NorthEast is 0.44.

As discussed above, the algorithm was tested with different density thresholds, which set the minimum density value for a descriptor to be considered as candidate. In table 3, we can see why Aberdeen (of the NamedAreas frame) was selected for a setting where density threshold was set to 0.4.

Frame of Reference	Descriptor	Point Count		Density
		Event	Frame	
CoastalProximity	Coastal	27	44	0.61
	Inland	17	83	0.20
Directions	NorthWest	7	27	0.26
	SouthEast	18	27	0.67
	SoutWest	1	41	0.02
	NorthEast	18	32	0.56
NamedAreas	Aberdeen	9	9	1.00
	Aberdeenshire	27	88	0.31
	Moray	8	30	0.27

Table 3: Event densities of a dataset used in the evaluations.

Following the description of the algorithm (in Section 4), the algorithm receives the set of points that 'are raining' as well as what descriptors can be assigned to each point. It counts the event density of each descriptor and attempts to reject any descriptor whose density is lower than the threshold. When the density threshold is set to 0, no descriptor is rejected so no frame can be selected. However, when we set the threshold to 0.4, Inland, NorthWest, SouthWest, Aberdeenshire and Moray get rejected. Because each frame now contains a rejected descriptor, all frames are good candidates as SREs. To break the tie, the algorithm resorts to frame weights and densities (i.e. utility). It computes that the utility score of Aberdeen is higher than that of the other non-rejected descriptors, NorthEast, SouthEast, and Coastal, so it selects the descriptor Aberdeen (and the NamedAreas Frame of Reference).

5 Conclusions and future work

In this paper we described an initial version of an algorithm that is able to select one or more Frames of Reference – and appropriate descriptors thereof – to describe an event taking place at a geographic scene. The current state of the algorithm seems promising insofar that it prefers the frame that humans also prefer: NamedAreas. This preference was better observed when the event-density threshold of the algorithm was set to 0.4. However this performance is only verified for first-focus frames, those that are used to reduce the global region to a smaller sub-region.

To enable the algorithm to compute second-focus frames, the key aspect will be *mereology*. A Frame of Reference mix is, at the current state of the algorithm, the geometrical union of two or more descriptors, which in turn share the same global region. Take for instance Texas and North; they belong to different Frames of Reference – StateNames and Directions respectively – but, in isolation, assume the same global area: the US. Although this may be a good mechanism to mix frames in some cases, our corpora are abundant of examples where one descriptor assumes another descriptor as its global region. Take the expression "northern Texas" for instance. It is not the case that the expression refers to the union of Texas and the north of the US. While "Texas" has the entire US as its global region, "northern" refers to the sub-area within Texas. In experiment 1 (see Section 3.2) we showed how names are very frequently the first meorological level when frames are mixed meorologically. We believe that a systematic approach to compute meorological Frames of Reference will substantially improve the performance of the algorithm. Based on evidence found, we also believe that named areas will play a particularly important role in meorological operations.

6 Related Work

The subtask of generating referring expressions such as *the green plastic chair* and *the tall bearded man* has been extensively studied by the NLG research community (Dale and Reiter, 1995; Van Deemter, 2002; Krahmer and Van Deemter, 2012). However, relatively fewer studies have been reported on SREs. A notable work is that of Turner and colleagues (2010), which implements the notion of FoR to generate approximate descriptions of geographical regions. As such Turner's algorithm seem to be too domain specific, as it covers only a subset of FoR that exist.

The algorithm we propose aims to **not** be domain specific but it may be constrained to generating expression that refer to locations of geographical scale such as regions of a country. Initially we are not concerned with describing the position of small-scale scenes such as a cup on a table. Below we describe how these *spaces* can be significantly different for our task. We also review the *backbone* concept for the algorithm, that of FoR, and we finally list some existing implementations for generating spatial referring expressions.

6.1 Spatial frames of reference

When choosing how to represent space with words, we need to select not only spatial entities but a spatial relation between them. Choosing a spatial relation depends largely on the perspective with which one looks at (or imagines) a scene. In cognitive sciences, people have used the term *Frames of Reference* (FoR) to refer to such perspectives. Levinson (2003) classifies cognitive FoR into 3 types:

Intrinsic Objects *have* spatial parts such as front or top.

Relative The 3rd object position is taken into account.

Absolute Fixed bearings such as latitude longitude coordinates.

In this work, we take the same position as (Turner et al., 2010), which perceives the absolute FoR as the one employed by humans when surveying geographical spaces.

6.2 Generation of spatial referring expressions

The first systems to use an SREG module date back to the 1990s. FOG (Goldberg, 1995) was the first large scale commercial application of NLG and it generated weather forecasts in English and French.

Similar to FOG, many other systems focus on generating descriptions for weather data (Coch, 1998; Reiter et al., 2005; Bohnet et al., 2007). We can expect the spatial language in the output of such systems to employ the absolute FoR, given the geo-referenced input data. The other type of systems normally use SREG modules to describe a medium-scale (e.g. street) or a small-scale (e.g. room) space (Ebert et al., 1996; Dale et al., 2005; Kelleher and Kruijff, 2006). In such systems, we can expect intrinsic and relative frames.

RoadSafe (Turner et al., 2010), is to the best of our knowledge the most recent system to implement an SREG module. Output spatial language employs absolute FoR and geo-referenced data is processed using DE-9IM (Clementini et al., 1993). RoadSafe implements the most sophisticated SREG module to describe geographical scenes using non-named FoR. We need to enable NLG systems to generate named spatial references as well.

References

Anja Belz and Albert Gatt. 2008. Intrinsic vs. extrinsic evaluation measures for referring expression generation. In *Proceedings of the 46th Annual Meeting of the Association for Computational Linguistics on Human Language Technologies: Short Papers*, pages 197–200. Association for Computational Linguistics.

Bernd Bohnet, François Lareau, Leo Wanner, et al. 2007. Automatic production of multilingual environmental information. In *Proceedings of the 21st Conference on Informatics for Environmental Protection (EnviroInfo-07), Warsaw, Poland.*

Eliseo Clementini, Paolino Di Felice, and Peter van Oosterom. 1993. A small set of formal topological relationships suitable for end-user interaction. In *Advances in Spatial Databases*, pages 277–295. Springer.

Jose Coch. 1998. Multimeteo: multilingual production of weather forecasts. *ELRA Newsletter*, 3(2).

Robert Dale and Ehud Reiter. 1995. Computational interpretations of the gricean maxims in the generation of referring expressions. *Cognitive science*, 19(2):233–263.

Robert Dale, Sabine Geldof, and Jean-philippe Prost. 2005. Using Natural Language Generation in Automatic Route Description. *Journal of Research & Practice in Information Technology*, 37(1):89–105.

Christian Ebert, Ralf Meyer-klabunde, Daniel Glatz, Martin Jansche, and Robert Porzel. 1996. From Conceptualization to Formulation in Generating Spatial Descriptions. In *Proceedings fo the 5th European Conference on Cognitive Modelling*, pages 235–241.

Albert Gatt, Anja Belz, and Eric Kow. 2008. The tuna challenge 2008: Overview and evaluation results. In *Proceedings of the Fifth International Natural Language Generation Conference*, pages 198–206. Association for Computational Linguistics.

Adele E Goldberg. 1995. *Constructions: A construction grammar approach to argument structure*. University of Chicago Press.

John Kelleher and Geert-Jan Kruijff. 2006. Incremental generation of spatial referring expressions in situated dialog. In *Proceedings of the 21st International Conference on Computational Linguistics and the 44th annual meeting of the Association for Computational Linguistics*, pages 1041–1048. Association for Computational Linguistics.

Emiel Krahmer and Kees Van Deemter. 2012. Computational generation of referring expressions: A survey. *Computational Linguistics*, 38(1):173–218.

Stephen C Levinson. 2003. Frames of reference. In *Space in Language and Cognition: Explorations in Cognitive Diversity*, chapter 2, pages 24–61. Cambridge University Press.

Ehud Reiter, Somayajulu Sripada, Jim Hunter, Jin Yu, and Ian Davy. 2005. Choosing words in computer-generated weather forecasts. *Artificial Intelligence*, 167(1):137–169.

Ross Turner, Somayajulu Sripada, and Ehud Reiter. 2010. Generating approximate geographic descriptions. In *Empirical methods in natural language generation*, pages 121–140. Springer.

Ross Turner. 2009. *Georeferenced data-to-text: techniques and application*. Ph.D. thesis, University of Aberdeen.

Kees Van Deemter. 2002. Generating referring expressions: Boolean extensions of the incremental algorithm. *Computational Linguistics*, 28(1):37–52.

Narrative Generation from Extracted Associations

Pierre-Luc Vaudry and Guy Lapalme
RALI-DIRO – Université de Montréal
C.P. 6128, succ. Centre-Ville
Montréal, Québec, Canada, H3C 3J8
{vaudrypl,lapalme}@iro.umontreal.ca

Abstract

This paper describes a method for extracting potential causal relations from temporal data and using them to structure a generated report. The method is applied to the Activity of Daily Living domain. The extracted relations seem to be useful to locally link activities with explicit rhetorical relations. However, further work is needed to better exploit them for improving coherence at the global level.

1 Introduction

One way of presenting voluminous and heterogeneous temporal data is to use natural language generation (NLG) technology to produce a narrative text summarizing the events of a given period. Experiments have shown that a narrative written by a domain expert can be a better support for decision-making than a graphical presentation of the same data (Law et al., 2005). Unfortunately current automatically generated narratives fail to achieve the same level of performance (Portet et al., 2009). Experts in discourse analysis have concluded that the problem may lay in the narrative structure: deficiencies in narrative flow and narrative details impacted negatively on coherence (McKinlay et al., 2009).

How can the coherence of generated narratives be improved? Causal networks have been successfully used to explain the process of narrative comprehension in humans (Trabasso et al., 1989). This motivated their use in the automatic creation of fairy tales (Swartjes and Theune, 2006; Theune et al., 2007). Those causal networks are essentially composed of physical and mental events and states (of which goals and actions) connected by causal relations. Restrictions apply on which types of causal relation can connect which types of event or state. Some have suggested that causal relations also play an important role in improving narrative generation from real-life data (Hunter et al., 2012; Gervás, 2014). Several narrative generation systems already identify and make use of some causal relations (Hallett, 2008; Hunter et al., 2012; Bouayad-Agha et al., 2012; Wanner et al., 2010). Going one step further, Vaudry and Lapalme (2015) have raised the question of the possibility of extracting an appropriate causal network from real-life temporal data and use it to generate more coherent narratives. They briefly proposed a document planning method that could presumably be parameterised to generate texts of varied styles from a single causal network. However, they did not address the causal network extraction process.

The goal of the experiment described in this paper is to verify if it is possible to extract a form of causal network from temporal data and use it to generate a coherent narrative text. The experiment consisted of data mining for associations in Activity of Daily Living (ADL) data to produce a network of hypothesised causal relations. This causal network was then used to generate a report of unusual facts aiming at supporting anomaly assessment.

The content of this paper is divided as follows. To begin with, the context of application, ADLs, will be introduced. Then, we will present our approach to association rule data mining and how we applied it to the domain of ADLs. The main part of this paper will describe the data-to-text pipeline that uses the extracted association rules, including: data interpretation, document planning, microplanning and surface realisation. Finally, we will present and discuss the results of this experiment.

Proceedings of the 15th European Workshop on Natural Language Generation (ENLG), pages 136–145,
Brighton, September 2015.

2 Context of application

Ambient Assisted Living (AAL) technology can be used to help elderly people to live in their own house longer. Moreover, sensor equipment can be used to monitor an elderly person's Activities of Daily Living and detect anomalies associated with dementia early (Lalanda et al., 2010).

There are different ways of processing sensor data to detect and present possible anomalies. For example, Munstermann et al. (2012) achieve typical behaviour discovery by learning a transition network from the ADL sequence data. They then use it to measure how normal a given day is and map this metric to traffic light colours.

However the normalcy of a given day is measured, health care professionals would still need to assess if there were indeed anomalies and what was their nature. For this, a more detailed access to the data is required. In our experiment, we explore a way of presenting unusual facts using NLG technology. For that we extract association rules from the event data. We then use them to present a textual narrative summary of a given time interval that emphasises unusual facts. Health care professionals could then review this summary for potential anomalies with access to other sources of information. One advantage of natural language is that it can compactly express not only events but also multiple relations between events. By selecting for the generated text only the most important events and relations, the reader should not have to pore over unnecessarily detailed usual behaviour.

Since this was our first experiment both with generating a narrative from extracted associations and presenting unusual facts in ADLs, we wanted to work on as simple a dataset as possible. For this reason we chose the publicly available UCI ADL Binary Dataset (Ordóñez et al., 2013). This dataset was assembled to train activity classifiers that take as input raw sensor data. We do not address this task in this paper, relying instead on the reference annotations provided as our input (but see for example the paper just cited or Fleury et al., 2010). Generating from real data and not reference annotations would pose problems that are out of the scope of this paper.

This dataset includes the ADLs of two users (A and B) in their own homes. The data was recorded for 14 and 21 consecutive days, respectively. Binary sensor events and the corresponding activity labels are given. We used only the latter in this experiment. For each sensor event or activity, the start and end time are given. There is no overlap between sensor events and between activities (there was only one person per house).

The ADL label set is: *Leaving, Toileting, Showering, Sleeping, Breakfast, Lunch, Dinner, Snack, Spare_Time/TV, Grooming*. The ADL sequence for user A comprises 248 activities (average of 18 activities per day) and that for user B, 493 activities (average of 21 activities per day). As an example, Table 1 shows the 30 ADL labels for user B on 24 November 2012.

Sometimes the same label is repeated and one could think that it was just the same activity that continued. However, by looking at the sensor data we can understand why it was annotated in this way. For example, between the Grooming that finishes at 11:52 and the following activity, also Grooming, that begins at 11:59, the bedroom door was used twice. In any case, it is out of the scope of this paper to question the annotation process.

Start time	End time	Activity
00:33:00	10:02:59	Sleeping
10:04:00	10:12:59	Breakfast
10:17:00	10:18:59	Toileting
10:19:00	11:13:59	Spare_Time/TV
11:16:00	11:19:59	Snack
11:30:00	11:38:59	Showering
11:39:00	11:52:59	Grooming
11:59:00	12:00:59	Grooming
12:01:00	12:02:59	Toileting
12:09:00	12:23:59	Snack
12:31:00	13:18:59	Spare_Time/TV
13:50:00	14:31:59	Spare_Time/TV
14:32:00	14:32:59	Grooming
14:36:00	15:59:59	Leaving
16:00:00	16:00:59	Toileting
16:01:00	16:01:59	Grooming
16:02:00	16:02:59	Toileting
16:03:00	16:03:59	Grooming
16:04:00	19:57:59	Spare_Time/TV
19:58:00	19:59:59	Snack
20:08:00	20:31:59	Spare_Time/TV
22:01:00	22:01:59	Toileting
22:02:00	22:16:59	Spare_Time/TV
22:17:00	22:18:59	Dinner
22:19:00	23:20:59	Spare_Time/TV
23:21:00	23:22:59	Snack
23:23:00	00:44:59	Spare_Time/TV
00:45:00	00:47:59	Grooming
00:48:00	01:48:59	Spare_Time/TV
01:50:00	09:24:59	Sleeping

Table 1. The 30 ADL labels for user B on 24 November 2012.

3 Data mining for association rules

For finding significant association rules in the ADL data, we used the data mining techniques presented by Hamalainen and Nykanen (2008). This approach was selected because it has been successfully applied for the construction of a causal network from a video (Kwon and Lee, 2012). The video was first segmented spatially and temporally using only pixel information to form the nodes of the network. The causal network was then presented as a visual (non-textual) summary of the video.

Generating a textual video summary using a similar technique would be an interesting endeavour. However, for that we would have first needed a reliable way of producing a sufficiently accurate textual description of an arbitrary spatio-temporal segment of a video. Generating text from ADL labels and time-stamps is easier as a first step to test our narrative planning method.

In this experiment we considered a limited number of simple types of association rules in the ADL data. To select them we assumed that **temporal proximity and temporal precedence were indicators of potential causality**. Although it is far from being a guaranty of causality, it is simple enough to apply as a first step. Also, the causal relation could very well be indirect or the relation may instead imply a common cause between the two events. Nevertheless, it does not necessarily make the relation less relevant to hint at in the generated text. The relations extracted from sensor data can only be imperfect, because sensor data contain only a fraction of the relevant information. However, the causal relations that count in the end are those the human reader reconstructs in his mind with the help of other sources of information, not the exact ones the machine identified.

The types of association rule considered are shown in Table 2. In the following, A and H are categorical variables and stand respectively for activity and hour of the day (hours 0-23, not considering minutes). $A_{i,p}$ stands for a particular type of activity i at position p in the event sequence. Association rule type 1 evaluates the influence of the last activity on the choice of the current activity. Type 2 does the same for the penultimate activity and type 3 for the last two activities. Type 4 takes into account the influence of the current hour of the day on the choice of activity. Lastly, type 5 combines the current hour and the last activity to try to predict the current activity. Each rule is accompanied by an example with the first *Toileting* activity of Table 1.

To be able to describe the algorithm in more general terms, events and states will in this paper be called eventualities (after Bach, 1986). This includes activities and hours of the day.

For selecting significant association rules, we computed three properties for each candidate (Hamalainen and Nykanen, 2008):

- **frequency**: the probability of encountering an instance of the association rule in the data; it is estimated from counts;
- **confidence**: the conditional probability of encountering an instance of the association, given that we just encountered an instance of the left part of the association rule;
- **significance**: the probability of obtaining the observed counts if the events on the right part of the rule were actually independent of the events on the left part of the rule. It is measured by computing the p-value according to the binomial distribution.

We computed two p-values: one to indicate positive association rules (significantly high counts) and the other to indicate negative association rules (significantly low counts). By the latter we mean cases in which the presence of the events on the left part of the rule can be used as a predictor of the absence of the events on the right part of the rule. In other words, actual instances of these association rules are unexpected.

Those properties are formalised in Figure 1.

To compute frequency, confidence and significance, we counted in the data $m(L_i, R_j)$ and $m(L_i)$ for each value i,j for each association candidate $L_i \rightarrow R_j$. Those counts were made using all the data available for a given user.

Type	Association rule	Example association rule candidate
1	$A_{i,p-1} \rightarrow A_{j,p}$	$A_{Breakfast,p-1} \rightarrow A_{Toileting,p}$
2	$A_{i,p-2} \rightarrow A_{j,p}$	$A_{Sleeping,p-2} \rightarrow A_{Toileting,p}$
3	$A_{i,p-2} \wedge A_{j,p-1} \rightarrow A_{k,p}$	$A_{Sleeping,p-2} \wedge A_{Breakfast,p-1} \rightarrow A_{Toileting,p}$
4	$H_{i,p} \rightarrow A_{j,p}$	$H_{10,p} \rightarrow A_{Toileting,p}$
5	$A_{i,p-1} \wedge H_{j,p} \rightarrow A_{k,p}$	$A_{Breakfast,p-1} \wedge H_{10,p} \rightarrow A_{Toileting,p}$

Table 2. Association rule types and examples.

Count for value i of variable X: $m(X_i)$ Total count for variable X: $n(X) = \sum_i m(X_i)$

Probability for value i of variable X: $P(X_i) = \frac{m(X_i)}{n(X)}$

Joint count for values i,j of left (L) and right (R) parts of association rule $L_i \rightarrow R_j$: $m(L_i, R_j)$

Total joint count for an association rule of type $L \rightarrow R$: $n(L,R) = \sum_{i,j} m(L_i, R_j)$

Frequency of an association rule $L_i \rightarrow R_j$: $fr(L_i \rightarrow R_j) = P(L_i, R_j) = \frac{m(L_i,R_j)}{n(L,R)}$

Confidence of an association rule $L_i \rightarrow R_j$: $cf(L_i \rightarrow R_j) = P(R_j|L_i) = \frac{P(L_i,R_j)}{P(L_i)}$

Significance (p-value using the binomial distribution) of $L_i \rightarrow R_j$:

$$p(L_i \rightarrow R_j) = \sum_{l=l_{min}}^{l_{max}} \binom{n(L,R)}{l} \left(P(L_i)P(R_j)\right)^l \left(1 - P(L_i)P(R_j)\right)^{n(L,R)-l}$$

With $l_{min} = m(L_i, R_j)$ and $l_{max} = m(L_i)$ for an expected association ($p_{expected}$)

and $l_{min} = 0$ and $l_{max} = m(L_i, R_j)$ for an unexpected association ($p_{unexpected}$).

Figure 1. Notation and formulas for counts, frequency, confidence and significance.

Next, we filtered the association rule candidates using the following criteria. To get the expected association rules, we retained only candidates $L_i \rightarrow R_j$ for which $cf(L_i \rightarrow R_j) > cf_{min}$ and $p_{expected}(L_i \rightarrow R_j) < 0.05$. To get the unexpected association rules, we retained only candidates $L_i \rightarrow R_j$ for which $cf(L_i \rightarrow R_j) < cf_{max}$ and $p_{unexpected}(L_i \rightarrow R_j) < 0.05$. We tried different values of cf_{min} and cf_{max} and settled for $cf_{min} = 0.3$ and $cf_{max} = 0.07$. This seemed reasonable because there were 10 ADL labels, which would give an *a priori* probability of 0.1 for each without any knowledge about the data. This means that associations that have a conditional probability of having their right part happen with a probability around 0.1 given their left part do not give much information. They are thus less relevant.

We also had to filter the candidates to eliminate redundancy: $L_i^1 \rightarrow R_j$ is considered more general than $L_k^2 \rightarrow R_j$ if and only if the events of L_i^1 are included in the events of L_k^2. For example, the rule $A_{Breakfast,p-1} \rightarrow A_{Toileting,p}$ is more general than $A_{Sleeping,p-2} \wedge A_{Breakfast,p-1} \rightarrow A_{Toileting,p}$. We considered a rule candidate non-redundant only if all more general rule candidates were less significant (had a higher p-value). We still kept a more general rule candidate too if it was significant enough (p-value < 0.05).

For example, among the five example rule candidates with *Toileting* given in Table 2, only $H_{10,p} \rightarrow A_{Toileting,p}$ ($cf = 0.365$, $p_{expected} = 0.002$) was selected as an expected association rule and none as an unexpected association rule. An example of a rule candidate that was selected as an unexpected rule is $A_{Toileting,p-1} \wedge H_{10,p} \rightarrow A_{Spare\_Time/TV,p}$ ($cf = 0.044$, $p_{unexpected} = 0.028$). Those numbers come from the counting of all the 21 days of data available for user B.

4 The data-to-text pipeline

To generate a report from the ADL data for a given period, we roughly follow a standard data-to-text pipeline (Reiter, 2007). Since we take as input the ADL labels, we do not have to analyse the underlying sensor signals. Therefore we begin with data interpretation, which consists of finding instances of the previously selected association rules in the input. For each of those, one or more logico-semantic relations are introduced as part of a hypothetic interpretation of the input data.

Following Bouayad-Agha et al. (2012), in this paper the term logico-semantic relation designates very abstract semantic relations between eventualities that are independent from pragmatic factors. They are to be distinguished from rhetorical relations in the sense of the Rhetorical Structure Theory (RST) (Mann and Thompson, 1987), which have an intentional load. According to Kosseim and Lapalme (2000), the many-to-many mapping between semantic relations and rhetorical relations requires placing them into separate representation levels in an NLG system.

Next the logico-semantic relations are used to plan the document as a whole in the document planning stage. The output is a rhetorical structure featuring rhetorical relations. Follows the microplanning stage that plans the phrases and lexical units expressing the events and rhetorical relations. This produces a lexico-syntactic specification that is realised as natural language text in the last stage: surface realisation.

In our case there is one more operation, which takes place between document planning and microplanning: summarisation. Here the rhetorical structure is pruned to keep only the most important events and relations. This produces a summary of the initially planned text.

The five pipeline stages are thus in order: data interpretation, document planning, summarising, microplanning and surface realisation. The following sections describe them in more detail.

5 Data interpretation

In data interpretation, each activity and its context in the input ADL sequence are examined to find instances of application of an association rule. When there is a match, the algorithm postulates one or more corresponding logico-semantic relations and adds them to the document content. When an expected association instance is found, a *pseudo-causal* relation is created between the left and right part of the rule. It is not necessary that the relation really be a direct causation. More precisely, the relation could be paraphrased as: *It does not seem a coincidence that this event is followed by that event.* The real explanation may be much more complex. For short, we will retain the terms *cause* and *result*. For example, in the example day of Table 1, the third activity matches the expected rule $H_{10,p} \rightarrow A_{Toileting,p}$.

1) Hour of Day 10 **causes** Toileting 10:17

When an unexpected association instance is found (including associations never encountered before), an *unexpected result* relation is created. For example, from Table 1 the following two relations are created from the unexpected rule $A_{Toileting,p-1} \wedge H_{10,p} \rightarrow A_{Spare\_Time/TV,p}$.

2) Toileting 10:17 **unexpectedly results in** Spare_Time/TV 10:19
3) Hour of Day 10 **unexpectedly results in** Spare_Time/TV 10:19

In addition, an *instead* relation is created with the best available prediction of what activity would have been expected in the same context, according to the expected association rules:

4) Spare_Time/TV 10:19 **instead of** Grooming

When the left part of the association rule includes the hour of the day variable and a match is found, a time mention is introduced and added to the document content. This time mention references the start time of the corresponding activity.

The algorithm also introduces a *repetition* relation when the activity type in the right part of a matching association rule is included in its left part. For example, because of a match of expected rule $A_{Grooming,p-2} \rightarrow A_{Grooming,p}$, a repetition relation is created:

5) Grooming 16:03 **is a repetition of** Grooming 16:01

To be able later to compare the importance of activities, time mentions and relations, a probability is assigned to each of them. The probability of a logico-semantic relation is the confidence of the corresponding matching association rule. For example, relation 1 is assigned as probability $cf(H_{10,p} \rightarrow A_{Toileting,p}) = 0.365$. An activity at the right side of one or more matching association rules is assigned as probability the highest confidence of those association rules. This probability is called posterior probability, in the sense that it takes into account the context (the left side of the rules). For example, *Toileting 10:17* is assigned probability 0.365. For other activities, the prior probability is used, that is, the frequency without looking at the context. For example, *Showering 11:30* does not correspond to the right side of any matching association rules and so it is assigned as probability its frequency. Time mentions use the frequency of the hour of the day.

6 Document planning

In this experiment, document planning and microplanning are done in essentially the same way as proposed by Vaudry and Lapalme (2015). The main difference is that there are only two types of eventualities: activity and hour of the day. This leads to a lesser number of *causal* and *unexpected result* subtypes (those subtypes are differentiated by the type of their arguments). On the other hand, we use two logico-semantic relations not mentioned in Vaudry and Lapalme (2015) : *instead* and *repetition*.

Document planning is done in four steps: derivation of additional logico-semantic relations, building of an unordered tree structure by clustering, logico-semantic to rhetorical relation mapping, and ordering of the tree. The following subsections describe each of them.

6.1 Deriving additional logico-semantic relations

Before building the rhetorical structure, Vaudry and Lapalme (2015) mention using rules to infer additional logico-semantic relations, such as volitional causation, contrast and conjunction. With only activities and hours of the day as eventualities, only the addition of conjunction relations was relevant for this experiment.

A *conjunction* relation applies to items that play a comparable role (Mann and Taboada, 2005). In the case of a logico-semantic network, this can be interpreted as the following: if two or more eventualities $e_1, e_2, \ldots, e_n$ that are part of the same type of logico-semantic relation r with another eventuality e_0, then they can be said to be in a relation of conjunction with each other. For example, if two activities are hypothesised to be caused by the same preceding activity, they are in a *conjunction* relation.

6.2 Clustering

The first step in document planning is to build an unordered tree structure by performing agglomerative hierarchical clustering. This is parameterized by adjacency preferences. Those must be specified for the *instead* and *repetition* relations, as well as for the *causal* and *unexpected result* relation subtypes resulting from data interpretation. Adjacency preferences are expressed in terms of how much a given relation prefers to have its arguments appear in the same sentence, the same paragraph or another paragraph.

The adjacency preferences used in the ADL report generation are presented in Table 3. They reflect the following choices. A time mention coming from a relation between the hour of the day and an activity must be mentioned very close to that activity so as not to generate ambiguity. Two related activities can be mentioned in separate sentences with the appropriate markers, except for the *instead* relation which calls for greater proximity. This makes for relatively short sentences. The conjunction relation must appear one level deeper in the tree than its related relation to avoid ambiguity.

In our experiment, average linkage clustering is used. The distance between two eventualities is computed from the average of the adjacency preferences of the logico-semantic relations holding between them. The more a relation prefers to have its arguments adjacent, the smaller the distance. When no logico-semantic relation holds between two eventualities, the sum of distances on the shortest path between them is used. If no such path exists, then the maximal distance is assigned. The temporal distance relative to the total duration of the period to be narrated is also taken into account, although with a low weight. In this way temporal distance helps order eventuality pairs that would have the same distance otherwise. For example, suppose activities A and B on one hand, and B and C on the other hand, have between them the same logico-semantic relation(s). If B is temporally closer to A than to C, this will tip the balance so that A and B will be clustered together first. At each iteration, the two closest clusters are merged to form a new cluster, until all clusters are merged into one. The resulting hierarchy forms the basis of the rhetorical structure.

Looking up the logico-semantic relations given in section 5, relation 2 has a lower adjacency preference than relation 3. This means that *Spare_Time/TV 10:19* will be clustered with *Hour of Day 10* before being clustered with *Toileting 10:17*. Also, *Toileting 10:17* will be in a different sentence than *Spare_Time/TV 10:19*.

6.3 Logico-semantic to rhetorical mapping

The second step is to map each logico-semantic relation to a rhetorical relation with respect to communicative constraints.

Logico-semantic relation	Adjacency preference	Rhetorical relation(s)	Satellite
Activity *causes* activity	0.60	Sequence	n/a (multinuclear)
Hour of day *causes* activity	1.00	Circumstance	first argument
Activity *unexpectedly results in* activity	0.60	Sequence, Concession	n/a (multinuclear), first argument
Hour of day *unexpectedly results in* activity	0.90	Concession	first argument
Instead	0.95	Instead	second argument
Conjunction (with p the adjacency preference of the relation that the coordinates have in common)	$1.50 \times p$	Conjunction	n/a (multinuclear)
Repetition	0.60	Repetition	first argument

Table 3. Adjacency preferences and logico-semantic to rhetorical mapping for ADL report. 0.0 means as far as possible, 1.0 mean as close as possible and 0.5 means in the same paragraph, but not the same sentence. The actual adjacency preference for conjunction is a coefficient applied to the adjacency preference of the relation that the coordinates have in common. This has usually the effect of keeping each conjunction relation just one level deeper in the tree than the common relation.

Generating a factual report such as an ADL report requires caution. There is no guarantee that the extracted association rules translate directly to causal relations. Therefore we judged it was appropriate to simply suggest a possible unnamed relation between the arguments of logico-semantic causal or unexpected result relations. Bouayad-Agha et al. (2012, p. 3:9) observed that a neutral perspective could be obtained by using a rhetorical temporal circumstance instead of a rhetorical cause. We also used the rhetorical temporal sequence relation for the same reason. This is because the presence of a causal relation implies that the cause precedes the effect. Thus, when a temporal relation is explicitly mentioned, it can suggest a possible causal relation without it being logically implied.

Except in the case of multinuclear relations, the parameters specifying the logico-semantic to rhetorical mapping must include how to choose which logico-semantic argument will be the rhetorical nucleus and which will be the satellite. According to RST, in a rhetorical argument pair, the nucleus is the one that is more essential to the writer's purpose and the other is termed the satellite. For example, the logico-semantic relation *hour of day* ***causes*** *activity* is expressed implicitly by putting forward the activity and mentioning the hour of day as only a rhetorical circumstance. The activity is judged more important because the central character of the narrative accomplishes it. Some relations such as contrast or sequence are considered multinuclear, which means that neither argument is more essential than the other (Mann and Thompson, 1987, pp. 31–38). Two observed activities are *a priori* no more important than the other; therefore the sequence rhetorical relation is used as a temporal relation between activities.

The parameters used for the logico-semantic to rhetorical mapping for the generation of the ADL report are presented in Table 3.

6.4 Ordering

Ordering preferences are specified for each type of rhetorical relation in terms of which of the satellite or the nucleus tends to come first and how strong this tendency is. The ordering preferences used in this experiment for the generation of the ADL report are presented in Table 4. In addition, a temporal ordering preference specifies to what extent chronological or reverse chronological order should be followed. In this experiment, chronological order was preferred.

Rhetorical relation	Ordering preference
Sequence	no preference
Circumstance	satellite first
Concession	no preference
Instead	nucleus first
Conjunction	no preference
Repetition	nucleus first

Table 4. Ordering preferences for ADL report. *No preference* means chronological order.

During ordering, the ordering preferences associated with the rhetorical and temporal relations are treated similarly to the adjacency preferences in the clustering step. Sibling clusters in the hierarchy produced by the clustering are ordered by averaging the ordering preferences of all the relations holding between them. For this purpose, a *nucleus first* preference has a value of 1.0 while a *satellite first* preference has a value of -1.0. The result of this step is an ordered tree.

7 Summarisation

To summarise the ADLs of a given period, we retain the most important facts from the rhetorical tree. At first we used the minimum tree depth at which a leaf is *promoted* as a criteria to generate a partial ordering of the eventualities (Marcu, 2000). The promotion set of a text span is the union of the promotion sets of its nuclei, except if it is a leaf. The promotion set of a leaf is the singleton containing only the leaf itself. This method gave interesting results, but tended to eliminate potentially anomalous facts that were located deep in the tree. This happened often because interesting logico-semantic relations tended to occur between the firstly created clusters, which placed them deep in the resulting tree.

Since the goal is to produce a report of unusual facts, we suppose that less typical facts are more important. Following this hypothesis, we used the probability according to the extracted association rule set as a measure of importance. As mentioned in section 5, the probability of an eventuality that does not appear in the right part of an instance of an association rule is its prior probability. Otherwise, it is the best prediction (the highest probability) given by those association rules, i.e. the posterior probability. A satellite text span was included in the summary if the probability of its promoted eventuality or the minimum probability of its relations with the nucleus was below a certain threshold. Otherwise, only the nucleus was kept. This method had the benefit of pruning less important text spans regardless of their depth in the tree.

Stage	Statistic	User A	User B
Data mining	Number of mined expected association rules	51	62
	Number of mined unexpected association rules	2	11
Data interpretation	Average number of logico-semantic relations	39.1	32.5
Document planning	Average number of linking rhetorical relations	22.1	25.3
	Av. num. of internal tree nodes without linking relations	7.8	12.9

Table 5. Statistics on the performance of data mining, data interpretation and document planning.

For example, with a threshold of 0.4, *Grooming 11:39* will be pruned, because the relation *Showering 11:30 causes Grooming 11:39* has probability 0.91. We can assume the reader can infer the grooming from the preceding showering if he is already familiar with user B's routine.

8 Microplanning and realisation

During microplanning, the rhetorical structure is translated into a lexico-syntactic specification. For this the microplanning algorithm traverses the document plan tree depth-first. When a leaf is visited, a specification of a description of the corresponding eventuality is produced from lexico-syntactic templates. When an internal node is visited, the rhetorical relations that link the two children nodes are expressed with appropriate discourse markers. The marker (or absence of marker) depends on the rhetorical relation and the aggregation level (same sentence, same paragraph or other paragraph). Those markers are then used to assemble the lexico-syntactic specifications obtained from the children nodes.

For now, only the rhetorical relations holding between the promoted leaves of the two children nodes are taken into account. When there are none, in the future we plan to take other relations between the two children nodes into account. Our hypothesis is that it could lead to more coherent texts provided that anaphora is used judiciously to avoid adding ambiguity.

Sentence and paragraph segmentation are a function of clustering distance. The latter reflects adjacency preferences, which are defined in terms of sentences and paragraphs.

Surface realization was performed using the SimpleNLG-EnFr Java library (Vaudry and Lapalme, 2013). During surface realization, the syntactic and lexical specifications are combined with the output language grammar and lexicon to generate formatted natural language text. Because SimpleNLG-EnFr can realise text in both English and French, we were able to generate a report in both languages. For that a version of the lexico-syntactic templates used in microplanning had to be written for each language.

9 Results

Table 5 presents some statistics on the performance of the data mining, data interpretation and document planning stages. Data interpretation and document planning were tested by generating one report per 24-hour period in the ADL data for each user. We can note that not all mined association rules apply each day. Moreover, not all logico-semantic relations were translated to a rhetorical relation in the rhetorical structure. This leads to a number of text spans being clustered together without a linking rhetorical relation. Those correspond mostly to the tree nodes closest to the root of the tree.

The example report of Figure 2 was generated from the data of Table 1. The maximum probability threshold used for summarisation was 0.4. At the top is displayed the start and end time of the period considered for the report. The dis-

Saturday, 24 November 2012 10:04 AM -
Sunday, 25 November 2012 09:24 AM

At 10:04 AM he ate his breakfast.

13 minutes later at 10:17 AM he went to the toilet. Then, nevertheless he spent time in the living room although it was 10:19 AM.

1 hour later at 11:16 AM he had a snack.

14 minutes later he took a shower.

1 hour later he went to the toilet.

8 minutes later he had a snack.

2 hours later he left.

1 hour later at 4:00 PM he went to the toilet. Then he groomed and at 4:02 PM went to the toilet. Then he groomed again.

1 minute later he spent time in the living room.

4 hours later he had a snack.

2 hours later he went to the toilet and at 10:02 PM spent time in the living room. Then at 10:17 PM he dined.

1 hour later he had a snack.

1 hour later he spent time in the living room.

Figure 2. ADL report generated from Table 1 with a maximum probability threshold of 0.4.

course markers (*at*, *although*, *then*, *nevertheless*, *and*, *again*) express the rhetorical relations that hold between sibling text spans in the rhetorical tree. The only exception is the default marker in the form of *X time later* that is used when no such relation exists between two text spans.

Out of 18 activities, 8 are mentioned singly in their own paragraph, without a discourse marker other than the default one. In other words, almost half of the mentioned activities are not connected closely to another part of the text. Paragraphs that do contain more than one activity have their content internally connected with discourse markers. However, they are not connected with the other paragraphs. This is consistent with the statistics of Table 5. From this we conclude that although the generated text expresses some rhetorical relations locally, it fails to explicitly achieve global coherence. This may leave a heavy burden on the reader in forming a representation of what happened during that day. Analysing the proposed data-to-text pipeline, there are several places where this may be improved.

Before generation itself, data mining could search for more diverse types of association rules so that more logico-semantic relations could be created during data interpretation. One possibility is to mine for associations where the implication goes backward in time, in order to indirectly capture underlying goals. For example: *He went to the toilet before going to bed. (He went to the toilet because he wanted to go to bed.)* Going to the toilet may not imply going to bed afterwards, but going to bed may imply having probably gone to the toilet beforehand. Moreover, associations where the implication goes in both directions should then be treated differently. They should probably be expressed as a conjunction.

A problem is that the summarisation stage has the effect of removing relations with a probability higher than the threshold. So the more we summarise, the less coherent the text may become. A possible solution to explore would be to select important relations and events based on logico-semantic relations alone, before document planning.

Maybe the key to achieve coherence at a higher level would be to detect more abstract eventualities and relations in the data. Those more abstract eventualities, such as routines, would include more concrete ones, like activities. This would create a hierarchy that could be used to build texts that are coherent at a higher level.

In a different vein, we did not concentrate our efforts on microplanning and it could certainly be improved. For example, as the input data is in the form of temporal intervals, the text could possibly be improved if the ADLs were described in the same way instead of as specific points in time.

10 Conclusion

We designed and implemented a method that extracts association rules from ADL data and uses them for the data-to-text generation of unusual fact reports. The extracted association rules were used to locally to link eventualities with rhetorical relations. However, more work will be needed to see how they could be used to enhance the global coherence of generated texts.

Future work will consist first of systematically testing different values for the confidence and significance thresholds with different datasets. Richer, bigger and more varied datasets could lead to more interesting rules being learned and more real anomalies being found. Then we will explore possible improvements, such as mining for more diverse types of association rules and detecting more abstract eventualities in the data. We will also try shifting summarization before document planning.

In this work, we have focused on providing a summary of a single factual time interval, as opposed to generating a summary of a typical (but necessarily fictitious) day. The latter is an interesting and complementary idea, but the extracted associations presented were not designed to do this kind of prediction. Moreover, the training data available may be insufficient to do this accurately enough. Incorporating recent work on activity prediction, such as Minor et al. (2015), is an avenue that should be explored.

A more thorough evaluation, including an appropriate baseline, will also be needed to see if the generated texts are perceived as more coherent and more useful for their intended role than with other generation methods.

References

Emmon Bach. 1986. The algebra of events. *Linguistics and philosophy*, 9(1):5–16.

Nadjet Bouayad-Agha, Gerard Casamayor, Simon Mille, and Leo Wanner. 2012. Perspective-oriented Generation of Football Match Summaries: Old Tasks, New Challenges. *ACM Trans. Speech Lang. Process.*, 9(2):3:1–3:31, August.

A. Fleury, M. Vacher, and N. Noury. 2010. SVM-Based Multimodal Classification of Activities of Daily Living in Health Smart Homes: Sensors, Algorithms, and First Experimental Results. *IEEE Transactions on Information Technology in Biomedicine*, 14(2):274–283, March.

Pablo Gervás. 2014. Composing narrative discourse for stories of many characters: A case study over a chess game. *Literary and Linguistic Computing*, August.

Catalina Hallett. 2008. Multi-modal presentation of medical histories. In *Proceedings of the 13th international conference on Intelligent user interfaces*, pages 80–89.

W. Hamalainen and M. Nykanen. 2008. Efficient Discovery of Statistically Significant Association Rules. In *ICDM '08 Proceedings of the 2008 Eighth IEEE International Conference on Data Mining*, pages 203–212. December.

James Hunter, Yvonne Freer, Albert Gatt, Ehud Reiter, Somayajulu Sripada, and Cindy Sykes. 2012. Automatic generation of natural language nursing shift summaries in neonatal intensive care: BT-Nurse. *Artificial intelligence in medicine*.

Leila Kosseim and Guy Lapalme. 2000. Choosing Rhetorical Structures To Plan Instructional Texts. *Computational Intelligence*, 16(3):408–445.

Junseok Kwon and Kyoung Mu Lee. 2012. A unified framework for event summarization and rare event detection. In *CVPR*, pages 1266–1273.

P. Lalanda, J. Bourcier, J. Bardin, and S. Chollet. 2010. Smart Home Systems. *Grenoble University, France*.

Anna S Law, Yvonne Freer, Jim Hunter, Robert H Logie, Neil McIntosh, and John Quinn. 2005. A comparison of graphical and textual presentations of time series data to support medical decision making in the neonatal intensive care unit. *Journal of clinical monitoring and computing*, 19(3):183–194, June. PMID: 16244840.

William C. Mann and Maite Taboada. 2005. Rhetorical Structure Theory : Relation definitions. Retrieved August 26, 2014, from http://www.sfu.ca/rst/01intro/definitions.html

William C. Mann and Sandra A. Thompson. 1987. *Rhetorical structure theory: A theory of text organization*. University of Southern California, Information Sciences Institute.

Daniel Marcu. 2000. *The theory and practice of discourse parsing and summarization*. MIT Press, Cambridge, Massachusetts, USA.

A. McKinlay, C. McVittie, E. Reiter, Y. Freer, C. Sykes, and R. Logie. 2009. Design Issues for Socially Intelligent User Interfaces: A Discourse Analysis of a Data-to-text System for Summarizing Clinical Data. *Methods of Information in Medicine*, 49(4):379–387, December.

Bryan Minor, Janardhan Rao Doppa, and Diane J. Cook. 2015. Data-Driven Activity Prediction: Algorithms, Evaluation Methodology, and Applications. In *Proceedings of the 21th ACM SIGKDD International Conference on Knowledge Discovery and Data Mining*, pages 805–814. ACM Press.

Marco Munstermann, Torsten Stevens, and Wolfram Luther. 2012. A Novel Human Autonomy Assessment System. *Sensors*, 12(6):7828–7854, June.

Fco Javier Ordóñez, Paula de Toledo, and Araceli Sanchis. 2013. Activity Recognition Using Hybrid Generative/Discriminative Models on Home Environments Using Binary Sensors. *Sensors*, 13(5):5460–5477, April.

François Portet, Ehud Reiter, Albert Gatt, Jim Hunter, Somayajulu Sripada, Yvonne Freer, and Cindy Sykes. 2009. Automatic generation of textual summaries from neonatal intensive care data. *Artificial Intelligence*, 173(7):789–816.

Ehud Reiter. 2007. An Architecture for Data-to-text Systems. In *Proceedings of the Eleventh European Workshop on Natural Language Generation*, pages 97–104, Stroudsburg, PA, USA. Association for Computational Linguistics.

Ivo Swartjes and Mariët Theune. 2006. A fabula model for emergent narrative. In *Technologies for Interactive Digital Storytelling and Entertainment*, pages 49–60. Springer.

Mariët Theune, Nanda Slabbers, and Feikje Hielkema. 2007. The Narrator: NLG for digital storytelling. In *Proceedings of the Eleventh European Workshop on Natural Language Generation*, pages 109–112. Association for Computational Linguistics.

Tom Trabasso, Paul Van den Broek, and So Young Suh. 1989. Logical necessity and transitivity of causal relations in stories. *Discourse Processes*, 12(1):1–25.

Pierre-Luc Vaudry and Guy Lapalme. 2013. Adapting SimpleNLG for bilingual English-French realisation. In *Proceedings of the 14th European Workshop on Natural Language Generation*, pages 183–187, Sofia, Bulgaria, August. Association for Computational Linguistics.

Pierre-Luc Vaudry and Guy Lapalme. 2015. Causal networks as the backbone for temporal data-to-text. Presented at the First International Workshop on Data-to-Text Generation, Edinburgh, United-Kingdom, March.

Leo Wanner, Bernd Bohnet, Nadjet Bouayad-Agha, François Lareau, and Daniel Nicklaß. 2010. Marquis: Generation of User-Tailored Multilingual Air Quality Bulletins. *Applied Artificial Intelligence*, 24(10):914–952.

Topic Transition Strategies for an Information-Giving Agent

Nadine Glas
Institut Mines-Télécom, Télécom ParisTech,
CNRS, LTCI
46 Rue Barrault, 75013 Paris, France
glas@telecom-paristech.fr

Catherine Pelachaud
CNRS, LTCI, Télécom ParisTech
46 Rue Barrault, 75013 Paris, France
pelachaud@
telecom-paristech.fr

Abstract

We have explored how a conversational agent can introduce a selected topic in an ongoing non-task oriented interaction with a user, where the selected topic has little to do with the current topic. Based on the reasoning process of the agent we have constructed a set of transition strategies to introduce the new topic. We tested the effects of each of these strategies on the perception of the dialogue and the agent.

1 Introduction

The choice of the dialogue topics that an agent initiates in non-task oriented human-agent interaction is important for several aspects of the interaction such as the coherence of the interaction (Macias-Galindo et al., 2012) and the user's engagement (Glas and Pelachaud, 2015). Multiple efforts are oriented towards the selection of the appropriate topic at a specific point in the interaction. However, *how* the selected topic can or should be introduced by the agent has not been given much consideration in non-task oriented dialogue.

In this work we will explore the latter aspect by looking at utterances that may be used to initiate a transition from one topic to another. We shall call these utterances *transition strategies*. By comparing a selection of transition strategies we try to answer two questions: 1) What strategies have the potential of keeping/making the dialogue coherent? And 2) what effect do the use of the different transition strategies have on the perception of the conversational agent? The answers to these questions will serve to automatically generate agent strategies to connect one topic to another in non-task oriented dialogue.

2 Domain

This research is performed for the French project 'Avatar 1:1' that aims at developing a human-sized virtual agent in a museum. The goal of the agent is to engage human visitors in interaction about the artworks of the museum. In this information-giving chat (Glas and Pelachaud, 2015) each artwork that is discussed is defined as a topic of the interaction. The discussion of an artwork's characteristic corresponds to a subtopic (Glas et al., 2015).

Previously, we found out that the topic of the interaction has an important influence on the user's level of engagement (Glas and Pelachaud, 2015). We had human users talk with a virtual agent that addressed several topics, correponding to different artworks. The users indicated that they were more engaged when the agent talked about artworks for which the users have a stronger preference (defined here as degree of liking) than when the agent talked about less preferred topics (Glas and Pelachaud, 2015). We are therefore working on an engagement driven topic manager that dynamically selects topics for the ongoing interaction taking into account the user's preferences (Glas et al., 2015). In the present work we are interested in agent strategies that may be used to connect the newly selected topic to the current topic of interaction. This is necessary as the topics are primarily selected according to their potential of engaging the user instead of their coherence with respect to the previous topic. Where other dialogue systems look at what topic is coherent at a specific point in the interaction (e.g. Macial-Galindo et al., 2012; Breuing and Wachsmuth, 2012; Wong et al., 2012), we are looking at possible strategies to introduce a topic coherently.

3 Related Work

3.1 Transition Strategies in Theory

Literature about transition strategies outside task-oriented applications can be found in the domains of conversational analysis and social sci-

Proceedings of the 15th European Workshop on Natural Language Generation (ENLG), pages 146–155,
Brighton, September 2015.

ences, where they are studied from an observational (detection) point of view. Downing (2000) distinguishes two forms of introducing a topic: by means of an *informative statement*, and by *asking a question*. By informing the speaker assigns him/herself the role of topic supplier, whereas by questioning or eliciting a topic this role is offered to an interlocutor in the discourse.

Similarly, Button and Casey (1985) define two global ways of introducing a topic that is not related to the prior topic in a conversation: by a *topic initial elicitor* that is used to elicit a candidate topic from the next speaker while being mute with respect to what that topic may be, and by *topic nominations* that are oriented to particular newsworthy items. Two sequence types that may be used for topic nomination are *itemised news enquires* and *news announcements*. An itemised news inquiry is oriented to a recipient's newsworthy item where a news announcement is oriented to a speaker's newsworthy item.

Maynard and Zimmerman (1984) identified four topic initiation strategies in dyadic human-human conversations. For acquainted parties: *displaying prior experience* and *using setting talk*, and for unacquainted parties: *categorisation question-answer pairs* (e.g. year in school, academic major, etc.) and *question-answer pairs involving activities* that are related to the categories.

Hobbs (1990) focuses on three coherence relations that he claims are responsible for most of the so-called topic drift in dialogue: *parallelism*, *explanation* and *metatalk*. Parallelism between two segments occur when the two segments assert propositions from which we can infer that identical properties hold of similar entities, or that similar properties hold for identical entities. An *explanation* occurs when one segment functions as the explanation of a previous segment and *metatalk* asserts a relation between some segment and the goals of the conversation.

3.2 Transition Strategies in Dialogue Systems

To our knowledge, existing dialogue systems that explicitly consider different strategies to introduce a particular topic have been developed exclusively for task oriented interaction, in particular in the form of task interruption strategies. In this context McFarlane (2002) defines four primary methods: *immediate*, *negotiated*, *mediated*, and *scheduled interruption*. Yang et al. (2008) found out that dialogue partners usually use *discourse markers* and *prosody cues* to signal task switching. Guided by these works Heinroth et al. (2011) looked at 4 different task switching strategies: *unassisted immediate topic shift*, *discourse markers combined with prosody cues*, and two full sentence initialising topic shifts to produce a more natural dialogue flow and to increase the timespan the user has for task switching: *explanation* and *negotiation* strategies. The explanation strategy explains what task is about to be started and the negotiation strategy asks for permission to switch a task. They evaluated the use of these four strategies on several dimensions and found that the explanation strategy showed high scores regarding efficiency and user-friendless and supports the user to memorise the tasks. Other strategies showed advantages such as being less irritating.

3.3 Guidelines for Topic Transitions

The above mentioned research demonstrates that there does not exist one overall taxonomy of transition strategies that can be used as a recipe for transition strategy generation in non-task oriented dialogue. This lack shows the need of our own research towards transition strategies and makes us fall back to the following generally accepted ideas about topic switching: According to Clark (1996) a topic can be described as a joint project as it is jointly established during ongoing conversations. Svennevig (2000) adds that every spoken contribution may raise new potential topics whose actual realisation depends on the co-participant's acceptance by picking up one of these topics within his or her reply. To conclude, Sacks (1971, April 5 in: Levinson, 1983:313) made an overall remark that what seems to be preferred for a topic shift is that if A has been talking about X, B should find a way to talk about Z (if Z is the subject he wants to introduce) such that X and Z can be found to be natural fellow members of some category Y. In the current work we try to collect more precise indications about how to generate transition strategies in non-task oriented dialogue.

4 Methodology

In order to find out what strategies a conversational agent can use to initiate topic transitions in non-task oriented dialogue we follow Heinroth et al. (2011) (Section 3.2) by testing a set of potential transition strategies with respect to their effects on

Speaker	Dialogue about "Luncheon on the Grass" by Claude Monet	Subtopic
	[...]	
Agent:	Claude Monet was a French painter. He lived his entire life at Giverny, a beautiful village north of Paris.	Artist
User:	Yes I know. I visited Giverny last year.	
Agent:	This painting was made around 1865.	Period
User:	Yes, I've read so too.	

Table 1: An example of a dialogue fragment preceding a topic switch initiated by a transition strategy. In the experiment this dialogue fragment (translated) serves as the context of scenario 1 (Section 4.3).

the perception of the dialogue and the agent. In the subsections below we respectively discuss the steps to achieve this: the specification of the context of the transition strategies (Section 4.1), the design of the transition strategies themselves (Section 4.2), the setup of the experiment to test the set of strategies (Section 4.3), and the questionnaire that will be used for this (Section 4.4).

4.1 Context of the Transition Strategies

The strategies that have been mentioned in previous work vary with respect to the context. Some strategies work for topics that are interesting for the listener and others for those that are interesting for the speaker (Button and Casey, 1985). Some strategies are used by acquainted parties and others by unacquainted parties (Maynard and Zimmerman, 1984). Explanation strategies in the sense of Hobbs (1990), as well as metatalk only work for a specific set of topics.

These constraints imply that the strategies that can be used to introduce a topic in a conversation depend on the relation between the current topic of the dialogue and the new topic that is to be introduced. The first step in generating transition strategies is thus to define this relation. In the context of project Avatar 1:1 (Section 2) we are looking at strategies that an agent can employ in interaction with an unacquainted user to make the transition between two discussion phases about two different artworks. In the current work we will focus on what seems the most extreme case, namely the transition between discussion phases of two very different artworks: Artworks that have nothing in common except from the fact that they are both artworks in the same museum. In this way we test if the agent's topic manager can indeed be allowed the flexibility to select any given artwork of the museum as next topic of the discussion. Such flexibility helps finding (initiating) the topic that engages the user most (Glas et al., 2015).

To be more precise, in Table 1 we give an example of a dialogue fragment that proceeds the moment at which the new topic, corresponding to a very different artwork than the one discussed, is to be introduced. As the timing of introducing a new topic may have an influence on the perception of the topic switch (Clark, 1996) we limit this research to a topic switch that occurs after the conversation has addressed respectively the artist and the period of the former discussed artwork.

4.2 Design of Potential Transition Strategies

Due to the nature of the context we are dealing with, the potential transition strategies to introduce a discussion phase of another artwork are limited to the following categories from the literature: explanations in the sense of Heinroth et al. (2011), informative statements (Downing, 2000), itemised news enquires and news announcements (Button and Casey, 1985), categorisation question-answer pairs and question-answer pairs involving activities (Maynard and Zimmerman, 1984), and parallelism (Hobbs, 1990). It is however not prescribed how we could generate formulations for each of these detection-based categories for the context we are looking at. We thus base the manual creation of a set of potential transition strategies that belong to one or multiple of these categories, on the general guideline by Sacks (1971, Section 3.3).

According to Sacks (1971) we need to find a way to let the former (current) and the next (selected) topic be members of some category Y. We try to do this by (indirectly) referring to an element that is used in the agent's reasoning process to talk about the next topic. The agent disposes of a knowledge base that holds information about certain artworks from the museum. From this set of artworks it selects dynamically a new topic of discussion with the goal of maximising the user's engagement level, taking into account the characteristics of the artworks (e.g. period, artist), the

Nr.	Strategy	Element in Topic Manager	Orientation
1.	$Pol(PrefA(i)) == Pol(PrefA(j))$ E.g. *I also like the Balloon Dog by Jeff Koons*	Preferences Agent (i, j)	Agent
2.	$(PrefA(j) > PrefA(i))$ E.g. *Personally, I prefer the Balloon Dog by Jeff Koons*	Preferences Agent (i, j)	Agent
3.	$AssociationA(i, j)$ E.g. This work reminds me of the Balloon Dog by Jeff Koons	Associations Agent (i, j)	Agent
4.	$(Pol(PrefU(i)) == +) \rightarrow (Pol(PrefU(j)) == +)$ E.g. *If you like this work, maybe you also like the Balloon Dog by Jeff Koons*	Preferences User (i, j)	User
5.	$(PrefU(j) > PrefA(i))?$ E.g. *Maybe you prefer the Balloon Dog by Jeff Koons.*	Preferences User (i, j)	User
6.	$ExperienceA(i) + ExperienceA(j)$ E.g. *I've also seen the Balloon Dog by Jeff Koons*	i, j in Knowledge Base	Agent
7.	$ExperienceU(i) + ExperienceU(j)?$ E.g. *Have you also seen the Balloon Dog by Jeff Koons?*	i, j in Knowledge Base	User
8.	$\exists\,(j) \wedge (j \neq i)$ E.g. *Another artwork is the Balloon Dog by Jeff Koons*	i, j in Knowledge Base	Object
9.	$\exists\,(j) \wedge (Artist(j) \neq Artist(i))$ E.g. *An artwork from another artist is the Balloon Dog by Jeff Koons*	Characteristics(i, j) in Knowledge Base	Object
10.	$\exists\,(j) \wedge (Period(j) \neq Period(i))$ E.g. *An artwork from another period is the Balloon Dog by Jeff Koons*	Characteristics(i, j) in Knowledge Base	Object

Table 2: Potential transition strategies to connect the discussion phases of two very different artworks (translated). i is the current topic of the interaction and j is the one to be introduced. A = Agent, U = User, Pol = Polarity, $Pref$ = Preference.

preferences of the user and the agent for an artwork (degree of liking), and the agent's associations (Glas et al., 2015). The set of potential transition strategies that we created by referring to these elements is listed in Table 2. For each of the strategies we formulated an agent utterance to realise the strategy.

Strategies 9 and 10 that insist on the (in this case contrasting) characteristics of the artworks are added as a reference to the strategies that we would use for the transition between artworks that have characteristics in common (the category Y).

4.3 Experimental Setup

Inspired by the existing literature we have created a set of potential transition strategies for the context we are looking at. In order to verify if each of these strategies is suitable to be generated by the agent to switch the topic in the information-giving chat with the user we perform an empirical study. By means of an online questionnaire we test the effect that the different transition strategies have on the perception of the dialogue and the agent.

To this end we present each participant with 2 different dialogue fragments (i.e. contexts) consisting of agent utterances and simulated user inputs (as e.g. Macias-Galindo et al., 2012). Each scenario is followed by 3 randomly assigned transition strategies, displayed next to each other. We do not show the utterances that may follow the transition strategies. In this way we do not show an acceptance or rejection of the topic by the user (Clark, 1996; Svennevig, 2000). Directly after each of the 3 transition strategies we ask the participants to answer several questions (Section 4.4). Appendix A shows a fragment of the website for this experiment. We use a written setup to allow the participants to consider multiple strategies at the same time in the same context, enabling cross-comparison and rereading as much as desired. Besides, in this way the judgements are not disturbed by unnatural text-to-speech realisations.

As mentioned before, the dialogue fragment that represent the former topic in the context and the topic that is addressed in the transition strategies (next topic) are about very different artworks. We test 2 topic pairs for each participant (i.e. 2 different scenarios) to anticipate possible effects that are due to individual characteristics of a particular context. Scenario 1 consists of the discussion of a painting by Monet (shown in table 1) followed by transition strategies introducing a statue by Jeff Koons (listed in Table 2). Scenario 2 consists of the discussion of a painting by Mondrian followed by transition strategies introducing David, the statue by Michelangelo. The alternation of agent-user utterances, the number of utterances and the order of the subtopics are the same in both context fragments. The order in which the scenarios are presented to the participants is random. Pictures of the artworks next to the questionnaire make sure that all the participants know what the artworks look like (Appendix A).

4.4 Questionnaire

For each of the 3 selected transition strategies we ask questions on a scale from 1-9 (shown in Appendix A) (following Bickmore and Cassell, 2005). The first 3 questions relate to the perception of the dialogue and serve to answer the first question we try to answer (Section 1): What strategies have the potential of keeping/making the dialogue coherent? We ask respectively if the participant finds the dialogue natural (Nakano and Ishii, 2010; Bickmore and Cassell, 2005), coherent (Macias-Galindo et al., 2012), and smooth (Higashinaka et al., 2008; Nakano and Ishii, 2010).

The following 5 questions serve to answer our second question (Section 1): What effect do the use of the different transition strategies have on the perception of the conversational agent? We ask respectively to what extent the participants find the agent friendly, warm, fun (in French "stimulant"), competent and informed (in French "cultivé) (Bickmore and Cassell, 2005). These measures are related to 2 important social aspects, warmth and competence (Fiske et al., 2007).

5 Results

83 subjects filled out the questionnaire: 56 female, all native speakers of French, aged 19-69. In the subsections below we show the results of the experiment specified for the two issues we are looking at: the perception of the dialogue and the perception of the agent.

5.1 Dialogue Perception

For each strategy, the perception of the dialogue has been questioned for the two scenarios and on three dimensions: naturalness, coherence, and smoothness. For each of these dimensions the results show no significant difference between the two scenarios (Kruskal-Wallis). This means that we can take the data for both scenarios together, as shown in Figures 1, 2, and 3.

For all three dimensions the scores differ significantly among the strategies (Kruskal-Wallis $p < 0.01$). Regarding the level of naturalness and smoothness, Kruskal-Wallis multiple comparisons show that the significant differences are due to the strategies 9 and 10 that score significantly lower than some others, indicated by the horizontal brackets in the graphs. Regarding the coherence of the dialogue, strategy number 10 leads to a significantly lower level than other strategies.

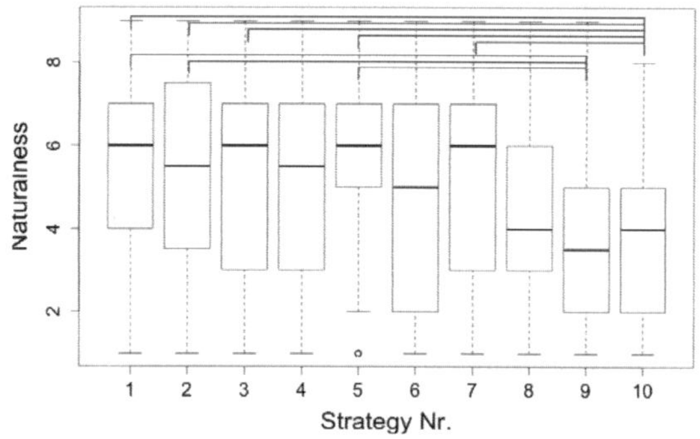

Figure 1: Naturalness for each strategy, $p < 0.01$.

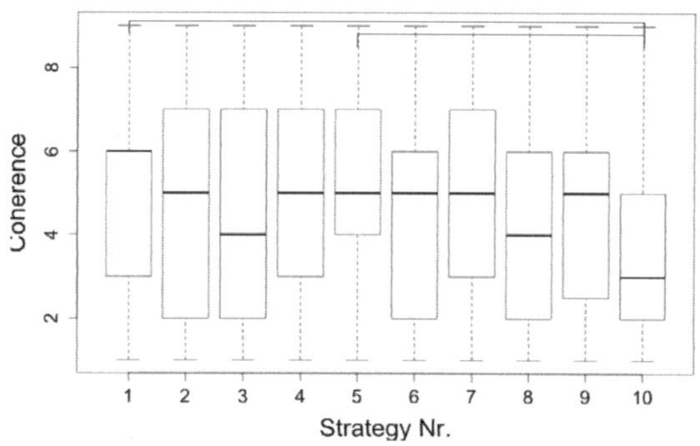

Figure 2: Coherence for each strategy, $p < 0.01$.

Only strategies 1 to 7 show a higher mean than the average level (4.5 on a scale of 9) on the dimensions of naturalness and smoothness. With respect to the level of coherence, except from strategies the 8, 9 and 10, strategy 3 also scores lower than average (mean).

As mentioned in Section 4.2 the strategies are either oriented towards the agent, the user, or the (characteristics) of the object (artwork). The strategies from the latter group lead to significantly lower levels of naturalness, coherence

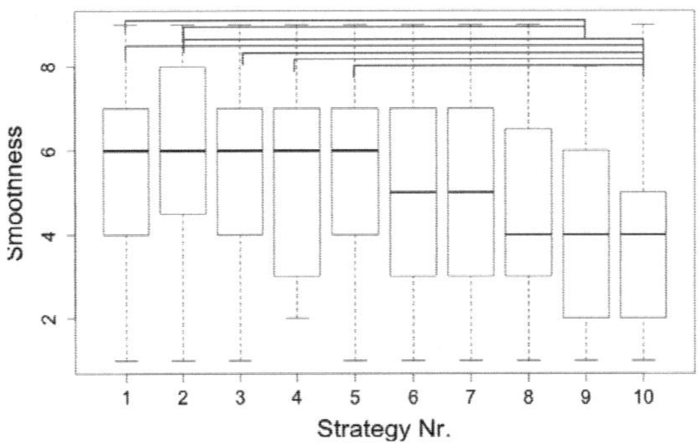

Figure 3: Smoothness for each strategy, $p < 0.01$.

and smoothness in comparison to the strategies with another orientation (both scenarios, Kruskal-Wallis $p < 0.01$). There is no significant difference in the scoring of the strategies that are agent oriented versus the ones that are user oriented with respect to the perception of the dialogue.

5.2 Agent Perception

Questions 4 to 8 are about the way the participants of the experiment perceive the social competence (Fiske et al., 2007) of an agent that would use the transition strategies in the context in which they are presented. The results show that between the two scenarios, the participants find the agent not significantly different with respect to its level of friendliness and knowledge ("informed") (Kruskal-Wallis). For these dimensions we can thus analyse the data for both scenarios together. Figure 4 and 5 specify the distributions of these dimensions for every strategy. The level of friendliness differs significantly among the strategies (Kruskal-Wallis $p < 0.01$), which is due to strategies 8, 9, and 10 (Kruskal-Wallis multiple comparisons). However, only strategy 10 scores below average for the level of friendliness (mean < 4.5). For all strategies the agent is not perceived significantly different with respect to its knowledge ("informed") and all of the strategies score above average on this dimension (mean < 4.5).

In contrast to the agent's level of friendliness and knowledge ("informed"), for the dimensions of warmth, fun and competence, some strategies are significantly differently judged among both scenarios (Kruskal-Wallis $p < 0.05$). Figure 6, 7 and 8 show the distribution of the results specified for both scenarios. The circled numbers indicate the strategies that are judged differently between

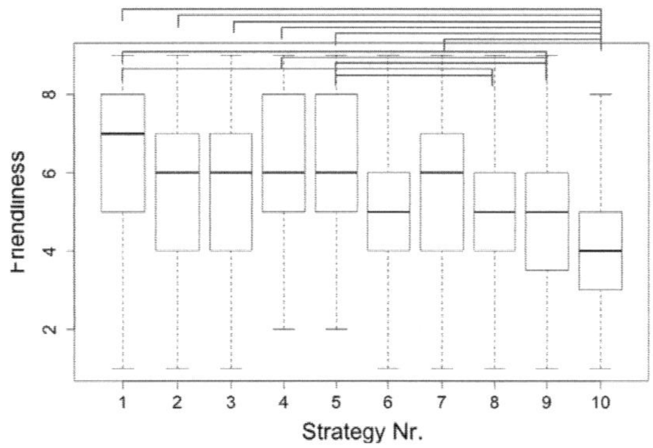

Figure 4: Friendliness for each strategy, $p < 0.01$.

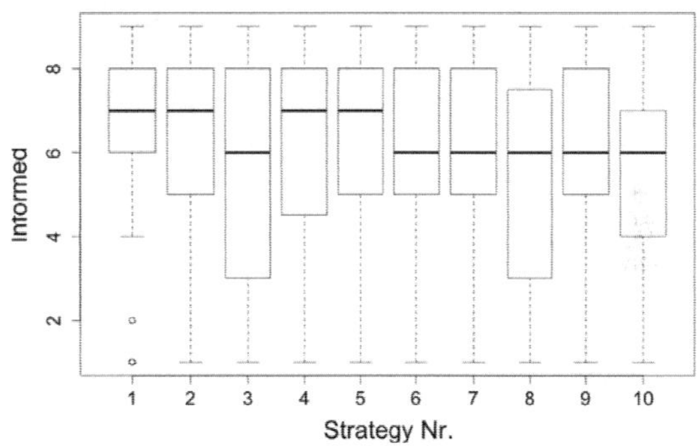

Figure 5: Agent being informed for each strategy.

both scenarios. On the dimension of warmth, strategy number 8 scores significantly higher in the second scenario (Monet-Koons) than in the first (Mondian-Michelangeloo). Together with strategy 6, strategy 8 also scores higher in the second scenario with respect to the level of fun that the participants perceived in the agent. Further, in the second scenario strategies 4 and 6 score higher on the dimension of competence than in the first scenario.

With respect to the agent's perceived level of warmth as well as fun, in scenario 1, strategies 8, 9 and 10 score significantly lower than other strategies (Kruskal-Wallis $p < 0.01$). In this scenario strategies 6, 8 and 10 also score below average (mean < 4.5). For scenario 2 strategy 10 scores significantly lower than other strategies (Kruskal-Wallis $p < 0.01$) and falls below average.

Scenario 1 shows significant differences between the scorings of the agent's perceived level of competence (Kruskal-Wallis $p < 0.01$). Multiple comparisons (Kruskal-Wallis) do not indicate a specific pair of strategies that is responsible for this difference. Strategy 3 is the only strategy that

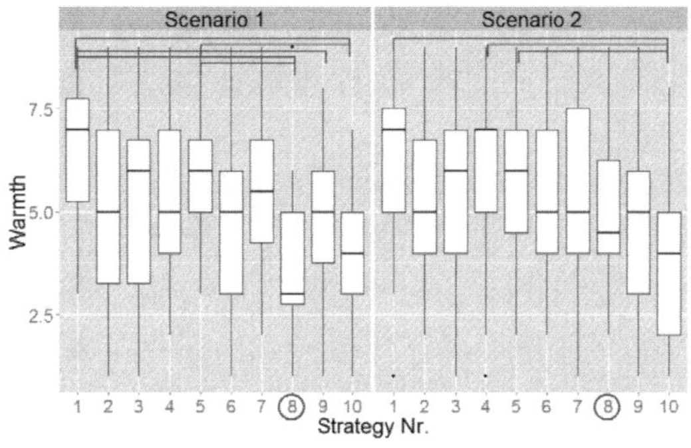

Figure 6: Warmth for each strategy, $p < 0.01$. Between scenarios strategy 8 differs $p < 0.05$.

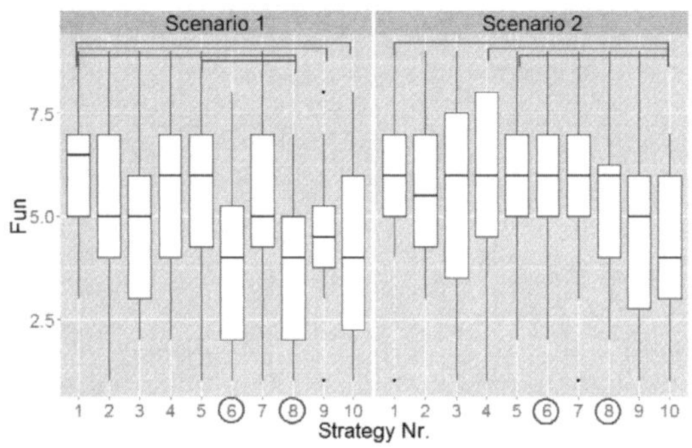

Figure 7: Fun for each strategy, $p < 0.01$. Between scenarios strategies 6, $p < 0.05$, and 8, $p < 0.01$, differ.

scores below average (mean < 4.5). In scenario 2 the strategies show no significant differences or scorings below average.

Comparing the strategies that are oriented towards the agent with those that oriented towards the user (Table 2) does not lead to a significant difference with respect to the perception of the agent (both scenarios, Kruskal-Wallis). The strategies that are not oriented towards the agent or user, but refer to the (characteristics) of the object (artwork) lead to significantly lower levels of friendliness, warmth and fun in comparison with the strategies that are oriented towards the interaction participants (both scenarios, Kruskal-Wallis $p < 0.01$).

Within the group of strategies that are agent or user oriented, we can make another grouping according to the element of the agent's reasoning process that is referred to: preferences (1,2,4,5), associations (3) and the presence of an artwork in the agent's knowledge base (6,7). A comparison between these groups leads to one significant result: in scenario 1, strategies that use preferences score significantly higher on competence than the strategies from the other groups (Kruskal-Wallis $p < 0.01$, Kruskal-Wallis multiple comparisons).

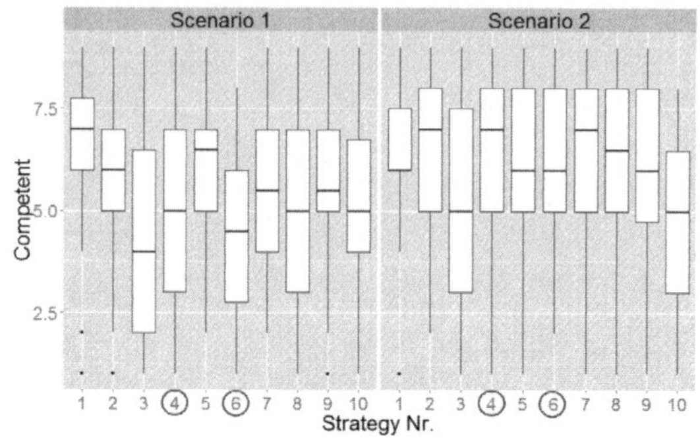

Figure 8: Competence for each strategy, $p < 0.01$ for scenario 1. Between scenarios strategies 4, $p < 0.05$, and 6, $p < 0.01$, differ.

6 Discussion

The results show that the transition strategies that insist on contrasting characteristics of the artworks such as a different artist (strategy 9) or period (strategy 10) lead to scores below average (4.5 on a scale of 9) with respect to the level of naturalness, coherence and smoothness. On the level of naturalness and smoothness the difference with the other strategies is significant. This demonstrates that even when the artist and period of the former artwork have been discussed just before the transition strategies, making transition strategies that are based on (referring back to) the earlier discussed characteristics (subtopics), does not guarantee a natural, coherent and smooth dialogue.

The fact that strategy 8, that presents another artwork as just being another artwork, scores below average on naturalness and coherence, shows that "being an artwork" is not a category that can sufficiently bind both topics ("category Y" by Sacks, 1971 in Levinson, 1983). This can have several reasons: The transition strategy may not succeed in presenting the former and latter artwork in being natural fellow members of some category Y, in this case being an artwork. Category Y may need to be a more restrictive (distinctive) category than one to which all topics belong (all topics are artworks) in order to bind two specific topics. Or, making both topics natural fellow members of some category Y may not be sufficient in general to establish a natural and coherent dialogue.

A reason why strategy 3 that is based on the associations of the agent, scores bad on coherence but well on naturalness and smoothness may be due to the fact that the participants can find the association itself incoherent. Due to the contrasting characteristics of the artworks the participants may find it incoherent that the first artwork reminds the agent of the second. However, given that the strategy is considered natural and smooth implies that it might be a suitable strategy to connect the discussions of two similar artworks.

The same explanation can be given for the low scoring of this strategy (3) with respect to the perception of the agent's level of competence (scenario 1). When the agent associates two artworks that do not seem alike the agent is perceived less competent than average.

The strategies that lead to low scores on naturalness, coherence and smoothness of the dialogue (8, 9 and 10) also score relatively low with respect to the perception of friendliness, fun and warmth of the agent. This gives us reasons to suspect that both aspects are related: when a dialogue is not considered natural, coherent or smooth, the agent is not considered as very friendly, fun and warm.

The participants do not perceive the agent significantly more or less informed when it uses certain transition strategies instead of others. This shows that referring explicitly to the characteristics of the artworks such as its artist (9) or period (10) does not make the agent look more informed than when the strategies refer to more subjective aspects of the agent's reasoning process, such as its preferences or associations.

On the contrary, strategies that refer to the preferences of the interaction participants score significantly higher with respect to the agent's level of competence than the strategies that use other variables from the agent's reasoning process.

With respect to the consequences of the transition strategies on the perception of the dialogue the results have shown no significant difference among both scenarios. The effects on the perception of the dialogue that are discussed in this Section seem thus generalisable for the domain we are looking at (Section 4.1). However, for some transition strategies the perception of the agent is judged significantly differently among the two scenarios. For example, strategy 6, a statement of the fact that the agent has seen some other artwork, has in some contexts a negative influence on the agent's level of fun and competence, where this is not the case in other contexts. In the two scenarios that were used for this experiment the type of information, the utterance types, and the number of utterances are equal. Therefore, further research will be needed to show what exactly the underlying reason is that the same strategies lead, in a different scenario, to a difference in the perception of the agent.

7 Conclusion

In this work we have looked at how a selected topic of discussion can be introduced by an agent in an ongoing non-task oriented dialogue. In the context we are looking at, each topic consists of the discussion of an artwork from a museum. Inspired by social and conversational analytic literature we first constructed a set of candidate transition strategies. We then checked the consequences of each of these transition strategies on the perception of the dialogue and the agent.

We have found that the strategies that score well on all dimensions and all tested circumstances are those that ask for the experience of the user, and those that refer to the preferences of the interaction participants. Whether the preference is the agent's or the user's, and whether or not the new topic is preferred over the current one, transition strategies that integrate any type of preference maintain the coherence of the dialogue while maintaining/establishing a positive perception of the agent. The fact that certain transition strategies can connect topics about very different artworks while maintaining positive perceptions of the dialogue and the agent, shows that the agent's topic manager can indeed be allowed to select any topic required to engage the user at any moment in the conversation (Glas et al., 2015).

We plan to use the observations we obtained in this study by automatically generating appropriate transition strategies for the conversational agent whenever the topic manager initiates a topic switch. The automatic generation of the transition strategies could be performed by means of templates where the object names and characteristics can be generated from the agent's knowledge base. In the future we would like to explore the effects of the timing of the topic switch on the perception of the topic transition (Clark, 1996). Lastly, we would like to consider the agent's non-verbal behaviour with respect to topic switching. Non-verbal behaviour plays an important role in topic switching (Kendon, 1972) and in the perception of verbal behaviour in general (Sidner et al., 2005).

Acknowledgements

We would like to thank Sophie Rosset and Andrew Kehler for valuable discussion, and Brice Donval and Caroline Langlet for technical support. We would also like to thank all the participants of the experiment. This research is partially funded by the French project Avatar 1:1, ANR MOCA, and the Labex SMART (ANR-11-LABX-65) supported by French state funds managed by the ANR, within the Investissements d'Avenir program under reference ANR-11-IDEX-0004-02.

References

Timothy Bickmore and Justine Cassell. 2005. Social dialongue with embodied conversational agents. In *Advances in natural multimodal dialogue systems*, pages 23–54. Springer.

Alexa Breuing and Ipke Wachsmuth. 2012. Let's talk topically with artificial agents! providing agents with humanlike topic awareness in everyday dialog situations. In *Proceedings of the 4th international conference on agents and artificial intelligence (ICAART)*, volume 2.

Graham Button and Neil Casey. 1985. Topic nomination and topic pursuit. *Human studies*, 8(1):3–55.

Herbert H Clark. 1996. *Using language*, volume 1996. Cambridge university press Cambridge.

Angela Downing. 2000. Talking topically. *CIRCLE of Linguistics Applied to Communication (CLAC)*, 3:31–50.

Susan T Fiske, Amy JC Cuddy, and Peter Glick. 2007. Universal dimensions of social cognition: Warmth and competence. *Trends in cognitive sciences*, 11(2):77–83.

Nadine Glas and Catherine Pelachaud. 2015. User engagement and preferences in information-given chat with virtual agents. In *Workshop on Engagement in Social Intelligent Virtual Agents*. Forthcoming.

Nadine Glas, Ken Prepin, and Catherine Pelachaud. 2015. Engagement driven topic selection for an information-giving agent. In *Workshop on the Semantics and Pragmatics of Dialogue (SemDial)*, pages 48–57.

Tobias Heinroth, Savina Koleva, and Wolfgang Minker. 2011. Topic switching strategies for spoken dialogue systems. In *INTERSPEECH*, pages 2077–2080.

Ryuichiro Higashinaka, Kohji Dohsaka, and Hideki Isozaki. 2008. Effects of self-disclosure and empathy in human-computer dialogue. In *Spoken Language Technology Workshop, 2008. SLT 2008. IEEE*, pages 109–112. IEEE.

Jerry R Hobbs. 1990. Topic drift. *Conversational organization and its development*, 38:3–22.

Adam Kendon. 1972. Some relationships between body motion and speech. *Studies in dyadic communication*, 7:177.

Stephen C Levinson. 1983. *Pragmatics (Cambridge textbooks in linguistics)*. Cambridge University Press.

Daniel Macias-Galindo, Wilson Wong, John Thangarajah, and Lawrence Cavedon. 2012. Coherent topic transition in a conversational agent. In *Proceedings of the 13th Annual Conference of the International Speech Communication Association (InterSpeech), Oregon, USA*.

Douglas W Maynard and Don H Zimmerman. 1984. Topical talk, ritual and the social organization of relationships. *Social psychology quarterly*, pages 301–316.

Daniel McFarlane. 2002. Comparison of four primary methods for coordinating the interruption of people in human-computer interaction. *Human-Computer Interaction*, 17(1):63–139.

Yukiko I Nakano and Ryo Ishii. 2010. Estimating user's engagement from eye-gaze behaviors in human-agent conversations. In *Proceedings of the 15th international conference on Intelligent user interfaces*, pages 139–148. ACM.

Candace L Sidner, Christopher Lee, Cory D Kidd, Neal Lesh, and Charles Rich. 2005. Explorations in engagement for humans and robots. *Artificial Intelligence*, 166(1):140–164.

Jan Svennevig. 2000. *Getting acquainted in conversation: a study of initial interactions*, volume 64. John Benjamins Publishing.

Wilson Wong, Lawrence Cavedon, John Thangarajah, and Lin Padgham. 2012. Flexible conversation management using a bdi agent approach. In *Intelligent Virtual Agents*, pages 464–470. Springer.

Fan Yang, Peter A Heeman, and Andrew Kun. 2008. Switching to real-time tasks in multi-tasking dialogue. In *Proceedings of the 22nd International Conference on Computational Linguistics-Volume 1*, pages 1025–1032. Association for Computational Linguistics.

Appendix A. Website for the experiment

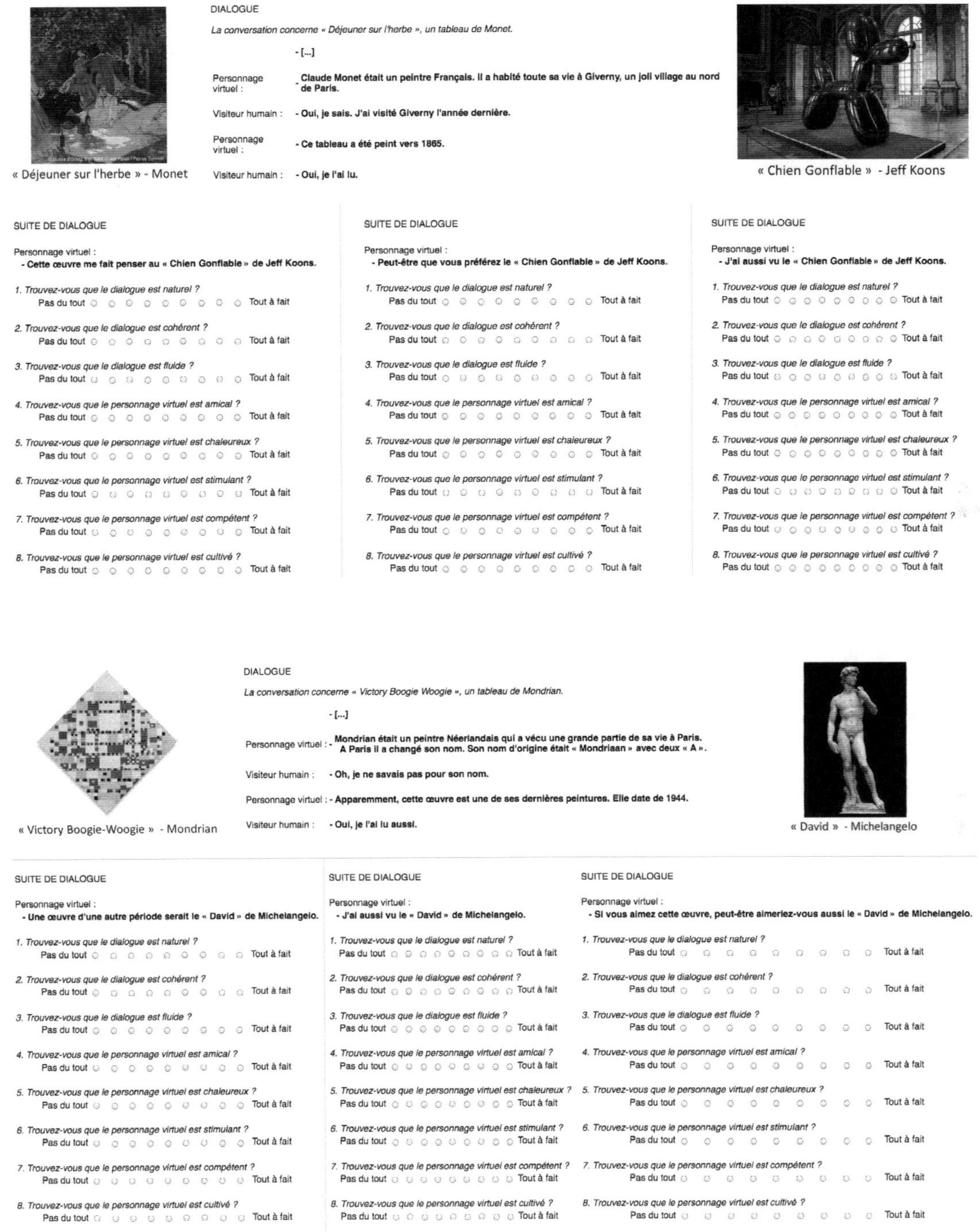

Figure 9: A screenshot of the website for the online experiment. The order of the scenarios and the selection of transition strategies differ among participants.

Creating Textual Driver Feedback from Telemetric Data

Daniel Braun Ehud Reiter Advaith Siddharthan
Department of Computing Science
University of Aberdeen
{r01db14, e.reiter, advaith}@abdn.ac.uk

Abstract

Usage based car insurances, which use sensors to track driver behaviour, are enjoying growing popularity. Although the data collected by these insurances could provide detailed feedback about the driving style, this information is usually kept away from the driver and is used only to calculate insurance premiums. In this paper, we explored the possibility of providing drivers with textual feedback based on telemetric data in order to improve individual driving, but also general road safety. We report that textual feedback generated through NLG was preferred to non-textual summaries currently popular in the field and specifically was better at giving users a concrete idea of how to adapt their driving.

1 Introduction

Although the number of road deaths in the UK is steadily decreasing, 1,713 people died in road accidents in 2013 and 21,657 were seriously injured according to the Department for Transport (2014). Nearly 35% of those who died were under the age of 30. Modern cars are often equipped with numerous driving assistance systems that detect and resolve dangerous situations, but these systems are not available in cheaper and older cars, which are particularly popular among younger drivers. In this group so called *"black box"* or *"telematic"* car insurances are becoming more and more popular and insurance companies expect that by 2020 nearly 40% of all car insurances in the UK will be telemetric (Rose, 2013).

Telematic insurances use different sensors installed in the car to track the individual driving style of their customers. Instead of calculating insurance premiums based on statistical risk groups, insurance companies can use these data to create individual risk profiles and calculate insurance premiums accordingly. This offers drivers who belong to a high-risk group, like young male drivers, the opportunity to save money. Very detailed feedback could be produced from these data which could be able to help drivers to improve their driving and hence road safety. However the feedback insurance companies give to their customers, if they give any feedback at all, is often very sparse: The current state of the art of driver feedback, as used by insurance policies like *AXA Drivesave*[1] and *Aviva Drive*[2], are scores (e.g. from 0 to 100) in general categories like "pace" and "smoothness" or maps where incidents are marked with pins, as used by *Intelligent Marmalade*[3]. As we show in Section 4, this feedback is not perceived as helpful by drivers.

Drivers who use such an insurance have a particularly high motivation (i.e. money) to change their behaviour. However a system which provides helpful feedback could also be useful for other drivers, especially for example for learners and young drivers. Therefore, in this paper, we explored the possibility of providing drivers with individual textual feedback based on telemetric data, in order to improve road safety. We evaluated the concept of textual driver feedback against the current state of the art feedback mechanisms, to find out if a textual feedback system is perceived as more helpful by drivers.

From an NLG point of view there are two main challenges in creating such a system: Driving one hour can create up to 300,000 data points, which have to be grouped and analysed in a way that allows us to describe important information within

[1] https://play.google.com/store/apps/details?id=com.mydrive.axa.drivesave
[2] https://play.google.com/store/apps/details?id=com.aviva.ukgi.avivadrive
[3] https://play.google.com/store/apps/details?id=com.wantstudios.marmalade

Proceedings of the 15th European Workshop on Natural Language Generation (ENLG), pages 156–165,
Brighton, September 2015.

this huge amount of data in a short text. And, like all systems that try to achieve a behaviour change, the texts produced by such a feedback system should take psychological considerations into account, in order to increase the likelihood to achieve a behaviour change. This distinguised our work from NLG systems summarising spatio-temporal data in other domains (Turner et al., 2008; Ponnamperuma et al., 2013).

2 Related Work

Although earlier work, like Reiter et al. (2003), has shown that behaviour changes are difficult to achieve, we believe that concrete individual driver feedback, based on telemetric data, could contribute to a more secure driving style.

2.1 Psychological Aspects of Behaviour Change

There are many theories about how behaviour changes can be achieved. Fogg (2009), for example, identifies three factors which control human behaviour: motivation, ability, and triggers. A similar point was made by Fishbein (2000), who postulated that "any given behaviour is most likely to occur if one has a strong intention to perform the behaviour, if one has the necessary skills and abilities required to perform the behaviour, and if there are no environmental constraints preventing behavioural performance". Abraham and Michie (2008) defined 26 "generally-applicable behavior change techniques", like providing information on consequences and providing general encouragement.

2.2 Giving Feedback

There is also a huge amount of literature about how to formulate feedback in order to increase the likelihood of having an impact on the recipient. Three popular advices, which were used in this work, are:

Positive feedback is in general perceived as more accurate and correct than negative feedback (Ilgen et al., 1979). **Starting with positive feedback** therefore gives the feedback source more credibility in general, what has a positive influence of the perception and acceptance of possibly following negative feedback (Steelman and Rutkowski, 2004). This technique is often used in clinical settings as part of the so called "feedback sandwich" (Dohrenwend, 2002).

Hattie and Timperley (2007) pointed out, that "**specific goals** are more effective than general or nonspecific ones" (emphasis added).

Ye and Johnson (1995), Teach and Shortliffe (1987), Weiner (1980) and many others pointed out, that it is crucial for the acceptance of feedback from computer systems, that the **feedback is justified** in a way that allows the user to reconstruct how conclusions were drawn.

2.3 Feedback Generation

NLG systems that generate feedback have proven to be helpful in many different areas. Gkatzia et al. (2013) for example showed that an NLG system can provide students with feedback that is perceived as helpful as feedback from lecturers, using reinforcement learning. The SkillSum system (Williams and Reiter, 2008), which generates feedback about basic reading skills and performed significantly better than a comparable system that used canned texts. In the context of citizen science, automatically generated feedback has been shown to improve both skill levels and motivation levels among participants (Blake et al., 2012; van der Wal et al., 2016).

As Eugenio et al. (2005) have shown, aggregation is one important factor that influences the effectiveness of feedback generation systems. This is especially important for the system we present in this paper, since it will deal with a huge amount of data.

Another important task, that is closely related to the aggregation, is the identification of important information which will also be an important part of our system. The approach that we present in Section 3.2.2 and Section 3.2.3 is similar to the work from Gatt et al. (2009) and Hallett et al. (2006)

2.4 Automotive Behaviour Change Support Systems

Some projects with focus on ecological driving have already successfully used feedback in order to influence driving behaviour: Like Tulusan et al. (2012), who were able to achieve an improvement in fuel efficiency of more than 3% by providing drivers with numerical feedback that was calculated after each route. Boriboonsomsin et al. (2010), who used a combination of instant and non-instant feedback, achieved an average improvement of 6% on city streets and 1% on highways. And Endres et al. (2010) improved fuel efficiency by using social networks and gamification elements.

There are also systems which use instant feedback, like the CarCoach project from Arroyo et al. (2006). CarCoach uses numerous sensors, like cameras and pressure sensors, to provide immediate feedback on incidents like not looking at the road or being distracted by handling the radio while driving. However, Sharon et al. (2005) showed that negative feedback from the system is easily perceived as frustrating. And there is also always a risk that the feedback itself is a further distraction, when given immediately.

3 Methods

3.1 Data Collection

Insurance companies use mainly two different approaches to collect their data: They either use permanently installed sensors, often called *"black box"*, or smart phone applications. In both cases GPS timestamps and coordinates as well as acceleration data are logged. Although especially smart phone solutions, but to a less extent also black box solutions, raise a lot of questions about data reliability and integrity, as pointed out by Händel et al. (2014) and others, according to Nol (2015) these two approaches have together a worldwide market share of nearly 80% of all telematic insurances.

As our research is focused on data analysis and presentation, rather than the collection, we decided to choose a smart phone based approach, as this method is less intrusive for the car owner and can be used by any driver interested in feedback, without going through an insurance company. The application we used for the data collection was based on previous work by Braun et al. (2011).

The data corpus we used to develop our prototype consisted of about 600 road miles, driven by five different drivers in four different countries. Table 1 shows an example of the data logged by the acceleration sensor, Table 2 shows data logged by the GPS receiver. The acceleration sensor logs the date, the time and the acceleration in $\frac{m}{s^2}$. The GPS receiver logs the latitude and longitude coordinates, the accuracy of the localization in meters and the GPS timestamp. Additional information that is needed during the data analysis, like street names, street types and speed limits, are obtained from *OpenStreetMap*. In order to access these data, we used *Nominatim*[4], to match GPS coordinates to streets in OpenStreetMap.

[4]https://nominatim.openstreetmap.org

3.2 Data Analysis

In order to provide feedback, we first have to decide which behaviour should be classified as "right" and which as "wrong" and when wrong behaviour is relevant or significant enough to be taken into account for the feedback generation.

3.2.1 Specification of Relevant Behaviour

The most obvious approach would probably be to expect law-abiding behaviour. However it is worth considering different points of view before specifying which behaviour should be regarded as "good" and which should be regarded as "bad". From the police's point of view the naive approach of law-abidance may be sufficient, from a driving instructor's point of view other things are also important, like energy-saving and smoothness. As our research is closely related to telematic insurances, particular attention should be paid to the point of view of insurance companies. Although their exact metrics are secret, we know that they take into account speeding, time of day, day of week, acceleration, braking, elapsed distance, road type and other parameters (cf. Händel et al. (2014) for a more extensive list). On one hand we understandably wanted to stick close to the insurance metrics, on the other hand, from a motivational point of view, it is strongly advised to analyse these parameters critically. It would be, for example, very frustrating for a driver who needs to drive to work at 6 a.m. every weekday, to be told that he should not drive before 9 a.m., because it could increase his insurance premium.

After taking all these different considerations into account, we decided to concentrate on speeding and acceleration and braking behaviour. These are three of the most important parameters for insurance companies, because wrong behaviour in these categories often causes accidents. They are also important for driving instructors. There are, of course, many other important parameters, like distraction and safety distance, which can not be taken into account due to the limitation of the available data.

Speeding, acceleration and braking also have quantitative dimensions, which are very important for feedback generation. While it is reasonable to define driving 30 mph where 20 mph are allowed as wrong behaviour it is arguable if that is the case for driving 21 mph too. In the UK, there is no com-

date	time	x	y	z
08.01.2015	12:07:10.838	1.4939818	2.1068976	9.768343
08.01.2015	12:07:10.858	1.4556746	2.183512	9.730036
08.01.2015	12:07:10.879	1.6472107	2.1452048	9.653421

Table 1: Data logged by the acceleration sensor (in $\frac{m}{s^2}$)

lat	lon	accuracy (in m)	timestamp
57.16042614	-2.09462595	10.0	1420718831921
57.1604265	-2.0946818	6.0	1420718832933
57.16042663	-2.0946828	6.0	1420718833934

Table 2: Data logged by the GPS receiver

pulsory law about how to handle these issues and the decision is up to the police officer's discretion. The Association of Chief Police Officers (2015) suggest a tolerance of 10% of the speed limit + 2mph. Other countries have fixed tolerance, like Germany, with a tolerance of 3%, or no tolerance at all, like Switzerland. Due to the limited accuracy of our measuring method, we decided to adopt a tolerance of 10% of the speed limit, before an incident is classified as speeding. We also decided to ignore violations of the speed limit with a length under 10 meters.

While the quantification of speeding incidents can be derived from laws, the situation is less obvious for inappropriate acceleration or braking. After numerous test, we decided to adopt the guidelines we derived from the *AXA Drivesave* app, which categorises speeding and braking incidents in 4 classes: An acceleration up to +/- $2\frac{m}{s^2}$ is permissible. Non-permissible behaviour is classified in three categories: Acceleration between +/- $2-3\frac{m}{s^2}$, +/- $3-4\frac{m}{s^2}$ and >+/<- $4\frac{m}{s^2}$.

3.2.2 Detection of Relevant Behaviour

After finishing a trip, the raw sensor data, obtained by the smart phone application, is parsed for incidents that meet the above described criteria. While acceleration and braking incidents can be detected directly from the sensor data, the recognition of speeding needs further information, namely the speed limit. The prototype we developed uses speed limits provided by the OpenStreetMap project. As the speed limit is not available for all streets in the OpenStreetMap-data, we also implemented a fall-back-mechanism, which sets the speed limit to the general national limit for the road type, for example 60 mph for single carriageways in the UK, if no further information is provided. Although data from OpenStreetMap has shown to be relatively reliable (Neis et al., 2011) user generated data can always have flaws. But since our analysis focuses on recurring behaviour patterns, rather than single incidents, the impact of single failures is minimized. However, for a commercial system, more reliable data sources could be used.

Each detected incident is stored in a database, as shown in Figure 1. The saved data set contains two timestamps and two GPS coordinate-pairs (start and end), the distance of the incident, the maximum value during the incident (either maximum speed or maximum acceleration) and the average value, as well as a unique ID that links to the street the incident happened on.

Based on these information an importance value is calculated for each incident. The importance of an incident is expressed as a number between 0 and 100 and is based on the type of the incident (speeding incidents are more important than braking incidents, which are more important than acceleration incidents), the distance, the maximum and average value and the type of the road the incident happened on.

3.2.3 Aggregation through Clustering

Common feedback systems for drivers, like lane departure warning systems or distance alert systems, give instant feedback about current or even upcoming situations. Our approach however is based on non-instant feedback and aims for a weekly feedback period. The significance of a single incident is therefore considerably lower in our system. As past behaviour can not be changed anyway, we focus on influencing future behaviour. We try to achieve this goal by identifying recurring behaviour patterns in the driving as these patterns

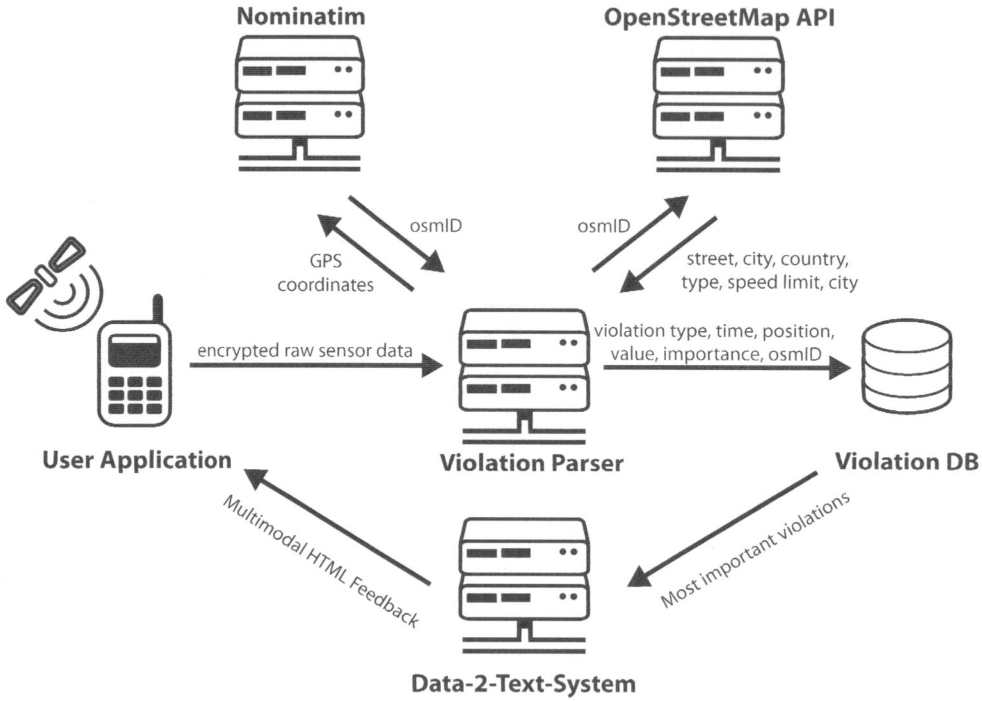

Figure 1: System architecture

are likely to occur again in the future. In this way we hope to not only achieve a change of behaviour in a current situation, but a long-term behaviour change.

Together with domain experts (i.e. driving instructors), we identified features which are suitable to group incidents by, in order to find behaviour patterns: street names, road types, speed limits, time of the day and day of the week. Some of the most common behaviour patterns, according to our domain experts, can be identified by these features. For example the tendency to speed on roads with "extreme" (i.e. very high or very low) speed limits, carelessness on well known routes and dangerous behaviour at certain times (e.g. late in the night or after work).

In order to detect these patterns in the database of all incidents, we use an agglomerative clustering algorithm, where the distance between two incidents is defined by the weighted similarity of all above mentioned features. The algorithm also has a minimal cluster size, which is influenced by the total number of incidents, and a maximum distance, which are used to decide, when to stop the agglomeration and which clusters are irrelevant. In this way we try to balance the interest between greatest possible and tightest possible clusters, since neither very small nor very loose clusters represent significant behaviour patterns.

3.3 NLG

The Data-2-Text module of our prototype follows the three-stage pipelined architecture, as described by Reiter (2007), and uses simpleNLG (Gatt and Reiter, 2009) as surface realiser.

3.3.1 Psychological Background

Since we try to achieve a behaviour change, we use different psychological techniques for the verbalisation of feedback, which have been shown to be useful in the literature (cf. Section 2.1) to maximize the likelihood of achieving this goal. This is reflected particularly in the document plan, which follows mainly the three techniques described in Section 2.2. Another psychological aspect was already taken into account during the specification of relevant behaviour. We try to avoid unnecessary frustration by only reporting behaviour that can be easily influenced by the driver, as described in Section 3.2.1.

3.3.2 Document Plan

The high level organisation of the document is based on these ideas. While the number of com-

Summary
Comparison
Map
Single Speeding Incidents
Speeding Clusters
Acceleration Clusters

Table 3: Content order

municated messages differs, depending on the total number of incidents, the order in which the five different messages types (in terms of "message types" as used by Reiter and Dale (2000)) are communicated is fixed, as shown in Table 3. The report always starts with a summary, which sums up facts about the reporting period, like the length of the period and the driven distance during this time. The summary is followed, whenever possible, by pointing out a positive development, compared to the last reporting period. This can be very general, if the driver improve broadly, like in Figure 2, *"you reduced the number of speeding incidents per mile by more than 10%"*, or can also be more specific, if the driver did not improve overall, but in one particular aspect, like *"you reduced the number of speeding incidents per mile in residential areas by 20%"*.

After this, a map follows, the main purpose of which is to justify the presented feedback. Each incident is marked with a pin on the map. By clicking on the description of a cluster or a violation type in the text, the map shows only the selected group of incidents and visualizes the frequency of the selected incidents to the user.

Below the map, up to five of the "worst" speeding incidents are reported, described by the amount of speeding and the names of the streets they occurred on. This is only shown if serious speeding, which means exceeding the speed limit by 20 mph or more, happened. Thereupon follows a phrase that specifies how much shorter the braking distance would be, if the driver obeys the speed limit, like *"Going 30 mph slower could shorten your braking distance by 108 yards."* in the example in Figure 2.

At the end of the report the behaviour patterns, found in form of clusters, are reported. As a short length of the reports is crucial to potential users (c.f. Section 4.6), the number of reported clusters is strictly limited to two of each type, which are selected by their importance. The importance of a

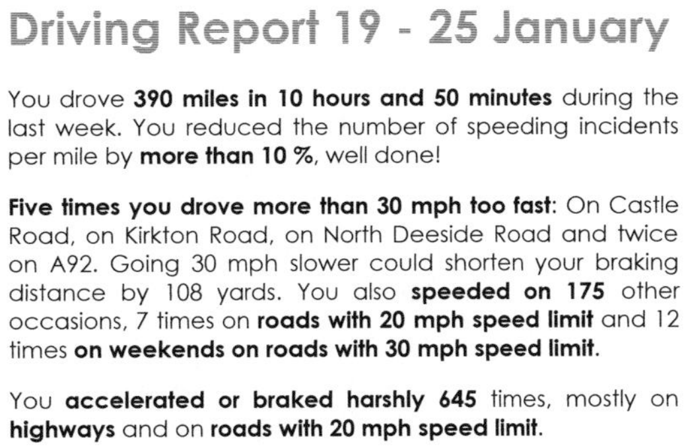
Driving Report 19 - 25 January

You drove **390 miles in 10 hours and 50 minutes** during the last week. You reduced the number of speeding incidents per mile by **more than 10 %**, well done!

Five times you drove more than 30 mph too fast: On Castle Road, on Kirkton Road, on North Deeside Road and twice on A92. Going 30 mph slower could shorten your braking distance by 108 yards. You also **speeded on 175** other occasions, 7 times on **roads with 20 mph speed limit** and 12 times **on weekends on roads with 30 mph speed limit.**

You **accelerated or braked harshly 645** times, mostly on **highways** and on **roads with 20 mph speed limit.**

Figure 2: Feedback type text

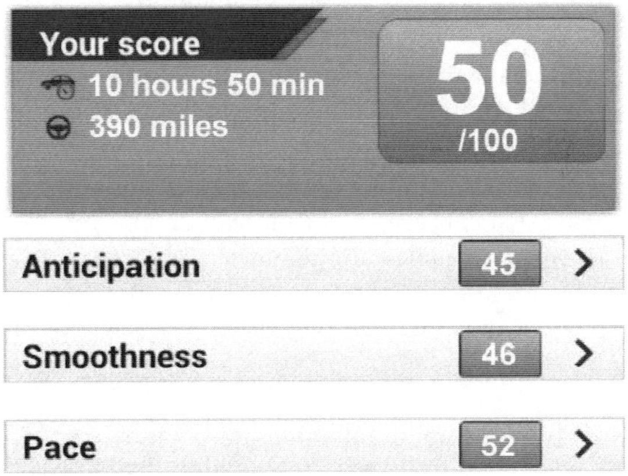

Figure 3: Feedback type score

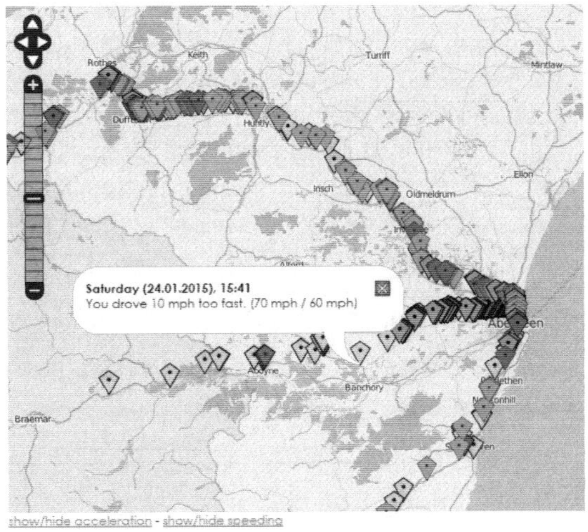

Figure 4: Feedback type map

cluster is a combination of the importance values of the single incidents within the cluster and the size of the cluster.

3.3.3 Variation

Due to the fixed structure and the brevity of the text, the space for variation is limited. Nevertheless, as feedback reports will be generated weekly, we added some variation to the text generation. As we expect behaviour changes, there should be a "natural" variation, because of the change of the underlying messages. The most static text, with regard to the underlying data, is the summary at the beginning, therefore there are nine different possibilities how the content of the same message can be realised as text, by changing the order of the sentence, formulations or leaving less important facts, like the driven time, out. In the second part, which starts after the map and consists of two sections, there is also a possible structural variation, as there is either one section about speeding and one about acceleration or one section with single incidents and one with clusters.

4 Evaluation

In order to evaluate our approach, we developed a questionnaire to find out how potential users perceive textual feedback, compared to the two state of the art types of feedback, maps and scores.

4.1 Data

For this evaluation we used two real datasets recorded in Aberdeen and Aberdeenshire each of which was used twice, once in full length and once by selecting a smaller subset. The feedback that was evaluated by the participants of our study was based on these datasets. These trips were not part of the training dataset we used to develop our prototype.

4.2 Questionnaire

We presented feedback reports for four configurations to every participant:

1. low (i.e. short) driven distance, low number of incidents (LL)
2. low driven distance, high number of incidents (LH)
3. high (i.e. long) driven distance, low number of incidents (HL)

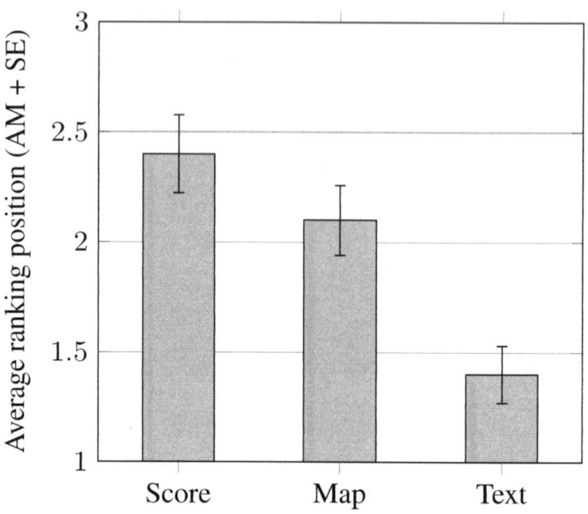

Figure 5: Ranking results

4. high driven distance, high number of incidents (HH)

For each of these four configurations, which were shown in a random order, we presented three types of feedback, which were also shown in a random order: A score, a map and a text. Figures 2, 3 and 4 show the three different types of feedback for the configuration HH. For each type of feedback three statements were given: "The feedback is helpful.", "The feedback gives me an idea how I could adapt my driving behaviour." and "The feedback encourages me to change my driving behaviour.". Participants were asked to indicate how much they agree or disagree with each statement on a Likert scale with seven options. After that, we asked the participants to give a ranking, which type of feedback would be their first, second and third choice, if they had to choose one. We also asked which type(s) of feedback they would choose if they could choose a combination of different types (only one, two or all three). In the end, participants were asked about their attitude towards telematic car insurances in general.

4.3 Participants

The survey was completed by 21 participants between the age of 20 and 52. The average age of the participants was 25. About 19% of all participants were female, 81% male. In average the participants had 7 years of driving experience and more than 66% of them drive every day.

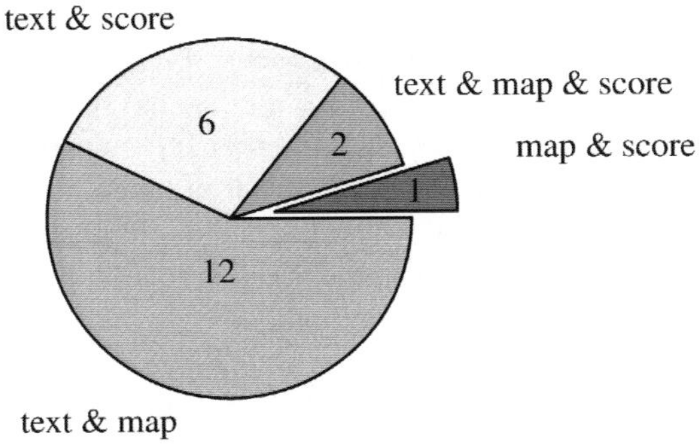

Figure 6: Preferred combination of feedback types

4.4 Basic Findings

The most basic conclusion that we can draw from the results of this survey is, that our participants preferred the textual feedback over the two other feedback types: 13 participants chose textual feedback as their first preference, 4 the score and 4 the map ($\chi^2 = 7.722; df = 2; p = 0.02$). The average ranking position for the text was 1.4, for the map 2.1 and 2.4 for the score (cf. Figure 5). When asked to choose a combination of feedback types, only one participant chose a combination without textual feedback. The most chosen combination was text and map (12 times). Only two people chose a combination of all three types of feedback (cf. Figure 6).

4.5 Likert Scale Results

We ran three ANOVA analyses, one with each of the three statements ("The feedback is helpful.", "The feedback gives me an idea how I could adapt my driving behaviour." and "The feedback encourages me to change my driving behaviour.") as dependent variables (Likert scale of 1-7) and feedback type (score, map or text), distance travelled and number of incidents (low/high) as fixed factors and the participant as a random factor. We found an overwhelming main effect of the feedback type ($p < 0.0001$). No other effects or interactions were significant at $p < 0.05$. Post hoc analysis by TukeyHSD confirmed that the textual feedback was more helpful, encouraging and provided more ideas than either the map or the score ($p < 0.0001$ in all cases, except text-map, $p = 0.0002$). Figures 7a to 7c display the differences graphically.

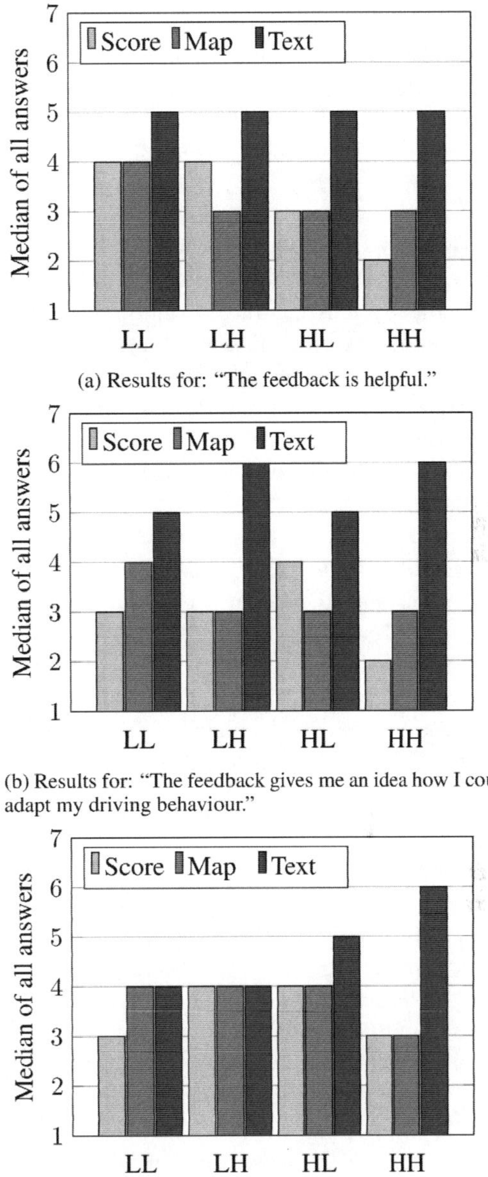

(a) Results for: "The feedback is helpful."

(b) Results for: "The feedback gives me an idea how I could adapt my driving behaviour."

(c) Results for: "The feedback encourages me to change my driving behaviour."

Figure 7: Evaluation of the Likert scale questions (1 = completely disagree, 4 = neutral, 7 = completely agree; LL = distance low & incidents low, LH = distance low & incidents high, HL = distance high & incidents low, HH = distance high & incidents high)

4.6 Comments

Six participants used the possibility to give additional comments via a free text field. Three participants said that the length of the text is important and should not be too long. Two participants expressed concerns about the score and that they do not trust the score, because they are not able to reconstruct how it is calculated.

4.7 Privacy

Although it was not the focus of our work, we were, of course, aware of the privacy issues that come with a system that tracks locations and analyse behaviour patterns. In our survey, more than 76% of the participants agreed that they would have privacy concerns if they would use a telematic car insurance. Our system itself can run completely autonomously on the phone of the user. That means, in order to guarantee the utmost privacy, no user data will be transmitted. If used in combination with a telematic car insurance, our system does not produce any additional personal data. Instead it processes existing data in a way that, as our evaluation has shown, is more helpful and preferred by users. In this way, the user profits more from his own data and also gets a better understanding of which data is collected.

5 Conclusion and Outlook

The results of our evaluation show, that textual driver feedback is perceived as more helpful than the currently used forms of feedback. It also gives drivers a more concrete idea how to adapt their driving. We are confident that textual feedback could not only increase acceptance for automatic generated driver feedback, but could also have a bigger impact on the behaviour than other forms of feedback.

The upcoming EU-legislation "eCall"[5], which will make telematic sensors mandatory in new cars from April 2018, will lead to a rapid spread of telematic devices in cars within the European Union and will make feedback systems, like the one presented in this paper, even more attractive. Besides the possible applications mentioned above, textual feedback systems could also be used in driving training.

At the moment we are conducting a field study in order to evaluate whether the perceived advantages of the textual feedback also manifest in a bigger influence on the behaviour of drivers. For this study, we equipped the experimental subjects with smart phone applications, so that each participant will evaluate feedback that is based on his or her own driving and we will be able to analyse if their is a change in behaviour.

[5] http://ec.europa.eu/digital-agenda/ecall-time-saved-lives-saved

References

Charles Abraham and Susan Michie. 2008. A taxonomy of behavior change techniques used in interventions. *Health psychology*, 27(3):379.

Ernesto Arroyo, Shawn Sullivan, and Ted Selker. 2006. Carcoach: A polite and effective driving coach. In *CHI '06 Extended Abstracts on Human Factors in Computing Systems*, CHI EA '06, pages 357–362, New York, NY, USA. ACM.

Association of Chief Police Officers. 2015. Acpo speed enforcement policy guidelines 2011 - 2015: Joining forces for safer roads. Technical report.

Steven Blake, Advaith Siddharthan, Hien Nguyen, Nirwan Sharma, Anne-Marie Robinson, Elaine O'Mahony, Ben Darvill, Chris Mellish, and Rene Van Der Wal. 2012. Natural language generation for nature conservation: Automating feedback to help volunteers identify bumblebee species. In *COLING*, pages 311–324.

Kanok Boriboonsomsin, Alexander Vu, and Matthew Barth. 2010. Eco-driving: pilot evaluation of driving behavior changes among us drivers. *University of California Transportation Center*.

Daniel Braun, Christoph Endres, and Christian Müller. 2011. Determination of mobility context using low-level data. In *Adjunct Proceedings of the 3rd International Conference on Automotive User Interfaces and Interactive Vehicular Applications (AutomotiveUI 2011)*, pages 41–42.

Department for Transport. 2014. Reported road casualties great britain: 2013 annual report. Technical report.

Anne Dohrenwend. 2002. Serving up the feedback sandwich. *Family practice management*, 9(10):43–50.

Christoph Endres, Jan Miksatko, and Daniel Braun. 2010. Youldeco-exploiting the power of online social networks for eco-friendly driving. In *Adjunct proceedings of the 2nd International Conference on Automotive User Interfaces and Interactive Vehicular Applications (AutomotiveUI 2010)*, page 5.

Barbara Di Eugenio, Davide Fossati, Dan Yu, Susan Haller, and Michael Glass. 2005. Aggregation improves learning: experiments in natural language generation for intelligent tutoring systems. In *Proceedings of the 43rd Annual Meeting on Association for Computational Linguistics*, pages 50–57. Association for Computational Linguistics.

Martin Fishbein. 2000. The role of theory in hiv prevention. *AIDS care*, 12(3):273–278.

Brian J Fogg. 2009. A behavior model for persuasive design. In *Proceedings of the 4th international Conference on Persuasive Technology*, page 40. ACM.

Albert Gatt and Ehud Reiter. 2009. Simplenlg: A realisation engine for practical applications. In *Proceedings of the 12th European Workshop on Natural Language Generation*, pages 90–93. Association for Computational Linguistics.

Albert Gatt, Francois Portet, Ehud Reiter, Jim Hunter, Saad Mahamood, Wendy Moncur, and Somayajulu Sripada. 2009. From data to text in the neonatal intensive care unit: Using nlg technology for decision support and information management. *Ai Communications*, 22(3):153–186.

Dimitra Gkatzia, Helen Hastie, Srinivasan Janarthanam, and Oliver Lemon. 2013. Generating student feedback from time-series data using reinforcement learning. *ENLG 2013*, page 115.

Catalina Hallett, Richard Power, and Donia Scott. 2006. Summarisation and visualisation of e-health data repositories.

Peter Händel, Isaac Skog, Johan Wahlström, Farid Bonawiede, Richard Welch, Jens Ohlsson, and Martin Ohlsson. 2014. Insurance telematics: opportunities and challenges with the smartphone solution. *Accepted in IEEE Intell. Transport. Syst. Mag., 2014*.

John Hattie and Helen Timperley. 2007. The power of feedback. *Review of educational research*, 77(1):81–112.

Daniel R Ilgen, Cynthia D Fisher, and M Susan Taylor. 1979. Consequences of individual feedback on behavior in organizations. *Journal of applied psychology*, 64(4):349.

Pascal Neis, Dennis Zielstra, and Alexander Zipf. 2011. The street network evolution of crowdsourced maps: Openstreetmap in germany 2007–2011. *Future Internet*, 4(1):1–21.

Matthieu Nol. 2015. The role of obd in the 2015 connected car market. *SMis Telematics for Usage-Based Insurance Conference*.

Kapila Ponnamperuma, Advaith Siddharthan, Cheng Zeng, Chris Mellish, and René Van Der Wal. 2013. Tag2blog: Narrative generation from satellite tag data. In *ACL (Conference System Demonstrations)*, pages 169–174.

Ehud Reiter and Robert Dale. 2000. *Building natural language generation systems*, volume 33. Cambridge university press.

Ehud Reiter, Roma Robertson, and Liesl M Osman. 2003. Lessons from a failure: Generating tailored smoking cessation letters. *Artificial Intelligence*, 144(1):41–58.

Ehud Reiter. 2007. An architecture for data-to-text systems. In *Proceedings of the Eleventh European Workshop on Natural Language Generation*, pages 97–104. Association for Computational Linguistics.

Stuart Rose. 2013. Telematics: How big data is transforming the auto insurance industry. Technical report, SAS.

Taly Sharon, Ted Selker, Lars Wagner, and Ariel J Frank. 2005. Carcoach: a generalized layered architecture for educational car systems. In *Software-Science, Technology and Engineering, 2005. Proceedings. IEEE International Conference on*, pages 13–22. IEEE.

Lisa A Steelman and Kelly A Rutkowski. 2004. Moderators of employee reactions to negative feedback. *Journal of Managerial Psychology*, 19(1):6–18.

Randy L Teach and Edward H Shortliffe. 1987. An analysis of physician attitudes regarding computer-based clinical consultation systems. In *Use and impact of computers in clinical medicine*, pages 68–85. Springer.

Johannes Tulusan, Thorsten Staake, and Elgar Fleisch. 2012. Providing eco-driving feedback to corporate car drivers: what impact does a smartphone application have on their fuel efficiency? In *Proceedings of the 2012 ACM Conference on Ubiquitous Computing*, pages 212–215. ACM.

Ross Turner, Somayajulu Sripada, Ehud Reiter, and IanP Davy. 2008. Selecting the content of textual descriptions of geographically located events in spatio-temporal weather data. In Richard Ellis, Tony Allen, and Miltos Petridis, editors, *Applications and Innovations in Intelligent Systems XV*, pages 75–88. Springer London.

Rene van der Wal, Nirwan Sharma, Anne-Marie Robinson, Chris Mellish, and Advaith Siddharthan. 2016. The role of automated feedback in training and retaining conservation volunteers: a case study of bumblebee recording. *To appear in Conservation Biology*.

JL Weiner. 1980. Blah, a system which explains its reasoning. *Artificial intelligence*, 15(1):19–48.

Sandra Williams and Ehud Reiter. 2008. Skillsum: basic skills screening with personalised, computer-generated feedback.

L Richard Ye and Paul E Johnson. 1995. The impact of explanation facilities on user acceptance of expert systems advice. *Mis Quarterly*, pages 157–172.

A personal storytelling about your favorite data

Cyril Labbé, Claudia Roncancio, Damien Bras
Univ. Grenoble Alpes, LIG, F-38000 Grenoble, France
first.last@imag.fr

Abstract

A controlled use of omnipresent data can leverage a potential of services never reached before. In this paper, we propose a user driven approach to take advantage of massive data streams. Our solution, named *Stream2Text*, relies on a personalized and continuous refinement of data to generate texts (in natural language) that provide a tailored synthesis of relevant data. It enables monitoring by a wide range of users as text streams can be shared on social networks or used individually on mobile devices.

1 Introduction

Considering a user-centered point of view, taking advantage of Big Data may be quite difficult. Managing data volume, variety and velocity to extract the adequate information is still challenging. The information extraction needs customization to adapt both, content and form, so to fit user's current profile. For content, data volume can be reduced by using user preferences, regarding the form, answers should be adapted to be displayed on the available user devices.

This paper focuses on improving stream data monitoring by proposing the construction of adhoc abstracts of data. This paper presents the generation of short texts which summarize (in natural language) the result of continuous complex data monitoring. Text summaries can be shared in social networks or can be delivered to personal devices in various context (e.g. listen to summaries while driving). Such a solution facilitates monitoring, even for disabled users.

Let's consider a running example on stock options monitoring involving data on volatility of the stock options, transactions and information about the country emitting the actions. This information represents a large volume of streamed data which could not be handled by an individual user. Rather than getting data about all the transaction of the day, users would prefer to focus on those which are the most *relevant* to him. This paper proposes a way to produce personalized summaries of the monitored data which fits better the user's current preferences. We adopt contextual preferences to integrate user's priority. For example:

In the IT category, I'm more interested in stock options that had low volatility during the last 3 days

Our system named, **Stream2text** will produce a stream of personalized summaries to provide important information to the user. Knowledge on the concepts of the application domain and a continuous query evaluation allows to serve queries such as the following.

Every two hours, I would like a summary of the last 50 transactions on my preferred stock options.

To the best of our knowledge, **Stream2text** is the first effort proposing a comprehensive solution that produces a stream of summaries based on a continuous analysis of streamed and persistent data[1]. . Section 2 details our running example. Section 3 provides a global picture of Stream2text. Section 4 and 5 respectively presents the theoretical basis for personalized continuous querying and the *text generator* operator. Section 6 exposes implementation and experimental results, sections 7 and 8 present related work and our conclusions.

2 Motivation and running example

This work adopts an unified model to query persistent relational data and streams. A precise definition of streams and relational data is given in section 4. In our running example, Luc, a cautious investor, likes to follow stock exchange information. He has access to real-time quotations and volatility rates as well as real-time transactions. These data involve the following streams and persistent relations (see the conceptual schema in

[1] A french version of this paper has been presented in the french conference on Information Systems INFORSID'14.

Proceedings of the 15th European Workshop on Natural Language Generation (ENLG), pages 166–174,
Brighton, September 2015. ©2015 Association for Computational Linguistics

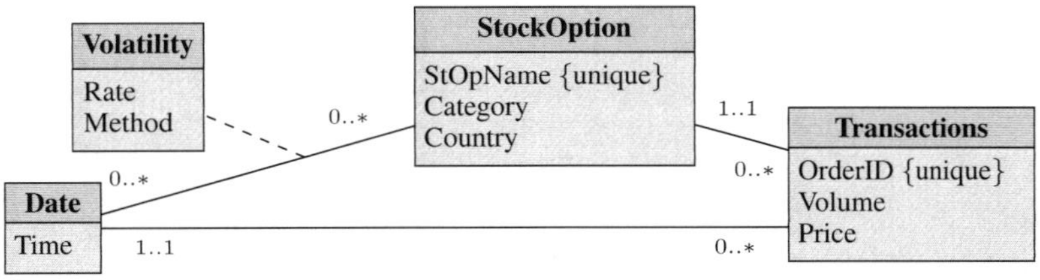

Figure 1: Data model for stock exchange information

figure 1):
– Relation *StockOption(StOpName, Category, Country)*: stores the stock option name, its category (e.g. Commodities (*Co*), Technologie (*IT*)), and the country where the company headquarters are located.
– Stream *Transactions(OrderID, TTime, StOpName, Volume, Price)*: a data stream providing real-time information about stock options transactions. It includes the transaction time ($TTime$), the quantity of shares ($Volume$) and the ($Price$) of the stock option share.
– Stream *Volatility(StOpName, ETime, Rate, Method)*: a data stream providing real-time information about the estimated volatility ($rate$) of stock options. It includes the time of the estimation $ETime$ and the estimation $Method$.

Luc wants to access such data any where, any time from any device (mobile, with or without screen). He has some preferences he wants to be taken into account so to get only the most appropriate data in order to facilitate and speed up his decisions. His preferences are described by the following statements:
[P1] Concerning stocks of category 'Co', Luc prefers those with a volatility-rate less than 0.25. On the other hand, concerning IT stocks, Luc prefers those with a volatility-rate greater than 0.35.
[P2] For stock options with volatility greater than 0.35 at present (calculated according to some method), Luc prefers those from Brazil than Venezuela's one.
[P3] For stock options with volatility-rate greater than 0.35 at present, Luc is interested in transactions carried out during the last 3 days concerning these stock options, preferring those transactions with quantity exceeding 1000 shares than those with a lower amount of shares.

Luc's preferences will be expressed in the system by means of *rules* of form `IF` *some context is verified* `THEN` *Luc prefers something to something else*. For [P1] the context is $StockOption.Category = \text{`}Co'$ and for Luc $Volatility.Rate \leq 0.25$ *is better than* $Volatility.Rate > 0.25$.

Preference rules may involve streams or relational data on both context side and preference side of the rule. Luc's summary requirements may also involve queries on relational data and streams and can be "one-shot" or continuous.
[Q1] Every day, a summary concerning the stock $Total$ over the last two days.
[Q2] Every hour, a summary, over the last hour, for the category IT inside the 100 transactions that fits the best my preferences.
[Q3] Every hour, a summary of the last hour, of the 100 preferred transactions in the category 'IT'.
[Q4] A summary of the last 1000 transactions for French stock options having a $rate > 0.8$ and with at least one transaction with $volume > 100$.

Data extraction can be precisely customized according to the current user preferences. For example [Q2] identifies Luc's 100 most preferred transactions and then extracts those being from the 'IT' category. Whereas [Q3] selects transactions of category 'IT' and among them extracts Luc's 100 most preferred. The rate of summary production is given either with a temporal pattern (e.g. Q1, Q2, Q3) either with a positional pattern (e.g. Q4: every 1000 transactions).

3 Overview of *Stream2text*

This section presents the global picture of *Stream2text*, illustrated in Figure 2.

Users provide queries and preferences on streams and persistent data. *Stream2text* evaluates the continuous queries by integrating user's preferences and generates a text stream summarizing the most pertinent data. User's query for the summary creation include a "point of view", the scope and the frequency of the summary production. The scope allows to limit the volume of data to consider in the production of one summary.

The support of users queries on streams and persistent data rely on the use of a formal model. Such model provides a non-ambiguous represen-

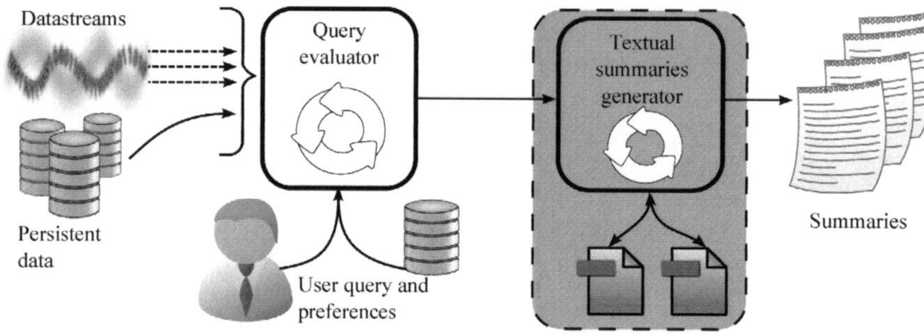

Figure 2: Architecture of *Stream2text*

tation of the data to be summarized. User's preferences allows to limit the volume of data to produce very customized summaries that fitts the current user's interest. Data summarization involves first, a data aggregation step to produce a structured summary and second, a natural language summary generation which leads to the text sent to the user.

Architecture of the text generator. This component (see Figure 3) relies on information about the conceptual schema of the data and the aggregation functions used to create the structured summary.

The main information about the schema concern the textual description of the properties of the entities. For example, *StOpName=v* can be expressed in a text by "*The stock option v*". A stock option, represented as a tuple $t \in StockOption$, can be described in a text as "*The stock option* $t.StOpName$ *is of category* $t.Category$ *and it's home country is* $t.Country$". Such phrases are usually available during the design phases of applications.

As text generation phase relies on the structured summary, it requires textual descriptions of the aggregation functions being used. For example, if the summary of the values of a property A includes $Avg(A)$, then the associated text could be "*The average value of A is* $Avg(A)$" or "*the average A is* $Avg(A)$".

4 Theoretical foundation for query evaluation

This section introduces the theoretical foundations for query evaluation with contextual preferences (query and user preferences in Figure 2).

4.1 Stream algebra

Let us first consider the queries introduced in Section 2 in a version without preferences and summarization aspects:

[Q1'] Every day, information concerning the share $Total$ over the last two days.

[Q2']/[Q3'] Every hour, informations related to the category 'IT'.

[Q4'] Informations for the last 1000 transactions concerning french stocks option having $rate > 0.8$ and with at least one transaction with $volume > 100$.

These queries are written using (Petit et al., 2012b). This algebra formalizes expressions of continuous and instantaneous queries combining streams and relational data. In the following, we present the basics of query expression.

Streams and relations (hereafter resp. denoted by S and R) are different concepts (Arasu et al., 2004). A *stream* S is an infinite set of tuples with a common schema and two special attributes: a timestamp and the position in the stream[2]. A *temporal relation* R is a function that maps a time identifier t to a set of tuples $R(t)$ having a common schema. Classical relational operators (selection σ, projection π, join $\bowtie$) are extended to temporal relations and π and σ to streams. For example, $\sigma_{Volume>10}(Transactions)$ is the stream of transactions having $Volume > 10$.

A temporal relation is extracted from a stream using windows operators. The algebra provides an extended model for windows operators including positional, temporal and cross domain windows (e.g. slide n tuples every δ seconds). The following expressions represent some very useful windows:

– $S[L]$ contains the last tuple of a stream (L standing for $Last$);

– $S[N$ slide $\Delta]$ is a sliding window of size N sliding Δ every Δ. N and Δ are either a time duration or a number of tuples.

A stream is generated from a temporal relation using a *streamer* operator. Among them, $I_S(R)$ produces the stream of tuples inserted in R. Given a window description, a streamer and a join con-

[2]These definitions can be extended using the notion of batch (Petit et al., 2012b).

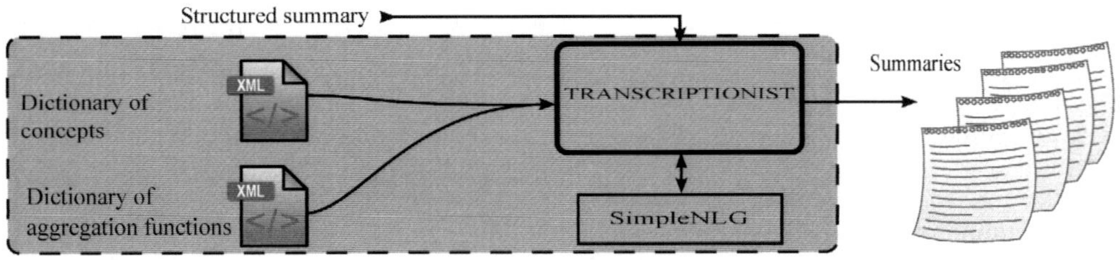

Figure 3: Architecture of the text generator

dition c, a join operator between two streams or between a stream and a relation can be defined. In the following we will use:

$$S \bowtie_c R = I_S(S[L] \bowtie_c R).$$

The stream $S \bowtie_c R$ may have new tuples originated by tuple arrivals in S or updates in R. The semi-sensitive-join operator ($\blacktriangleright\!\!\blacktriangleleft$) produces a stream resulting from a join between the last tuple of the stream and the relation by the time the tuple arrives:

$$S \blacktriangleright\!\!\blacktriangleleft_c R = I_S(S[L] \bowtie_c R(\tau_S(S[L])))$$

where τ_S denotes the function that gives the timestamp of a tuple in the stream S (see (Petit et al., 2012b) for more details). In the following, the stream-join that joins tuples from two different streams will be defined as follows:

$$S_1 \underset{\leq}{\bowtie} S_2 = I_S(S_1[\infty] \underset{\leq}{\bowtie} S_2[L])$$

where $\underset{\leq}{\bowtie}$ joins the tuple of $S_2[L]$ with the single tuple of S_2 having the maximal timestamps lower or equal to the timestamp of $S_2[L]$ (i.e. $\tau_S(S_2[L])$). Previously defined queries can be written as:

$$\textbf{[Q1']}((Volatility \underset{\leq}{\bowtie} Transaction) \blacktriangleright\!\!\blacktriangleleft \sigma_{StOpName='Total'} StockOption) [2day \text{ slide } 1day] \quad (1)$$

$$\textbf{[Q3']}((Volatility \underset{\leq}{\bowtie} Transaction) \blacktriangleright\!\!\blacktriangleleft \sigma_{Category='IT'} StockOption)[1h \text{ slide } 1h] \quad (2)$$

$$\textbf{[Q4']}((\sigma_{rate>0.8} Volatility \underset{\leq}{\bowtie} \sigma_{Volume>100} Transaction) \blacktriangleright\!\!\blacktriangleleft \sigma_{Country='FR'} StockOption)[1000n \text{ slide } 1n] \quad (3)$$

4.2 The Preference Model

In this section we present the main concepts concerning the logical formalism for *specifying and reasoning* with preferences (see (de Amo and Pereira, 2010; Petit et al., 2012a) for details). Intuitively speaking, a *rule of contextual preference* (a cp-rule) allows to compare two tuples of a relation R both of them fitting a particular context.

$$\varphi : u \rightarrow C_1(X) \succ C_2(X)[W]$$

Where $X \subseteq Attr(R)$, $W \subseteq Attr(R)$ et $X \notin W$; $C_i(X)$ (for $i = 1, 2$) is an evaluable condition over tuples of R. u is also a condition in which neither X nor W are involved (cf. exemple 1). Two tuples are comparable using a cp-rule, if they have the same value for the so-called *ceteris paribus* (noted with [ ]).

A *contextual preference theory* (*cp-theory* for short) over R is a finite set of cp-rules. Under certain consistency constraints a cp-theory induce a *strict partial order* over tuples allowing to rank them according to the user preferences.

Example 1 *Let us consider the two preference statements P1 and P2 of our motivating example. They can be expressed by the following cp-theory over the schema* $T(StOpName, Cat, Country, ETime, Rate, Method)$:
– φ_1: $Cat = co \rightarrow (Rate < 0.25 \succ Rate \geq 0.25), [Method]$
– φ_2: $Cat = it \rightarrow (Rate \geq 0.35 \succ Rate < 0.35), [Method]$
– φ_3: $Rate > 0.35 \rightarrow (Country = Brazil \succ Country = Venezuela)$

The user preferences of Figure 2 are cp-theories. The algebra integrates them in a streaming context. The semantics is the one called *with constraints*.

4.3 Preference Operator

Preference operators are algebraic and can be used on instantaneous and continuous queries on streams and relations. User preferences, represented as a cp-theory, can be seen as part of a user profil. Preferences are used only if personalization of queries is asked by the use of a "top-k" query in which the operator ***KBest*** is used. ***KBest*** selects the subset of k preferred data according to the hierarchy specified by the cp-theory. For example, **Q2** of Section 2 is expressed as

$$(\sigma_{Category='IT'}(\mathbf{KBest_{100}}((Volatility \underset{\leq}{\bowtie} Transaction) \blacktriangleright\!\!\blacktriangleleft StockOption)))[1h \text{ slide } 1h]$$

Whereas **Q3** can be written as:

$KBest_{100}(Q2')$.

4.4 Aggregation functions and structured data summary

To generate textual summaries, *Stream2text* first builds a structured summary of data by using aggregation functions provided by the query evaluator. The choice of functions may depend of the application domain. Intuitively, an aggregation function f associates to a set of tuples a unique tuple for which attributes and values are determined by f. We will use definition 1, which includes a resulting attribute named after the function used to compute the aggregated value.

Definition 1 (Aggregation Operator) *Let R be a temporal relation with schema $A = \{a_i\}_{i=1..n}$, Let $f^j(\{A_i\}_{i\in\{1,n\}})_{j=1..m}$, be m aggregation functions. The aggregation operator $\mathcal{G}_{f^1,f^2,...f^m}$ aggregates the set of tuples R in one tuple using the functions f^j.*

$$\mathcal{G}_{f^1,f^2,...f^m}(R) = \{\cup_{j=1}^{m}(f^j, f^j(\{A_i\}_{i\in\{1,n\}}))\}$$

5 Text generation operator

We define several functions and operators to associate text to data. Sections 5.1 and 5.2 show how the schema knowledge and structured summary can be related to text. Section 5.3 defines the transcription operator.

5.1 Dictionary of concepts

We will consider a database dealing with n_e entities/classes $\{E_i\}_{i=1..n_e}$. Each of which has a set n_i de property/attributes $\{A_{i,j}\}_{j=1..n_i}^{i=1..n_e}$, some of them being identifiers or key attributs.

Schema knowledge is mandatory to be able to express facts about data. A text fragment is associated to each property of the data model. It may be used to *name* the referred concept in a text. These texts are managed in a *Dictionary of concepts*.

Definition 2 (Dictionary of Concepts) *It is a function $\mathcal{D}_c$ which associates to each database concept (ie. property $A_{i,j}$) a noun phrase NP. This noun phrase can be use to name the concept (property $A_{i,j}$) in a text.*

$$\mathcal{D}_c(A_{i,j}) = \{NP\}_{i,j}$$

where $\{NP\}_{i,j}$ is a noun phrase naming concept $A_{i,j}$ in natural language.

The example 2 illustrates some possible values for $\mathcal{D}_c$ (in french).

Example 2 (Dictionary of concepts (french entries))

$$\mathcal{D}_c(StOpName) = \left\{ \begin{array}{cc} le & action \\ det. & noun \end{array} \right\}$$

$$\mathcal{D}_c(Price) = \left\{ \begin{array}{cc} le & prix \\ det. & noun \end{array} \right\}$$

$$\mathcal{D}_c(Price) = \left\{ \begin{array}{cc} le & cours \\ det. & noun \end{array} \right\}$$

$\mathcal{D}_c$ may associate several values to a given concept. This can be used to improve diversity in the generated texts.

5.2 Dictionary of aggregation functions

The textual summary is based on a structured summarization computed using aggregation functions. A dictionary with sentence structures is used as the basis to reflect the meaning of the aggregation functions. A sentence structure is composed of sub fragments that can be used by a *realization engine* (cf. (Gatt and Reiter, 2009) and example 3) i.e. the generation of a correct sentence regarding the grammatical rules of the targeted natural language.

Example 3 (Sentence structure and realization) *A sentence structure (in french), represented as a graph, followed by its realization is presented in figure 5.*

The definition 3 formalizes the function used to associate a text to the result of an aggregation function F over a set of k attributes $\{a_i\}_{i=1..k}$. The text is function of the texts $\mathcal{D}_c(a_i)_{i=1..k}$ and the result of the aggregation function $F(\{a_i\}_{i=1..k})$.

Definition 3 (Dictionary of aggregation functions) *It is a function $\mathcal{D}_f$ that, given an aggregation function $F(\{a_i\}_{i=1..k})$, returns a sentence structure SP. The realization of SP describes the aggregation function in natural language.*

$$\mathcal{D}_f(F) = \{\{\mathcal{D}_c(a_i)\}_{i=1..k}, VP, \{Co_i\}_{i=1..x}, F(\{a_i\}_{i=1..k}), \{R_j\}_{j=1..y}\} \quad (4)$$

where VP is a verb phrase explaining the relation between attributes $\{a_i\}_{i=1..k}$ and the value $F(\{a_i\}_{i=1..k})$. $\{Co_i\}_{i=1..x}$ is a set of x complements (noun, direct object, indirect object) and $\{R_j\}_{j=1..y}$ is a set of y relations between sentence elements.

Example 4 *Hereafter a simplified example of sentence structure in french for the $MostFreq(A)$ function which calculates* the most frequent value. *Other sentence structures are possible.*

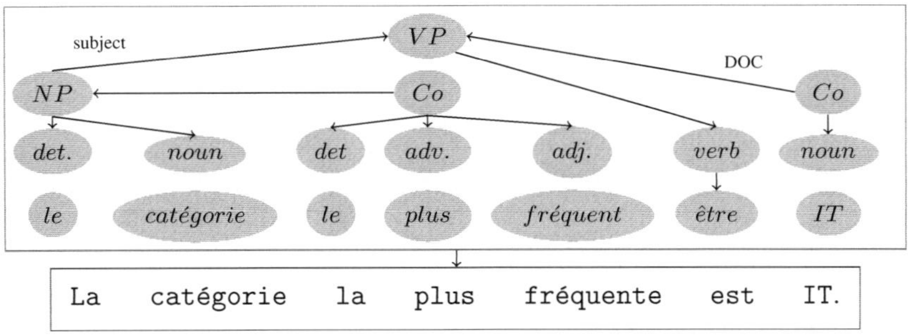

Figure 4: sentence structure

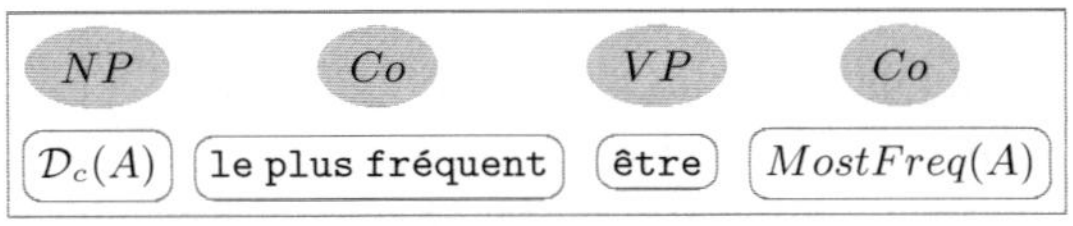

A possible realization of this sentence structure is presented in Example 3 with the attribute $Category$. The same aggregation function used with an other attribute would give a different realization. For example, given the attribute $Country$ the realization in french could be (given that $MostFreq(Country) = France$):

`Le pays le plus fréquent est France.`

The text generation for an aggregation function requires the realization of the entry of the dictionary of functions and the computation of the function itself.

5.3 Transcription operator

A temporal relation (i.e. a function of time) is said to be *transcriptable* if it is possible to generate a set of sentence structures concerning this relation. Thus, transcribing in natural language the signification of a set of data is equivalent to produce a set of sentence structures describing this data set. The transcription is a step that comes after the computation of a structured summary, which has the form of a unique tuple. Definition 4 gives the form of relation that will be considered for transcription.

Definition 4 (A transcriptable relation) *is a temporal relation R that contains a unique tuple such that: $\forall (A, v) \in t$:*
– either A is a concept for which an entry exists in the dictionary of concepts (ie. $A \in Dom(\mathcal{D}_c)$)
– either $A = F$ where $F(\{a_i\}_{i=1..n})$ is an aggregation function used to aggregate a set of values $\{a_i\}_{i=1..n}$ in a value v and such that $F \in Dom(\mathcal{D}_f)$ and $(F, v) \in \mathcal{G}_F(R)$).

A transcription operator is defined to generate a set of sentence structures given a transcriptable relation.

Definition 5 *The transcription operator $\mathcal{T}$ provides a set of sentence structures given a temporal relation R having a schema F_i:*

$$\mathcal{T}(R) = \bigcup_i \mathcal{D}_f(F_i)$$

R being a temporal relation, $\mathcal{T}(R)$ is a set of sentence structures evolving with time. The use of a streamer to create a stream on this set allows the insertion in a stream of texts timestamped with the time when R is modified.

Generally speaking, a function identity $\mathcal{I}d$ is used as name of attributes of a transcriptable relation gives the "point of view" chosen to summarize the data. The dictionary of functions has to include an entry for such function $\mathcal{I}d$. This could be a starting sentence for the textual summary.

Remark 1 (Special case for key attributes) *When the function $\mathcal{I}d$, in the list of attributes of a transcriptable relation, is applied to a key, then the transcription must describe a particular object and not the "point of view" adopted to summarize the data. In that case, it is not a summary but an object of the data base. It is thus necessary to specify an entry in the dictionary of functions for such cases: i.e. $\mathcal{I}d$ on key attributes. As an example, $\mathcal{D}_f(\mathcal{G}_{\mathcal{I}d(Name),\mathcal{I}d(Country)})$ could be defined in french as follows:*

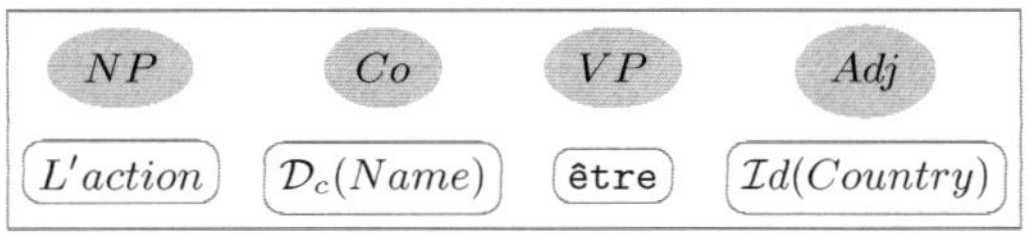

So the realization of

$$\mathcal{T}(\mathcal{G}_{\mathcal{I}d(Name),\mathcal{I}d(Country)}(\pi_{Name,Country}(\sigma_{Name='Total'}(StOpName))))$$

is *L' action Total est française.*

The transcription operator builds texts for ASTRAL queries (with or without preferences). The

$$\mathcal{T}(\mathcal{G}_{\mathcal{I}d(Name),\mathcal{I}d(Country),\mathcal{I}d(Category),Avg(Volume),MostFreq(Methode)}(\pi_{Name,Country,Category,Volume,Methode}(Q1'))) \quad (5)$$

$$\mathcal{T}(\mathcal{G}_{MostFreq(Name),MostFreq(Country),\mathcal{I}d(Category),Avg(Volume),MostFreq(Methode)}(\pi_{Name,Country,Category,Volume,Methode}(Q3'))) \quad (6)$$

$$\mathcal{T}(\mathcal{G}_{MostFreq(Name),\mathcal{I}d(Country),MostFreq(Category),Avg(Volume),MostFreq(Methode)}(\pi_{Name,Country,Category,Volume,Methode}Q4')) \quad (7)$$

generated text depends only on data content and on the functions used for the structure summary. The query itself is not directly transcripted (see example 5).

Example 5 (Transcription) *Assuming that numerical (resp. non-numerical) attributes are aggregated using the average function Avg (resp. most frequent $MostFreq$), queries Q1, Q3 and Q4 are written as presented in equations 5,6,7.*

6 Implementation and experimentation of Stream2text

This section describes our prototype and the experimentations realized (in french) as a proof-of-concept. We focus here on the transcription as the query evaluation part is based on existing software (PostegreSQL and Asteroide (Petit, 2012)).

6.1 Data to text transcription

The transcriptionist component of *Stream2text* has been developed in Java. It produces textual summaries of the data provided by the query manager. The conceptual entities are used to establish the structure of the text. The transcriptionist prepares the grammatical structure of the sentences and uses the french version of SimpleNLG (Gatt and Reiter, 2009) for the text realization. The transcriptionist assembles the sentences issued by SimpleNlg and produces the paragraphs. The summaries include an introduction to give information on treated data and one paragraph per entity involved in the summary. Each paragraph includes several sentences reflecting the meaning of the aggregation functions used for the structured data summary.

The current **dictionary of functions** includes: – $MostFreq$ to calculate the most frequent value in a data set. – Avg, Med and $Count$ with usual mathematical semantics. – $Part(v, A)$ to indicate the % of a value v in the values of A. – $\mathcal{I}d(Key\_Attribute)$ to handle key attributes cases which require particular text generation (see remark 1). This is done for each entity of the database schema. Except for $\mathcal{I}d$, the dictionary contains generic sentence structures. There is no need of redefinition when the functions are used for different attributes and the dictionary is independent from the data schema and may be shared by many applications and users. Nevertheless, the functions can be personalized to produce customized summaries.

6.2 Experiment with stock exchange data

From `http://www.abcbourse.com/`, an experimental data set (5000 transactions) was created. Data involves twelve stock options belonging to ten categories and three countries. Data have timestamps used in the streams (ie. $TTime$ and $ETime$). Quantity, price of transactions, volatility, the category and the country of the stock options are available.

The dictionary of concepts has entries for all attributes and concepts, such as $StOpName$ and $Category$, for the three entities (cf. section 2). We experimented summary generation for queries as in the running example. To illustrate the result, see hereafter a summary for [Q1].

Example 6 (Summary for Q1) *For its summary, let consider that Luc wishes the average and the median for the volume of transactions, prices, etc. [Q1] is evaluated as specified in equation 5. Figure 5 shows the summary for a 2 day period.*

7 Related work

This work is related to several subjects including continuous query evaluation, structured data summarization and natural language generation.

Many theoretical (Krishnamurthy et al., 2010) and practical (Arasu et al., 2006) works have been done to master continuous querying on datastreams. We use (Petit et al., 2012a) which presents the advantage of a non-ambiguous semantics for querying streams and temporal relations. This is particularly important for joins (Petit et al., 2012b) and windows (Petit et al., 2010).

Résumé de l'action *Total*

Ce résumé est construit à partir de *17* transactions.

L'action est dans la catégorie Energie et Produits de base et est française.

Concernant les transactions, le volume moyen d'une transaction est de 155 actions. De plus, la moitié des transactions ont un volume supérieur à 141 actions. Le prix moyen d'une action est de 41,57 euros. De plus, la moitié des transactions ont un prix supérieur à 42,69 euros. Ensuite, l'action Total représente 14 pour cent des transactions. Enfin, l'action Total représente 2 pour cent du volume.

En ce qui concerne la volatilité, l'action Total a la plus forte variation avec 1.22 pour cent. L'action a 1 méthode de calcul de la volatilité. La méthode M1 a une volatilité moyenne de 1,04 pour cent. La méthode M1 a une valeur médiane de 1,00 pour cent. Pour terminer, la méthode de calcul la plus fréquente est M1.

} Summarize title $\mathcal{T}(\mathcal{G}_{\mathcal{I}d(Name)}(Q1))$

} *Head* of summarize with data informations.

} *StockOption* entity paragraph : gives category and country of the share *Total*. $\mathcal{T}(\mathcal{G}_{\mathcal{I}d(Name),\mathcal{I}d(Country),\mathcal{I}d(Cat)}(Q1))$

} *Transactions* entity paragraph : average volume, median price ...

$$\mathcal{T}(\mathcal{G}_{Avg(Vol),Med(Vol),Avg(Price),Med(Price),..}(\pi_{Volume,Price}(Q1)))$$

} Last entity : this paragraph groups data about $Volatility$ entity like number of calculation method of volatility, average volatility ...

Figure 5: Summary for query Q1 according to the example 6

There are also several efforts on summarizing or synthesizing numerical and structured data. In this context, we can understand preferences models and $top-k$ operators as a way to reduce the volume of data. Our proposition supports $top-k$ queries combined to aggregation functions to produce a structured summary. This phase could use other works of this nature as (Cormode et al., 2012; Cormode and Muthukrishnan, 2005). The choice of another preferences model (Koutrika et al., 2010) is compatible with the natural language transcription phase but impacts the structured summary. The use of the CPrefSQL model is motivated by the qualitative approach it proposes and it's support of "contexts" in dominant tuple calculation. This differs from approaches by score functions (Borzsonyi et al., 2001; Papadias et al., 2005; Kontaki et al., 2010).

Concerning automatic text generation, the $text-to-text$ approach is used to automatically summarize texts (Rotem, 2003) or opinions (Labbé and Portet, 2012) expressed in natural language. Our proposal follows a $data-to-text$ approach which consists in text generation to explain data. To the best of our knowledge, current proposals are specific to an application domain such as medicine (Portet et al., 2009; Gatt et al., 2009) or weather report (Turner et al., 2010). The NLG community focuses on language aspects as sentence aggregation, enumerative sentence construction or referential expressions. These works are independent of the application domain whereas the upstream phase including the determination of the content and document planing (Reiter and Dale, 2000), still require domain experts help. However, (Androutsopoulos et al., 2013) proposed, recently, natural language descriptions of individuals or classes of an OWL ontology. In our context, this is analogous to the description of a single tuple in a relation but does not include information summarization as proposed in this paper. *Stream2text* facilitates concept determination and sentence generation by using the conceptual knowledge on data schema and aggregation functions used for the structured summary. The domain specific knowledge required for text generation can be extracted from the data analysis phase. The knowledge relative to the aggregation functions is mostly domain independent. Our proposal combines data model knowledge and data sets to produce summaries by using the realization engine proposed by (Gatt and Reiter, 2009).

8 Conclusion and future research

Our work joins a global effort in mastering big data. We propose the automatic generation of short texts to summarize streamed and persistent data. Such textual summaries allow new information access possibilities. For example, sharing in social networks, access through mobile devices and the use of text-to-speech software.

We propose *Stream2text* which is a generic solution including the whole process, from continuous data monitoring until the generation of a natural language summary. The personalization of the service and, the reduction of the volume of data, rely on the integration of user preferences on data and some knowledge on the conceptual model and the aggregation functions. *Stream2text* has been experimented for texts in French. A version for texts in English is in progress.

Our future research targets the combination of complex data management and appropriate text generation. For example, the contextualization of complex event detection and the production of texts referring to present and past situations.

References

Ion Androutsopoulos, Gerasimos Lampouras, and Dimitrios Galanis. 2013. Generating natural language descriptions from owl ontologies: the naturalowl system. *Journal of Artificial Intelligence Research*, 48:671–715.

Arvind Arasu, Brian Babcock, Shivnath Babu, John Cieslewicz, Mayur Datar, K. Ito, R. Motwani, U. Srivastava, and J. Widom. 2004. STREAM: The Stanford Data Stream Management System. Technical report, Stanford InfoLab.

Arvind Arasu, Shivnath Babu, and Jennifer Widom. 2006. The CQL continuous query language: semantic foundations and query execution. In *Proc. of 32nd int. conf. on Very Large Data bases (VLDB '06)*, volume 15.

S. Borzsonyi, D. Kossmann, and K. Stocker. 2001. The skyline operator. In *Proceedings of the 17th International Conference on Data Engineering (ICDE 2001)*, pages 412–430.

Graham Cormode and S. Muthukrishnan. 2005. An improved data stream summary: the count-min sketch and its applications. *J. Algorithms*, 55(1):58–75.

Graham Cormode, Minos N. Garofalakis, Peter J. Haas, and Chris Jermaine. 2012. Synopses for massive data: Samples, histograms, wavelets, sketches. *Foundations and Trends in Databases*, 4(1-3):1–294.

Sandra de Amo and Fabiola Pereira. 2010. Evaluation of conditional preference queries. *Journal of Information and Data Management (JIDM). Proceedings of the 25th Brazilian Symposium on Databases, 2010, Belo Horizonte, Brazil.*, 1(3):521–536.

Albert Gatt and Ehud Reiter. 2009. Simplenlg: A realisation engine for practical applications. In *Proceedings of the 12th European Workshop on Natural Language Generation*, ENLG '09, pages 90–93, Stroudsburg, PA, USA. Association for Computational Linguistics.

Albert Gatt, François Portet, Ehud Reiter, James Hunter, Saad Mahamood, Wendy Moncur, and Somayajulu Sripada. 2009. From data to text in the neonatal intensive care unit: Using NLG technology for decision support and information management. *AI Communications*, 22(3):153–186.

M. Kontaki, A.N. Papadopoulos, and Y. Manolopoulos. 2010. Continuous processing of preference queries on data streams. In *Proc. of the 36th Int. Conf. on Current Trends in Theory and Practice of Computer Science (SOFSEM 2010)*, pages 47–60. Springer Berlin Heidelberg.

Georgia Koutrika, Evaggelia Pitoura, and Kostas Stefanidis. 2010. Representation, composition and application of preferences in databases. In *Proceedings of International Conference on Data Engineering (ICDE)*, pages 1214–1215.

Sailesh Krishnamurthy, M.J. Franklin, Jeffrey Davis, Daniel Farina, Pasha Golovko, Alan Li, and Neil Thombre. 2010. Continuous analytics over discontinuous streams. In *SIGMOD '10: Proc. of the 2010 ACM SIGMOD int. conf. on Management of data*, pages 1081–1092. ACM.

Cyril Labbé and François Portet. 2012. Towards an Abstractive Opinion Summarisation of Multiple Reviews in the Tourism Domain. In *The First International Workshop on Sentiment Discovery from Affective Data (SDAD 2012)*, pages 87–94, Bristol, UK, sep.

D. Papadias, Y. Tao, G. Fu, and B. Seeger. 2005. Progressive skyline computation in database systems. *ACM Transactions on Database Systems*, 30:41–82.

Loïc Petit, Cyril Labbé, and Claudia Lucia Roncancio. 2010. An Algebric Window Model for Data Stream Management. In *Proceedings of the 9th Int. ACM Workshop on Data Engineering for Wireless and Mobile Access (MobiDE '10)* , pages 17–24. ACM.

Loïc Petit, Sandra de Amo, Claudia Roncancio, and Cyril Labbé. 2012a. Top-k context-aware queries on streams. In *Proc. of Int. Conf. on Database and Expert Systems Applications (DEXA 12)*, pages 397–411.

Loïc Petit, Cyril Labbé, and Claudia Lucia Roncancio. 2012b. Revisiting Formal Ordering in Data Stream Querying. In *Proc. of the 2012 ACM Symp. on Applied Computing*, New York, NY, USA. ACM.

Loïc Petit. 2012. *Gestion de flux de donnés pour l'observation de systèmes*. Thèse de doctorat, Université de Grenoble, Décembre.

F. Portet, E. Reiter, A Gatt, J. Hunter, S. Sripada, Y. Freer, and C. Sykes. 2009. Automatic generation of textual summaries from neonatal intensive care data. *Artificial Intelligence*, 173(7–8):789–816.

Ehud Reiter and Robert Dale. 2000. *Building Natural Language Generation Systems*. Cambridge University Press, New York, NY, USA.

N Rotem. 2003. Open text summarizer (ots). June, 2012, http://libots.sourceforge.net.

Ross Turner, Somayajulu Sripada, and Ehud Reiter. 2010. Generating approximate geographic descriptions. In Emiel Krahmer and Mariët Theune, editors, *Empirical Methods in Natural Language Generation*, volume 5790 of *Lecture Notes in Computer Science*, pages 121–140. Springer Berlin Heidelberg.

Author Index

Association for Computational Linguistics
209 N. Eighth Street
Stroudsburg, Pennsylvania 18360

CURRAN ASSOCIATES INC.
proceedings.com

ISBN 978-1-5108-1401-1
9 781510 814011